POINTS OF VIEW

POINTS OF VIEW

READINGS IN AMERICAN GOVERNMENT AND POLITICS

THIRD EDITION

Edited by **ROBERT E. DiCLERICO**
and **ALLAN S. HAMMOCK**

West Virginia University

Random House New York

Third Edition
9 8 7 6 5 4 3 2 1
Copyright © 1980, 1983, 1986 by Newbery Award Records, Inc.

Library of Congress Cataloging-in-Publication Data
Main entry under title:

Points of view.
  Includes bibliographies.
  1. United States—Politics and government—
Addresses, essays, lectures. I. DiClerico, Robert E.
II. Hammock, Allan S., 1938–
JK21.P59 1986   320.973   85-19323
ISBN 0-394-35408-7

Cover design: Jeanette Jacobs

Manufactured in the United States of America

PREFACE

We have made numerous changes in this, the third edition of *Points of View*. The selections in chapters 4, 5, 8, 9, 11, and 12 of the previous edition—dealing with public opinion, voting, political parties, interest groups, presidential power, and the bureaucracy—have all been replaced with new selections. In addition, we have updated the selection in Chapter 10 on congressional ethics; and updated and expanded the debate, begun more than a decade ago, between Sidney Hook and Howard Zinn on democracy in Chapter 1. We have also added new topics to several chapters: Chapter 2 now contains selections dealing with the desirability of having a new constitutional convention; and in the area of civil liberties and civil rights; chapters 14 and 15 now feature articles focusing on school prayer and comparable worth. These changes have for the most part been dictated by the press of events. At the same time however, we have retained those articles, which by now have become "classics" in the field.

The basic goals of the book remain the same, namely, to provide students with a manageable number of selections that present readable, thoughtful, and diverse perspectives across the broad range of subject matter related to American government.

We would like to express our appreciation to J. Patrick Hagan and Rodger D. Yeager, colleagues at West Virginia University, who provided valuable recommendations for the third edition. A debt of gratitude is also owed to Cheryl Flagg whose secretarial assistance—always offered unselfishly—enabled us to meet a tight deadline. Finally, our thanks also goes to Bert Lummus, Dorchen Leidholdt, Anna Marie Muskelly, and Lionel Dean—all at Random House—for shepherding this project through to completion.

Morgantown, West Virginia   R.E.D.
February 1985   A.S.H.

A NOTE TO
THE INSTRUCTOR

For some years now, both of us have jointly taught the introductory course to American government. Each year we perused the crop of existing readers, and while we adopted several different readers over this period, we were not wholly satisfied with any of them. It is our feeling that the fifty or so readers currently on the market suffer from one or more of the following deficiencies: (1) Some contain selections which are difficult for students to comprehend because of the sophistication of the argument, the manner of expression, or both. (2) In many instances, readers do not cover all of the topics typically treated in an introductory American government course. (3) In choosing selections for a given topic, editors do not always show sufficient concern for how—or whether—one article under a topic relates to other articles under the same topic. (4) Most readers contain too many selections for each topic—indeed, in several cases the number of selections for some topics exceeds ten. Readers are nearly always used in conjunction with a textbook. Thus, to ask a student to read a lengthy chapter—jammed with facts—from a textbook and then to read anywhere from five to ten selections on the same topic from a reader is to demand that students read more than they can reasonably absorb in a meaningful way. Of course, an instructor need not assign all of the selections under a given topic. At the same time, however, this approach justifiably disgruntles students who, after purchasing a reader, discover that they may only be asked to read one-half or two-thirds of it.

Instead of continuing to complain about what we considered to be the limitations of existing American government readers, we decided to try our own hand at putting one together. In doing so, we were guided by the following considerations.

Readability

Quite obviously, students will not read dull, obtuse articles. As well as having something important to say, we feel that each of the articles in *Points of View* is clearly written, well organized, and free of needless jargon.

Comprehensiveness

The sixteen topics included in *Points of View* constitute all the major areas of concern that are typically treated in the standard introductory course to American government.

Economy of Selections

We decided, in most instances, to limit the number of selections to two per topic, although we did include four selections for some topics that we deemed especially important. The limitation on selections will, we feel, maximize the possibility that students will read them. It has been our experience that when students are assigned four, five, or more selections under a given topic, they simply do not read them all. In addition, by limiting the selections for each topic, there is a greater likelihood that students will be able to associate an argument with the author who made it.

Juxtaposition

The two selections for each topic will take *opposing* or *different* points of view on some aspect of a given topic. This approach was chosen for three reasons. First, we believe that student interest will be enhanced by playing one article off against the other. Thus, the "interest" quality of a given article will derive not only from its own content but also from its juxtaposition with the other article. Second, we think it is important to sensitize students to the fact that one's perspective on an issue will depend upon the values that he or she brings to it. Third, by having both selections focus on a particular issue related to a given topic, the student will have a greater depth of understanding about that issue. We think this is preferable to having five or six selections under a topic, with each selection focusing on a different aspect, and with the result that the student ultimately is exposed to "a little of this and a little of that"—that is, if the student even bothers to read all five or six selections.

   While the readers currently available take into account one or, in some instances, several of the considerations identified above, we believe that the uniqueness of *Points of View* lies in the fact that it has sought to incorporate *all* of them.

Morgantown, West Virginia   R.E.D.
February 1979   A.S.H.

CONTENTS

CHAPTER ONE

DEMOCRACY

Any assessment of a society's democratic character will be fundamentally determined by what the observer chooses to use as a definition of democracy. While the concept of democracy has commanded the attention of political thinkers for centuries, the following selections by Howard Zinn and Sidney Hook serve to demonstrate that there continues to be considerable disagreement over its meaning. Each of them has scanned the American scene and reached different conclusions regarding the democratic character of our society. This difference of opinion is explained primarily by the fact that each approaches his evaluation with a different conception of what democracy is.

For Zinn, the definition of democracy includes not only criteria which bear upon how decisions get made, but also upon what results from such decisions. Specifically, he argues that such results must lead to a certain level of human welfare within a society. In applying these criteria of human welfare to the United States, he concludes that we fall short of the mark in several areas.

Although Sidney Hook is willing to acknowledge that democracy may indeed function more smoothly in societies where the conditions of human welfare are high, he insists that these conditions do not themselves constitute the definition of democracy. Rather, he maintains that democracy is a process—a way of making decisions. Whether such decisions lead to the conditions of human welfare that Zinn prescribes is irrelevant. The crucial test, according to Hook, is whether or not the people have the right, by majority rule, to make choices about the quality of their lives—whatever those choices may be.

How Democratic Is America?

Howard Zinn

To give a sensible answer to the question "How democratic is America?" I find it necessary to make three clarifying preliminary statements. First, I want to define "democracy," not conclusively, but operationally, so we can know what we are arguing about, or at least what I am talking about. Second, I want to state what my criteria are for measuring the "how" in the question. And third, I think it necessary to issue a warning about how a certain source of bias (although not the only source) is likely to distort our judgments.

Our definition is crucial. This becomes clear if we note how relatively easy is the answer to our question when we define democracy as a set of formal institutions and let it go at that. If we describe as "democratic" a country that has a representative system of government, with universal suffrage, a bill of rights, and party competition for office, it becomes easy to answer the question "how" with the enthusiastic reply, "Very!" . . .

I propose a set of criteria for the description "democratic" which goes beyond formal political institutions, to the quality of life in the society (economic, social, psychological), beyond majority rule to a concern for minorities, and beyond national boundaries to a global view of what is meant by "the people," in that rough, but essentially correct view of democracy as "government of, by, and for the people."

Let me list these criteria quickly, because I will go on to discuss them in some detail later:

1. To what extent can various people in the society participate in those decisions which affect their lives: decisions in the political process and decisions in the economic structure?

Originally published in Robert A. Goldwin, ed., *How Democratic Is America?* pp. 39–60 (Chicago: Rand McNally, 1971). The author has revised and updated this essay for *Points of View*.

2. As a corollary of the above: do people have equal access to the information which they need to make important decisions?

3. Are the members of the society equally protected on matters of life and death—in the most literal sense of that phrase?

4. Is there equality before the law: police, courts, the judicial process—as well as equality *with* the law-enforcing institutions, so as to safeguard equally everyone's person, and his freedom from interference by others, and by the government?

5. Is there equality in the distribution of available resources: those economic goods necessary for health, life, recreation, leisure, growth?

6. Is there equal access to education, to knowledge and training, so as to enable persons in the society to live their lives as fully as possible, to enlarge their range of possibilities?

7. Is there freedom of expression on all matters, and equally for all, to communicate with other members of the society?

8. Is there freedom for individuality in private life, in sexual relations, family relations, the right of privacy?

9. To minimize regulation: do education and the culture in general foster a spirit of cooperation and amity to sustain the above conditions?

10. As a final safety feature: is there opportunity to protest, to disobey the laws, when the foregoing objectives are being lost—as a way of restoring them? . . .

Two historical facts support my enlarged definition of democracy. One is that the industrialized Western societies have outgrown the original notions which accompanied their early development: that constitutional and procedural tests sufficed for the "democracy" that overthrew the old order; that democracy was quite adequately fulfilled by the Bill of Rights in England at the time of the glorious Revolution, the Constitution of the United States, and the declaration of the Rights of Man in France. It came to be acknowledged that the rhetoric of these revolutions was not matched by their real achievements. In other words, the limitations of that "democracy" led to the reformist and radical movements that grew up in the West in the middle and late nineteenth centuries. The other historical note is that the new revolutions in our century, in Africa, Asia, Latin America, while rejecting either in whole or in part the earlier revolutions, profess a similar democratic aim, but with an even broader rhetoric. . . .

My second preliminary point is on standards. By this I mean that we can judge in several ways the fulfillment of these ten criteria I have listed. We can measure the present against the past, so that if we find that in 1985 we are doing better in these matters than we were doing in 1860 or 1910, the society will get a good grade for its "democracy." I would adjure such an approach because it supports complacency. With such a standard, Russians in 1910 could point with pride to how much progress they had made toward parliamentary democracy; as Russians in 1985 can point to their poststudent progress away from the gulag; as Americans could point in 1939 to how far they had come toward solving the problem of economic equality; as Americans in the South could point in 1950 to the progress of the southern Negro. Indeed, the American government gives military aid to brutal regimes in Latin America on the ground that a decrease in the murders by semiofficial death squads is a sign of progress.

Or, we could measure our democracy against other places in the world. Given the high incidence of tyranny in the world, polarization of wealth, and lack of freedom of expression, the United States, even with very serious defects, could declare itself successful. Again, the result is to let us all off easily; some of our most enthusiastic self-congratulation is based on such a standard.

On the other hand, we could measure our democracy against an ideal (even if admittedly unachievable) standard. I would argue for such an approach, because, in what may seem to some a paradox, the ideal standard is the pragmatic one; it affects what we *do*. To grade a student on the basis of an improvement over past performance is justifiable if the intention is to encourage someone discouraged about his ability. But if he is rather pompous about his superiority in relation to other students (and I suggest this is frequently true of Americans evaluating American "democracy"), and if in addition he is a medical student about to graduate into a world ridden with disease, it would be best to judge him by an ideal standard. That might spur him to an improvement fast enough to save lives. . . .

My third preliminary point is a caution based on the obvious fact that we make our appraisals through the prism of our own status in society. This is particularly important in assessing democracy, because if "democracy" refers to the condition of masses of people, and if we as the assessors belong to a number of elites, we will tend (and I am not declaring an inevitability, just warning of a tendency) to see the present situation in America more benignly than it deserves. To be more specific, if democracy requires a keen awareness of the condition of black people, of poor people, of young people, of that majority of the world who are not American—and we are white, prosperous, beyond draft age, and American—then we have a number of pressures tending to dull our sense of inequity. We are, if not doomed to err, likely to err on the side of complacency—and we should try to take this into account in making our judgments.

1. PARTICIPATION IN DECISIONS

We need to recognize first, that whatever decisions are made politically are made by representatives of one sort or another: state legislators, congressmen, senators, and other elected officials, governors and presidents; also by those appointed by elected officials, like Supreme Court justices. These are important decisions, affecting our lives, liberties, and ability to pursue happiness. Congress and the president decide on the tax structure, which affects the distribution of resources. They decide how to spend the monies received, whether or not we go to war; who serves in the armed forces; what behavior is considered a crime; which crimes are prosecuted and which are not. They decide what limitations there should be on our travel, or on our right to speak freely. They decide on the availability of education and health services.

If representation by its very nature is undemocratic, as I would argue, this is an important fact for our evaluation. Representative government is *closer* to democracy than monarchy, and for this reason it has been hailed as one of the great political advances of modern times; yet, it is only a step in the direction of democracy, at its best. It has certain inherent flaws—pointed out by Rousseau in the eighteenth century, Victor Considerant in the nineteenth century, Robert Michels in the beginning of the twentieth century, Hannah Arendt in our own time. No representative can adequately represent another's needs; the representative tends to become a member of a special elite; he has privileges which weaken his sense of concern at others' grievances; the passions of the troubled lose force (as Madison noted in *The Federalist 10*) as they are filtered through the representative system; the elected official develops an expertise which tends toward its own perpetuation. Leaders develop what Michels called "a mutual insurance contract" against the rest of society. . . .

If only radicals pointed to the inadequacy of the political processes in the United States, we might be suspicious. But established political scientists of a moderate bent talk quite bluntly of the limitations of the voting system in the United States. Robert Dahl, in *A Preface to Democratic Theory*, drawing on the voting studies of American political scientists, concludes that "political activity, at least in the United States, is positively associated to a significant extent with such variables as income, socio-economic status, and education." He says:

> By their propensity for political passivity the poor and uneducated disfranchise themselves. . . . Since they also have less access than the wealthy to the organizational, financial, and propaganda resources that weigh so heavily in campaigns, elections, legislative, and executive decisions, anything like equal control over government policy is triply barred to the members of Madison's unpropertied masses. They are barred by their relative greater inactivity, by their relatively

limited access to resources, and by Madison's nicely contrived system of constitutional checks.[1]

Dahl thinks that our society is essentially democratic, but this is because he expects very little. (His book was written in the 1950s, when lack of commotion in the society might well have persuaded him that no one else expected much more than he did.) Even if democracy were to be superficially defined as "majority rule," the United States would not fulfill that, according to Dahl, who says that "on matters of specific policy, the majority rarely rules."[2] After noting that "the election is the critical technique for insuring that governmental leaders will be relatively responsive to nonleaders," he goes on to say that "it is important to notice how little a national election tells us about the preferences of majorities. Strictly speaking, all an election reveals is the first preferences of some citizens among the candidates standing for office."[3] About 45 percent of the potential voters in national elections, and about 60 percent of the voters in local elections do not vote, and this cannot be attributed, Dahl says, simply to indifference. And if, as Dahl points out, "in no large nation state can elections tell us much about the preferences of majorities and minorities," this is "even more true of the interelection period.". . .

Dahl goes on to assert that the election process and interelection activity "are crucial processes for insuring that political leaders will be *somewhat* responsive to the preferences of *some* ordinary citizens."[4] I submit (the emphasized words are mine) that if an admirer of democracy in America can say no more than this, democracy is not doing very well.

Dahl tells us the election process is one of "two fundamental methods of social control which, operating together, make governmental leaders so responsive to nonleaders that the distinction between democracy and dictatorship still makes sense." Since his description of the election process leaves that dubious, let's look at his second requirement for distinguishing democracy: "The other method of social control is continuous political competition among individuals, parties, or both." What it comes down to is "not minority rule but minorities rule."[5]

If it turns out that this—like the election process—also has little democratic content, we will not be left with very much difference—by Dahl's own admission—between "dictatorship" and the "democracy" practiced in the United States. Indeed, there is much evidence on this: the lack of democracy within the major political parties, the vastly disproportionate influence of wealthy groups over poorer ones (what consumers' group in 1983 could match the $1 million spent by the Natural Gas Supply Association to lobby, in fifteen key congressional districts, for full control of natural gas prices?);[6] the unrepresentative nature of the major lobbies (the wealthy doctors speaking for all through the AMA, the wealthy farmers speaking for the poorer ones through the American Farm Bureau Federation, the most affluent trade unions speaking for all workers). All of this, and more, supports the idea of a "decline of American pluralism" that Henry Kariel has written about. What Dahl's democracy comes down to is "the steady appeasement of relatively small groups."[7] If these relatively small groups turn out to be the aircraft industry far more than the aged, the space industry far more than the poor, the Pentagon far more than the college youth—what is left of democracy?

Sometimes the elitism of decision-making is defended (by Dahl and by others) on the ground that the elite is enacting decisions passively supported by the mass, whose tolerance is proof of an underlying consensus in society. But Murray Levin's studies in *The Alienated Voter* indicate how much nonparticipation in elections is a result of hopelessness rather than approval. And Robert Wiebe, a historian at Northwestern University, talks of "consensus" becoming a "new stereotype." He approaches the question historically.

Industrialization arrived so peacefully not because all Americans secretly shared the same values or implicitly willed its success but because its millions of bitter enemies lacked the mentality and the means to organize an effective counterattack.[8]

Wiebe's point is that the passivity of most Americans in the face of elitist decision-making has not been due to acquiescence but to the lack of resources for effective combat, as well as a gulf so wide between the haves and have-nots that there was no ground on which to dispute. Americans neither revolted violently nor reacted at the polls; instead they were subservient, or else worked out their hostilities in personal ways. . . .

Presidential nominations and elections are more democratic than monarchical rule or the procedures of totalitarian states, but they are far from some reasonable expectation of democracy. The two major parties have a monopoly of presidential power, taking turns in the White House. The candidates of minority parties don't have a chance. They do not have access to the financial backing of the major parties, and there is not the semblance of equal attention in the mass media; it is only the two major candidates who have free access to prime time on national television.

More important, both parties almost always agree on the fundamentals of domestic and foreign policy, despite the election-year rhetoric which attempts to find important differences. Both parties arranged for United States intervention in Vietnam in the 1950s and 1960s, and both, when public opinion changed, promised to get out (note the Humphrey–Nixon contest of 1968). In 1984, Democratic candidate Walter Mondale agreed with Republican candidate Ronald Reagan that the United States (which had ten thousand thermonuclear warheads) needed to continue increasing its arms budget, although he asked for a smaller increase than the Republicans. Such a position left Mondale unable to promise representatives of the black community (where unemployment was over 20 percent) that he would spend even a few billion dollars for a jobs program. Meanwhile, Democrats and Republicans in Congress were agreeing on a $297 billion arms bill for the 1985 fiscal year.[9]

With all the inadequacies of the representative system, it does not even operate in the field of foreign policy. In exactly those decisions which are the most vital—matters of war and peace, life and death—power rests in the hands of the President and a small group of advisers. We don't notice this when wars seem to have a large degree of justification (as World War II); we begin to notice it when we find ourselves in the midst of a particularly pointless war.

I have been talking so far about democracy in the political process. But there is another serious weakness that I will only mention here, although it is of enormous importance: the powerlessness of the American to participate in economic decision-making, which affects his life at every moment. As a consumer, that is, as the person whom the economy is presumably intended to serve, he has virtually nothing to say about what is produced for him. The corporations make what is profitable; the advertising industry persuades him to buy what the corporations produce. He becomes the passive victim of the misallocation of resources, the production of dangerous commodities, the spoiling of his air, water, forests, beaches, cities.

2. ACCESS TO INFORMATION

Adequate information for the electorate is a precondition for any kind of action (whether electoral or demonstrative) to affect national policy. As for the voting process, Berelson, Lazarsfeld, and McPhee tell us (in their book, *Voting*) after extensive empirical research: "One persistent conclusion is that the public is not particularly well informed about the specific issues of the day." . . .

Furthermore, . . . there are certain issues which never even reach the public because they are decided behind the scenes. . . .

Consider the information available to voters on two major kinds of issues. One of them is the tax structure, so bewilderingly complex that the corporation, with its corps of accountants and financial experts, can prime itself for lobbying activities, while the average voter, hardly able to comprehend his own income tax, stands by helplessly as the President, the Bureau of the Budget, and the Congress decide the tax laws. The dominant influences are those of big business, which has the resources both to understand and to act.

Then there is foreign policy. The government leads the citizenry to believe it has special expertise which, if it could only be revealed, would support its position against critics. At the same time, it hides the very information which would reveal its position to be indefensible. The mendacity of the government on the Bay of Pigs operation, the secret operations of the CIA in Iran, Indonesia, Guatemala, and other places, the withholding of vital information about the Tonkin Gulf events are only a few examples of the way the average person becomes a victim of government deception.

When the United States invaded the tiny island of Grenada in the fall of 1983, no reporters were allowed to observe the invasion, and the American public had little opportunity to get independent verification of the reasons given by the government for the invasion. As a result, President Reagan could glibly tell the nation what even one of his own supporters, journalist George Will, admitted was a lie: that he was invading Grenada to protect the lives of American medical students on the island. He could also claim that documents found on the island indicated plans for a Cuban–Soviet takeover of Grenada; the documents showed no such thing.[10]

Furthermore, the distribution of information to the public is a function of power and wealth. The government itself can color the citizens' understanding of events by its control of news at the source: the presidential press conference, the "leak to the press," the White Papers, the teams of "truth experts" going around the country at the taxpayers' expense. As for private media, the large networks and mass-circulation magazines have the greatest access to the public mind. There is no "equal time" for critics of public policy. . . .

3. EQUAL PROTECTION

Let us go now from the procedural to the substantive, indeed to the *most* substantive of questions: the right of all the people to life itself. Here we find democracy in America tragically inadequate. The draft, which has been a part of American law since 1940 (when it passed by one vote) decides, in wartime, who lives and who dies. Not only Locke, one of the leading theorists of the democratic tradition, declared the ultimate right of any person to safeguard his own life when threatened by the government; Hobbes, often looked on as the foe of democratic thought, agreed. The draft violates this principle, because it compels young people to sacrifice their lives for any cause which the leaders of government deem just; further it discriminates against the poor, the uneducated, the young.

It is in connection with this most basic of rights—life itself, the first and most important of those substantive ends which democratic participation is designed to safeguard—that I would assert the need for a global view of democracy. One can at least conceive of a democratic decision for martial sacrifice by those ready to make the sacrifice; a "democratic" war is thus a theoretical possibility. But that presumption of democracy becomes obviously false at the first shot because then *others* are affected who did not decide. . . . Nations making decisions to slaughter their own sons are at least theoretically subject to internal check. The victims on the other side fall without any such chance. For the United States today, this failure of democracy is total; we have the capacity to destroy the world without giving it a chance to murmur a dissent; we did, in fact, destroy a part of southeast Asia on the basis of a unilateral decision made in Washington. There is no more pernicious manifestation of the lack of democracy in America than this single fact.

4. EQUALITY BEFORE THE LAW

Is there equality before the law? At every stage of the judicial process—facing the policeman, appearing in court, being freed on bond, being sentenced by the judge—the poor person is treated worse than the rich, the black treated worse than the white, the politically or personally odd character is treated worse than the orthodox. The details are given in the 1963 report of the Attorney General's Committee on Poverty and the Administration of Federal Criminal Justice. There a defendant's poverty is shown to affect his preliminary hearing, his right to bail, the quality of his counsel. The evidence is plentiful in the daily newspapers, which inform us that a Negro boy fleeing the scene of a two-dollar theft may be shot and killed by a pursuing policeman, while a wealthy man who goes to South America after a million-dollar swindle, even if apprehended, need never fear a scratch. The wealthy price-fixer for General Motors, who costs consumers millions, will get ninety days in jail, the burglar of a liquor store will get five years. A Negro youth, or a bearded white youth poorly dressed, has much more chance of being clubbed by a policeman on the street than a well-dressed white man, given the fact that both respond with equal tartness to a question. . . .

Aside from inequality among citizens, there is inequality between the citizen and his government, when they face one another in a court of law. Take the matter of counsel: the well-trained government prosecutor faces the indigent's court-appointed counsel. Four of my students did a study of the City Court of Boston several years ago. They sat in the court for weeks, taking notes, and found that the average time spent by court-appointed counsel with his client, before arguing the case at the bench, was seven minutes.

5. DISTRIBUTION OF RESOURCES

Democracy is devoid of meaning if it does not include equal access to the available resources of the society. In India, democracy might still mean poverty; in the United States, with a Gross National Product of $3 trillion a year, democracy should mean that every American, working a short work-week, has adequate food, clothing, shelter, health care, education for himself and his family—in short, the material resources necessary to enjoy life and freedom. Even if only 20 percent of the American population is desperately poor . . . in a country so rich, that is an inexcusable breach of the democratic principle. Even if there is a large, prosperous middle class, there is something grossly unfair in the wealthiest fifth of the population getting 40 percent of the nation's income, and the poorest fifth getting 5 percent (a ratio virtually unchanged from 1947 to 1980). . . .[11]

Whether you are poor or rich determines the most fundamental facts about your life: whether you are cold in the winter while trying to sleep, whether you suffocate in the summer; whether you live among vermin or rats; whether the smells around you all day are sweet or foul; whether you have adequate medical care; whether you have good teeth; whether you can send your children to college; whether you can go on vacation or have to take an extra job at night; whether you can afford a divorce, or an abortion, or a wife, or another child. . . .

6. ACCESS TO EDUCATION

In a highly industrialized society, education is a crucial determinant of wealth, political power, social status, leisure, and the ability to work in one's chosen field. Educational resources in our society are not equitably distributed. Among high-school graduates of the same IQ levels, a far higher percentage of the well-to-do go on to college than the poor.[12] A mediocre student with money can always go to college. A mediocre student without money may not be able to go, even to a state college, because he may have to work to support his family. Furthermore, the educational resources in the schools—equipment, teachers, etc.—are far superior in the wealthy suburbs than in the poor sections of the city, whether white or black.

7. FREEDOM OF EXPRESSION

Like money, freedom of expression is available to all in America, but in widely varying quantities. The First Amendment formally guarantees freedom of speech, press, assembly, and petition to all—but certain realities of wealth, power, and status stand in the way of the equal distribution of these rights. Anyone can stand on a street corner and talk to ten or a hundred people. But someone with the resources to buy loudspeaker equipment, go through the necessary red tape, and post a bond with the city may hold a meeting downtown and reach a thousand or five thousand people. A person or a corporation with $100,000 can buy time on television and reach 10 million people. A rich person simply has much more freedom of speech than a poor person. The government has much more freedom of expression than a private individual, because the President can command the airwaves when he wishes, and reach 60 million people in one night.

Freedom of the press also is guaranteed to all. But the student selling an underground newspaper on the street with a nude woman on the cover may be arrested by a policeman, while the airport newsstand selling *Playboy* and ten magazines like it will remain safe. Anyone with $10,000 can put out a newspaper to reach a few thousand people. Anyone with $10 million can buy a few newspapers that will reach a few million people. Anyone who is penniless had better have a loud voice; and then he might be arrested for disturbing the peace.

8. FREEDOM FOR INDIVIDUALITY

The right to live one's life, in privacy and freedom, in whatever way one wants, so long as others are not harmed, should be a sacred principle in a democracy. But there are hundreds of laws, varying from state to state, and sometimes joined by federal laws, which regulate the personal lives of people in this country: their marriages, their divorces, their sexual relations. Furthermore, both laws and court decisions protect policemen and the FBI in their use of secret devices which listen in on private conversations, or peer in on private conduct.

9. THE SPIRIT OF COOPERATION

The maintenance of those substantive elements of democracy which I have just sketched, if dependent on a pervasive network of coercion, would cancel out much of the benefit of that democracy. Democracy needs rather to be sustained by a spirit in society, the tone and the values of the culture. I am speaking of something as elusive as a mood, alongside something as hard as law, both of which would have to substitute cooperation tinged with friendly competition for the fierce combat of our business culture. I am speaking of the underlying drive that keeps people going in the society. So long as that drive is for money and power, with no ceiling on either, so long as ruthlessness is built into the rules of the game, democracy does not have a chance. If there is one crucial cause in the failure of American democracy—not the only one, of course, but a fundamental one—it is the drive for corporate profit, and the overwhelming influence of money in every aspect of our daily lives. That is the uncontrolled libido of our society from which the rape of democratic values necessarily follows.

The manifestations are diverse and endless: the Kefauver hearings on the drug industry in 1961 disclosed that the drive for profit in that industry had led to incredible overpricing of drugs for consumers (700 percent markup, for instance, for tablets to arthritic patients) as well as bodily harm resulting from "the fact that they market so many of their failures."

It was disclosed in 1979 that Johns-Manville, the nation's largest asbestos manufacturer, had deliberately withheld from its workers X-ray results which showed they were developing cancer.[13] The careless disposition of toxic wastes throughout the country and the repeated accidents at nuclear plants were testimony to the concern for corporate profit over human life.

If these were isolated cases, reported and then eliminated, they could be dismissed as unfortunate blemishes on an otherwise healthy social body. But the major allocations of resources in our society are made on the basis of money profit rather than social use. . . .

Recent news items buttress what I have said. The oil that polluted California's beautiful beaches in the 1960s . . . was produced by a system in which the oil companies' hunger for profit has far more weight than the ordinary person's need to swim in clean water. This is not to be attributed to Republicanism overriding the concern for the little fellow of the Democratic Party. Profit is master whichever party is in power; it was the liberal Secretary of the Interior Stewart Udall who allowed the dangerous drilling to go on. . . .

In 1984, the suit of several thousand veterans against the Dow Chemical Company, claiming that they and their families had suffered terrible illnesses as a result of exposure in Vietnam to the poisonous chemical Agent Orange, was settled. The Dow corporation avoided the disclosures of thousands of documents in open court by agreeing to pay $180 million to the veterans. One thing seemed clear: the company had known that the defoliant used in Vietnam might be dangerous, but it held back the news, and blamed the government for ordering use of the chemical. The government itself, apparently wanting to shift blame to the corporation, declared publicly that Dow Chemical had been motivated in its actions by greed for profit.

10. OPPORTUNITY TO PROTEST

The first two elements in my list for democracy—decision-making and information to help make them—are procedural. The next six are substantive, dealing with the consequences of such procedures on life, liberty, and the pursuit of happiness. My ninth point, the one I have just discussed, shows how the money motive of our society corrupts both procedures and their consequences by its existence and suggests we need a different motive as a fundamental requisite of a democratic society. The point I am about to discuss is an ultimate requisite for democracy, a safety feature if nothing else—neither procedures nor consequences nor motivation—works. It is the right of citizens to break through the impasse of a legal and cultural structure, which sustains inequality, greed, and murder, to initiate processes for change. I am speaking of civil disobedience, which is an essential safeguard even in a successful society, and which is an absolute necessity in a society which is not going well.

If the institutional structure itself bars any change but the most picayune and grievances are serious, it is silly to insist that change must be mediated through the processes of that legal structure. In such a situation, dramatic expressions of protest and challenge are necessary to help change ways of thinking, to build up political power for drastic change. A society that calls itself democratic (whether accurately or not) must, as its ultimate safeguard, allow such acts of disobedience. If the government prohibits them (as we must expect from a government committed to the existent) then the members of a society concerned with democracy must not only defend such acts, but encourage them. Somewhere near the root of democratic thought is the theory of popular sovereignty, declaring that government and laws are instruments for certain ends, and are not to be deified with absolute obedience; they must constantly be checked by the citizenry, and challenged, opposed, even overthrown, if they become threats to fundamental rights.

Any abstract assessment of *when* disobedience is justified is pointless. Proper conclusions depend on empirical evidence about how bad things are at the moment, and how adequate are the institutional mechanisms for correcting them. . . .

One of these is the matter of race. The intolerable position of the black person, in both North and South, has traditionally been handled with a few muttered apologies and tokens of reform. Then the civil disobedience of militants in the South forced our attention on the most dramatic (southern) manifestations of racism in America. The massive black urban uprisings of 1967 and 1968 showed that nothing less than civil disobedience (for riots and uprisings go beyond that) could make the nation see that the race problem is an American—not a southern—problem and that it needs bold, revolutionary action.

As for poverty: it seems clear that the normal mechanisms of congressional pretense and presidential rhetoric are not going to change things very much. Acts of civil disobedience by the poor will be required, at the least, to make middle-class America take notice, to bring national decisions that begin to reallocate wealth.

The war in Vietnam showed that we could not depend on the normal processes of "law and order," of the election process, of letters to *The Times*, to stop a series of especially brutal acts against the Vietnamese and against our own sons. It took a nationwide storm of protest, including thousands of acts of civil disobedience (14,000 people were arrested in one day in 1971 in Washington, D.C.) to help bring the war to an end. The role of draft resistance in affecting Lyndon Johnson's 1968 decision not to escalate the war further is told in the Defense Department secret documents of that period. In the 1980s civil disobedience continues, with religious pacifists and others risking prison in order to protest the arms race and the plans for nuclear war.

The great danger for American democracy is not from the protesters. That democracy is too poorly realized for us to consider critics—even rebels—as the chief problem. Its fulfillment requires us all, living in an ossified system which sustains too much killing and too much selfishness, to join the protest.

NOTES

1. Robert A. Dahl, *A Preface to Democratic Theory* (Chicago: University of Chicago Press, 1963), p. 81.

2. *Ibid.*, p. 124.
3. *Ibid.*, p. 125.
4. *Ibid.*, p. 131.
5. *Ibid.*, pp. 131–32.
6. Thomas B. Edsall, *The New Politics of Inequality* (New York: Norton, 1984), p. 112.
7. Dahl, *A Preface to Democratic Theory*, p. 146.
8. Robert Wiebe, "The Confinements of Consensus," *TriQuarterly*, 1966, Copyright by TriQuarterly 1966. All rights reserved.
9. *New York Times*, September 25, 1984.
10. The *New York Times*, reported, November 5, 1983: "There is nothing in the documents, however, that specifically indicates that Cuba and the Soviet Union were on the verge of taking over Grenada, as Administration officials have suggested."
11. Edsall, *The New Politics of Inequality*, p. 221.
12. See the Carnegie Council on Children study, *Small Futures*, by Richard deLore, 1979.
13. *Los Angeles Times*, May 3, 1979.

How Democratic Is America?
A Response to Howard Zinn

Sidney Hook

Charles Peirce, the great American philosopher, once observed that there was such a thing as the "ethics of words." The "ethics of words" are violated whenever ordinary terms are used in an unusual context or arbitrarily identified with another concept for which other terms are in common use. Mr. Zinn is guilty of a systematic violation of the "ethics of words." In consequence, his discussion of "democracy" results in a great many methodological errors as well as inconsistencies. To conserve space, I shall focus on three..

I

First of all, he confuses democracy as a political *process* with democracy as a political *product* or state of welfare; democracy as a *"free* society" with democracy as a *"good* society," where good is defined in terms of equality or justice (or both) or some other constellation of values. One of the reasons for choosing to live under a democratic political system rather than a nondemocratic system is our belief that it makes possible a better society. That is something that must be empirically established, something denied by critics of democracy from Plato to Santayana. The equality which is relevant to democracy as a *political process* is, in the first instance, political equality with respect to the rights of citizenship. Theoretically, a politically democratic community could vote, wisely or unwisely, to abolish, retain, or establish certain economic inequalities. Theoretically, a benevolent despotism could institute certain kinds of social and even juridical equalities. Historically, the Bismarckian political dictatorship introduced social welfare legislation for the masses at a time when such legislation would have been repudiated by

Originally published in *How Democratic Is America?* ed. Robert A. Goldwin, pp. 62–75 (Chicago: Rand McNally, 1971). The author has revised and updated this essay for *Points of View.*

the existing British and American political democracies. Some of Mr. Zinn's proposed reforms could be introduced under a dictatorship or benevolent despotism. Therefore, they are not logically or organically related to democracy.

The second error in Mr. Zinn's approach to democracy is "to measure our democracy against an ideal (even if inadvertently unachievable) standard . . . even if utopian . . ." without *defining* the standard. His criteria admittedly are neither necessary nor sufficient for determining the presence of democracy since he himself admits that they are applicable to societies that are not democratic. Further, even if we were to take his criteria as severally defining the presence of democracy—as we might take certain physical and mental traits as constituting a definition of health—he gives no operational test for determining whether or not they have been fulfilled. For example, among the criteria he lists for determining whether a society is democratic is this: "Are the members of the society equally protected on matters of life and death— in the most literal sense of that phrase?" A moment's reflection will show that here—as well as in other cases where Zinn speaks of equality—it is impossible for all members to be equally protected on matters of life and death—certainly not in a world in which men do the fighting and women give birth to children, where children need *more* protection than adults, and where some risk-seeking adults require and deserve less protection (since resources are not infinite) than others. As Karl Marx realized, "in the most literal sense of that phrase," there cannot be absolute equality even in a classless society. . . .

The only sensible procedure in determining the absence or presence of equality from a democratic perspective is comparative. We must ask whether a culture is more or less democratic in comparison to the past with respect to some *desirable* feature of equality (Zinn ignores the fact that not all equalities are desirable). It is better for some people to be more intelligent and more knowledgeable than others than for all to be unintelligent and ignorant. There never is literally equal access to education, to knowledge and training in any society. The question is: Is there more access today for more people than yesterday, and how can we increase the access tomorrow?

Mr. Zinn refuses to take this approach because, he asserts, "it supports complacency." It does nothing of the sort! On the contrary, it shows that progress is possible, and encourages us to exert our efforts in the same direction if we regard the direction as desirable.

It will be instructive to look at the passage in which Mr. Zinn objects to this sensible comparative approach because it reveals the bias in his approach:

"With such a standard," he writes, "Russia in 1910 could point with pride to how much progress they had made towards parliamentary democracy: as Russians in 1984 could point to their post-Stalin progress away from the gulag; as Americans could point in 1939 to how far they had come in solving the problem of equality; as Americans in the South could point in 1950 to the progress of the American Negro."

a. In 1910 the Russians were indeed moving toward greater progress in local parliamentary institutions. Far from making them complacent, they moved towards more inclusive representative institutions which culminated in elections to the Constituent Assembly in 1918, which was bayoneted out of existence by Lenin and the Communist Party, with a minority party dictatorship established.

b. Only Mr. Zinn would regard the slight diminution in terror from the days of Stalin to the regime of Chernenko as progress toward democracy. Those who observe the ethics of words would normally say that the screws of repression had been slightly relaxed. Mr. Zinn seems unaware that as bad as the terror was under Lenin it was not as pervasive as it is today. But no one with any respect for the ethics of words would speak of "the progress of democracy" in the Soviet Union from Lenin to Stalin to Khrushchev to Chernenko. Their regimes were varying degrees of dictatorship and terror.

c. Americans could justifiably say that in 1939 progress had been made in giving workers a greater role, not as Mr. Zinn says in "solving the problem of economic equality" (a meaningless phrase) but in determining the conditions and rewards of work that prevailed in 1929 or previously because the existence of the Wagner Labor Relations Act made collective bargaining the law of the land. They could say this *not* to rest in complacency but to use the organized force of their trade unions to influence further the political life of the country. And indeed, it was the organized labor movement in 1984 which in effect chose the candidate of the Democratic Party.

d. Americans in the South in 1950 could rightfully speak of the progress of the Southern Negro over the days of unrestricted Jim Crow and lynching bees of the past, *not* to rest in complacency, but to agitate for further progress through the Supreme Court decision of *Brown v. Board of Education in Topeka* and through the Civil Rights Act of Congress. This has not made them complacent, but more resolved to press further to eliminate remaining practices of invidious discrimination.

Even Mr. Zinn should admit that with respect to some of his other criteria this is the only sensible approach. Otherwise we get unhistorical answers, the hallmark of the doctrinaire. He asks—criterion 1—"To what extent can various people in the society participate in those decisions which affect their lives?" and—criterion 7—"Is there freedom of expression on all matters, and equally for all, to communicate with other members of the society?" Why doesn't Mr. Zinn adopt this sensible comparative approach? Because it would lead him to inquire into the extent to which people are free to participate in decisions that affect their lives *today*, free to express themselves, free to organize, free to protest and dissent today, *in comparison with the past.* It would lead him to the judgment *which he wishes to avoid at all costs,* to wit, that despite the grave problems, gaps, and tasks before us, the United States is *more* democratic today than it was a hundred years ago, fifty years ago, twenty years ago, five years ago with respect to every one of the criteria he has listed. To recognize this is *not* an invitation to complacency. On the contrary, it indicates the possibility of broadening, deepening, and using the democratic political process to improve the quality of human life, to modify and redirect social institutions in order to realize on a wider scale the moral commitment of democracy to an equality of concern for all its citizens to achieve their fullest growth as persons. This commitment is to a process, not to a transcendent goal or a fixed, ideal standard.

In a halting, imperfect manner, set back by periods of violence, vigilantism, and xenophobia, the political democratic process in the United States has been used to modify the operation of the economic system. The improvements and reforms won from time to time make the still-existing problems and evils more acute in that people become more aware of them. The more the democratic process extends human freedoms, and the more it introduces justice in social relations and the distribution of wealth, the greater grows the desire for *more* freedom and justice. Historically and psychologically, it is false to assume that reforms breed a spirit of complacency. . . .

The third and perhaps most serious weakness in Mr. Zinn's view is his conception of the nature of the formal political democratic process. It suffers from several related defects. First, it overlooks the central importance of majority rule in the democratic process. Second, it denies in effect that majority rule is possible by defining democracy in such a way that it becomes impossible. . . .

"Representation by its very nature," claims Mr. Zinn, "is undemocratic." This is Rousseauistic nonsense. For it would mean that no democracy—including all societies that Mr. Zinn ever claimed at any time to be democratic—could possibly exist, not even the direct democracies or assemblies of Athens or the New England town meetings. For all such assemblies must elect officials to carry out their will. If no representative (and an official is a representative, too) can adequately represent another's needs, there is no assurance that in the actual details of governance, the selectmen, road commissioners, or other town or assembly officials will, in fact, carry out their directives. No assembly or meeting can sit in continuous session or collectively carry out the common decision. In the nature of the case, officials, like representatives, constitute an elite and their actions *may* reflect their interests more than the interests of the governed. This makes crucial the questions whether and how an elite can be removed, whether the consent on which the rule of the officials or representatives rests is free or coerced, whether a minority can peacefully use these mechanisms, by which freely given consent is registered, to win over or become a majority. The existence of representative assemblies makes democracy difficult, not impossible.

Since Mr. Zinn believes that a majority never has any authority to bind a minority as well as itself by decisions taken after free discussion and debate, he is logically committed to anarchy. Failing to see this, he confuses two fundamentally different things—the meaning or definition of democracy, and its justification.

1. A democratic government is one in which the general direction of policy rests directly or indirectly upon the freely given consent of a majority of the adults governed. Ambiguities and niceties aside, that is what democracy means. It is not anarchy. The absence of a unanimous consensus does not entail the absence of democracy.

2. One may reject on moral or religious or personal grounds a democratic society. Plato, as well as modern totalitarians, contends that a majority of mankind is either too stupid or vicious to be entrusted with self-government, or to be given the power to accept or reject their ruling elites, and that the only viable alternative to democracy is the self-selecting and self-perpetuating elite of "the wise," or "the efficient," or "the holy," or "the strong," depending upon the particular ideology of the totalitarian apologist. The only thing they have in common with democrats is their rejection of anarchy.

3. No intelligent and moral person can make an *absolute* of democracy in the sense that he believes it is always, everywhere, under any conditions, and no matter what its consequences, ethically legitimate. Democracy is obviously not desirable in a head-hunting or cannibalistic society or in an institution of the feeble-minded. But wherever and whenever a principled democrat accepts the political system of democracy, he must accept the binding authority of legislative decisions, reached after the free give-and-take of debate and discussion, as binding upon him whether he is a member of the majority or minority. Otherwise the consequence is incipient or overt anarchy or civil war, the usual preface to despotism or tyranny. Accepting the decision of the majority as binding does not mean that it is final or irreversible. The processes of freely given consent must make it possible for a minority to urge amendment or repeal of any decision of the majority. Under carefully guarded provisions, a democrat may resort to civil disobedience of a properly enacted law in order to bear witness to the depths of his commitment in an effort *to reeducate* his fellow citizens. But in that case he must voluntarily accept punishment for his civil disobedience, and so long as he remains a democrat, voluntarily abandon his violation or noncompliance with law at the point where its consequences threaten to destroy the democratic process and open the floodgates either to the violent disorders of anarchy or to the dictatorship of a despot or a minority political party.

4. That Mr. Zinn is not a democrat but an anarchist in his views is apparent in his contention that not only must a democracy allow or tolerate civil disobedience within limits but that "members of a society concerned with democracy must not only defend such acts, but encourage them." On this view, if Southern segregationists resort to civil disobedience to negate the long-delayed but eminently just measures adopted by the government to implement the amendments that outlaw slavery, they should be encouraged to do so. On this view, any group that defies any law that violates its conscience—with respect to marriage, taxation, vaccination, abortion, education—should be encouraged to do so. Mr. Zinn, like most anarchists, refuses to generalize the principles behind his action. He fails to see that if all fanatics of causes deemed by them to be morally just were encouraged to resort to civil disobedience, even our imperfect existing political democracy would dissolve in chaos, and that civil disobedience would soon become quite uncivil. He fails to see that *in a democracy the processes of intelligence, not individual conscience, must be supreme.*

II

I turn now to some of the issues that Mr. Zinn declares are substantive. Before doing so I wish to make clear my belief that the most substantive issue of all is the procedural one by which the inescapable differences of interests among men, once a certain moral level of civilization has been reached, are to be negotiated. The belief in the validity of democratic procedures rests upon the conviction that where adult human beings have freedom of access to relevant information, they are, by and large, better judges of their own interests than are those who set themselves up as their betters and rulers, that, to use the homely maxim, those who wear the shoes know best where they pinch and therefore have the right to change their political shoes in the light of their experience. . . .

Looking at the question "How democratic is America?" with respect to the problems of poverty, race, education, etc., we must say "Not democratic enough!", but not for the reasons Mr. Zinn gives. For he seems to believe that the failure to adopt *his* solutions and proposals with respect to foreign policy, slum clearance, pollution, etc., is evidence of the failure of the democratic process itself. He overlooks the crucial difference between the procedural process and the substantive issues. When he writes that democracy is devoid of meaning if it does not include "equal access to the available resources of the society," he is simply abusing language. Assuming such equal access is desirable (which some might question who believe that access to *some* of society's resources—for example, to specialized training or to scarce supplies—should go not equally to all but to the most needful or sometimes to the most qualified), a democracy may or may not legislate such equal access. The crucial question is whether the electorate has the power to make the choice, or to elect those who would carry out the mandate chosen. . . .

When Mr. Zinn goes on to say that "in the United States . . . democracy should mean that every American, working a short work-week, has adequate food, clothing, shelter, health care, . . ." he is not only abusing language, he is revealing the fact that the procedural processes that are essential to the meaning of democracy, in ordinary usage, are not essential to his conception. He is violating the basic ethics of discourse. If democracy "should mean" what Zinn says it should, then were Huey Long or any other dictator to seize power and introduce a "short work-week" and distribute "adequate food, clothing, shelter, health care" to the masses, Mr. Zinn would have to regard his regime as democratic.

After all, when Hitler came to power and abolished free elections in Germany, he at the same time reduced unemployment, increased the real wages of the German worker, and provided more adequate food, clothing, shelter, and health care than was available under the Weimar Republic. On Zinn's view of what democracy "should mean," this made Hitler's rule more democratic than that of Weimar. . . .

Not surprisingly, Mr. Zinn is a very unreliable guide even in his account of the procedural features of the American political system. In one breath he maintains that not enough information is available to voters to make intelligent choices on major political issues like tax laws. (The voter, of course, does not vote on such laws but for representatives who have taken stands on a number of complex issues.) "The dominant influences are those of big business, which has the resources both to understand and to act." In another breath, he complains that the electorate is at the mercy of the propagandist. "The propagandist does not need to lie; he overwhelms the public with so much information as to lead it to believe that it is all too complicated for anyone but the experts."

Mr. Zinn is certainly hard to please! The American political process is not democratic because the electorate hasn't got enough information. It is also undemocratic because it receives too much information. What would Zinn have us do so that the public gets just the right amount of information and propaganda? Have the government control the press? Restrict freedom of propaganda? But these are precisely the devices of totalitarian societies. The evils of the press, even when it is free of government control, are many indeed. The great problem is to keep the press free and responsible. And as defective as the press and other public media are today, surely it is an exaggeration to say that with respect to tax laws "the dominant influences are those of big business." If they were, how can we account for the existence of the income tax laws? If the influence of big business on the press is so dominant and the press is so biased, how can we account for the fact that although 92 percent of the press opposed Truman's candidacy in 1948, he was re-elected? How can we account for the profound dissatisfaction of Vice President Agnew with the press and other mass media? And since Mr. Zinn believes that big business dominates our educational system, especially our universities, how can we account for the fact that the universities are the centers of the strongest dissent in the nation to public and national policy, that the National Association of Manufacturers bitterly complained a few years ago that the economics of the free enterprise system was derided, and often not even taught, in most Departments of Economics in the colleges and universities of the nation?

Mr. Zinn's exaggerations are really caricatures of complex realities. Far from being controlled by the monolithic American corporate economy, American public opinion is today marked by a greater scope and depth of dissent than at any time in its history, except for the days preceding the Civil War. The voice and the votes of Main Street still count for more in a democratic polity than those of Wall Street. Congress has limited, and can still further limit, the influence of money on the electoral process by federal subsidy and regulations. There are always abuses needing reforms. By failing to take a comparative approach and instead focusing on some absolute utopian standard of perfection, Mr. Zinn gives an exaggerated, tendentious, and fundamentally false picture of the United States. There is hardly a sentence in his essay that is free of some serious flaw in perspective, accuracy, or emphasis. Sometimes they have a comic effect, as when Mr. Zinn talks about the lack of "equal distribution of the right of freedom of expression." What kind of "equal distribution" is he talking about? Of course, a person with more money can talk to more people than one with less, although this does not mean that more persons will listen to him, agree with him, or be influenced by him. But a person with a more eloquent voice or a better brain can reach more people than you or I. What shall we therefore do to insure equal distribution of the right of freedom of expression? Insist on equality of voice volume or pattern, and equality of brain power? More money gives not only greater opportunity to talk to people than less money but the ability to do thousands of things barred to those who have less money. Shall we then decree that all people have the same amount of money all the time and forbid anyone from depriving anyone else of any of his money even by fair means? "The government," writes Mr. Zinn, "has much more freedom of expression than a private individual because the President can command the airwaves when he wishes, and reach 60 million people in one night."

Alas! Mr. Zinn is not joking. Either he wants to bar the President or any public official from using the airwaves or he wants all of us to take turns. One wonders what country Mr. Zinn is living in. Nixon spoke to 60 million people several times, and so did Jimmy Carter. What was the result? More significant than the fact that 60 million people hear the President is that 60 million or more can hear his critics, sometimes right after he speaks, and that no one is compelled to listen.

Mr. Zinn does not understand the basic meaning of equality in a free, open democratic society. Its philosophy does not presuppose that all citizens are physically or intellectually equal or that all are equally gifted in every or any respect. It holds that all enjoy a *moral* equality, and that therefore, as far

as is practicable, given finite resources, the institutions of a democratic society should seek to provide an equal opportunity to all its citizens to develop
themselves to their full desirable potential.

Of course, we cannot ever provide complete equal opportunity. More
and more is enough. For one thing, so long as children have different parents
and home environments, they cannot enjoy the same or equal opportunities.
Nonetheless, the family has compensating advantages for all that. Let us
hope that Mr. Zinn does not wish to wipe out the family to avoid differences
in opportunity. Plato believed that the family, as we know it, should be
abolished because it did not provide equality of opportunity, and that all
children should be brought up by the state.

Belief in the moral equality of men and women does not require that all
individuals be treated identically or that equal treatment must be measured
or determined by equality of outcome or result. Every citizen should have an
equal right to an education, but that does not mean that, regardless of capacity and interest, he or she should have the same amount of schooling beyond
the adolescent years, and at the same schools, and take the same course of
study. With the increase in national wealth, a good case can be made for an
equal right of all citizens to health care or medical treatment. But only a
quack or ideological fanatic would insist that therefore all individuals should
have the same medical regimen no matter what ails them. This would truly
be putting all human beings in the bed of Procrustes.

This conception of moral equality as distinct from Mr. Zinn's notions of
equality is perfectly compatible with intelligent recognition of human inequalities and relevant ways of treating their inequalities to further both the
individual and common good. Intelligent and loving parents are equally concerned with the welfare of all their children. But precisely because they are,
they may provide different specific strategies in health care, education, psychological motivation, and intellectual stimulation to develop the best in all
of them. The logic of Mr. Zinn's position—although he seems blissfully unaware of it—leads to the most degrading kind of egalitarian socialism, the
kind which Marx and Engels in their early years denounced as "barracks socialism."

It is demonstrable that democracy is healthier and more effective where
human beings do not suffer from poverty, unemployment, and disease. It is
also demonstrable that to the extent that property gives power, private property in the means of social production gives power over the lives of those
who must live by its use, and, therefore, that such property, whether public
or private, should be responsible to those who are affected by its operation.
Consequently one can argue that political democracy depends not only on
the extension of the franchise to all adults, not only on its active exercise, but
on programs of social welfare that provide for collective bargaining by free
trade unions of workers and employees, unemployment insurance, minimum wages, guaranteed health care, and other social services that are integral to the welfare state. It is demonstrable that although the existing

American welfare state provides far more welfare than was ever provided in the past—my own lifetime furnishes graphic evidence of the vast changes—it is still very far from being a genuine welfare state. Political democracy can exist without a welfare state, but it is stronger and better with it.

The basic issue that divides Mr. Zinn from others no less concerned about human welfare, but less fanatical than he, is how a genuine welfare state is to be brought about. My contention is that this can be achieved by the vigorous exercise of the existing democratic process, and that by the same coalition politics through which great gains have been achieved in the past, even greater gains can be won in the future.

For purposes of economy, I focus on the problem of poverty, or since this is a relative term, hunger. If the presence of hunger entails the absence of the democratic political process, then democracy has never existed in the past—which would be an arbitrary use of words. Nonetheless, the existence of hunger is always a *threat* to the continued existence of the democratic process because of the standing temptation of those who hunger to exchange freedom for the promise of bread. This, of course, is an additional ground to the even weightier moral reasons for gratifying basic human needs.

That fewer people go hungry today in the United States than ever before may show that our democracy is better than it used to be but not that it is as good as it can be. Even the existence of one hungry person is one too many. How then can hunger or the extremes of poverty be abolished? Certainly not by the method Mr. Zinn advises: "Acts of civil disobedience by the poor will be required, at the least, to make middle-class America take notice, to bring national decisions that begin to reallocate wealth."

This is not only a piece of foolish advice, it is dangerously foolish advice. Many national decisions to reallocate wealth have been made through the political process—what else is the system of taxation if not a method of reallocating wealth?—without resort to civil disobedience. Indeed, resort to civil disobedience on this issue is very likely to produce a backlash among those active and influential political groups in the community who are aware that normal political means are available for social and economic reform. The refusal to engage in such normal political processes could easily be exploited by demagogues to portray the movement towards the abolition of hunger and extreme poverty as a movement towards the confiscation and equalization of all wealth.

The simplest and most effective way of abolishing hunger is to act on the truly revolutionary principle, enunciated by the federal government, that it is responsible for maintaining a standard of relief as a minimum beneath which a family will not be permitted to sink. . . .

For reasons that need no elaboration here, the greatest of the problems faced by American democracy today is the race problem. Although tied to the problems of poverty and urban reconstruction, it has independent aspects exacerbated by the legacy of the Civil War and the Reconstruction period.

Next to the American Indians, the American Negroes have suffered most from the failure of the democratic political process to extend the rights and privileges of citizenship to those whose labor and suffering have contributed so much to the conquest of the continent. The remarkable gains that have been made by the Negroes in the last twenty years have been made primarily through the political process. If the same rate of improvement continues, the year 2000 may see a rough equality established. The growth of Negro suffrage, especially in the South, the increasing sense of responsibility by the white community, despite periodic setbacks resulting from outbursts of violence, opens up a perspective of continuous and cumulative reform. The man and the organization he headed, chiefly responsible for the great gains made by the Negroes, Roy Wilkins and the NAACP, were convinced that the democratic political process can be more effectively used to further the integration of Negroes into our national life than by reliance on any other method. . . .

The only statement in Mr. Zinn's essay that I can wholeheartedly endorse is his assertion that the great danger to American democracy does not come from the phenomena of protest as such. Dissent and protest are integral to the democratic process. The danger comes from certain modes of dissent, from the substitution of violence and threats of violence for the mechanisms of the political process, from the escalation of that violence as the best hope of those who still have grievances against our imperfect American democracy, and from views such as those expressed by Mr. Zinn which downgrade the possibility of peaceful social reform and encourage rebellion. It is safe to predict that large-scale violence by impatient minorities will fail. It is almost as certain that attempts at violence will backfire, that they will create a climate of repression that may reverse the course of social progress and expanded civil liberties of the last generation. . . .

It is when Mr. Zinn is discussing racial problems that his writing ceases to be comic and silly and becomes irresponsible and mischievous. He writes:

> The massive black urban uprisings of 1967 and 1968 showed that nothing less than civil disobedience (for riots and uprisings go beyond that) could make the nation see that the race problem is an American—not a southern—problem and that it needs bold, revolutionary action.

First of all, every literate person knows that the race problem is an American problem, not exclusively a southern one. It needs no civil disobedience or "black uprisings" to remind us of that. Second, the massive uprisings of 1967 and 1968 were violent and uncivil, and resulted in needless loss of life and suffering. The Civil Rights Acts, according to Roy Wilkins, then head of the NAACP, were imperiled by them. They were adopted despite, not because, of them. Third, what kind of "revolutionary" action is Mr. Zinn calling for? And by whom? He seems to lack the courage of his confusions. Massive civil disobedience when sustained becomes a form of civil war.

Despite Mr. Zinn and others, violence is more likely to produce reaction than reform. In 1827 a resolution to manumit slaves by purchase (later, Lincoln's preferred solution) was defeated by three votes in the House of Burgesses of the State of Virginia. It was slated to be reintroduced in a subsequent session with excellent prospects of being adopted. Had Virginia adopted it, North Carolina would shortly have followed suit. But before it could be reintroduced, Nat Turner's rebellion broke out. Its violent excesses frightened the South into a complete rejection of a possibility that might have prevented the American Civil War—the fiercest and bloodiest war in human history up to that time, from whose consequences American society is still suffering. Mr. Zinn's intentions are as innocent as those of a child playing with matches.

III

One final word about "the global" dimension of democracy of which Mr. Zinn speaks. Here, too, he speaks sympathetically of actions that would undermine the willingness and capacity of a free society to resist totalitarian aggression.

The principles that should guide a free democratic society in a world where dictatorial regimes seek to impose their rule on other nations were formulated by John Stuart Mill, the great defender of liberty and representative government, more than a century ago:

> *To go to war for an idea, if the war is aggressive not defensive, is as criminal as to go to war for territory or revenue, for it is as little justifiable to force our ideas on other people, as to compel them to submit to our will in any other aspect. . . .* The doctrine of non-intervention, to be a legitimate principle of morality, must be accepted by all governments. *The despots must consent to be bound by it as well as the free states. Unless they do, the profession of it by free countries comes but to this miserable issue, that the wrong side may help the wrong side but the right may not help the right side. Intervention to enforce non-intervention is always right, always moral* if not always prudent. *Though it may be a mistake to give freedom (or independence—S. H.) to a people who do not value the boon, it cannot but be right to insist that if they do value it, they shall not be hindered from the pursuit of it by foreign coercion* (Fraser's Magazine, *1859, emphasis mine).*

Unfortunately, these principles were disregarded by the United States in 1936 when Hitler and Mussolini sent troops into Spain to help Franco overthrow the legally elected democratic Loyalist regime. The U.S. Congress, at the behest of the administration, adopted a Neutrality Resolution which prevented the democratic government of Spain from purchasing arms here. This compelled the Spanish government to make a deal with Stalin, who not only demanded its entire gold supply but the acceptance of the dread Soviet secret police, the NKVD, to supervise the operations. The main operation of the NKVD in Spain was to engage in a murderous purge of the democratic ranks of anti-Communists which led to the victory of Franco. The story is told in George Orwell's *Homage to Catalonia*. He was on the scene.

The prudence of American intervention in Vietnam may be debatable but there is little doubt that Adlai Stevenson, sometimes referred to as the liberal conscience of the nation, correctly stated the American motivation when he said at the UN on the very day of his death: "My hope in Vietnam is that resistance there may establish the fact that changes in Asia are not to be precipitated by outside force. This was the point of the Korean War. This is the point of the conflict in Vietnam."

Today the Soviet Union and Communist Cuba are engaged in extensive operations to help indigenous elements overthrow regimes in Central America. Mr. Zinn's remarks about Grenada show he is opposed to the liberal principles expressed by J. S. Mill in the passage cited above. His report of the facts about Grenada is as distorted as his account of present-day American democracy. On tiny Grenada, whose government was seized by Communist terrorists, were representatives of every Communist regime in the Kremlin's orbit, Cuban troops, and a Soviet general. I have read the documents captured by the American troops. They conclusively establish that the Communists were preparing the island as part of the Communist strategy of expansion.[1]

It is sad but significant that Mr. Zinn, whose heart bleeds for the poor Asians who suffered in the struggle to prevent the Communist takeover in Southeast Asia, has not a word of protest, not a tear of compassion for the hundreds of thousands of tortured, imprisoned, and drowned in flight after the victory of the North Vietnamese "liberators," not to mention the even greater number of victims of the Cambodian and Cuban Communists.

One summary question may be asked whose answer bears on the issue of how democratic America is. Suppose all the iron and bamboo and passport curtains of the world were lifted today, in what direction would freedom loving and democratic people move? Anyone is free to leave the United States today, except someone fleeing from the law, but in the countries arrayed against the United States people are penned in like animals and cannot cross a boundary without risking death. Has this no significance for the "global" aspect of our question?

NOTES

1 *THE GRENADA PAPERS: The Inside Story of the Grenadian Revolution—and the Making of a Totalitarian State as Told in Captured Documents* (San Francisco: Institute of Contemporary Studies, 1984).

Rebuttal to Sidney Hook

Howard Zinn

Mr. Hook *does* have the courage of his confusions. I have space to point out only a few.

1. He chooses to define democracy as a "process," thus omitting its substance. Lincoln's definition was quite good—"government of, by, and for the people." Mr. Hook pooh-poohs the last part as something that could be done by a despot. My definition, like Lincoln's, requires "of" and "by" as well as "for," process as well as content. Mr. Hook is wild about voting, which can also be allowed by despots. Voting is an improvement over autocracy, but insufficient to make any society democratic. Voting, as Emma Goldman said (true, she was an anarchist), and as Helen Keller agreed (true, she was a socialist), is "our modern fetish." It is Mr. Hook's fetish.

Mr. Hook's "democracy" is easily satisfied by hypocrisy, by forms and procedures which look good on paper, and behind which the same old injustices go on. Concealed behind the haughty pedant's charge of "methodological errors" is a definition of democracy which is empty of human meaning, a lifeless set of structures and procedures, which our elementary school teachers tried to pawn off on us as democracy—elections, checks and balances, how a bill becomes a law. Of course, we can't have perfect democracy, and can't avoid representation, but we get closer to democracy when representation is supplemented by the direct action of citizens.

The missing heart, the flowing blood, the life-giving element in democracy is the constant struggle of people inside, around, outside, and despite the ordinary political processes. That means protest, strikes, boycotts, demonstrations, petitions, agitation, education, sometimes the slow buildup of public opinion, sometimes civil disobedience.

2. Mr. Hook seems oblivious of historical experience in the United States. His infatuation with "political process" comes out of ancient textbooks in which presidents and congresses act in the nick of time to save us when we're

Howard Zinn's rebuttal was written specifically for this volume.

in trouble. In fact, that political process has never been sufficient to solve any crucial problem of human rights in our country: slavery, corporate despotism, war—all required popular movements to oppose them, movements outside those channels into which Mr. Hook and other apologists for the status quo constantly invite us, so we can get lost. Only when popular movements go into action do the channels themselves suddenly come to life.

The test is in history. When Mr. Hook says blacks got their gains "primarily through the political process" he simply does not know what he is talking about. The new consciousness of the rights of blacks, the gains made in the past twenty years—were they initiated by the "political process"? That process was dead for one hundred years while five thousand blacks were lynched, segregation flourished, and presidents, Congress, and the Supreme Court turned the other cheek. Only when blacks took to the streets by the tens of thousands, sat-in, demonstrated, even broke the law, did the "political process" awaken from its long lethargy. Only then did Congress rush to pass civil rights laws, just in time for Mr. Hook to say, cheerily, "You see, the process works."

Another test. Mr. Hook talks about the progress made "because the existence of the Wagner Labor Relations Act made collective bargaining the law of the land." He seems unaware of the wave of strikes in 1933–34 throughout the nation that brought a dead labor relations act to life. Peter Irons, in his prize-winning study, *The New Deal Lawyers*, carefully examines the chronology of 1934, and concludes: "It is likely that the existing National Labor Relations Board would have limped along, unable to enforce its orders, had not the industrial workforce erupted in late April, engulfing the country in virtual class war. . . . Roosevelt and the Congress were suddenly jolted into action." Even after the act was passed in 1935, employers resisted it, and it took the sit-down strikes of 1936–37—yes, civil disobedience—to get contracts with General Motors and U.S. Steel.

A third test. The political process was pitifully inept as a handful of decision-makers, telling lies, propelled this country into the ugly war in Vietnam. (Mr. Hook joins them, when he quotes Adlai Stevenson that we were in Vietnam to act against "outside force"; the overwhelming "outside force" in Vietnam was the United States, with 525,000 troops, dropping 7 million tons of bombs on Southeast Asia.) A President elected in 1964 on his promises to keep the peace took us into war; Congress, like sheep, voted the money; the Supreme Court enveloped itself in its black robes and refused to discuss the constitutionality of the war. It took an unprecedented movement of protest to arouse the nation, to send a surge of energy moving through those clogged processes, and finally bring the war to an end.

3. Mr. Hook doesn't understand civil disobedience. He makes the common error of thinking that a supporter of Martin Luther King's civil disobedience must also support that of the Ku Klux Klan. He seems to think that if you

believe civil disobedience is sometimes justified, for some causes, you must support civil disobedience done any time, by any group, for any reason. He does not grasp that the principle is not one of absolute civil disobedience; it simply denies absolute obedience. It says we should not be fanatics about "law and order" because sometimes the law supports the disorder of poverty, or racism, or war.

We can certainly distinguish between civil disobedience for good causes and for bad causes. That's what our intelligence is for. Will this lead to "chaos," as Mr. Hook warns? Again, historical experience is instructive: Did the civil disobedience of blacks in the sixties lead to chaos? Or the civil disobedience of antiwar protesters in the Vietnam years? Yes, they involved some disorder, as all social change does; they upset the false tranquility of segregation, they demanded an end to the chaos of war.

4. Mr. Hook thinks he is telling us something new when he says we can't, and sometimes should not, have perfect equality. Of course. But the point of having ideals is not that they can be perfectly achieved, but that they do not let us rest content, as Mr. Hook is, with being somewhat better off today than yesterday. By his standard, we can give just enough more to the poor to appease anger, while keeping the basic injustice of a wealthy society. In a country where some people live in mansions and others in slums, should we congratulate ourselves because the slums now have TV antennas sticking out of the leaky roofs? His prescription for equality would have us clean out the Augean stables with a spoon, and boast of our progress, while comparing us to all the terrible places in the world where they don't even have spoons. Mr. Hook tries to avoid this issue of inequality by confusing inequality in intellect and physique, which obviously can't be helped much, with inequality of wealth, which is intolerably crass in a country as wealthy as ours.

Mr. Hook becomes ludicrous when he tries to deny the crucial importance of wealth in elections and in control of the media. When he says, "The voice and votes of Main Street still count for more in a democratic polity than those of Wall Street," I wonder where he has been. If Main Street counts more than Wall Street, how come congressional cutbacks in social programs in 1981–82 brought the number of people officially defined as poor to its highest level since 1965—25.3 million—while at the same time eight thousand millionaires saved a billion dollars in lowered taxes? And how can we account for this news item of October 16, 1984, in the *New York Times:* "Five of the nation's top dozen military contractors earned profits in the years 1981, 1982, and 1983, but paid no Federal income taxes." Can you name five schoolteachers or five social workers who paid no federal income taxes?

What of the system of justice—has it not always favored Wall Street over Main Street? Compare the punishment given to corporation executives found guilty of robbing billions from consumers by price-fixing with the punishment given to auto thieves and house burglars.

Money talks loudly in this "democratic polity." But, Mr. Hook says, in an absurd defense of the control of the media, you don't have to listen! No, the mother needing medical aid doesn't have to listen, but whether her children live or die may result from the fact that the rich dominate the media, control the elections, and get legislation passed which hurts the poor. A *Boston Globe* dispatch, May 24, 1984:

> *Infant mortality, which had been declining steadily in Boston and other cities in the 1970s, shot up suddenly after the Reagan Administration reduced grants for health care for mothers and children and cut back sharply on Medicaid eligibility among poor women and children in 1981, according to new research.*

5. As for "the global dimension of democracy," Mr. Hook's simple view of the world as divided between "free society" and "totalitarian aggression" suggests he is still living back in the heroic battles of World War II. We are now in the nuclear age, and that neat division into "free" and "totalitarian" is both factually wrong and dangerous. Yes, the United States is a relatively free society, and the Soviet Union is a shameful corruption of Marx's dreams of freedom. But the United States has established or supported some of the most brutal totalitarian states in the world: Chile, South Africa, El Salvador, Guatemala, South Korea, the Philippines. Yes, the Soviet Union has committed cruel acts of aggression in Hungary, Czechoslovakia, and especially Afghanistan. But the United States has also, whether by the military or the CIA, committed aggression in Iran, Guatemala, Cuba, and the Dominican Republic, and especially in Vietnam, Laos, and Cambodia.

You cannot draw a line across the globe, as Mr. Hook does, to find good on one side and evil on the other. We get a sense of Mr. Hook's refusal to face the complexities of evil when he passes off the horror of the American invasion of Southeast Asia, which left a million dead, with: "The prudence of American intervention in Vietnam may be debatable." One can hear Mr. Hook's intellectual counterparts in the Soviet Union saying about the invasion of Afghanistan: "Our prudence . . . may be debatable." Such moral blindness will have to be overcome if there is to be movement toward real democracy in the United States, and toward real socialism in the Soviet Union. It is the fanaticism on both sides, justifying war "to defend freedom," or "to defend socialism," or simply, vaguely, "national security," that may yet kill us all. That will leave the issue of "how democratic we are" for archeologists of a future era.

Rejoinder to Howard Zinn

Sidney Hook

I may have been mistaken about Mr. Zinn's courage. I am not mistaken about his confusion—his persistent confusion of a free or democratic society with a good society as he defines a good society. Zinn has not understood my criticism and therefore not replied to it. Perhaps on rereading it he will grasp the point.

1. Of course, there is no guarantee that the democratic process will yield a good society regardless of how Zinn or anyone else defines it. Democracies, like majorities, may sometimes be wrong or unwise. But if the decision is a result of a free and fair discussion and vote, it is still democratic. If those who lose in the electoral process resort to civil disobedience, democratic government ultimately breaks down. Even though the processes of democracy are slow and cumbersome and sometimes result in unwise action, its functioning Bill of Rights makes it possible to set them right. That is why Churchill observed, "Democracy is the worst of all forms of government except all the others that have been tried," including, we should add, anarchism.

Zinn dismisses our democratic processes as "a lifeless set of structures and procedures." But it is these very structures and procedures which have enabled us to transform our society from one in which only white men with property voted to one in which all white men voted, then all men, then all men and women. It is these structures and procedures which have extended and protected the right to dissent, even for all sorts of foolishness like Zinn's. They currently protect Mr. Zinn in his academic freedom and post, in his right to utter any criticism of the democratic system under which he lives—a right he would never enjoy in any so-called socialist society in the world today.

Mr. Zinn gives his case away when he refers to the democratic process, which requires voting in *free* elections, as a "fetish." A fetish is an object of irrational and superstitious devotion which enlightened persons reject. Like

Sidney Hook's rejoinder was written specifically for this volume.

Marx, Zinn rejects "the fetishism of commodities." Is he prepared to reject the democratic process, too, if its results do not jibe with *his* conception of the good society?

How, one wonders, does Zinn know that his conception is inherently more desirable than that of his fellow citizens? The democrat says: *Let us leave this choice to the arbitrament of the democratic process.* Zinn has a shorter way. He labels any conception other than his own as undemocratic; and if it prevails, he urges the masses to take to the streets.

2. The space allotted to me does not permit adequate discussion of the international aspects of the struggle for a free society. (I refer students to my *Philosophy and Public Policy* and *Marxism and Beyond.*) Suffice it to say here that sometimes when the feasible alternatives are limited, the wisest choice between evils is the lesser one. This is the same principle, supported by Zinn, that justified military aid to the Soviet Union when Nazi Germany invaded, although Stalin's regime at the time oppressed many more millions than Hitler's. From the standpoint of the free society, Stalin was the lesser evil then. Today Nazism is destroyed and globally expanding communism has taken its place. If, and only if, we are anywhere confronted by a choice of support between an authoritarian regime and a totalitarian one, the first is the lesser evil. This is not only because the second is far more oppressive of human rights (compare Batista to Castro, Thieu to Hanoi, Syngman Rhee to North Korea, Lon Nol to Pol Pot) but because authoritarian regimes sometimes develop peacefully into democracies (Spain, Portugal, Greece, Argentina) whereas no Communist regime allied to the Kremlin so far has.

3. Within narrowly prescribed limits, a democracy may tolerate civil disobedience of those who on grounds of conscience violate its laws and willingly accept their punishment. (Cf. the chapter in my *Revolution, Reform and Social Justice.*) But Zinn does not advocate civil disobedience in this sense. He urges what is clearly *uncivil* disobedience like the riotous actions that preceded the Civil Rights Acts from which the blacks, not white racists, suffered most, and the extensive destruction of property from factory sit-ins. Roy Wilkins, who should know, is my authority for asserting that the Civil Rights Acts were adopted by Congress not because of, but despite of, these disorders. The most significant racial progress since 1865 was achieved by *Brown v. Topeka Board of Education* without "the disorders" Zinn recommends—a sly term that covers broken heads, loss of property, and sometimes loss of life, which are no part of civil disobedience.

Until now, the most charitable thing one could say of Zinn's position is what Cicero once said of another loose thinker: there is no absurdity to which a person will not resort to defend another absurdity. But when Zinn with calculated ambiguity includes "disorders" in the connotation of civil disobedience, *without denouncing violence as no part of it as Gandhi and Martin Luther King did,* he is verging on moral irresponsibility. From the safety of his white suburbs, he is playing with fire.

Law and order are possible without justice; but Mr. Zinn does not seem to understand that justice is impossible without law and order.

CHAPTER TWO

THE CONSTITUTION AND THE FOUNDING FATHERS

Of the many books that have been written about the circumstances surrounding the crea-
tion of our Constitution, none generated more controversy than the publication of Charles
Beard's An Economic Interpretation of the Constitution of the United States
(1913). A historian by profession, Beard challenged the belief that our Constitution was
fashioned by men of democratic spirit. On the contrary, in what appeared to be a system-
atic marshaling of evidence, Beard sought to demonstrate: (1) that the impetus for a new
constitution came from individuals who saw their own economic interests threatened by a
growing trend in the population toward greater democracy; (2) that the Founding Fathers
themselves were men of considerable "personalty" (i.e., holdings other than real estate),
who were concerned not so much with fashioning a democratic constitution as they were
with protecting their own financial interests against the more democratically oriented
farming and debtor interests within the society; and, finally, (3) that the individuals
charged with ratifying the new Constitution also represented primarily the larger eco-
nomic interests within the society. While space limitations prevent a full development of
Beard's argument, the portions of his book that follow should provide some feel for both
the substance of his argument and his method of investigation.

Beard's analysis has been subject to repeated scrutiny over the years. The most sys-
tematic effort in this regard came in 1956 with the publication of Robert Brown's
Charles Beard and the Constitution: A Critical Analysis of an Economic Interpretation of the Constitution. *Arguing that the rigor of Beard's examination was*
more apparent than real, Brown accuses him of citing only the facts that supported his
case while ignoring those that did not. Moreover, he contends that even the evidence that
Beard provided did not warrant the interpretation he gave to it. Brown concludes that
the best evidence now available does not support the view that "the Constitution was put
over undemocratically in an undemocratic society by personal property."

An Economic Interpretation of the Constitution of the United States

Charles A. Beard

Suppose it could be shown from the classification of the men who supported and opposed the Constitution that there was no line of property division at all; that is, that men owning substantially the same amounts of the same kinds of property were equally divided on the matter of adoption or rejection—it would then become apparent that the Constitution had no ascertainable relation to economic groups or classes, but was the product of some abstract causes remote from the chief business of life—gaining a livelihood.

Suppose, on the other hand, that substantially all of the merchants, money lenders, security holders, manufacturers, shippers, capitalists, and financiers and their professional associates are to be found on one side in support of the Constitution and that substantially all or the major portion of the opposition came from the nonslaveholding farmers and the debtors—would it not be pretty conclusively demonstrated that our fundamental law was not the product of an abstraction known as "the whole people," but of a group of economic interests which must have expected beneficial results from its adoption? Obviously all the facts here desired cannot be discovered, but the data presented in the following chapters bear out the later hypothesis, and thus a reasonable presumption in favor of the theory is created.

Of course, it may be shown (and perhaps can be shown) that the farmers and debtors who opposed the Constitution were, in fact, benefited by the general improvement which resulted from its adoption. It may likewise be shown, to take an extreme case, that the English nation derived immense advantages from the Norman Conquest and the orderly administrative processes which were introduced, as it undoubtedly did; nevertheless, it does not follow that the vague thing known as "the advancement of general welfare" or some abstraction known as "justice" was the immediate, guiding purpose of the leaders in either of these great historic changes. The point is, that the direct, impelling motive in both cases was the economic advantages which the beneficiaries expected would accrue to themselves first, from their action. Further than this, economic interpretation cannot go. It may be that some larger world process is working through each series of historical events: but ultimate causes lie beyond our horizon. . . .

THE FOUNDING FATHERS: AN ECONOMIC PROFILE

A survey of the economic interests of the members of the Convention presents certain conclusions:

A majority of the members were lawyers by profession.

Most of the members came from towns, on or near the coast, that is, from the regions in which personalty was largely concentrated.

Not one member represented in his immediate personal economic interests the small farming or mechanic classes.

The overwhelming majority of members, at least five-sixths, were immediately, directly, and personally interested in the outcome of their labors at Philadelphia, and were to a greater or less extent economic beneficiaries from the adoption of the Constitution.

1. Public security interests were extensively represented in the Convention. Of the fifty-five members who attended no less than forty appear on the Records of the Treasury Department for sums varying from a few dollars up to more than one hundred thousand dollars. . . .

    It is interesting to note that, with the exception of New York, and possibly Delaware, each state had one or more prominent representatives in the Convention who held more than a negligible amount of securities, and who could therefore speak with feeling and authority on the question of providing in the new Constitution for the full discharge of the public debt. . . .

2. Personalty invested in lands for speculation was represented by at least fourteen members. . . .

3. Personalty in the form of money loaned at interest was represented by at least twenty-four members. . . .

4. Personalty in mercantile, manufacturing, and shipping lines was represented by at least eleven members. . . .

5. Personalty in slaves was represented by at least fifteen members. . . .

It cannot be said, therefore, that the members of the Convention were "disinterested." On the contrary, we are forced to accept the profoundly significant conclusion that they knew through their personal experiences in economic affairs the precise results which the new government that they were setting up was designed to attain. As a group of doctrinaires, like the Frankfort assembly of 1848, they would have failed miserably; but as practical men they were able to build the new government upon the only foundations which could be stable: fundamental economic interests.[1]. . . .

RATIFICATION

New York

There can be no question about the predominance of personalty in the contest over the ratification in New York. That state, says Libby, "presents the problem in its simplest form. The entire mass of interior counties . . . were solidly Anti-federal, comprising the agricultural portion of the state, the last settled and the most thinly populated. There were however in this region two Federal cities (not represented in the convention [as such]), Albany in Albany county and Hudson in Columbia county. . . . The Federal area centred about New York city and county: to the southwest lay Richmond county (Staten Island); to the southeast Kings county, and the northeast Westchester county; while still further extending this area, at the northeast lay the divided county of Dutchess, with a vote in the convention of 4 to 2 in favor of the Constitution, and at the southeast were the divided counties of Queens and Suffolk. . . . These radiating strips of territory with New York city as a centre form a unit, in general favorable to the new Constitution; and it is significant of this unity that Dutchess, Queens, and Suffolk counties broke away from the anti-Federal phalanx and joined the Federalists, securing thereby the adoption of the Constitution."[2]

Unfortunately the exact distribution of personalty in New York and particularly in the wavering districts which went over to the Federalist party cannot be ascertained, for the system of taxation in vogue in New York at the period of the adoption of the Constitution did not require a state record of property.[3] The data which proved so fruitful in Massachusetts are not forthcoming, therefore, in the case of New York; but it seems hardly necessary to demonstrate the fact that New York City was the centre of personalty for the state and stood next to Philadelphia as the great centre of operations in public stock.

This somewhat obvious conclusion is reinforced by the evidence relative to the vote on the legal tender bill which the paper money party pushed through in 1786. Libby's analysis of this vote shows that "no vote was cast against the bill by members of counties north of the county of New York. In the city and county of New York and in Long Island and Staten Island, the combined vote was 9 to 5 against the measure. Comparing this vote with the vote on the ratification in 1788, it will be seen that of the Federal counties 3 voted against paper money and 1 for it; of the divided counties 1 (Suffolk) voted against paper money and 2 (Queens and Dutchess) voted for it. Of the anti-Federal counties none had members voting against paper money. The merchants as a body were opposed to the issue of paper money and the Chamber of Commerce adopted a memorial against the issue."[4]

Public security interests were identified with the sound money party. There were thirty members of the New York constitutional convention who voted in favor of the ratification of the Constitution and of these no less than sixteen were holders of public securities. . . .

South Carolina

South Carolina presents the economic elements in the ratification with the utmost simplicity. There we find two rather sharply marked districts in antagonism over the Constitution. "The rival sections," says Libby, "were the coast or lower district and the upper, or more properly, the middle and upper country. The coast region was the first settled and contained a larger portion of the wealth of the state; its mercantile and commercial interests were important; its church was the Episcopal, supported by the state." This region, it is scarcely necessary to remark, was overwhelmingly in favor of the Constitution. The upper area, against the Constitution, "was a frontier section, the last to receive settlement; its lands were fertile and its mixed population was largely small farmers. . . . There was no established church, each community supported its own church and there was a great variety in the district."[5]

A contemporary writer, R. G. Harper, calls attention to the fact that the lower country, Charleston, Beaufort, and Georgetown, which had 28,694 white inhabitants, and about seven-twelfths of the representation in the state convention, paid £28,081:5:10 taxes in 1794, while the upper country, with 120,902 inhabitants, and five-twelfths of the representation in the convention, paid only £8390:13:3 taxes.[6] The lower districts in favor of the Constitution therefore possessed the wealth of the state and a disproportionate share in the convention—on the basis of the popular distribution of representation.

These divisions of economic interest are indicated by the abstracts of the tax returns for the state in 1794 which show that of £127,337 worth of stock in trade, faculties, etc. listed for taxation in the state, £109,800 worth was in Charleston, city and county—the stronghold of Federalism. Of the valuation of lots in towns and villages to the amount of £656,272 in the state, £549,909 was located in that city and county.[7]

The records of the South Carolina loan office preserved in the Treasury Department at Washington show that the public securities of that state were more largely in the hands of inhabitants than was the case in North Carolina. They also show a heavy concentration in the Charleston district.

At least fourteen of the thirty-one members of the state-ratifying convention from the parishes of St. Philip and Saint Michael, Charleston (all of whom favored ratification) held over $75,000 worth of public securities. . . .

Conclusions

At the close of this long and arid survey—partaking of the nature of catalogue—it seems worthwhile to bring together the important conclusions for political science which the data presented appear to warrant.

The movement for the Constitution of the United States was originated and carried through principally by four groups of personalty interests which had been adversely affected under the Articles of Confederation: money, public securities, manufactures, and trade and shipping.

The first firm steps toward the formation of the Constitution were taken by a small and active group of men immediately interested through their personal possessions in the outcome of their labors.

No popular vote was taken directly or indirectly on the proposition to call the Convention which drafted the Constitution.

A large propertyless mass was, under the prevailing suffrage qualifications, excluded at the outset from participation (through representatives) in the work of framing the Constitution.

The members of the Philadelphia Convention which drafted the Constitution were, with a few exceptions, immediately, directly, and personally interested in, and derived economic advantages from, the establishment of the new system.

The Constitution was essentially an economic document based upon the concept that the fundamental private rights of property are anterior to government and morally beyond the reach of popular majorities.

The major portion of the members of the Convention are on record as recognizing the claim of property to a special and defensive position in the Constitution.

In the ratification of the Constitution, about three-fourths of the adult males failed to vote on the question, having abstained from the elections at which delegates to the state conventions were chosen, either on account of their indifference or their disfranchisement by property qualifications.

The Constitution was ratified by a vote of probably not more than one-sixth of the adult males.

It is questionable whether a majority of the voters participating in the elections for the state conventions in New York, Massachusetts, New Hampshire, Virginia, and South Carolina, actually approved the ratification of the Constitution.

The leaders who supported the Constitution in the ratifying conventions represented the same economic groups as the members of the Philadelphia Convention; and in a large number of instances they were also directly and personally interested in the outcome of their efforts.

In the ratification, it became manifest that the line of cleavage for and against the Constitution was between substantial personalty interests on the one hand and the small farming and debtor interests on the other.

The Constitution was not created by "the whole people" as the jurists have said; neither was it created by "the states" as Southern nullifiers long contended; but it was the work of a consolidated group whose interests knew no state boundaries and were truly national in their scope.

NOTES

1. The fact that a few members of the Convention, who had considerable economic interests at stake, refused to support the Constitution does not invalidate the general conclusions here presented. In the cases of Yates, Lansing, Luther Martin, and Mason, definite economic reasons for their action are forthcoming; but this is a minor detail.
2. O. G. Libby, *Geographical Distribution of the Vote of the Thirteen States on the Federal Constitution*, p. 18. Libby here takes the vote in the New York convention, but that did not precisely represent the popular vote.
3. *State Papers: Finance*, vol. 1, p. 425.
4. Libby, *Geographical Distribution*, p. 59.
5. *Ibid.*, pp. 42–43.
6. "Appius," *To the Citizens of South Carolina* (1794), Library of Congress, Duane Pamphlets, vol. 83.
7. *State Papers: Finance*, vol. 1, p. 462. In 1783 an attempt to establish a bank with $100,000 capital was made in Charleston, S.C., but it failed. "Soon after the adoption of the funding system, three banks were established in Charleston whose capitals in the whole amounted to twenty times the sum proposed in 1783." D. Ramsey, *History of South Carolina* (1858 ed.), vol. 2, p. 106.

Charles Beard and the Constitution: A Critical Analysis

Robert E. Brown

At the end of Chapter XI [of *An Economic Interpretation of the Constitution of the United States*], Beard summarized his findings in fourteen paragraphs under the heading of "Conclusions." Actually, these fourteen conclusions merely add up to the two halves of the Beard thesis. One half, that the Constitution originated with and was carried through by personalty interests—money, public securities, manufactures, and commerce—is to be found in paragraphs two, three, six, seven, eight, twelve, thirteen, and fourteen. The other half—that the Constitution was put over undemocratically in an undemocratic society—is expressed in paragraphs four, five, nine, ten, eleven, and fourteen. The lumping of these conclusions under two general headings makes it easier for the reader to see the broad outlines of the Beard thesis.

Before we examine these two major divisions of the thesis, however, some comment is relevant on the implications contained in the first paragraph. In it Beard characterized his book as a long and arid survey, something in the nature of a catalogue. Whether this characterization was designed to give his book the appearance of a coldly objective study based on the facts we do not know. If so, nothing could be further from reality. As reviewers pointed out in 1913, and as subsequent developments have demonstrated, the book is anything but an arid catalogue of facts. Its pages are replete with interpretation, sometimes stated, sometimes implied. Our task has been to examine Beard's evidence to see whether it justifies the interpretation which Beard gave it. We have tried to discover whether he used the historical method properly in arriving at his thesis.

If historical method means the gathering of data from primary sources, the critical evaluation of the evidence thus gathered, and the drawing of conclusions consistent with this evidence, then we must conclude that Beard has done great violation to such method in this book. He admitted that the evidence had not been collected which, given the proper use of historical method, should have precluded the writing of the book. Yet he nevertheless proceeded on the assumption that a valid interpretation could be built on secondary writings whose authors had likewise failed to collect the evidence. If we accept Beard's own maxim, "no evidence, no history," and his own admission that the data had never been collected, the answer to whether he used historical method properly is self-evident.

Neither was Beard critical of the evidence which he did use. He was accused in 1913, and one might still suspect him, of using only that evidence which appeared to support his thesis. The amount of realty in the country compared with the personalty, the vote in New York, and the omission of the part of *The Federalist*, No. 10, which did not fit his thesis are only a few examples of the uncritical use of evidence to be found in the book. Sometimes he accepted secondary accounts at face value without checking them with the sources; at other times he allowed unfounded rumors and traditions to color his work.

Finally, the conclusions which he drew were not justified even by the kind of evidence which he used. If we accepted his evidence strictly at face value, it would still not add up to the fact that the Constitution was put over undemocratically in an undemocratic society by personalty. The citing of property qualifications does not prove that a mass of men were disfranchised. And if we accept his figures on property holdings, either we do not know what most of the delegates had in realty and personalty, or we know that realty outnumbered personalty three to one (eighteen to six). Simply showing that a man held public securities is not sufficient to prove that he acted only in terms of his public securities. If we ignore Beard's own generalizations and accept only his evidence, we have to conclude that most of the country, and that even the men who were directly concerned with the Constitution, and especially Washington, were large holders of realty.

Perhaps we can never be completely objective in history, but certainly we can be more objective than Beard was in this book. Naturally the historian must always be aware of the biases, the subjectivity, the pitfalls that confront him, but this does not mean that he should not make an effort to overcome these obstacles. Whether Beard had his thesis before he had his evidence, as some have said, is a question that each reader must answer for himself. Certain it is that the evidence does not justify the thesis.

So instead of the Beard interpretation that the Constitution was put over undemocratically in an undemocratic society by personal property, the following fourteen paragraphs are offered as a possible interpretation of the Constitution and as suggestions for future research on that document.

1. The movement for the Constitution was originated and carried through by men who had long been important in both economic and political affairs in their respective states. Some of them owned personalty, more of them owned realty, and if their property was adversely affected by conditions under the Articles of Confederation, so also was the property of the bulk of the people in the country, middle-class farmers as well as town artisans.

2. The movement for the Constitution, like most important movements, was undoubtedly started by a small group of men. They were probably interested personally in the outcome of their labors, but the benefits which they expected were not confined to personal property or, for that matter, strictly to things economic. And if their own interests would be enhanced by a new government, similar interests of other men, whether agricultural or commercial, would also be enhanced.

3. Naturally there was no popular vote on the calling of the convention which drafted the Constitution. Election of delegates by state legislatures was the constitutional method under the Articles of Confederation, and had been the method long established in this country. Delegates to the Albany Congress, the Stamp Act Congress, the First Continental Congress, the Second Continental Congress, and subsequent congresses under the Articles were all elected by state legislatures, not by the people. Even the Articles of Confederation had been sanctioned by state legislatures, not by popular vote. This is not to say that the Constitutional Convention should not have been elected directly by the people, but only that such a procedure would have been unusual at the time. Some of the opponents of the Constitution later stressed, without avail, the fact that the Convention had not been directly elected. But at the time the Convention met, the people in general seemed to be about as much concerned over the fact that they had not elected the delegates as the people of this country are now concerned over the fact that they do not elect our delegates to the United Nations.

4. Present evidence seems to indicate that there were no "propertyless masses" who were excluded from the suffrage at the time. Most men were middle-class farmers who owned realty and were qualified voters, and, as the men in the Convention said, mechanics had always voted in the cities. Until credible evidence proves otherwise, we can assume that state legislatures were fairly representative at the time. We cannot condone the fact that a few men were probably disfranchised by prevailing property qualifications, but it makes a great deal of difference to an interpretation of the Constitution whether the disfranchised comprised 95 percent of the adult men or only 5 percent. Figures which give percentages of voters in terms of the entire population are misleading, since less than 20 percent of the people were adult men. And finally, the voting qualifications favored realty, not personalty.

5. If the members of the Convention were directly interested in the outcome of their work and expected to derive benefits from the establishment of the new system, so also did most of the people of the country. We have many statements to the effect that the people in general expected substantial benefits from the labors of the Convention.

6. The Constitution was not just an economic document, although economic factors were undoubtedly important. Since most of the people were middle class and had private property, practically everybody was interested in the protection of property. A constitution which did not protect property would have been rejected without any question, for the American people had fought the Revolution for the preservation of life, liberty, and property. Many people believed that the Constitution did not go far enough to protect property, and they wrote these views into the amendments to the Constitution. But property was not the only concern of those who wrote and ratified the Constitution, and we would be doing a grave injustice to the political sagacity of the Founding Fathers if we assumed that property or personal gain was their only motive.

7. Naturally the delegates recognized that protection of property was important under government, but they also recognized that personal rights were equally important. In fact, persons and property were usually bracketed together as the chief objects of government protection.

8. If three-fourths of the adult males failed to vote on the election of delegates to ratifying conventions, this fact signified indifference, not disfranchisement. We must not confuse those who could *not* vote with those who *could* vote but failed to exercise their right. Many men at the time bewailed the fact that only a small portion of the voters ever exercised their prerogative. But this in itself should stand as evidence that the conflict over the Constitution was not very bitter, for if these people had felt strongly one way or the other, more of them would have voted.

Even if we deny the evidence which I have presented and insist that American society was undemocratic in 1787, we must still accept the fact that the men who wrote the Constitution believed that they were writing it for a democratic society. They did not hide behind an iron curtain of secrecy and devise the kind of conservative government that they wanted without regard to the views and interests of "the people." More than anything else, they were aware that "the people" would have to ratify what they proposed, and that therefore any government which would be acceptable to the people must of necessity incorporate much of what was customary at the time. The men at Philadelphia were practical politicians, not political theorists. They recognized the multitude of different ideas and interests that had to be reconciled and compromised before a constitution would be acceptable. They were far too practical, and represented far too many clashing interests themselves, to fashion a government weighted in favor of personalty or to believe that the people would adopt such a government.

9. If the Constitution was ratified by a vote of only one-sixth of the adult men, that again demonstrates indifference and not disfranchisement. Of the one-fourth of the adult males who voted, nearly two-thirds favored the Constitution. Present evidence does not permit us to say what the popular vote was except as it was measured by the votes of the ratifying conventions.

10. Until we know what the popular vote was, we cannot say that it is questionable whether a majority of the voters in several states favored the Constitution. Too many delegates were sent uninstructed. Neither can we count the towns which did not send delegates on the side of those opposed to the Constitution. Both items would signify indifference rather than sharp conflict over ratification.

11. The ratifying conventions were elected for the specific purpose of adopting or rejecting the Constitution. The people in general had anywhere from several weeks to several months to decide the question. If they did not like the new government, or if they did not know whether they liked it, they could have voted *no* and there would have been no Constitution. Naturally the leaders in the ratifying conventions represented the same interests as the members of the Constitutional Convention—mainly realty and some personalty. But they also represented their constituents in these same interests, especially realty.

12. If the conflict over ratification had been between substantial personalty interests on the one hand and small farmers and debtors on the other, there would not have been a constitution. The small farmers comprised such an overwhelming percentage of the voters that they could have rejected the new government without any trouble. Farmers and debtors are not synonymous terms and should not be confused as such. A town-by-town or county-by-county record of the vote would show clearly how the farmers voted.

13. The Constitution was created about as much by the whole people as any government could be which embraced a large area and depended on representation rather than on direct participation. It was also created in part by the states, for as the *Records* show, there was strong state sentiment at the time which had to be appeased by compromise. And it was created by compromising a whole host of interests throughout the country, without which compromises it could never have been adopted.

14. If the intellectual historians are correct, we cannot explain the Constitution without considering the psychological factors also. Men were motivated by what they believe as well as by what they have. Sometimes their actions can be explained on the basis of what they hope to have or hope that their children will have. Madison understood this fact when he said that the universal hope of acquiring property tended to dispose people to look favorably upon property. It is even possible that some men support a given economic system when they themselves have nothing to gain by it. So we would want to know what the people in 1787 thought of their class status. Did workers and small farmers believe that they were lower class, or did they, as many workers do now, consider themselves middle class? Were the common people trying to eliminate the Washingtons, Adamses, Hamiltons, and Pinckneys, or were they trying to join them?

As did Beard's fourteen conclusions, these fourteen suggestions really add up to two major propositions: the Constitution was adopted in a society which was fundamentally democratic, not undemocratic; and it was adopted by a people who were primarily middle-class property owners, especially farmers who owned realty, not just by the owners of personalty. At present these points seem to be justified by the evidence, but if better evidence in the future disproves or modifies them, we must accept that evidence and change our interpretation accordingly.

After this critical analysis, we should at least not begin future research on this period of American history with the illusion that the Beard thesis of the Constitution is valid. If historians insist on accepting the Beard thesis in spite of this analysis, however, they must do so with the full knowledge that their acceptance is founded on "an act of faith," not an analysis of historical method, and that they were indulging in a "noble dream," not history.

A NEW CONSTITUTIONAL CONVENTION?

When the Founding Fathers wrote our Constitution, they provided that amendments to it could be proposed in either of two ways: (1) by a two-thirds vote of both Houses of Congress; or (2) by a constitutional convention called at the request of two-thirds of the state legislatures. Not since the Founding Fathers convened in 1787, however, has our nation held a constitutional convention. Rather, all amendments to our Constitution have been proposed by Congress.

In the last several years, the growing federal deficit has become a matter of national concern in this country. As a solution to this critical problem, some have advocated a constitutional amendment which would require the federal government to balance its budget each year. That this solution commands considerable support within the population is indicated by the fact that thirty-two state legislatures—just two short of the necessary two-thirds—have already passed resolutions calling for a constitutional convention for the purpose of formally proposing this amendment.

Not only has the wisdom of the balanced budget proposal been questioned by some, but so has the call for a constitutional convention to propose it. In the first selection which follows, Melvin Laird gives voice to these concerns, arguing that a convention could lead to fundamental and undesirable changes in our political system and have damaging international consequences as well. Griffin Bell, on the other hand, feels that Laird and others are creating a tempest in a teapot. He believes there is little likelihood that a convention will actually be called, but even if it is, that we have little to fear. In his judgment, the option of a convention provides the population with a needed check over a potentially unresponsive Congress. Moreover, given the history of constitutional conventions at the state level, there is every reason to believe that a national constitutional convention would act prudently and responsibly.

James Madison Wouldn't Approve

Melvin R. Laird

> *. . . The prospect of a second [constitutional] convention would be viewed by all Europe as a dark and threatening Cloud hanging over the Constitution.*

These are the words of James Madison, the father of the U.S. Constitution; they were written in 1787, upon the adjournment of the only federal constitutional convention held in our nation's history. Although Madison, as it turned out, worried needlessly over the possible disruptive impact on our foreign relations of a constitutional convention in the 1700s, he along with "all Europe"—certainly the free nations of Europe—would have cause to worry in 1984. And so should America. In fact, most Americans may be surprised to learn that we may be on the verge of convening the Second Constitutional Convention.

As a former member of both the legislative and executive branches, I am concerned . . . about the drastic and divisive consequences of action that would lead to the call for a constitutional convention.

Under Article V, there are two procedures for amending the U.S. Constitution. Under the only procedure used in our history, Congress considers, passes, and submits a proposed amendment to the states for ratification. If ratified by three-quarters of the states, the amendment becomes a part of the Constitution. That has proved to be a responsive and orderly procedure.

The second procedure requires the convening of a full constitutional convention whose scope and authority are not defined or limited by our Constitution. If thirty-four states submit valid petitions to Congress for a convention, it must be convened. Any and all amendments that are considered and passed by such a convention are then forwarded to the states for ratification.

Reprinted from the *Washington Post*. From Melvin R. Laird, "James Madison Wouldn't Approve," *Washington Post*, February 13, 1984.

Our citizens understandably have been wary of a constitutional convention, and there is little or no historical or constitutional guidance as to its proper powers and scope. The Constitution does not spell out, for example, how delegates would be chosen or time limits for the convention or payment of costs.

The only precedent we have for a constitutional convention took place in Philadelphia in 1787. That convention, it must be remembered, broke every legal restraint designed to limit its power and agenda. It violated specific instructions from Congress to confine itself to amending the Articles of Confederation and instead discarded the Articles and wrote our present Constitution. Moreover, that convention acted in violation of the existing Articles of Confederation by devising a new method for ratifying the proposed Constitution, specifically prohibited by the Articles of Confederation.

Reputable scholars have recently grappled with these complexities, but the realistic fact remains that two hundred years later there is no certainty that our nation would survive a modern-day convention with its basic structures intact and its citizens' traditional rights retained. The convening of a federal constitutional convention would be an act of the greatest magnitude for our nation. I believe it would be an act fraught with danger and recklessness.

Today, thirty-two of the required thirty-four states have petitioned Congress for a convention to draft an amendment requiring the federal government to maintain a balanced budget. Well-meaning and learned people differ on the desirability of mandating a balanced federal budget. I favor the adoption of an amendment through the traditional congressional procedure that would require the federal government to live within its means. Nevertheless, I cannot support and will oppose any attempt to force this issue upon Congress through petitions for a convention.

Ironically, while a constitutional convention could totally alter our way of life, the petitions for a convention regrettably have often been acted upon hastily at the state legislature level in a cavalier manner. Over one-half of the states calling for a convention have done so without the benefit of public hearings, debate, or recorded vote. This momentous decision, in other words, is being made surreptitiously, as if it cannot withstand the scrutiny and discussion of a concerned and intelligent citizenry.

In addition to its perils for the internal workings of our nation, a constitutional convention would have serious, frequently overlooked, international repercussions. The United States is the oldest, largest, and most stable republic in the world. It is also the cornerstone of the entire economic life of the Western world and a significant factor in the economy of almost every country on the globe.

If Madison were justifiably concerned over the foreign policy implications of a U.S. constitutional convention in the eighteenth century, our concern should be multiplied by the infinitely more prominent world role our country plays in the twentieth century. The potential disruptions to our vital foreign policy interests—NATO is an example—are disturbing to contemplate.

If a convention were called, our allies and foes alike would soon realize the new pressures imposed upon our republic. The mere act of convening a constitutional convention would send tremors throughout all those economies that depend on the dollar; would undermine our neighbors' confidence in our constitutional integrity; and would weaken not only our economic stability but the stability of the free world. That is a price we cannot afford.

The domestic and international instability engendered by a convention cannot be justified by the prospect of a balanced federal budget. Even if the convention passed a balanced budget amendment in short order and then disbanded, the ratification process would take years. In addition, it is unlikely that an amendment would require a balanced budget in its first effective year: each of the drafts historically considered to date has allowed a multiyear phasing in of the limitations.

So even in the best case, a convention would not cure our budget deficit problems quickly. And the price for a long-term solution achieved through a convention would be incalculable domestic and international confusion.

The concept that a constitutional convention would be harmless is not conservative, moderate, or liberal philosophy. That concept is profoundly radical, born either of naiveté or the opportunistic thought that the end justifies the means. Our duty, as citizens of this nation, is to guard and protect our Constitution, to uphold its integrity, and to weigh the impact not only of proposed revisions but also of the means proposed to adopt them. We must work together to preserve all that is good in our system and to resolve problems by rational means. This nation certainly does not need a constitutional crisis; it should not take the first steps toward a possible wholesale revision of its Constitution; it must not, by moving closer to a constitutional convention, engender crippling domestic and international uncertainty.

Especially now, when international relations are precarious and global economies are struggling to regain the momentum of growth, a convention would divert our domestic attentions from pressing national problems and legislative and executive branch responsibilities, while focusing global attention on what would certainly appear, to friends and enemies alike, as a profound weakness in our national fabric. To say a constitutional convention should be called to balance the federal budget is a deception. A convention cannot perform magic; at best, it could offer an over-the-horizon possibility of a balanced budget amendment, while creating the certainty of profound mischief.

Constitutional Convention: Oh, Stop the Hand-Wringing

Griffin B. Bell

Like most Americans, I am deeply concerned by the federal government's continuing failure to control the budget deficits. The interest payments on the debt now amount to 12 percent of the current budget. Basic to this failure is that no counterforce exists against the special interest groups that are the driving force behind excessive government spending.

Because Congress has failed to control runaway government deficits, the people have acted through their state legislatures, 32 of which have called for a constitutional convention to draft a balanced federal budget amendment. When 34 states have so acted, Congress, under Article V of the Constitution, must call a convention.

We are now hearing predictions of doom and gloom that have not been heard since the passage of the Seventeenth Amendment seventy-two years ago. . . . In our original Constitution, senators were appointed by the state legislatures rather than elected by the people. By 1912, the people had concluded by a wide margin that the Senate should be elected, not appointed. The House of Representatives agreed, five times passing a proposed constitutional amendment to make the Senate elective.

But five times the Senate killed the amendment in committee, thereby forcing the people to take action. State legislatures began passing conditional calls for a convention, if Congress did not approve the amendment.

At that time, the two-thirds required was 32 state legislatures. When 31 states had acted, the Senate read the handwriting on the wall and passed the amendment. Without the use of the alternative route in Article V of our Constitution, the Seventeenth Amendment would not have been passed and senators would still be appointed.

Reprinted from the *Washington Post*. From Griffin B. Bell, "Constitutional Convention: Oh, Stop the Hand-Wringing," *Washington Post*, April 14, 1984.

This is precisely what the Founding Fathers had in mind. They provided for amendment through action of the state legislatures to deal with those situations in which Congress was part of the problem and would not act. That situation prevailed in 1912. It prevails equally in 1984.

Aside from the specious argument that a convention is "alien" to the constitutional process, we also hear other objections. It is argued that our friends abroad would recoil in horror at the prospect of a U.S. constitutional convention that would presumably destabilize America. But the free world has been decimated by our interest rates and the dollar exchange rate, which foreign financial experts attribute to our huge deficits and general fiscal profligacy. A serious effort to install long-term constitutional control over U.S. fiscal practices would be welcomed by our friends abroad.

Also, we are bombarded with ominous stories about a "runaway" constitutional convention that, presumably, would repeal the Bill of Rights, dismantle the Constitution, and install some sort of totalitarian regime. Well, while we have not had a federal convention since 1787, there have been over two hundred conventions held in various states, many of whose constitutions provide for periodic conventions to propose amendments. Such gatherings have brought out the best, not the worst, in people's government.

It is claimed that James Madison said a "new" constitutional convention would be a cloud over the Constitution. He did in fact utter those words, but in response to critics who declared that the Constitution written in Philadelphia in 1787 should be rejected and a new convention be held immediately. Thomas Jefferson, author of the Declaration of Independence, assumed that we would have a new convention about every twenty years.

In fact, fears about a "runaway" convention are groundless. The various state applications to Congress not only exhort Congress to pass the Tax Limitation–Balanced Budget Amendment but limit the scope of a convention to the sole and exclusive purpose of the balanced budget issue.

Those who wring their hands over the prospects of a convention run the risk of exposing their elitism, implying that the average citizen cannot be trusted. At the same time, they are willing to place their full faith in Congress, the very institution that has precipitated the fiscal mess that, in turn, has prompted the Tax Limitation–Balanced Budget movement.

But, suppose that other resolutions were offered at the Balanced Budget Convention. Congress would not be compelled, nor would it have any incentive, to send along to the states for ratification any proposals emanating from the convention that exceeded the scope of the call. And thirty-eight states are not about to ratify any proposal that does violence to or seeks to dismantle fundamental constitutional protections and guarantees.

Finally, it is important to understand that a convention will not necessarily take place upon the application of thirty-four states. The state calls have said: if Congress does not pass the amendment, then a convention for that purpose is called. The calls are conditional, not absolute. I believe there will not be a balanced budget constitutional convention. Congress simply will not abide letting mere citizens decide its taxing and spending power. Congress will act, I predict, as it did on the issue of the direct elections of senators—when overwhelming pressure from the states and the people can no longer be ignored.

CHAPTER THREE

FEDERALISM

The making of decisions within the American governmental system has always been complicated by the fact that formal governmental powers are divided between the national government and the states. This arrangement, mandated by the Constitution, frequently leads to conflict between the states and the national government over which level should perform a given function. Thus, when government leaders have debated such issues as health care for the elderly, welfare benefits for the poor, the financing of public education, or civil rights for racial minorities, they have been compelled to consider not only "What should we do?" but also "At which level of government should it be done?" This debate has grown particularly intense lately in light of President Reagan's call for a New Federalism—a plan that calls for turning as many as forty federal government programs over to the states.

The two selections in this chapter consider the desirability of returning power to the states. In the first, Gregg Easterbrook, a contributing editor of the Washington Monthly *magazine, argues that, since the states already have a demonstrated record of waste, corruption, and inefficiency, little is to be gained by conferring additional responsibilities upon them. In the second selection, Daniel Elazar, a long-time defender of the states, maintains that the states' reputation for corruption and inefficiency is undeserved. He contends that an objective examination of the evidence shows that the states are no less capable of performing governmental functions than the federal government. Indeed, they are perhaps better able to serve the public's needs more effectively.*

50 Miniature Washingtons: The Flaw in Reagan's New Federalism

Gregg Easterbrook

"A lot of people view state government with more alarm than they do Washington," Senator Paul Laxalt observed recently. Whoa! *That* will never do. To the woodshed with you, Paul. Surely you've heard about New Federalism, strategic fulcrum of former Governor Ronald Reagan's master plan to end government incompetence and strangling bureaucracy. Reagan considers states the most efficient and proper units of government; he wants to turn significant amounts of federal authority over to them. The President likes to suggest that this would solve once and for all the problems of "unmanageable, unaccountable" government agencies. New Federalism, Reagan has said, "is my dream."

What does Laxalt, also a former governor, know that Reagan doesn't? Perhaps some basic figures. For instance, state government is a larger and much faster growing organism than federal government. There are 3.5 million state workers compared to 2.8 million at the federal level. While federal employment changed little through the 1970s, state employment grew more than three percent annually. In fact, during the last decade, when Reagan was pounding the stump with his anti-Washington message, federal employment as a pecentage of total government employment *declined* steadily.

Laxalt probably also knows about state spending. Last year state government broke the $1,000 barrier, spending an average of $1,010 per capita (North Dakota spends $1,307 per resident, Delaware $1,378, Hawaii $1,594, and Alaska $4,827). To obtain this kind of money, states have begun borrowing at a furious rate. Total state deficits hit $119 billion in 1980; the percentage increase in state deficits has run *ahead* of the federal deficit seven of the last ten years. State and local government spending accounted for 8 percent of the gross national product in 1950; by 1975, as Reagan was stepping down from control of California's government, it was up to 15 percent of the GNP.

States are also surging forward in their drive to become as much like Washington as possible. Forty-two states now have agencies modeled after the federal EPA; they serve mainly to issue rules conflicting with other states' rules, forcing the federal EPA (and the courts) in to mediate. Thirty-five states have agencies patterned after the federal Department of Transportation, which since its creation in 1966 has served mainly to slow highway and subway construction to a crawl while presiding over countless service cutbacks and cost overruns. Most states have agency analogs for the departments of agriculture, commerce, energy, housing, interior (usually called "parks and wildlife"), labor, and even defense, considering the 50 different administrations of the National Guard. Thirty-six states now have "cabinet government," the system that is a standing joke at the federal level. From the Colorado Board of Abstractors to the Dormitory Authority of New York, miscellaneous manifestations of state government are proliferating as well.

States are also imitating Washington's most maddening flaws by sheltering their workers under civil service programs: some 75 percent of those 3.5 million state employees have "merit" protections, meaning lifetime job guarantees regardless of whether they perform well, poorly, or at all. Like federal workers, they continue to get hefty raises, oblivious to the hard times that prevail elsewhere. While Virginia Governor John Dalton was cutting $3 million from state Medicaid spending early this year, he was also ordering a $47 million across-the-board raise for state employees. At the same time he upped his own salary 33 percent to $80,000 and bestowed even larger raises on other state officials.

"Our nation of sovereign states has come dangerously close to becoming one great national government," Reagan warns. Not really. In truth the sovereign states are dangerously close to becoming 50 miniature Washingtons.

As the White House staff has ballooned in recent years, so have its 50 miniature counterparts, the staffs of governors. Jerry Brown has a personal staff of 83. New Mexico's governor had 3 aides in 1950 and now has 21; Oklahoma has gone from 12 to 43; Kentucky has zoomed from 7 to 54 and North Carolina from 8 to 57. In 17 states, the governor has a personal budget of $1 million or more.

Washington affectations have extended even to lieutenant governors, our miniature vice presidents. Maryland's Sam Bogley makes $52,500 and has a staff of six—including two bodyguards and a full-time chauffeur. Bogley recently described himself as having practically no responsibilities. "For what I'm doing," Bogley told a reporter, "I don't feel I'm justifying my salary." Bogley was then asked why he didn't return some of the money. "That's a good question," he replied.

As the states expand into 50 miniature Washingtons, thousands of HO-gauge D.C.s are springing up at the local level, too; local governments, being state-funded and state-regulated, follow in the states' wake. (New York has eleven major laws and six thousand pages of regulations controlling local governments.) While Reagan has vowed that New Federalism will bring government closer to the people, what it may really do is bring Washington closer to the people, planting a Washington-like bureaucracy on every Main Street in America.

But why take my word for it? Instead, let's examine the states (and their local mini-festations) for the very things Reagan finds most offensive about the federal government—waste, fraud, and inefficiency. Let's go around the country for a closer look at your tax dollars at play.

STATE WASTE

In Reagan's home state, Illinois, the Department of Public Aid has been leasing office buildings for more *per year* than they would cost to buy. In one case the agency paid $750,000 in rent for a building that was appraised at $90,000. In another case it rented a building from a "landlord" who, it turned out, did not own the property.

Meanwhile James Jeffers, director of the Illinois Division of Vocational Rehabilitation took $250,000 from a fund earmarked for the handicapped to purchase "psychocybernetics" training sessions. Psychocybernetics is a self-actualizing encounter system devised by the late lamented plastic surgeon Dr. Maxwell Maltz. Records show the psychocybernetics sessions were attended mainly by members of the DVR staff. And while the DVR group was groping itself on taxpayers' time, Vincent Toolen, Illinois's chief purchasing officer, was using taxpayers' money to buy himself $11,000 worth of office furniture, including a $600 chair and a $2,300 African mahogany credenza. Toolen, asked to explain his excesses, noted, "I needed a desk." He also paid for the furniture out of the wrong fund, the state's computer-services budget. Remember, this is the guy in charge of purchasing.

In Wisconsin, there is a state agency called the Solid Waste Recycling Authority. It was created for the purpose of issuing bonds for recycling projects. The agency has existed since 1973 and has spent $1.5 million. It has yet to issue a bond.

In New York, state workers go about their appointed tasks in the $1.5 billion Albany mall built by former Governor Nelson Rockefeller. The mall features marble-covered skyscrapers poised on gravity (and budget) defying stilts. Up in Alaska the state continues to plan to spend $4.4 billion to construct an entirely new capital city at the inland rail stop known as Willow. . . .

But as creative as states can be when dispensing with their own proceeds, they save their highest fiduciary standards for other people's money; among the worst-managed programs anywhere are those financed by the federal government but administered by states and localities. When the money comes from somebody else, the state or city has no incentive to economize—in government, in fact, it has every reason to waste, since the more (of somebody else's money) spent, the bigger the spender's empire.

David Stockman seems to understand this. December's *Atlantic* describes the tennis courts in tiny Royalton, Michigan, Stockman's home. They were built with federal revenue-sharing funds, a program under which Washington went deeper into debt in order to make unrestricted gifts of cash to cities and states. Royalton's citizens "never would have taxed themselves to build that," Stockman said, looking out over the deserted courts. "But as long as somebody's giving them the money, sure, they're willing to spend it." Somebody plans to keep giving them the money: Reagan has recently pledged to retain (although at a lower level than Carter) the revenue-sharing program. His first concrete proposal for New Federalism, widespread use of "block grants," specifies that a larger share of federal funds be turned over to the states with no strings attached.

New York City's pending Westway project, funded by the federal government but administered by the state and city, will be a four-mile highway running along the southwest edge of Manhattan. It's slated to cost $2.2 billion. That's *$550 million a mile*—not only more expensive than any highway ever built (the previous record-holder was $145 million) but more expensive than any *subway*. Westway's four miles are also scheduled to take ten years to complete. Reagan has made a grand show of his backing for Westway, traveling to New York to present a giant cardboard check for $85 million to Mayor Edward Koch. Under New York's penny-pinching plan that $85 million will buy exactly 816 feet of highway; Westway is programmed to cost $8,680 per *inch*. Koch, for his part, complained that the federal government had double-crossed him by refusing to pay for the "amenities" like roadside parks and, perhaps, porcelain-inlaid drainage pipes.

California's federally funded but state-run Medi-Cal system (the state's version of Medicaid) continues to hum like a well-oiled machine. A California state commission recently said that 25 percent of Medi-Cal's $4 billion budget is waste—far higher than the 10 percent waste Reagan has said plagues the federal government.

State auditors have found doctors billing Medi-Cal for abortions performed on women who weren't pregnant; dentists billing to cap teeth they had already billed to extract; and psychiatrists billing an hour's fee after seeing patients for only 15 minutes. One Los Angeles doctor made $500,000 last year in Medi-Cal fees. Another, Dr. Leo Kenneally, sentenced to 125 days for claiming phony services, continued to submit bills to Medi-Cal while appealing his conviction. A hospital emergency room billed the state $76.30 for fitting a woman for a diaphragm. Now this might have seemed like an emergency situation to the patient (and the guy waiting for her in the car), but had the procedure been done in a clinic it would have cost only $12.

Medical billings and many other examples of federally funded state waste involve intangible circumstances that resist fiscal control. But some do not. Chicago's Deep Tunnel project recently managed to misplace 26 million tons of rock. Deep Tunnel is a megasewer financed by Washington but built by Chicago's Metropolitan Sanitary District. The district (on the advice of a federally funded study by the consulting firm of Booz-Allen) allegedly decided to give away all the limestone removed from its excavations. Limestone, it turns out, is selling for $4 a ton in Chicago; the decision cost federal taxpayers about $100 million. (Most of the stone, by the way, was carted off by contractors for use as roadfill in a federally funded, state-run highway project.)

FEDERALIST FRAUD

Okay, that gives you an idea of how states have taken command on the "waste" issue. Now let's move on to Reagan's second category, "fraud."

So far this year, 120 present or former county commissioners have been found guilty (or pleaded guilty) in Oklahoma's road-building kickback scandals. Oklahoma City's U.S. attorney says he hopes to nail 250 commissioners before it's over. The FBI estimates that at least $25 million in kickbacks and ill-spent money is involved. Road kickback investigations continue in Illinois, Tennessee, Florida, Virginia, North Carolina, Georgia, and other states.

Investigators found two basic types of scams in Oklahoma. One was a straight 10 percent kickback from contractor to public official. The other was a bit bolder—totally phony purchase documents, 100 percent profit. Kickbacks are a traditional way of doing business in many states, but apparently complete nondelivery of the goods crossed that fine ethical line. "I think the 10 percent kickback probably would have been accepted [by the public] if it had stopped at that," Oklahoma state Senator John Clifton, chairman of a special committee studying the affair, said recently.

Just before Tennessee Governor Ray Blanton left office in January 1980, three of his top aides were arrested (carrying marked FBI money) on charges of selling state pardons. One aide, state trooper Charles Taylor, displayed his sterling moral fiber when he told investigators he would sell a pardon to any criminal except one who had "molested a minor child."

Prosecutors from that incompetent, inefficient federal government you've heard so much about found that evidence of Blanton's pardon-selling apparatus had been given to a Nashville state attorney four years before; he had simply filed the information. Blanton expressed shock and outrage over the allegations. Then three days before leaving office he commuted the sentences of fifty-two felons, including twenty-six murderers and double-murderer Roger Humphreys, son of one of Blanton's friends. The good governor's successor, Lamar Alexander, was sworn into office ahead of schedule when the FBI learned that still more pardons were imminent.

Since then Blanton has also been charged with taking liquor license kickbacks. Shortly after the pardon-selling charges surfaced, Blanton complained that the FBI had violated executive courtesy by not informing him that a secret investigation of his activities was in progress. . . .

Down in Florida, Daniel Gonzales Roman was, until recently, director of Miami Cruz Outreach Center, a federally funded, state-supervised community facility. It was discovered that Roman had put himself on the payroll twice—as "Daniel Roman," director, and "Daniel Gonzales," clerk-typist.

When confronted, Roman said he deserved both salaries because he did his own typing.

INTERGOVERNMENTAL INEFFICIENCY

So much for "waste" and "fraud." Now how about Reagan's third dramatic charge against the federal government—"inefficiency"? If the states had greater authority, Reagan argues, government would be much more efficient. Let's begin testing his thesis in New England.

Recently the state-chartered Massachusetts Bay Transportation Authority declared a special crash program to get its notoriously faulty buses rolling again. During the two-week "all-out effort," the MBTA's bill for maintenance overtime increased from an average of $1,750 per week to about $15,000 weekly. Bus availability, running at 49 percent, fell to 41 percent.

The T is one of the many state-supervised mass transit systems that serve our great cities so magnificently. An extensive *Boston Globe* study showed that in 1979 the "cost per mile of vehicle operation" for Washington's Metro was $2.82; for Philadelphia's SEPTA, $3.13; for San Francisco's BART, $3.39; and for Boston's T, $6.22. The cost per mile of Toronto's subway system—which I can attest as a frequent visitor to Toronto is superior to any of the systems mentioned here—was $2.18.

The T's efficiency is greatly aided by its 28 union contracts, most of which forbid any changes in "established practices." When, for instance, T managers tried to coordinate bus drivers' schedules to cut down excessive overtime and drivers sitting idle, the Amalgamated Transit Union blocked this move, claiming that overlapping schedules were established practice. (Overtime cost the T $11 million in 1979, the *Globe* found, compared to $2.6 million for Toronto's system, which covers three times as many miles and has 2,000 more employees.) Getting a distributor changed in a T bus can require as many as ten workers—one to drive the bus to a repair shop, another (a "shifter") to drive it *into* the shop, a sheet metal worker to open the engine cover, a machinist to remove any parts in the way, an electrician to change the distributor, and sometimes an entirely new set of workers to reverse the sequence.

Lean, mean fighting machines like the T can be found in state governments throughout the country. In Michigan, 18 stages of state approval are required for a community to erect a stop sign. Back in Illinois, a scandal recently broke over poor care and unsanitary conditions in state-chartered nursing homes. There are seven different Illinois agencies that license and monitor nursing homes; each issued statements claiming it was another agency's responsibility to act.

California's Public Utilities Commission recently was charged with administering a law giving tax credits to homeowners who install solar heating systems. PUC's "checklist" to determine eligibility has 54 steps. And PUC will rule on whether a heater qualifies for the tax credit only *after* it has been installed. . . .

THAT'S ALL VOTERS UNDER THE BRIDGE

Overall, not exactly a shining portrait of the sovereign states. But there are other factors to consider besides waste, fraud, and inefficiency. States increasingly have regulatory responsibilities in business, the professions, the environment, and other fields. Consider the following great moments in state regulation:

Indiana's State Board of Health, its EPA-analog agency, is charged with monitoring water pollution discharge from landfills. The board does this by requiring landfill operators to send in periodic samples of ground water from their property. Vials of water are simply sent to state labs by the operators. The agency has no way of knowing whether the sample actually comes from a landfill, a garden hose, or a bottle of Perrier.

Last spring Florida's State Board of Pilots reinstated, without penalty, harbor Pilot John Lerro. Lerro had been guiding the freighter *Summit Venture* when it slammed into the Sunshine Skyway Bridge near Tampa, collapsing a 1,300-foot section of roadway and sending 35 people to their deaths. Lerro testified at an inquest that he had decided to sail under the bridge despite a blinding storm that reduced visibility to zero, and knowing full well that the ship's navigational radar had failed. Asked to describe his feelings after returning to the scene of the tragedy, Lerro told an Associated Press reporter, "It's nothing you could understand. I walk to the beat of a different drummer."

In Texas, the legislature became mildly displeased when reports surfaced that one-third of Dallas and Houston public school teachers could not pass high-school-level literacy tests. The legislature demanded teacher-competency testing and assigned the matter to the Texas Education Agency, which quickly convened its Commission on Standards.

Like many state regulatory bodies, the Texas Education Agency is staffed almost entirely by people with a great personal stake in making sure no reforms are imposed on whatever they regulate. TEA's Commission on Standards, for instance, is comprised of teacher's college administrators, public school administrators, and teacher's union representatives. Its first act was to ask for $1 million to study the vexing question of whether teachers should be required to read and write; it has yet to issue a ruling on competency testing. It has, however, proposed that if a test is ever staged, any teacher already certified will be allowed to keep his job regardless of how poorly he scores (the commission called this a "grandperson clause"). It also proposed that new teachers who flunk future tests be allowed to remain so long as they begin taking graduate-level education courses. The commission neglected to explain how someone who flunks a high-school literacy test could qualify for a graduate course. . . .

Some states have camouflaged the existence of their many essential boards and commissions through agency consolidation. Seldom are the functions eliminated; they are merely subsumed under a larger heading, creating the illusion of government streamlining. Connecticut, for instance, had 172 state agencies employing 17,000 people in 1950; today it has 26 agencies employing 53,000.

State professional "regulation" boards exist, of course, mainly to restrict entry into a trade, monopolize it, and thus drive up the earnings of those safely inside and certified. Michigan's constitution, for instance, specifies that state boards be controlled "by members of that profession." Members of the barbers' profession have decided to require 2,000 hours of instruction before anyone could take the state barber's exam. Before long a little off the sides may require a Ph.D.

WE SERVE AND PROTECT OTHERS

One of the most distinctively perverse qualities of Washington (and one Reagan has so often blasted) is the federal government's ironclad civil service system, which prevents firing bureaucrats, ensures perpetual raises for federal employees regardless of performance, and in general makes the federal government less and less accountable to the will of the people. Through 1979 and 1980, for instance, Oregon cut its budget 10 percent, a far more drastic reduction than Reagan imposed at the federal level. For 1981 and 1982, Oregon froze its budget exactly at 1980 levels. All told, this means more than a 30 percent loss of buying power after inflation. How many Oregon state employees have been let go? Two percent.

Texas Governor Bill Clements took office in 1978 vowing to slash 25,000 of the state's 187,000 workers. He settled for fewer than 3,000, a figure achieved not through dynamic cuts but by normal attrition (retirements, death from insect inhalation in Houston, and so on). If you count state-run colleges, Texas public employment has *increased* under Clements.

As in Washington, when the ax does fall, it usually falls on those doing productive work while sparing deskbound administrators. Eureka, California's city manager recently asked to combine his department of public works with his department of parks and recreation, thus saving one managerial salary. The city council refused. It did, however, fire three park maintenance workers. While Chicago's federally and state-funded school system was laying off 2,000 teachers in 1979 and 1980, it was increasing the number of top administrative posts (paying $40,000 or more) from 80 to 156. It also created a "Department of Employee Relations," with a $56,000 -a-year manager and three $40,000-plus aides whose jobs, apparently, are to find out where those 2,000 teachers went. When the state-chartered, federally funded Chicago Transit Authority lapsed into financial distress this summer, its first response was to fire all 107 of its transit policemen. Next it cut service and laid off 97 bus drivers. Only later did it lay off the first administrative workers—and those layoffs came from low-level clerical slots, not management.

And like the federal government, state and local governments are following the pattern of laying off some employees while granting raises to others, instead of trying to keep everybody working. Wayne County (Detroit) recently laid off 78 employees and simultaneously awarded 9 percent raises to those who got to stay. (In 1979 Wayne County was paying $18,300 for an entry-level accountant; private firms in Detroit were paying $14,000.)...

Public servants in the miniature Washingtons have perfected their self-protective instincts in other ways. Several lawyers for the New York Transit Authority recently were found to be doing private work during business hours; some even had private telephone listings at the public offices. The Houston Police Patrolmens Union wrote its members asking them to take their time in answering emergency calls. Rapid responses, the union said, could sabotage efforts to expand the force.

ESTATE OF THE STATES

State and local governments are more responsive, Reagan has said, because they are "closest to the people." Yet the miniature Washingtons can be especially adept at fouling up the things that concern people most directly.

One close-to-the-people issue affecting nearly everyone is the condition of America's physical plant—roads, bridges, dams, and sewers. While acid rain may be a faraway abstraction, everyone knows whether the roads are in good shape. Yet in recent years the states have succeeded in dramatically cutting back spending for construction and maintenance of the physical plant—the "infrastructure"—in order to channel money to civil servants' salaries and raises.

In 1970, state and local infrastructure spending was $29 billion; this year it will be $19 billion, a sheer plummet considering inflation. Two out of every five bridges in the country are said to be "structurally deficient"; one-fifth of the interstate highway system has already passed its expected service life. New York City's subway system simply stopped doing preventive maintenance in 1975; now it repairs only tracks and vehicles that are already out of order. The results are predictable—12,000 breakdowns in 1977, 36,000 last year. Raises for transit authority workers continue, however, as they do at Chicago's and Boston's troubled transit systems.

But as far as state governments themselves are concerned, the story of 1981 has had nothing to do with bureaucracy or inefficiency—it's been Reagan's budget cuts. New Federalism, while promising less supervision and red tape (a primary effect of block grants is to convert funds intended to serve some specific purpose into unrestricted gifts), also so far has promised less money. In Reagan's 1982 budget there is $82 billion for the states, down from $88 billion in Carter's final budget.

State and local officials had to be peeled off the ceiling after they heard about these cuts; Governor Richard Snelling of Vermont calls them a "tragedy" and an "economic Bay of Pigs." But in truth they had it coming. When it comes to wallowing up to the federal trough, states may be the most accomplished porkers of our time. Reagan's 1982 state funding level will still be 11 times higher than federal funding of states in 1960. The CPI has increased about 2.5 times since 1960. In 1955 states drew 20 percent of their revenue from Washington; now it's 37 percent.

It would be nice to think that channeling so much cash through Washington enables wealthy states to aid their less fortunate neighbors; this is seldom the case. Alaska, with rich oil revenues and a state treasury surplus of $1 billion last year, is in by far the best financial condition of any state. Yet it receives by far the highest proportion of federal assistance, reeling in $4,759 per resident in federal grants and expenditures, according to a *National Journal* study. The national average of per capita federal assistance to states, $2,101, is less than half Alaska's allotment. New Jersey gets $1,722 per capita, Iowa gets $1,602, and Michigan, supposed bailout capital of the world, gets only $1,556.

Another measure of funding logic is the "flow" of state-generated tax dollars—how much of the money a state sends to Washington eventually comes back to it in some form. Michigan finishes dead last in flow, getting only 66 cents back for every dollar it supplies Washington. Indiana gets 70 cents, Ohio 71 cents, Delaware 74 cents. Minnesota, with the worst short-term financial condition of any state (it projects a $180 million budget deficit next year), has a federal flow of just 85 cents. Pennsylvania gets 92 cents and New York 96 cents. Meanwhile booming Colorado has a positive flow of $1.06; Washington State gets $1.10, Georgia $1.11, Arizona $1.21, Hawaii $1.30, and Alaska $1.44. Clearly where the federal money is needed has little to do with where it goes.

If so much money is shipped back to the states (after, as Reagan has said, traveling "to Washington and back minus a carrying charge"), why, it's often asked, does it go to the federal government at all? Why don't states directly fund their own services like education and highway repair? Why, indeed. Although most governors claim to detest the Washington round trip of tax money and long to be left alone, more than likely nothing could be further from the truth.

When money is raised by Washington and then handed back to the states, it keeps governors and mayors from having to face the thing Reagan says they can handle best—political acccountability. That federal withholding line on your paycheck is big, unfathomable, unchallengeable, imposed by someone far away. The smaller state and local lines are, in contrast, much easier to understand and raise hell about. Witness the fact that there have been recent tax upheavals of one sort or another in California, Minnesota, New Jersey, South Dakota, and Massachusetts, but no serious grassroots political assault against federal taxes. Mayors and governors would rather keep it this way. The last thing they want to admit is how much they're *really* spending; they would rather continue to blame Washington for it all, calling press conferences to denounce that inflationary monster on the Potomac, even as they are subsidized by the national tax bookkeeping swindle. (Miniature Washington's favorite book-juggler is the industrial revenue bond, which allows *states* to grant exemption from *federal* taxes.)

Last summer there were signals from the Reagan administration that New Federalism's next step would be "tax turnbacks," ending the arrangement where Washington serves as the states' collection agency. It was never exactly clear what tax turnbacks would be. At first, the proposal seemed to be for some return of taxing authority directly to states. That made governors nervous, since it means voters could hold them responsible. Then it was suggested that Washington would turn back revenues collected from gasoline and cigarette taxes, handing the cash over as unrestricted grants; this prospect pleased the states no end, since Washington would continue to take the blame while states took the money.

Recent gloomy budget projections have, however, forced Reagan to put the tax turnback plan on hold. In October, Treasury Undersecretary Norman Ture recently said that turnbacks are far off; he noted, however, that Reagan has already effectively returned some revenue-raising power to states via federal income tax cuts. If states are really as badly racked as they claim, Ture said, they could raise their own taxes to soak up recently freed federal tax dollars.

This is accurate economic thinking and is, philosophically, just what Reagan's New Federalism preaches. The primary features of Ture's proposal—self-reliance, decentralized government, voter accountability—are just what nine out of ten governors would endorse, so long as it didn't apply to them. But states have become addicted to their federal handouts—just as many individuals and businesses have—and they reacted to the Ture statement with an intense flurry of lobbying. States succeeded in getting Reagan to make several reconciliatory statements and moderate his plans for the next round of state-aid cuts. Lobbying the full-scale Washington is something the miniature Washingtons seem better poised to do then getting their own houses in order. Thirty-one states now maintain their own offices in Washington, some states having different lobbies for different state agencies. They are joined by more than one hundred city lobbies representing everything from the metropolises to Natchez, Mississippi; even twenty-five or so *counties* have Washington lobbies, including Los Angeles County, King County (Seattle), Hennepin County (Minneapolis), and Pitkin County, Colorado, home of financially strapped Aspen.

The sorry state of today's state does not mean that New Federalism is a bad idea. In the abstract it is a very good idea—government decision making, financing, and functioning should be carried out at the levels where they are most keenly felt. The state of the state does indicate, however, that merely handing responsibility over to the country's 50 miniature Washingtons will not accomplish anything. Stagnant bureaucracy has pervaded American life right down to the local level, and until its causes—self-serving thinking, civil-service inefficiency, interest group paralysis—are attacked, the rest is just paper-shuffling. As it stands now, Reagan's New Federalism mainly calls for tossing administrative problems back to the states so the bomb will be in somebody else's hands when it goes off. That might please the tosser, but it doesn't help the rest of us.

Can the States Be Trusted?

Daniel J. Elazar

THE CRITICS' CASE

... In a single issue of the *New York Times* not long ago, Amitai Etzioni became the latest in a long succession of people who have attacked revenue-sharing on the ground that state and local government is especially corrupt, and Arthur Schlesinger, Jr., questioned the entire idea of enhancing the power of local government by claiming, as many have before him, that, because the national government is no less the government of the people than local government, there is no reason to believe that anything is better done locally than nationally.

The Etzioni and Schlesinger myths are but two of many. In other quarters, there are those who still argue that strengthening the hand of the states and localities is a way of perpetuating racial discrimination. Others repeat the myth that the federal government grew in power originally because of state and local failures, and that there is therefore no reason to reward the states and localities today. Tied closely with that myth is another one that claims that, because the states and localities have not made sufficient effort to come to grips with their problems on their own, they do not deserve to be bailed out by Washington.

I submit that a careful reading of the record belies each and every one of these criticisms, revealing most of them to have been untruths from the first and the rest to be criticisms that, whatever their original value, have long since become obsolete. There is more than enough evidence to show that the states and localities, far from being weak sisters, have actually been carrying

Reprinted with permission of the author from *The Public Interest* No. 35 (Spring 1974), pp. 89–102. © 1974 by National Affairs Inc. The author is Professor of Political Science, Bar-Ilan and Temple Universities; Senior Fellow, Center for the Study of Federalism, Temple University; President, Jerusalem Institute for Federal Studies.

the brunt of domestic governmental progress in the United States ever since the end of World War II, and have done so at an accelerated pace since the advent of America's direct combat involvement in Vietnam. Moreover, they have been largely responsible for undertaking the truly revolutionary change in the role of government in the United States that has occurred over the past decade.

In making this claim, I do not intend to argue from single examples, as people usually do when they want to "prove" the failure of the states and localities. Generally, when the claim is made that the states or the cities are failing, the claimant then points to Mississippi or Newark or some other state or community that does provide a sufficiently horrible case in point. Such arguments are no more accurate than a claim that the states are the most progressive governments in the country—which could easily be substantiated if one looked exclusively at New York, California, Wisconsin, or Massachusetts, which have been over the last 80 years far more progressive in many ways than the federal government—or that the cities are far more compassionate than any other governments, a contention that would be sustained if one looked only at San Francisco, New Orleans, Berkeley, or New York, which have been far more tolerant of individual social differences and deviations than Washington or any state. In these pages, therefore, I propose to evaluate state and local government, not by citing a few extreme examples, but by looking at the general record which state and local governments as a whole have built in each of the areas their critics have pointed to.

THE MYTH OF URBAN-RURAL WELFARE

Criticism # 1: The states are unmindful of local—particularly big-city—needs, while the cities distrust the states and refuse to cooperate with them. This argument had considerable merit during the two generations or so the country took to make the transition from rural to urban living. Not unreasonably, declining rural populations were reluctant to give up their dominance of state governments to the new urbanites, particularly since so many of the former genuinely believed in the moral superiority of rural life and so many of the latter belonged to ethnic or racial groups with decidedly different mores. Indeed, much of what posed as urban–rural conflict was really interethnic conflict set in a discreet juridical framework. . . .

Since the rural–urban transition took place at different times in different parts of the country, different states have been undergoing its pains since the late nineteenth century. Consequently, in the memories of those now living there have always been horrible examples of rural-dominated state political systems interfering with the burgeoning cities within their borders, and these examples have obscured the ever-growing number of states that were politically responsive to their cities.

By 1970 few, if any, states had yet to enter the transition period. Put simply, the record reveals that the transition begins when at least 40 percent of a state's population is urban and is completed when the urban places account for over 60 percent of the population total. No state is now below that 40 percent figure, and only eleven (seven of them in the South) are less than 50 percent urban, but these contain only a bit more than 10 percent of the country's population. Another nine fall between 50 and 60 percent. Before the 40 percent mark is attained, big cities find it very difficult to gain consideration in their state capitols. This is hardly surprising in a democracy, where majorities rule and overwhelming majorities tend to rule easily. After the 40 percent figure is reached, the cities can begin to bargain with increasing success. Georgia is a case in point, having passed the 40 percent mark in 1960 and closed on the 50 percent mark in 1970.

Past 60 percent, there is no longer any real contest. Minnesota and Indiana are good examples. Since they passed 60 percent, their legislatures, each in its own way, have opened up to every kind of prometropolitan legislation that has been proposed. Ten of the fifty states, containing some 79.4 million people (or nearly 40 percent of the country's total population), are 75 percent urban or more, which means that urban and state interests are essentially identical.

Cities—of varying sizes and with varying interests, to be sure—are in the saddle in virtually all of the states today, and rural–urban conflict has given way to new interurban conflicts in whose resolution the state government plays a legitimate and not unfair role, even if the losers, in the great tradition of American politics, holler "foul" at every opportunity. . . .

Even more significant than the fact of urban hegemony in contemporary state–city relations is the fact that state expenditures have grown extraordinarily since World War II, and that most of those expenditures, particularly in the last decade, have been funneled into urban areas, especially big cities. Unfortunately, the great fixed-cost programs such as public welfare, in which the fixed costs keep rising, have absorbed the greater part of these funds so that they are largely unavailable for more innovative uses. Worse for the public image of the states, the funds are so quickly absorbed in this manner that the public is not even aware that they have been increased—but this does not change the fact that they have been.

In fact, the states and the cities themselves have recognized that the day of conflicting state–city interests is past. For several years after it was seriously proposed, revenue-sharing itself was held up by a dispute as to whether the cities would receive funds directly from Washington or through their states. In 1971, the Council of State Governments and the National League of Cities reached an agreement which ended the conflict. In a manner entirely consonant with the whole idea of American federalism, they agreed to request that Congress appropriate the monies to the states without even a fixed passthrough formula but with the provision that the states would have to negotiate with their local governments to arrive at a satisfactory distribution of the funds, thereby effectively affirming the cities' new feeling of con-

fidence that the states will be alert to their needs through an ordinary nego-
tiation process. While this was not the formula adopted by Congress, the
agreement did pave the way for the passage of general revenue-sharing legislation in 1972.

THE MYTH OF ADMINISTRATIVE INCOMPETENCE

*Criticism #2: The states and localities are administratively incapable of properly uti-
lizing any additional powers that might be transferred to them.* This myth also has its
roots in a partial truth of the past. When the role of government in American
society underwent drastic expansion in the 1930s, Washington did indeed set
the pace in the development of a proper bureaucracy to manage the new government programs. Many of the states and localities were either unprepared
or too impoverished by the Depression to respond in kind, and some were
still too small in size to require so extensive an administrative apparatus.
Nevertheless, most states laid the foundations during the Depression years
for an administrative system appropriate to the mid-twentieth century, and
then built on those foundations after World War II, when the resources denied them by circumstances for fifteen years or more became available again.

Today, in my own talks with officials of federal agencies that work with
their state and local opposite numbers I have found, even among those not
particularly disposed to turn their functions over to other planes of government, a growing consensus affirming the competence of state and local administration. These insiders' arguments in favor of retaining a strong federal
presence are based on real or perceived policy differences between them and
the states and localities, not on the question of competence. Nor should this
cause any great surprise. The investigations of political scientists over the
past decade—totally ignored by the mythologists, of course—have consistently found no substantial difference among the three groups of bureaucrats
with respect to background, capability, and dedication to their respective
programs. All the studies have shown that, in most program areas, the administrative officials of all three planes of government are drawn from the
same professional backgrounds and are committed to the same professional
goals.

Perhaps most important, within the past decade the executive agencies
of general government in both the states and localities—that is, the offices of
the governors and mayors—have generally been strengthened in a manner
reminiscent of the strengthening of the President's office in the 1920s and
1930s. State planning agencies are being developed as arms of the office of
governor; executive office staffing has improved in cities as well as in states;
and mayors and governors are increasingly using their planning staffs as resources for controlling and coordinating the multifarious activities of their
governments, much as our presidents use the Office of Management and
Budget.

A good deal of this improvement has been the consequence of simple growth. While the states range in population from California's 19.7 million to Alaska's 300,000, six states, containing 40 percent of America's population, have over 10 million people each. Five more, containing some 15 percent of the total, have over 5 million people each. States of this size are bigger than most sovereign countries in today's world (California is almost as populous as Canada or Argentina, Pennsylvania nearly equals Australia and surpasses Belgium or Chile, New Jersey is larger than Austria, and Michigan is larger than any of the Scandinavian countries or Switzerland). All told, fully half the states have more than 3 million inhabitants, which means that they are as large or larger than Ireland, Israel, New Zealand, Norway, or Uruguay—all of them countries acknowledged to be able to sustain themselves as independent nations. This means that sheer growth in population has fostered a growth in social complexity and internal resources (human and material) that, in turn, has led to more sophisticated governmental responses.

It is true that smaller states may be unable to mobilize the resources necessary for across-the-board governmental sophistication (although all major programs, both in large states and small, are now managed by personnel of relatively equal competence). Yet in many such cases local norms and expectations do not encourage "sophisticated" government on the federal model. Supposed "deficiencies" in these states and localities are often mere reflections of the tastes and wishes of their citizens.

None of the foregoing is intended to suggest that there are no problems facing state and local administrations or that all business is efficiently conducted in the states and localities; but by the same token, no one is about to claim that the federal administration is without its serious problems either. Not many Americans would deny Washington the wherewithal to administer programs because of the TFX scandal or the Post Office mess or the lack of coordination within HEW. No government has a monopoly on efficiency—or inefficiency—in the United States today. Consequently, decisions as to where to locate responsibility must hinge on other criteria.

THE PROBLEM OF CORRUPTION

Criticism #3: Even if the states and localities now have enough in common and sufficient administrative skills to handle the additional powers, corruption and vested interests will prevent them from utilizing those powers well. The "local corruption" argument, another favorite myth in the American political repertoire, has at least two serious inadequacies. One is a question of fact. As a group, state and local governments today are far less corrupt in the usual sense of the term than at any time in the past one hundred years. When it comes to "conventional" corruption, the same can be said of the federal government. (The kind of corruption represented by Watergate is something new—and it is far more dangerous than old-fashioned graft and influence-peddling.) A whole host of factors having to do with changes in American society have operated to reduce at all planes of government the relatively crude forms of political payoff common at the turn of the century and earlier. . . .

The morality of public business—governmental or nongovernmental— is rightfully a matter of concern in the United States today, but strengthening the position of the states and localities should not be contingent on that question. It may indeed be argued with considerable justice that supposed differences in the extent of corruption at the various planes of government only reflect the fact that influence-peddling in Washington is usually more genteel—since it involves the country's great enterprises—than the simpler forms involving "common folk" in the states and localities. By the same token, it may be that corruption closer to home at least gets spread more widely among those who need money than corruption in high places, which tends to reward the already privileged only. And in any event, it is important to remember that corruption at the federal plane affects the entire country, whereas at the state and local planes the consequences stop at the state or city boundaries.

A second weakness of the "local corruption" argument is its tendency to overestimate the extent to which corruption, where it exists, affects the delivery of governmental services. There are many indications that corruption has far less influence on governmental performance today than it did eighty or one hundred years ago. This is because the nature of corruption has changed; the old days of straightforward bribery and "buying" of public officials have generally disappeared. Today, practices are more subtle; characteristically, they involve rewarding one's friends with favors rather than blocking proposed government activities. The lucrative business today is in the awarding of contracts for the delivery of services, a system which more or less guarantees that services will be delivered one way or another. Consequently, whether corruption exists or not, the services will.[1]

Corruption is a perennial governmental problem, and it is usually related to norms rooted in the local culture. By all accounts, states like Michigan, Minnesota, Virginia, and Utah are far less corrupt than the federal government. New York, North Carolina, and Pennsylvania are probably on a par with Washington in this respect, while Indiana, Louisiana, New Jersey, and Texas are probably more corrupt. Even the above list indicates that there is no simple correlation between corruption and the quality of government.

Much the same argument can be made in the case of waste. There are clearly no grounds for believing that one plane of government is more wasteful than the others, though the way in which their wastefulness is manifested may differ. Personal deficiencies of public officials cause waste and inefficiency in some of the smaller states and localities, but no more than is generated by red tape in very large bureaucracies like the federal government today.

Nor do vested interests in the states and localities cause more "distortions" of public policy than those in Washington. This proposition has been well tested in recent years as the federal government has extended its regulatory powers over coal mining, boating, flammable clothes, and, most recently, industrial safety, supposedly in response to state "failures." It has become increasingly apparent that federal regulation has meant not higher standards in these areas but an adjustment of standards toward a national mean that suits the interests of the parties being regulated, often to the dismay of those who championed federal intervention in the first place on the ground that federal action would obviously mean higher standards.

WHY ARE FEDERAL FUNDS NEEDED?

Criticism #4: The states and localities have failed to assume their proper fiscal obligations, and there is no reason why the federal government should bail them out. If the truth be known, the states and localities have borne the brunt of the effort to cope with increased demand for domestic services since the end of World War II. No matter what base period is used, the fiscal data confirm this. Since 1946, state and local revenues from their own sources have risen from under $10 billion to over $100 billion, or by more than 10 times, while federal revenues have only quadrupled. Between 1960 and 1969—a decade of great expansion of federal activities—federal expenditures rose 69 percent, including increases for the Vietnam war, but state and local expenditures rose 76 percent. For only a few brief years during the mid-1960s at the height of the Great Society did federal expenditures increase at the same rate as those of the states and cities. . . .

The diversion of federal resources to the Vietnam war increased the burden on the states and localities to support domestic government activities. (Under the Constitution, this is how it should be; those who believe in strong state and local government cannot find fault in an arrangement whereby the states and localities provide something like two-thirds of the funds for domestic purposes and the federal government approximately one-third.) The states and localities did not shirk their responsibility to provide this larger share. In any given year, approximately four-fifths of the states increase their taxes to pay for new services or added costs. Their problem is that they are caught either way. If they fail to provide adequate services, they are faulted for their failure. If they supply adequate services, the steady increase in fixed costs puts them near bankruptcy. . . .

At the same time, the federal government, with its foreign involvements taking precedence (and that is as it should be), has maintained its dominant role in the income tax field. There is where the crunch lies. Should Congress in its wisdom decide to drastically reduce the federal income tax, even without any formal provision for enhancing state revenue in the form of state tax credits or the like, there is little doubt that the states and localities would pick up the slack without any outside compulsion to do so. This thesis has even been tested in a limited way. When the federal government last cut taxes during the Kennedy administration, state and local revenues increased automatically as the released funds poured into the economy to be taxed by those governments under existing levies; but, in addition, after a year's delay, no more, most states and localities raised their own taxes to absorb an even bigger share of the reduction, primarily because of the demands placed upon them by their own citizens.

Even the argument about the regressiveness of state taxes has lost potency in the last decade. Forty-five states now collect a state income tax, and several of the remaining states, which rely exclusively on the sales tax, have made that tax a far less regressive instrument than it once was by exempting such necessities as food, clothing, and medicine. . . . Only in the case of local reliance on property taxes is serious regressiveness still built into the system, but even here many states are now providing some relief for low-income taxpayers to the extent that they are fiscally able to do so. . . .

WILL FEDERAL MONEY BE WISELY USED?

Criticism #5: The states and localities will dissipate federal money given them without any strings attached instead of using the funds where they are most needed. The governmental functions which generate the heaviest drains on the country's fiscal resources—education, welfare, health, transportation—are precisely the ones whose necessity is generally accepted in all parts of the country or which have well-established clientele and interest group support. The chances that any state or locality could easily ignore that public support is exceedingly slight. It has become entirely clear, in the study of federal aid programs, that once a program becomes routinized, there is rarely any difference of opinion among the planes of government as to the necessity for maintaining it. If anything, there is a tendency to freeze such programs in. There is absolutely no reason to doubt that the bulk of any shared revenues would be used to meet well-defined, well-established, and well-supported needs in these essential areas.

There is a historical precedent here which may be apt. In 1837, the federal government decided to distribute surplus revenue in the federal treasury to the states for use in meeting domestic needs that Congress felt the federal government was prohibited from undertaking directly. At that time, the great needs were for the creation of public elementary schools, the establishment of public welfare institutions, and the construction of internal improvements (particularly roads, canals, and railroads). There were those in Congress who wanted to specify, in the legislation granting the funds, that they would be used for these purposes, but the strict constitutional constructionists of the time felt that this would be an improper exercise of federal power. The money was ultimately distributed with no formal strings but with the understanding that it would be used for such purposes—and indeed it was. While not every penny was well used (what government can ever make that claim?), a substantial share was; much of it was invested in permanent funds, with the interest to be used to support the functions in question for many years. Many of the state and local public school systems, public institutions, and even highways of today trace their origins to the surplus distribution of 1837, and more than a few are still benefiting from it. . . .

THE CASE FOR LOCALISM

There are those who assert that, since the national government is in many respects as close to the people as local government, there is no need to sacrifice the virtues of national uniformity for the will-o'-the wisp of local control. Given the ease of nationwide communications today, it is reasonable to argue that national political figures can reach out to their constituents in ways that make them better known than their state and local counterparts. At the same time, however, one-way communication through the media is not the only— or even the best—measure of closeness. Granted that more people watch the President on television than the mayor, it is still questionable whether sheer visibility without the possibilities of interaction constitutes "closeness" in the sense that a democracy requires. Moreover, the sheer size of the national bureaucracy creates a degree of remoteness, inefficiency, and waste that rivals that of the least professionalized state government.

But efficiency is by no means the only value involved here. Part of the strength of the American political system derives from our understanding that where men are free it is not always necessary to use direct national action to achieve national goals. Often, they can be as effectively achieved through local or state action, and in such cases the results are almost certain to be more enduring because the decisions are more solidly rooted in public opinion. The history of the great innovations in the American federal system affirms the truth of this proposition. When we created a public education system in the United States over one hundred years ago, we did so as a matter of national policy, but we accomplished the task through local action accompanied by state and national assistance of various kinds. Our highway and welfare systems were built in essentially the same way. This general technique is an aspect of the genius of American politics.

Today there is much discussion of, and growing support for, the idea of local control—of the restoration of local self-government insofar as that is possible in our complex world. I believe this is a responsible and hopeful movement of opinion. It is not a question of whether the federal government shall abdicate its role in domestic policy; that would be as impossible as it is undesirable. The growing demand of Americans today is rather that the federal role be adjusted to accommodate the goal of local self-determination.

I do not doubt that, in some places, greater local responsibility for making and administering public policy will engender results that liberals and persons whose concern for a particular program is unmodified by other interests will find disagreeable. In other places, the result will be just as disturbing to conservatives and to those whose opposition to particular programs is untempered by any other interest. This is the price of democracy. No doubt it is a price worth arguing about. But those who choose to discuss the issue should do so on its merits, not on the basis of myths which have hitherto obscured them. Today there is simply no justification for thinking that the states and localities, either in principle or in practice, are less able to do the job than the federal government. In fact, there is some reason to believe that, even with their weaknesses, they will prove better able to restore public confidence in America's political institutions.

NOTE

1. Massachusetts may well be a case in point. While its politics are often described as seamy, its governmental record actually makes it by any measure one of the most progressive governments in the Union, and in pioneering new programs or setting higher standards it often outdoes Washington. In the case of the Bay State, the combination of the moralistic commitment to "good government" stemming from its Puritan heritage and the desire to utilize politics to gain material advantage which is strong among many of its "ethnic" politicians has served to enhance the progressive character of that commonwealth when it comes to the delivery of services, even as it maintains its reputation for shady politics.

CHAPTER FOUR

PUBLIC OPINION

The process of governing has always been a two-way street between those who rule and those who are ruled. In totalitarian countries, the relationship between the rulers and the ruled is tilted in favor of the rulers because they make decisions without much regard for the wishes of the people. In democratic countries, however, the relationship between the rulers and the ruled is presumed to be more reciprocal—the rulers must at all times be concerned about what the people want.

The United States, of course, is an example of a democratic system in which "representatives" are chosen to make decisions by and with the consent of the people. But how much influence ought the people to have? Should our representatives act on the basis of public opinion polls, a kind of national referendum on every issue, or should these officials be free to act on their beliefs and judgments without having to be responsive to their constituent's views?

This issue is addressed in a very unusual and interesting way in the following two articles. The authors have written commentaries on a significant technological development in our society—"teledemocracy." Teledemocracy is a concept which embraces the use of electronic devices for the purpose of instantly recording people's preferences on anything from consumer goods to political issues. In the first article, Ted Becker describes these new electronic devices, reviews their use in the United States and elsewhere, and presents an argument for their increased usage as a way of making our political system even more democratic.

Taking issue with Becker is Michael Malbin, who sees some danger in instant electronic polling. To Malbin, the act of governance is more than a simple recording of public opinion, electronically or otherwise; it involves "deliberation," which can only come with the give-and-take of discussion. According to him, pushing a button on a black box in the privacy of your living room will hardly lead to enlightened public discussion on the critical issues of the day.

Teledemocracy: Bringing Power Back to the People

Ted Becker

These are bad times for democracy. Only half those American citizens eligible to vote did so in the last presidential election, following a trend of declining voter participation in recent years. Many nonvoters in the United States feel powerless and forgotten, ignored by elected representatives and overwhelmed by what they perceive as the power and influence of special and vested interests.

These are good times for democracy. In Europe, there is a trend for national governments to put vital questions directly to the people for them to decide the destiny of their countries:

- England—join the Common Market?
- Spain—adopt a new constitution?
- Italy—allow abortion?

But whether the trend is favorable or not, there is a deep yearning in nations everywhere to increase the democratic essence of their political life.

Fortunately, new technologies and techniques present exciting prospects for involving people directly in governing themselves. Teledemocracy—the term coined for electronically aided, rapid, two-way political communication, could offer the means to help educate voters on issues, to facilitate discussion of important decisions, to register instantaneous polls, and even to allow people to vote directly on public policy.

Experiments in teledemocracy first began in earnest in the 1970s. The first tests were modest in scale, using small groups like apartment complexes and housing communities.

Perhaps the first successful large-scale adventure was Alternatives for

From "Teledemocracy: Bringing Power Back to the People," by Ted Becker, *The Futurist*, December 1981, pp. 6–9.

Washington (AFW), which ran from 1974 to 1976. The brainchild of Governor Dan Evans, AFW was a state-sponsored project that sought to involve as many of the state's citizens as possible in conceiving and choosing among a number of potential long-range futures for the state.

AFW started with meetings of a wide-based group of citizens in workshops and seminars, then employed several survey methods to involve even more people. To draw the public-at-large into the process, AFW sponsored programs on public television, then published over a million questionnaires in all the state's major newspapers that presented eleven futures and asked people for their views. Random-sample polls were conducted to determine what a representative group of citizens would choose as well.

As an exercise designed to provide broad-based, long-distance future planning, AFW was a huge success. More than 45,000 citizens answered the newspaper surveys and thousands more cooperated in the telephone random surveys. Perhaps hundreds of thousands of others watched some part of the TV programming. And many thousands participated in a multitude of meetings around the state.

AFW proved that people are eager to get involved in politics when they believe their opinions are valued and see how the decisions directly affect their futures. Despite the great response to the program, however, the state legislature proved recalcitrant in moving on the recommendations AFW developed.

INTERACTIVE TV INVOLVES PUBLIC

Perhaps the most famous teledemocratic experiment is the QUBE interactive cable TV system in Columbus, Ohio. Set up by Warner Communications Corporation in 1977 and still running, it is the most ambitious and glamorous such system in existence.

Each household subscribing to QUBE has a small black box with five buttons connected to its TV set. The viewing public can respond to questions put to it about programs by pushing the buttons as instructed.

The interaction mostly involves various kinds of entertainment (games) or marketing (the viewer as consumer), but QUBE does provide regular public affairs shows. In an interview program called "Columbus Alive" and special affairs programs, the public—the audience—is asked for opinions on selected issues. The results of this flash "polling" register instantaneously on the screen.

QUBE does have its flaws—it is mainly oriented to consumerism, merchandising, and entertainment. The home console, the black box, does cost money: it nearly doubles the cost of the basic service and would, in "real" voting, represent a "poll tax" that poor people might be hard pressed to pay. QUBE has tested in a rather well-to-do suburb that may not be a reliable gauge of how the rest of America would respond.

But look what QUBE proves! Between 80 and 90 pecent of the potential pool of users of this system opt to use it. The evidence is clear that these folks truly enjoy using this teledemocratic system: they express avid interest in participating in feedback; they find the use of the system easy and rewarding. And they are willing to pay for the service directly out of their own pockets.

Another future-planning exercise using television considered highly successful by its organizers, and by participating citizens, was conducted in Canada in 1978–79. "Talking Back" was mainly a network television extravaganza of the Canadian Broadcasting Company.

Telephones, television, and computers linked a large number of simultaneous conferences in a series of electronic meetings to generate a nationwide discussion on several topics of national concern.

Although the Canadian Parliament did not crank out relevant policies as a direct result of "Talking Back," the experiment was an enormous success. In large numbers, from coast to coast, people responded with interest, time, energy, and creative thought.

NEW ZEALANDERS PLAN THEIR FUTURE

New Zealand Televote added some new dimensions to teledemocratic experiments. It was conducted in mid-1981 by a permanent government agency, the Commission for the Future, that was created by New Zealand's parliament for the purpose of involving the public in long-range future studies.

The project used a new kind of public opinion survey—televote—that is two parts telephone survey and one part mail survey. Televote organizers do extensive research for the public, then present the best pro and con argumentation on a subject in easy-to-read formats. People phone in their replies, which gives them time to do the poll at their own convenience. The method is capable of obtaining informed and deliberated opinion from representative samples of citizenry on complicated issues.

Televote originated in Hawaii, where it was used to aid the constitutional convention of 1978 and the state legislature from 1978 to 1980. Hawaii Televote operated out of a university, making the college part of the public government decision-making system. This system has also been less costly than comparable efforts by conventional polling organizations.

To cover the entire country, New Zealand Televote used a three-university network of televote centers.

Although confronted with a complex set of philosophical and policy choices, New Zealanders took to teledemocracy like birds to trees.

Thousands of New Zealanders answered a newspaper televote (with the same information and questions as in the "official televote") that was printed in half of New Zealand's major dailies and promoted by a thirty-station community radio network.

New Zealand Televote showed, too, that all segments of the nation's population—all ages, races, economic, and educational levels—were willing to join in teledemocracy.

TWO TELEDEMOCRATIC SYSTEMS

These examples are not the only teledemocratic experiments of recent vintage, nor are they necessarily the most important. Taken together, though, they help reveal two models of teledemocracy—and demonstrate the even greater promise of teledemocracy given the new hardware already on line, waiting to be plugged in.

The first of these two types of teledemocratic systems might be called Television Talkback (TT). The other is a blend of groups (workshops, conferences, task forces, meetings); polling (random and newspaper); and electronic media involvement (radio and TV) that might be called the Public Participation (PP) model.

Improved teledemocratic projects in the not-so-distant future must combine both kinds to overcome shortfalls each has alone.

For example, the TT system tends to balkanize the public by isolating individuals and families in their homes in front of the TV. Also, printed material has greater versatility than material displayed on a TV screen—and perhaps greater staying power.

The PP models have lacked the flair of the TT model. The modernity, novelty, and spontaneity of Television Talkback—whether via home console, the new "votaphone" method, or conventional telephone—inspire great public participation.

Recent innovations in technology will entice even greater mass participation. By way of illustration, the dramatic increase in electronic games that plug into TV sets will recondition people to interact with their sets rather than sit passively in front of the tube.

Other advances that will stimulate teledemocracy are the video recording and playback systems and the personal home computer. The home is on the verge of becoming *the* major educational and informational center.

New electronic interactive systems are on line and ready for everyday use in several countries, including Canada (Teledon), France (Intelmatique), and Japan (Hi-Ovia). Cable television is ready to spread through the United States like wildfire. The forecast is nothing but bright for teledemocracy, thanks to modern science.

All systems are go for more and better teledemocratic experiments: the theory and knowledge are there; the enthusiasm and enthusiasts are there; the public is there; the paraphernalia are there. Future experimentation will bring us closer and closer to implementing pure electronic democracy in a real-life situation and allow us to transform public opinion as developed and measured by teledemocratic means into the law of some lands.

What is missing is a commitment by policymakers and planners to promote and respond to teledemocratically derived opinion. Such a commitment might arise in the business sector when it is understood that teledemocratic systems, combining these hard technologies and soft techniques, have enormous profit-making potential. Millions of people are already willing to "play and pay" for electronic town meetings, just as they are already paying to shoot down space invaders and enjoy ballets. A similar commitment from the political sector may be harder to come by.

Sometime in the near future the degree of alienation may be so great, the amount of social turbulence so distressing, and the threat of chaos so imminent that a drastic political realignment will be the only path open.

We could take the radical detour to the right and march down the iron road to totalitarianism, with a government akin to the Big Brotherism foreseen by George Orwell.

But it may be preferable to embrace greater and purer democracy, to let people in, to divest, diffuse, and decentralize power as never before. At that moment, teledemocracy will be ready for its greatest challenge and responsibility. The public will no longer expect those in power to ignore its will, because the real power will rest in the will of the public itself. With the help of teledemocratic processes, public opinion will become the law of the land, as in all places where referendums and initiatives are used.

Teledemocracy and Its Discontents

Michael Malbin

Professional survey researchers like to dismiss electronic straw polls as pseudoscientific. They're right, of course, but that only begins to get at what's most troubling about this new phenomenon. The more basic issues have to do with the proper function of issue polling in a representative democracy, and the future possibilities for electronic initiatives and referendums. These issues would have to be addressed even if straw polls could be made every bit as accurate as polls using standard sampling techniques.

Let's consider electronic referendums first. It would be easy to imagine every person in the country, in a few years or decades, having access to a cable or other system that would record his opinions on issues. It also would be easy to imagine that the owners of the various systems, or the Federal Communications Commission, could devise a technology—national identity cards, fingerprint readers, or whatever—that would prevent double voting and limit participation to eligible or registered voters. Of course, there would be political resistance to the central management that would be required, but let's ignore this impediment for the moment. The point is that technologically, the country is on the threshold of an era in which frequent and direct participation of the people in their government will be possible.

Some of the new technology's supporters look forward to the coming era with unfettered enthusiasm. One such person is University of Hawaii political scientist Ted Becker, who refers to the phenomenon as "teledemocracy." In an article in the December issue of *The Futurist*, Becker eagerly anticipates the day when "with the help of teledemocratic processes, public opinion will become the law of the land, as in all places where referendums and initiatives are used." Becker notes that where QUBE is in place, "folks truly enjoy using this teledemocratic system: they express avid interest in

From *Public Opinion*, June/July 1982, pp. 58–59.

participating in feedback; they find the use of the system rewarding. And they are willing to pay for the service."

Becker surely seems right on one point: as more people experience the joys of electronic political self-expression, the pressure for turning such expressions into law will increase. The way of the future seems clear. At least, the way is clear if no convincing case can be mounted to show that it should not be.

Just such a case was mounted successfully almost two hundred years ago in *The Federalist Papers*. It would be worthwhile to think once again about what *The Federalist* had to say—not because the work is old and venerated, but because its arguments are still alive and can help clarify the problems of today.

DRAWBACKS OF DIRECT DEMOCRACY

The first, and most important, thing to remember about the Constitution's framers is that democracy was less basic to them than liberty. They wanted to set up a democracy, to be sure, but it had to be one that worked toward securing the inalienable rights enumerated in the Declaration of Independence. Every form of government poses some danger to those rights, they thought, but some government is necessary to secure them. The threat to rights peculiar to democracies, the Founders believed, was that posed by majority tyranny. The Constitution is the framers' attempt to minimize that danger in a manner consistent with democratic principles. Representation was a key part of that solution in at least two different ways.

First, the framers thought majority tyranny is most likely if the majority gets swept up by a single, common special interest or passion. Their solution called for a large, economically complex republic where no one interest would be likely to predominate. But large republics obviously have to be representative. Two hundred million people cannot fit into one room. And if they could, the result would not be democracy but mob rule, in which an oligarchy inevitably would rise to the top and control the proceedings.

What makes electronic initiatives and referendums so attractive is that they seem on the surface to overcome these traditional objections to direct democracy. Through modern technology, people across a large republic can act in concert without taking on the characteristics of a mob. Technology, in other words, would seem to allow the country to enjoy the advantages of a large republic's diversity together with a small republic's direct participation.

UNREFINED OPINIONS

The problem with this argument is that it fails to deal with the second, and more important, reason for having a system of representation. Representatives were expected to be accountable to public opinion, but they were not simply to reflect it as if they were mere physical surrogates for the people. The need to form majorities out of multiple factions was supposed to force representatives, in the words of *Federalist* No. 10, "to refine and enlarge the public views"—that is, to modify and compromise legislative proposals *before* adopting or rejecting them. The process, in other words, was supposed to force legislators to deliberate and to think of the needs of others.

Modern mass communications cannot overcome these objections to direct democracy for two reasons. First, initiatives, like polls, place unwarranted power in the hands of those who frame the questions. Second, even if direct democracy were limited to referendums on questions drawn up by the legislature, the answers given by citizens isolated in their homes would add nothing worthwhile to the deliberative process. Political deliberation is not a solitary activity. Opinions only become refined through the give-and-take of discussion with people whose backgrounds and opinions differ from one's own. And discussion presupposes reasonably well-informed discussants. A "discussion" between a well- and an ill-informed person is nothing more than an exhortation. This is all one can expect from a referendum campaign, however. Referendums may be useful in small countries, or on statewide constitutional issues, or in local areas in which citizens may know almost as much as their representatives about the issues. But on complicated national and statewide legislative matters, referendums merely give special interest groups an opportunity to use demagogic advertising appeals to frustrate the legislative will.

There is no conceivable way the public could "refine and enlarge" its own views in a manner that would be conducive to sound legislation. The public is, and necessarily will remain, poorly informed on most issues. Even members of Congress, who devote their lives to public affairs, have to depend on committee specialists for most of their information. Think of how much more difficult it would be for the average citizen, for whom politics is only a passing interest. For confirmation, look at the level of public confusion shown by issue polls in which slightly different questions produce contradictory results, or those on which follow-ups yield little but gaps or "don't knows."

This is not meant as a slap at the American people. The question is not so much the people's ability as how people choose to use their time. The purpose of the Republic, after all, is not to make every citizen a public figure. The United States is not and was not meant to be another Switzerland. Rather, the purpose of our government is to use public action to secure the private rights to life, liberty, and the pursuit of happiness.

If referendums and initiatives are dismissed, what about the increased use of issue polls for purely advisory purposes? I have no doubt that both electronic and nonelectronic issue polling will continue their steady rate of growth. The problem with them is that the opinions they solicit are, in *The Federalist*'s terms, unrefined and unenlarged. They are raw pieces of data that deserve to be treated with extreme caution. Increasing the frequency of issue polling, through QUBE or other systems, cannot make their results more refined but it can add to the public pressure for taking unrefined results more seriously. It may become increasingly difficult for legislators to dismiss such polls without becoming labeled "enemies of democracy." Labeling of this sort should be resisted. Legislators who read issue polls with jaundiced eyes may be a democratic republic's best friends.

CHAPTER FIVE

VOTING

From 1960 to 1980, voting turnout in presidential elections declined by some 10 percent. Moreover, while turnout went up by seven-tenths of 1 percent in the 1984 presidential election, the fact remains that more than 80 million Americans continued to stay away from the polls. Despite the fact that our population is more highly educated and faces fewer procedural impediments to voting than ever before, a significant portion of the electorate does not participate.

Is nonvoting a source for concern? In the view of Austin Ranney, it is not. He contends that voters and nonvoters do not differ significantly in their policy and candidate preferences, nor in their degree of civic duty. Moreover, in his opinion, nonvoting does not offend any basic democratic principle, for the right not to vote is every bit as precious as the right to vote. In contrast, Curtis Gans believes that we should be disturbed about both the causes and the consequences of low turnout. While acknowledging that the mechanics of voting should be made easier, nevertheless, he insists that the fundamental reason for nonvoting is quite simple—citizens no longer believe that their vote has any importance in the political system. This attitude, he argues, can be altered only if fundamental changes are made in our institutions. Equally disturbing for him is the fact that a declining pool of voters leaves government vulnerable to the influence of special interests, thereby lessening its capacity to make decisions in the public interest.

Nonvoting Is Not a Social Disease

Austin Ranney

In 1980 only 53 percent of the voting-age population in the United States voted for president, and in 1982 only 38 percent voted for members of the House. As the statistics are usually presented, this rate is, on the average, from ten to forty points lower than in the democratic nations of Western Europe, Scandinavia, and the British Commonwealth—although such numbers involve major technical problems of which we should be aware.* We also know that the level of voter participation has been declining steadily since the early 1960s.

All forms of *in*voluntary nonvoting—caused by either legal or extralegal impediments—are violations of the most basic principles of democracy and fairness. Clearly it is a bad thing if citizens who want to vote are prevented from doing so by law or intimidation. But what about *voluntary* nonvoters— the 30 percent or so of our adult citizens who *could* vote if they were willing to

---

* European and American measures of voting and nonvoting differ significantly. In all countries the numerator for the formula is the total number of votes cast in national elections. In most countries the denominator is the total number of persons on the electoral rolls—that is, people we would call "registered voters"—which includes almost all people legally eligible to vote. In the United States, on the other hand, the denominator is the "voting-age population," which is the estimate by the Bureau of the Census of the number of people in the country who are eighteen or older at the time of the election. That figure, unlike its European counterpart, includes aliens and inmates of prisons and mental hospitals as well as persons not registered to vote. One eminent election analyst, Richard M. Scammon, estimates that if voting turnout in the United States were computed by the same formula as that used for European countries, our average figures would rise by eight to ten percentage points, a level that would exceed Switzerland's and closely approach those of Canada, Ireland, Japan, and the United Kingdom.

This selection was adapted from a paper delivered to the ABC/Harvard symposium on Voter Participation on October 1, 1983. *Public Opinion*, October/November 1983, pp. 16–19.

make the (usually minimal) effort, but who rarely or never do so? What does it matter if millions of Americans who could vote choose not to?

We should begin by acknowledging that suffrage and voting laws, extralegal force, and intimidation account for almost none of the nonvoting. A number of constitutional amendments, acts of Congress, and court decisions since the 1870s—particularly since the mid-1960s—have outlawed all legal and extralegal denial of the franchise to blacks, women, Hispanics, people over the age of eighteen, and other groups formerly excluded. Moreover, since the mid-1960s most states have changed their registration and voting laws to make casting ballots a good deal easier. Many states, to be sure, still demand a somewhat greater effort to register than is required by other democratic countries. But the best estimates are that even if we made our voting procedures as undemanding as those in other democracies, we would raise our average turnouts by only nine or so percentage points. That would still leave our voter participation level well below that of all but a handful of the world's democracies, and far below what many people think is the proper level for a healthy democracy.

Throughout our history, but especially in recent years, many American scholars, public officials, journalists, civic reformers, and other people of good will have pondered our low level of voting participation and have produced a multitude of studies, articles, books, pamphlets, manifestoes, and speeches stating their conclusions. On one point they agree: All start from the premise that voluntary, as well as involuntary, nonvoting is a bad thing for the country and seek ways to discourage it. Yet, despite the critical importance of the question, few ask *why* voluntary nonvoting is a bad thing.

Voluntary nonvoting's bad name stems from one or a combination of three types of arguments or assumptions. Let us consider these arguments in turn.

WHAT HARM DOES IT DO?

One of the most often-heard charges against nonvoting is that it produces unrepresentative bodies of public officials. After all, the argument runs, if most of the middle-class WASPs vote and most of the blacks, Hispanics, and poor people do not, then there will be significantly lower proportions of blacks, Hispanics, and poor people in public office than in the general population. Why is that bad? For two reasons. First, it makes the public officials, in political theorist Hanna Pitkin's term, "descriptively unrepresentative." And while not everyone would argue that the interests of blacks are best represented by black officials, the interests of women by women officials, and so on, many people believe that the policy preferences of the underrepresented groups will get short shrift from the government. Second, this not only harms the underrepresented groups but weakens the whole polity, for the underrepresented are likely to feel that the government cares nothing for them and they owe no loyalty to it. Hence it contributes greatly to the underclasses' feelings of alienation from the system and to the lawlessness that grows from such alienation.

This argument seems plausible enough, but a number of empirical studies comparing voters with nonvoters do not support it. They find that the distributions of policy preferences among nonvoters are approximately the same as those among voters, and therefore the pressures on public officials by constituents for certain policies and against others are about the same as they would be if everyone, WASPs and minorities, voted at the same rate.

Moreover, other studies have shown that the level of cynicism about the government's honesty, competence, and responsiveness is about the same among nonvoters as among voters, and an increased level of nonvoting does not signify an increased level of alienation or lawlessness. We can carry the argument a step further by asking if levels of civic virtue are clearly higher and levels of lawlessness lower in Venezuela (94 percent average voting turnout), Austria (94 percent), and Italy (93 percent) than in the United States (58 percent), Switzerland (64 percent), and Canada (76 percent). If the answer is no, as surely it is, then at least we have to conclude that there is no clear or strong relationship between high levels of voting turnout and high levels of civic virtue.

Another argument concerns future danger rather than present harm to the Republic. Journalist Arthur Hadley asserts that our great and growing number of "refrainers" (his term for voluntary nonvoters) constitutes a major threat to the future stability of our political system. In his words:

> These growing numbers of refrainers hang over the democratic process like a bomb, ready to explode and change the course of our history as they have twice in our past. . . . Both times in our history when there have been large numbers of refrainers, sudden radical shifts of power have occurred. As long as the present gigantic mass of refrainers sits outside of our political system, neither we nor our allies can be certain of even the normally uncertain future. This is why creating voters, bringing the refrainers to the booth, is important.

Hadley's argument assumes that if millions of the present nonvoters suddenly voted in some future election, they would vote for persons, parties, and policies radically different from those chosen by the regular voters. He asserts that that is what happened in 1828 and again in 1932, and it could happen again any time. Of course some might feel that a sudden rush to the polls that produces another Andrew Jackson or Franklin Roosevelt is something to be longed for, not feared, but in any case his assumption is highly dubious. We have already noted that the policy preferences of nonvoters do not differ greatly from those of voters, and much the same is true of their candidate preferences. For example, a leading study of the 1980 presidential election found that the five lowest voting groups were blacks, Hispanics, whites with family incomes below $5,000 a year, whites with less than high school educations, and working-class white Catholics. The study concluded that if all five groups had voted at the same rate as the electorate as a whole, they would have added only about one-and-a-half percentage points to Carter's share of the vote, and Reagan would still have been elected with a considerable margin. So Hadley's fear seems, at the least, highly exaggerated.

WHAT SOCIAL SICKNESS DOES NONVOTING MANIFEST?

Some writers take the position that, while a high level of voluntary nonvoting may not in itself do harm to the nation's well-being, it is certainly a symptom of poor civic health. Perhaps they take their inspiration from Pericles, who, in his great funeral oration on the dead of Marathon, said:

> . . . *Our ordinary citizens, though occupied with the pursuits of industry, are still fair judges of public matters; for, unlike any other nation, regarding him who takes no part in these duties not as unambitious but as useless.* . . .

One who holds a twentieth-century version of that view is likely to believe that our present level of voluntary nonvoting is a clear sign that millions of Americans are civically useless—that they are too lazy, too obsessed with their own selfish affairs and interests, and too indifferent to the welfare of their country and the quality of their government to make even the minimum effort required to vote. A modern Pericles might ask, How can such a nation hope to defend itself in war and advance the public welfare in peace? Are not the lassitude and indifference manifested by our high level of nonvoting the root cause of our country's declining military strength and economic productivity as well as the growing corruption and bungling of our government?

Perhaps so, perhaps not. Yet the recent studies of nonvoters have shown that they do not differ significantly from voters in the proportions who believe that citizens have a civic duty to vote or in the proportions who believe that ordinary people have a real say in what government does. It may be that nonvoters are significantly less patriotic citizens, poorer soldiers, and less productive workers than voters, but there is no evidence to support such charges. And do we accept the proposition that the much higher turnout rates for the Austrians, the French, and the Irish show that they are significantly better on any or all of these counts than the Americans? If not, then clearly there is no compelling reason to believe that a high level of nonvoting is, by itself, a symptom of sickness in American society.

WHAT BASIC PRINCIPLES DOES IT OFFEND?

I have asked friends and colleagues whether they think that the high level of voluntary nonvoting in America really matters. Almost all of them believe that it does, and when I ask them why they usually reply not so much in terms of some harm it does or some social illness it manifests but rather in terms of their conviction that the United States of America is or should be a democracy, and that a high level of voluntary nonvoting offends some basic principles of democracy.

Their reasoning goes something like this: The essential principle of democratic government is government by the people, government that derives its "just powers from the consent of the governed." The basic institution for ensuring truly democratic government is the regular holding of free elections at which the legitimate authority of public officials to govern is renewed or terminated by the sovereign people. Accordingly, the right to vote is the basic right of every citizen in a democracy, and the exercise of that right is the most basic duty of every democratic citizen.

Many have made this argument. For example, in 1963 President John F. Kennedy appointed an eleven-member Commission on Registration and Voting Participation. Its report, delivered after his death, began:

> Voting in the United States is the fundamental act of self-government. It provides the citizen in our free society the right to make a judgment, to state a choice, to participate in the running of his government. . . . The ballot box is the medium for the expression of the consent of the governed.

In the same vein the British political philosopher Sir Isaiah Berlin declares, "Participation in self-government is, like justice, a basic human requirement, an end in itself."

If these views are correct, then any nominal citizen of a democracy who does not exercise this basic right and fulfill this basic duty is not a full citizen, and the larger the proportion of such less-than-full citizens in a polity that aspires to democracy, the greater the gap between the polity's low realities and democracy's high ideals.

Not everyone feels this way, of course. Former Senator Sam Ervin, for example, argues:

> I'm not going to shed any real or political or crocodile tears if people don't care enough to vote. I don't believe in making it easy for apathetic, lazy people. I'd be extremely happy if nobody in the United States voted except for the people who thought about the issues and made up their own minds and wanted to vote. No one else who votes is going to contribute anything but statistics, and I don't care that much for statistics.

The issues between these two positions are posed most starkly when we consider proposals for compulsory voting. After all, if we are truly convinced that voluntary nonvoting is a violation of basic democratic principles and a major social ill, then why not follow the lead of Australia, Belgium, Italy, and Venezuela and enact laws *requiring* people to vote and penalizing them if they do not?

The logic seems faultless, and yet most people I know, including me, are against compulsory voting laws for the United States. All of us want to eradicate all vestiges of *in*voluntary nonvoting, and many are disturbed by the high level of voluntary nonvoting. Yet many of us also feel that the right to abstain is just as precious as the right to vote, and the idea of legally compelling all citizens to vote whether they want to or not is at least as disturbing as the large numbers of Americans who now and in the future probably will not vote without some compulsion.

THE BRIGHT SIDE

In the light of the foregoing considerations, then, how much should we worry about the high level of voluntary nonvoting in our country? At the end of his magisterial survey of voting turnout in different democratic nations, Ivor Crewe asks this question and answers, "There are . . . reasons for *not* worrying—too much."

I agree. While we Americans can and probably should liberalize our registration and voting laws and mount register-and-vote drives sponsored by political parties, civic organizations, schools of government, and broadcasting companies, the most we can realistically hope for from such efforts is a modest increase of ten or so percentage points in our average turnouts. As a college professor and political activist for forty years, I can testify that even the best reasoned and most attractively presented exhortations to people to behave like good democratic citizens can have only limited effects on their behavior, and most get-out-the-vote drives by well-intentioned civic groups in the past have had disappointingly modest results.

An even more powerful reason not to worry, in my judgment, is that we are likely to see a major increase in our voting turnouts to, say, the 70 or 80 percent levels, only if most of the people in our major nonvoting groups—blacks, Hispanics, and poor people—come to believe that voting is a powerful instrument for getting the government to do what they want it to do. The recent register-and-vote drives by the NAACP and other black-mobilization organizations have already had significant success in getting formerly inactive black citizens to the polls. These new black voters played a more important role in the congressional and other local elections in 1982 and 1983 than ever before, and they are likely to be even more significant in the elections of 1984. Organizations like the Southern Voter Registration Education Project have had some success with Hispanic nonvoters in Texas and New Mexico and may have more. Jesse Helms and Jerry Falwell may also have success in their newly launched efforts to urge more conservatives to register and vote.

But hard evidence that voting brings real benefits, not exhortations to be good citizens, will be the basis of whatever success any of these groups enjoy.

If we Americans stamp out the last vestiges of institutions and practices that produce *in*voluntary nonvoting, and if we liberalize our registration and voting laws and procedures to make voting here as easy as it is in other democracies, and if the group-mobilization movements succeed, then perhaps our level of voting participation may become much more like that of Canada or Great Britain. (It is unlikely ever to match the levels in the countries with compulsory voting or even those in West Germany or the Scandinavian countries.)

But even if that does not happen, we need not fear that our low voting turnouts are doing any serious harm to our politics or our country, or that they deprive us of the right to call ourselves a democracy.

The Problem of Nonvoting

Curtis B. Gans

Since 1960, with the exception of 1982 and 1984, voter turnout has declined by 10 percent in both presidential and congressional elections. Fully 20 million eligible Americans who previously voted regularly or sporadically have ceased voting. Even in 1982, 90 million eligible Americans failed to cast their ballots. And in the presidential year of 1984, more than 80 million Americans did not vote. Voting today in America has reached a level so low that of all the world's democracies, only Botswana has a consistently lower voter participation rate than the United States; although Switzerland, which referends all important issues and thus makes office holding meaningless, and India, which tends to have wars in one or more of its provinces at any given point, approach the United States's low participation rate.

This decline in voting affects all ages, races, and classes, with only two exceptions. The South, because of both the Voting Rights Act and the rise of two-party competition, has been increasing its vote, and younger women— between the ages of 25 and 44—are also increasing their share of the vote. Minorities voted more heavily in 1982, but it is too early to tell whether this trend will continue, absent Reagan as a national motivating and polarizing force.

This decline has occurred during precisely the time when the United States has made it easier to vote. We have abolished literacy tests and the poll tax; we have enfranchised our young and effectively enfranchised our minorities; we have adopted liberalized voting procedures, including shortening the time between the close of registration and voting, enacting in a majority of states postcard registration, and establishing in a few states election-

Excerpted from a speech delivered on September 26, 1983 to The Consultation on Citizen Responsibility, Political Participation and Government Accountability: Foundation Responsibility and Opportunity. Permission to use this speech has been granted to these authors only. All further permissions must be referred to Curtis Gans.

day registration. We have provided multilingual ballots in some places and voter outreach programs in others. . . .

In one sense, it would be a wonder had voter participation not declined during the past two decades. For in that period, we have had Watergate and Vietnam, Agnew and Abscam; we have had Johnson, Nixon, Carter, and Reagan and with them images of public leadership not commensurate with the high title of President; we have had early 1960s promises which were not fulfilled by programs or performance; we have had growing complexity in our national life and of our national problems and growing confusion about how to deal with it and them; we have had increasingly larger and larger political, economic, and social institutions and a corresponding feeling of citizen impotence in the face of them; and we have had an increasingly atomized society, increasingly confused about their choices, courtesy of the coaxial cable. Sadly but surely, nonvoting is growing to be an increasingly rational act. . . .

There are some who say that the size of the electorate is not important, that those who don't vote would not vote any differently than those who do. They are flatly and dangerously wrong.

There may well be no optimal level of participation in America, but:

(1) to the extent that fewer and fewer Americans bother to vote, the ability of organized political minorities, special interest and single-issue zealots to polarize American politics and influence the course of public policy will be enhanced;

(2) to the extent that American political participation dwindles and the business of politics is increasingly the province of organized interest groups, the ability of the political system to produce public policy in the interests of the society as a whole decreases correspondingly. (Perhaps an example is in order. If public employees constitute one-sixth of the nation but vote heavily, as they do, then when only a half of the rest of the nation votes, as they do in presidential elections, the force of the public employee vote is equal to one-third. If only one-third of the nation votes, as roughly they do in congressional elections, then public employees constitute one-half of the electorate. It is thus no wonder that it is difficult to modify civil service, abolish agencies, shrink unnecessary bureaucracy or devolve power to other levels of government);

(3) to the extent that interest and involvement with the political process declines and the citizenry is content to abdicate their responsibility to others, the potential for unstable, demagogic, and even authoritarian leadership increases;

(4) to the extent, as it has been shown, that voting is a lowest common denominator act—that people who don't vote tend not to participate in any

form of civil, social, or political activity—then any diminution of the voting force is also sapping the voluntary spirit of participation upon which the health and vitality of our institutions depend.

Democracy is not only the most humane form of government, it is also the most fragile. It depends not only for its legitimacy but also for its health and well-being on the involvement of the governed.

Government may not be, as many people now seem to feel, the answer to all of society's ills, but unless the American people wish to abdicate to oligarchic or authoritarian rule, the resolution of societal problems must come through the democratic political process.

The continuing withdrawal of American people from voting and political participation threatens not only wise governance, but the underlying vitality of the political process and the democratic ideal.

We are simply and bluntly in danger of becoming a nation governed of, for, and by the interested few.

Having said all of this, it might be well to look at who these nonvoters are. For if we are to begin to address both the general problem of nonparticipation or the more particular problem of participation of certain important subgroups, it would be well to know the lay of the land.

In 1976 [the Committee for the Study of the American Electorate] undertook a survey of a scientifically selected sample of nonvoters to attempt to ascertain who they were and why they weren't participating. And while I found that survey less than fully satisfying as a total answer to the problem (although surely more satisfying than anything which has been done before or since), it does provide some clues.

For the purposes of this discussion, I would like to categorize nonvoters in four broad groups. Any such categorizing is, of course, imperfect, but the categories may serve to show at least something of the nature of the problem which confronts us.

By far the largest group are chronic nonvoters, people who have never, or in Gilbert and Sullivan's phrase "hardly ever," voted. They tend to come from families who have never voted. They tend to be poorer, younger, less educated, more unorganized working class, more unemployed, more minority, more southern, more rural, and more urban underclass than the rest of the population. They are also likely to be participants in nothing else. With the exception of a few chronic nonvoters in the South who participate in fundamentalist religion (and who are likely to have been the source of the Reverend Jerry Falwell's additions to the voter rolls . . .), the chronic nonvoter tends to participate in no organized political, social, religious, or civic activities. They are a nation larger than France within our midst, who, if one were to describe them in the terms used by the Bureau of Labor Statistics to describe the elements of the labor force, would be out of the labor and voting force. It is unlikely that any substantial portion of these people will be engaged in the polity unless and until we make much greater strides than we have to address the problem of class in America and to integrate them not only politically, but economically and socially as well, into the mainstream of American society. Until then, politics is likely to appear to the chronic nonvoter as irrelevant.

The second group are those who have dropped out of the political process in the past two decades, some 20 million Americans. They are still more heavily weighted to the poorer and more minority segments of our population. But they also include a 40 percent component who are educated, middle-class, professional, and white-collar workers in the suburbs in the middle Atlantic, northeastern, and western states. These people were in our survey the most alienated and the most motivated by events and by a belief that their vote no longer had any efficacy either in the improvement of their individual lives or the conduct of public policy. They can be returned to the polity only when and if they come to believe that in the political marketplace there are choices that will truly affect their personal and the societal well-being.

The third group is the young. For the lowest participating group in America is the nation's youth. Bluntly, fewer young people are voting than ever before. They are becoming socialized to participate at a slower rate than previous generations and their interest in politics as a group is substantially lower than that of the rest of the nation. If they are to become participants, they need to be engaged early and often, something which is not being done either by our high schools or our extracurricular institutions.

Finally, there are those who are still impeded by procedures governing registration and voting and those for whom the word "apathetic" is an accurate description. For while in our survey, nonvoters by a margin of 4 to 1 gave substantive reasons for their nonparticipation, there were still some who felt intimidated at the polls or impeded from participation, by polling hours, registration procedures, and the like. And, of course, there are some who just don't give a damn.

But for the vast majority of Americans, nonvoting is an intentional act. . . .

If there are solutions to those problems, they must come from a variety of directions.

Having said earlier that the central problem of low and declining voting is not principally a matter of procedure, I would like to suggest that procedure is not altogether irrelevant. For it has been estimated that if the nation would adopt election day registration there would be an immediate 9 percent rise in voter participation. I believe such a claim is somewhat excessive. On the other hand, if we just accept the evidence of our eyes—that when Wisconsin, Minnesota, Oregon, and Maine adopted election day registration, they experienced initial increases of from 2 to 4 percent in the face of national voting declines—we know we could add from 4 to 9 million Americans to the voter rolls. Bluntly speaking, America need not be, as it is today, the only major democracy in the world which puts the principal onus for registration on the citizen rather than the state. We need not necessarily have a system in which we must advertise "Register and Vote," forcing the citizen into not one but two acts in order to participate and knowing that the two are increasingly no longer synonymous. We can explore election day registration in more states, or better still, universal enrollment, as they have in Canada, which offers the prospect of fraud-free elections while lifting the burden of registration from the citizen's back. And in the interim we can explore those things which will bring us closer to this ideal—further shortening the time between the close of registration and election, drivers' license registration, and the like. . . .

We should constructively reduce the length of our ballots. There are no good reasons that the secretaries of state and attorneys general should be elected—they are not policymaking but rather policy implementing positions. Similarly, we could reduce the number of other elected offices and the number of ballot propositions. With ballots a mile long and information about them scarce as hen's teeth, it is no wonder that the public says in public opinion polls that it is confused, and it is no wonder that there are discouragingly long lines at the polling places.

We can and should have, instead of more elections, more polling places and longer hours (although not a twenty-four-hour voting day).

We should be concerned about the information, or rather lack thereof, the average citizen has available to him or her in making voting decisions. If citizens depend on television for the bulk of their information, they may know a little about the candidates who are running for the offices of president, governor, and senator, but they have no means of knowing anything about the other offices and issues at stake in any particular election. If they read most newspapers, they have little prospect for learning much more (the *New York Times*, the *Los Angeles Times*, and a few others being notable exceptions.) Only through the continuing work of the League of Women Voters do some people in some places know what is going on. But that information ought to be available to everyone. We need, in short, to see whether the type of voter information pamphlets provided by the counties of Oregon, which provide information about each office and issue at stake in each election, pamphlets which can be carried into the voting booth, ought not to be used in every state in the union.

We should here and now begin the process of establishing a commission to look into and recommend remedies for those last vestiges of discrimination and intimidation which still plague our polls. There is no reason why the registration books of Upper Marlboro, Maryland, should be open for two unadvertised hours every two years. Jesse Jackson is right when he suggests that people should not be asked to register in one place for one election and in another for another. Eddie Williams is right when he decries the discriminatory effects of at-large elections, full slate requirements, and redistricting. We should be concerned about districting that effectively disenfranchises blacks from voting in their place of residence and on the officeholders and issues which will affect their lives. We should be concerned about students who are denied the vote in either their place of education or home because of discriminatory residency requirements in both places. . . .

We could, of course, do all of these things I have so far suggested and still not have a healthy democracy and high level of voter participation. For unless and until the public believes that it is voting for something meaningful and that its vote will make a difference, low voter participation will continue to be the order of the day.

The simple answer to this problem is, of course, to have candidates who speak relevantly to the issues of public concern and who can deliver upon their political promises once in office.

Life and reality are rarely so simple. For this relatively simple answer runs us smack against the five central political problems afflicting our political life—the problems of policy, parties, institutions, media, and governance.

A. POLICY

We may lament the quality of our candidates. Such laments have been common for the past twenty years. Yet leadership does not spring full blown upon the political scene. The business of a politician is, in its best sense, to move the center of America in creative directions and to preserve the option to move in other directions. It involves very fine antennae about how far one can move to the center without making one's self irrelevant. The problem within America today is that there is no such center of ideas to which the politician can repair. If all our politicians sound like throwbacks to the New Deal (or, as in the case of the President, to the 1920s) it is because they are repairing to the only safe grounds they know. The problem lies not with our leaders but with the state of the art.

For three decades, we had such a consensual center. Out of the two great crises of the 1930s and 1940s, the Great Depression and World War II, there emerged a national consensus. On the domestic side we had Keynesian economics and the New Deal, a programmatic federal response to each perceived problem taken ad seriatim. On the foreign side, we had an increasing American global role in the containment first of fascism and later of communism. We argued about issues but only in degree. Was this domestic program necessary? How much aid should we be sending abroad and should it be military or economic?

The consensus broke down in the 1960s. The war in Vietnam revealed the limits of American power and resources in the world to assume a truly global role. The blight of our cities, the pollution of our environment were but two ways which showed that treating our problems ad seriatim might bring by-products as bad as the disease the original programs were designed to cure. Burgeoning unresponsive bureaucracies showed the limits to the maxim "let the federal government do it.". . .

In retrospect, (President Franklin) Roosevelt had an easier time, because he could accomplish those changes in outlook in an atmosphere of perceived crisis. In many ways the problems confronting us are nearly as great, but the perceived sense of crisis is not there. Thus, it becomes an exercise in leadership, an exercise no less necessary because it is difficult.

B. PARTIES

If the candidate has difficulty in knowing what to say because of a lack of a central American consensus, then he also has difficulty as an officeholder in delivering upon his promises because there is no organizational force to discipline the individual officeholder and make him part of a collective.

That is the traditional role of the political party, which should serve as the training ground for leadership, the mobilizer of voters, the mediator of contending factions, the sorter of public program from contending interests, the disciplinarian of individual self-interest, the enactor of program, and the implementor of legislation.

But political parties are now in disarray. Their patronage functions have been supplanted by government, their informational functions by television, their role in the conduct of the campaigns by money, media, and political consultants.

They are in disarray also for other reasons—in that they either stand for something irrelevant or stand for nothing at all.

C. INSTITUTIONS

Related to the problem of parties is the problem of our institutions. Part of that problem is simply that the institutional base of our society has atrophied as people have been atomized by television. Part of the problem is that some of our institutions have grown so large as to make them unresponsive.

But perhaps a more critical problem is the degree to which traditional institutions no longer stand for what they once did. Rather than being adversaries, business and labor are in an entente for jobs and production to the detriment of other elements of society. Unions, once the place where the common man could repair, have too often (and not without significant exceptions) become the protector of the long-term employed at the expense of the unemployed or marginally employed. The middle-class liberals, once a reliable source of strength for redistributive policies, are increasingly literally and figuratively cultivating their own gardens. Because of this, it is unlikely that we will ever again have the type of coalition of interests that existed within the New Deal.

But we can and should have interest groups that accurately reflect the interests of their issue or class. We can and should have different coalitions for different societal problems. Too often now the institutional interests of one group tend to resist cooperation with another for the public good. We need to have some general recognition of the role of time in our politics—that it is possible to be on the same side tomorrow with today's enemy. We need, in short, to return civility to the way we conduct our politics and rekindle an outlook that seeks ways to cooperate with others in temporary coalition for the common good.

D. MEDIA

There is also the problem of media. For if the politician had the consensus through which to lead, the parties through which to implement program, the institutions in floating formation to back some or all of his or her program, there would still be the problem of communications.

. . . If there is one such development which acted to society's detriment, it has been television.

For not only has it served to atomize our society; weaken our institutions; reduce participation by making people spectators and consumers rather than involved participants; decrease reading, comprehension, and conversation; and increase public confusion by giving information in undifferentiated blips and by highlighting the most visually exciting—it has also established unreal expectations for our political system by creating heroes and as quickly destroying them and by offering in its advertising medical panaceas which give the society a belief it can have equally rapid social panaceas.

But perhaps most pertinent of all is the degree to which there is in the television message no sense of history, no sense of the slow pace of progress, no sorting out of the important from the unimportant. In the coverage of a political campaign, it is easier to focus on a politician's gaffe than on his record; it is easier to talk about James Watt's remarks related to the membership of a commission than his record in despoiling the environment. . . .

E. GOVERNANCE

Finally there is the problem of governance. For if we hail the exceedingly high black turnout for the races of Harold Washington and Wilson Goode, we should be sobered by the turnout rates in elections after such blacks as

Carl Stokes and Tom Bradley were in office. While we may look with some satisfaction at the slight increase in turnout in 1984, we can almost surely look for a decline in turnout in 1988 if a Democrat should be elected and find himself not quite up to government. For at the root of public cynicism about politics is a disillusionment with government. We need to make the politician in office as effective as he is appealing on the stump. And this, in turn, mandates a program of leadership education in the arts of administration, politics, and governance. . . .

CHAPTER SIX

CAMPAIGNS AND THE MEDIA

Probably nothing has so transformed American politics as commercial television. What used to be the experience of only a few—hearing and seeing a candidate at some campaign rally, for example—is now an experience of many millions of Americans. Since television enables political candidates literally to be seen and heard in every living room in the country, it is no wonder that politicians devote so much time to its use in their campaigns.

What impact has television had on the voter? Can voters be manipulated into voting blindly for candidates because of clever image making on the television screen? Or are voters more discerning than the political advertising executives would have us believe?

While not all of the evidence is in on the impact of television on the American voter, two well-known books have dealt with this question and arrived at different conclusions. One book, The Selling of the President 1968 *by Joe McGinniss, from which excerpts are presented here, presents a first-hand account of the 1968 television campaign of former President Richard M. Nixon—a campaign that, according to McGinniss, featured a carefully packaged television image of Nixon. The success of the Nixon campaign in 1968, as compared to 1960, convinced McGinniss and many others that all political campaigning was now merely a matter of projecting the right image on the television screen and "selling" the politician to the public.*

Political scientists Thomas Patterson and Robert McClure, on the other hand, after studying the 1972 presidential election campaigns of George McGovern and Richard Nixon, conclude that the public, far from being manipulated, is actually better informed and is better able to make decisions as a result of exposure to televised political commercials.

What accounts for the seemingly contradictory results of these two studies? The answer is probably to be found in the different perspectives of the authors. McGinniss is writing from the point of view of an insider in the Nixon campaign. Patterson and McClure base their findings on the results of some two thousand interviews conducted during the 1972 campaign.

Politics as a Con Game

Joe McGinniss

Politics, in a sense, has always been a con game.

The American voter, insisting upon his belief in a higher order, clings to his religion, which promises another, better life; and defends passionately the illusion that the men he chooses to lead him are of a finer nature than he.

It has been traditional that the successful politician honor this illusion. To succeed today, he must embellish it. Particularly if he wants to be President.

"Potential presidents are measured against an ideal that's a combination of leading man, God, father, hero, pope, king, with maybe just a touch of the avenging Furies thrown in," an adviser to Richard Nixon wrote in a memorandum late in 1967. Then, perhaps aware that Nixon qualified only as father, he discussed improvements that would have to be made—not upon Nixon himself, but upon the image of him which was received by the voter. . . .

Advertising, in many ways, is a con game, too. Human beings do not need new automobiles every third year; a color television set brings little enrichment of the human experience; a higher or lower hemline no expansion of consciousness, no increase in the capacity to love.

It is not surprising, then, that politicians and advertising men should have discovered one another. And, once they recognized that the citizen did not so much vote for a candidate as make a psychological purchase of him, not surprising that they began to work together. . . .

Advertising agencies have tried openly to sell presidents since 1952. When Dwight Eisenhower ran for reelection in 1956, the agency of Batton, Barton, Durstine and Osborn, which had been on a retainer throughout his first four years, accepted his campaign as a regular account. Leonard Hall, national Republican chairman, said: "You sell your candidates and your programs the way a business sells its products." . . .

With the coming of television, and the knowledge of how it could be used to seduce voters, the old political values disappeared. Something new, murky, undefined started to rise from the mists. "In all countries," Marshall McLuhan writes, "the party system has folded like the organization chart. Policies and issues are useless for election purposes, since they are too specialized and hot. The shaping of a candidate's integral image has taken the place of discussing conflicting points of view." . . .

The television celebrity is a vessel. An inoffensive container in which someone else's knowledge, insight, compassion, or wit can be presented. And we respond like the child on Christmas morning who ignores the gift to play with the wrapping paper.

Television seems particularly useful to the politician who can be charming but lacks ideas. Print is for ideas. Newspapermen write not about people but policies; the paragraphs can be slid around like blocks. Everyone is colored gray. Columnists—and commentators in the more polysyllabic magazines—concentrate on ideology. They do not care what a man sounds like; only how he thinks. For the candidate who does not, such exposure can be embarrassing. He needs another way to reach the people.

On television it matters less that he does not have ideas. His personality is what the viewers want to share. He need be neither statesman nor crusader; he must only show up on time. Success and failure are easily measured: How often is he invited back? Often enough and he reaches his goal—to advance from "politician" to "celebrity," a status jump bestowed by grateful viewers who feel that finally they have been given the basis for making a choice.

The TV candidate, then, is measured not against his predecessors—not against a standard of performance established by two centuries of democracy—but against Mike Douglas. How well does he handle himself? Does he mumble, does he twitch, does he make me laugh? Do I feel warm inside?

Style becomes substance. The medium is the message and the masseur gets the votes. . . .

"The success of any TV performer depends on his achieving a low-pressure style of presentation," McLuhan has written. The harder a man tries, the better he must hide it. Television demands gentle wit, irony, understatement: the qualities of Eugene McCarthy. The TV politician cannot make a speech; he must engage in intimate conversation. He must never press. He should suggest, not state; request, not demand. Nonchalance is the key word. Carefully studied nonchalance.

Warmth and sincerity are desirable but must be handled with care. Unfiltered, they can be fatal. Television did great harm to Hubert Humphrey. His excesses—talking too long and too fervently, which were merely annoying in an auditorium—became lethal in a television studio. The performer must talk to one person at a time. He is brought into the living room. He is a guest. It is improper for him to shout. Humphrey vomited on the rug.

It would be extremely unwise for the TV politician to admit such knowledge of his medium. The necessary nonchalance should carry beyond his appearance while *on* the show; it should rule his attitude *toward* it. He should express distaste for television; suspicion that there is something "phony" about it. This guarantees him good press, because newspaper reporters, bitter over their loss of prestige to the television men, are certain to stress anti-television remarks. Thus, the sophisticated candidate, while analyzing his own on-the-air technique as carefully as a golf pro studies his swing, will state frequently that there is no place for "public relations gimmicks" or "those show business guys" in his campaign. Most of the television men working for him will be unbothered by such remarks. They are willing to accept anonymity, even scorn, as long as the pay is good.

Into this milieu came Richard Nixon: grumpy, cold, and aloof. He would claim privately that he lost elections because the American voter was an adolescent whom he tried to treat as an adult. Perhaps. But if he treated the voter as an adult, it was as an adult he did not want for a neighbor.

This might have been excused had he been a man of genuine vision. An explorer of the spirit. Martin Luther King, for instance, got by without being one of the boys. But Richard Nixon did not strike people that way. He had, in Richard Rovere's words, "an advertising man's approach to his work," acting as if he believed "policies (were) products to be sold the public—this one today, that one tomorrow, depending on the discounts and the state of the market."

So his enemies had him on two counts: his personality, and the convictions—or lack of such—which lay behind. They worked him over heavily on both. . . .

But Nixon survived, despite his flaws, because he was tough and smart, and—some said—dirty when he had to be. Also, because there was nothing else he knew. A man to whom politics is all there is in life will almost always beat one to whom it is only an occupation.

He nearly became President in 1960, and that year it would not have been by default. He failed because he was too few of the things a President had to be—and because he had no press to lie for him and did not know how to use television to lie about himself.

It was just Nixon and John Kennedy and they sat down together in a television studio and a little red light began to glow and Richard Nixon was finished. Television would be blamed but for all the wrong reasons.

They would say it was makeup and lighting, but Nixon's problem went deeper than that. His problem was himself. Not what he said but the man he was. The camera portrayed him clearly. America took its Richard Nixon straight and did not like the taste.

The content of the programs made little difference. Except for startling lapses, content seldom does. What mattered was the image the viewers received, though few observers at the time caught the point. . . .

What the camera showed was Richard Nixon's hunger. He lost, and bitter, confused, he blamed it on his beard. . . .

He was afraid of television. He knew his soul was hard to find. Beyond that, he considered it a gimmick; its use in politics offended him. It had not been part of the game when he had learned to play, he could see no reason to bring it in now. He half suspected it was an eastern liberal trick: one more way to make him look silly. It offended his sense of dignity, one of the truest senses he had.

So his decision to use it to become President in 1968 was not easy. So much of him argued against it. But in his Wall Street years, Richard Nixon had traveled to the darkest places inside himself and come back numbed. He was, as in the Graham Greene title, a burnt-out case. All feeling was behind him; the machine inside had proved his hardiest part. He would run for President again and if he would have to learn television to run well, then he would learn it.

America still saw him as the 1960 Nixon. If he were to come at the people again, as a candidate, it would have to be as something new; not this scarred, discarded figure from their past.

He spoke to men who thought him mellowed. They detected growth, a new stability, a sense of direction that had been lacking. He would return with fresh perspective, a more unselfish urgency.

His problem was how to let the nation know. He could not do it through the press. He knew what to expect from them, which was the same as he had always gotten. He would have to circumvent them. Distract them with coffee and doughnuts and smiles from his staff and tell his story another way.

Television was the only answer, despite its sins against him in the past. But not just any kind of television. An uncommitted camera could do irreparable harm. His television would have to be controlled. He would need experts. They would have to find the proper settings for him, or if they could not be found, manufacture them. These would have to be men of keen judgment and flawless taste. He was, after all, Richard Nixon, and there were certain things he could not do. Wearing love beads was one. He would need men of dignity. Who believed in him and shared his vision. But more importantly, men who knew television as a weapon: from broadest concept to most technical detail. This would be Richard Nixon, the leader, returning from exile. Perhaps not beloved, but respected. Firm but not harsh; just but compassionate. With flashes of warmth spaced evenly throughout.

Nixon gathered about himself a group of young men attuned to the political uses of television. . . .

Harry Treleaven, hired as creative director of advertising in the fall of 1967, immediately went to work on the more serious of Nixon's personality problems. One was his lack of humor.

"Can be corrected to a degree," Treleaven wrote, "but let's not be too obvious about it. Romney's cornball attempts have hurt him. If we're going to be witty, let a pro write the words."

Treleaven also worried about Nixon's lack of warmth, but decided that "he can be helped greatly in this respect by how he is handled. . . . Give him words to say that will show his *emotional* involvement in the issues. . . . Buchanan wrote about RFK talking about the starving children in Recife. *That's* what we have to inject. . . .

"He should be presented in some kind of 'situation' rather than cold in a studio. The situation should look unstaged even if it's not."

Some of the most effective ideas belonged to Raymond K. Price, a former editorial writer for the *New York Herald Tribune*, who became Nixon's best and most prominent speech writer in the campaign. Price later composed much of the inaugural address.

In 1967, he began with the assumption that "the natural human use of reason is to support prejudice, not to arrive at opinions." Which led to the conclusion that rational arguments would "only be effective if we can get the people to make the *emotional* leap, or what theologians call (the) 'leap of faith.' "

Price suggested attacking the "personal factors" rather than the "historical factors" which were the basis of the low opinion so many people had of Richard Nixon.

"These tend to be more a gut reaction," Price wrote, "unarticulated, nonanalytical, a product of the particular chemistry between the voter and the *image* of the candidate. *We have to be very clear on this point: that the response is to the image, not to the man.* . . . It's not what's *there* that counts, it's what's projected—and carrying it one step further, it's not what *he* projects but rather what the voter receives. It's not the man we have to change, but rather the *received impression.* And this impression often depends more on the medium and its use than it does on the candidate himself."

So there would not have to be a "new Nixon." Simply a new approach to television.

"What, then, does this mean in terms of our uses of time and of media?" Price wrote.

"For one thing, it means investing whatever time RN needs in order to work out firmly in his own mind that vision of the nation's future that he wants to be identified with. This is crucial. . . ."

So, at the age of fifty-four, after twenty years in public life, Richard Nixon was still felt *by his own staff* to be in need of time to "work out firmly in his own mind that vision of the nation's future that he wants to be identified with."

"Secondly," Price wrote, "it suggests that we take the time and the money to experiment, in a controlled manner, with film and television techniques, with particular emphasis on pinpointing those *controlled* uses of the television medium that can *best* convey the *image* we want to get across. . . .

"The TV medium itself introduces an element of distortion, in terms of its effect on the candidate and of the often subliminal ways in which the image is received. And it inevitably is going to convey a partial image—thus ours is the task of finding how to control its use so the part that gets across is the part we want to have gotten across. . . .

"Voters are basically lazy, basically uninterested in making an *effort* to understand what we're talking about . . . ," Price wrote. "Reason requires a high degree of discipline, of concentration; impression is easier. Reason pushes the viewer back, it assaults him, it demands that he agree or disagree; impression can envelop him, invite him in, without making an intellectual demand. . . . When we argue with him we demand that he make the effort of replying. We seek to engage his intellect, and for most people this is the most difficult work of all. The emotions are more easily roused, closer to the surface, more malleable. . . ."

So, for the New Hampshire primary, Price recommended "saturation with a film, in which the candidate can be shown better than he can be shown in person because it can be edited, so only the best moments are shown; then a quick parading of the candidate in the flesh so that the guy they've gotten intimately acquainted with on the screen takes on a living presence—not saying anything, just being seen. . . .

"[Nixon] has to come across as a person larger than life, the stuff of legend. People are stirred by the legend, including the living legend, not by the man himself. It's the aura that surrounds the charismatic figure more than it is the figure itself, that draws the followers. Our task is to build that aura. . . .

"So let's not be afraid of television gimmicks . . . get the voters to like the guy and the battle's two-thirds won."

So this was how they went into it. Trying, with one hand, to build the illusion that Richard Nixon, in addition to his attributes of mind and heart, considered, in the words of Patrick K. Buchanan, a speech writer, "communicating with the people . . . one of the great joys of seeking the Presidency"; while with the other they shielded him, controlled him, and controlled the atmosphere around him. It was as if they were building not a President but an Astrodome, where the wind would never blow, the temperature never rise or fall, and the ball never bounce erratically on the artificial grass.

They could do this, and succeed, because of the special nature of the man. There was, apparently, something in Richard Nixon's character which sought this shelter. Something which craved regulation, which flourished best in the darkness, behind clichés, behind phalanxes of antiseptic advisers. Some part of him that could breathe freely only inside a hotel suite that cost a hundred dollars a day.

And it worked. As he moved serenely through his primary campaign, there was new cadence to Richard Nixon's speech and motion; new confidence in his heart. And, a new image of him on the television screen.

TV both reflected and contributed to his strength. Because he was winning he looked like a winner on the screen. Because he was suddenly projecting well on the medium he had feared, he went about his other tasks with assurance. The one fed upon the other, building to an astonishing peak in August as the Republican convention began and he emerged from his regal isolation, traveling to Miami not so much to be nominated as coronated. On live, but controlled, TV.

The Impact of Televised Political Commercials

Thomas E. Patterson and Robert D. McClure

One minute after a product commercial fades from the television screen, most viewers have forgotten what was advertised. They cannot recall whether the ad trumpeted aspirin, shaving cream, or automobiles. A particularly clever or amusing commercial may draw some notice, and linger in their thoughts, but most product ads pass from the mind as quickly as from the screen.[1]

Presidential ads affect viewers differently. On television only a month or two every four years, their novelty attracts attention. Also their subject matter. They picture and discuss men seeking the nation's highest office, and most Americans feel that choosing a President deserves more consideration than selecting a brand of antacid. A clear indication of presidential advertising's attention-getting ability is that most viewers can rather fully recall the message of a presidential spot. When asked to describe a commercial they had seen during the 1972 election, 56 percent of the viewers gave a remarkably full and complete description of one, and only 21 percent were unable to recall anything at all from political ads.[2] In market research, any product whose commercials are recalled with half this accuracy is considered to have had a very successful advertising campaign.[3]

People also evaluate presidential advertising differently than product advertising. A study conducted for the American Association of Advertising Agencies in the 1960s discovered that television viewers judge product commercials more on *how* they communicate their message than on *what* they say about a product.[4] A commercial for a soft drink or a paper towel is regarded as good or bad by the television audience more on whether it is enjoyable to watch than on the truthfulness of its message or the value of the information it contains. People judge presidential ads, on the other hand, primarily on *what* they say, not *how* they say it. Whether the techniques used in presidential spots are visually appealing or unappealing seems to matter little. Viewers seem concerned mainly with whether the advertising message is truthful and worth knowing. Where the American Association of Advertising Agencies' study found that only 46 percent of viewer reactions to product ads related to the information communicated, 74 percent of viewer reactions to presidential commercials shown in 1972 centered on the information contained in the message.[5]

Thus, presidential spots get noticed, and the attention centers on the message. But to what end? Does the viewer learn anything about the candidates? Does he find out anything about the issues?

For years, most political observers have been certain they knew the answers: Advertising builds false political images and robs the American electorate of important issue information. On both counts, this orthodox view is wrong. In a presidential campaign, spot commercials do much more to educate the public about the issues than they do to manipulate the public about the candidates.

ADVERTISING'S IMAGE IMPACT

In presidential politics, advertising image-making is a wasted effort. All the careful image planning—the coaching, the camera work, the calculated plea—counts for nothing. Just as with network news appearances, people's feelings about the candidate's politics—his party, past actions, and future policies—far outweigh the influence of televised commercials.

Strong evidence for advertising's ineffectiveness comes from a look at *changes* in voters' images during the 1972 campaign. Just before presidential ads began appearing on television and again when the candidates' ad campaigns were concluding, the same people were asked to judge the images of Nixon and McGovern. They evaluated each candidate on seven traits associated with personality and leadership. Because the same people were questioned each time, an exact measure exists of how their images changed during the time when the candidates' ads were appearing on television.

These changes in voters' images indicate that advertising image-making had no effect. . . . Among people who preferred Nixon, his image showed a 35 percent improvement and McGovern's image a 28 percent decline. This happened among people exposed to many of the candidates' ads and to those seeing few commercials, if any. Among people backing McGovern, however, his image made a 20 percent improvement and Nixon's had an 18 percent decline. And again, no significant difference occurred in the image changes of people heavily and lightly exposed to presidential advertising.

Thus, whether people watched television regularly, and constantly saw the advertised images of Nixon and McGovern, had no influence on their impressions of the two candidates. Whatever people were getting from political spots, it was not their image of the candidates. . . .

By projecting their political biases, people see in candidates' commercials pretty much what they want to see. Ads sponsored by the candidate who shares their politics get a good response. They like what he has to say. And they like him. Ads sponsored by the opposing candidate are viewed negatively. They object to what he says. And they object to him.

A sampling of viewers' reactions to the series of image commercials used by George McGovern throughout the general election campaign illustrates how strongly political bias affects viewers. These spots pictured McGovern among small groups of people in natural settings, discussing their problems and promising to help them if elected. The commercials were intended to project an image of McGovern as a man who cared about people. Whether viewers received this image, however, had little to do with what happened on the television screen. It was all in their minds:[6]

He really cares what's happened to disabled vets. They told him how badly they've been treated and he listened. He will help them.
—37-year-old, pro-McGovern viewer

McGovern was talking with these disabled vets. He doesn't really care about them. He's just using them to get sympathy.
—33-year-old, pro-Nixon viewer

It was honest, down-to-earth. People were talking and he was listening.
—57-year-old, pro-McGovern viewer

Those commercials are so phoney. He doesn't care.
—45-year-old, pro-Nixon viewer

McGovern had his coat off and his tie was hanging down. It was so relaxed, and he seemed to really be concerned with those workers.
—31-year-old, pro-McGovern viewer

He is trying hard to look like one of the boys. You know, roll up the shirt sleeves and loosen the tie. It's just too much for me to take.
—49-year-old, pro-Nixon viewer

I have seen many ads where McGovern is talking to common people. You know, like workers and the elderly. He means what he says. He'll help them.
—22-year-old, pro-McGovern viewer

He's with all these groups of people. Always making promises. He's promising more than can be done. Can't do everything for everyone.
—41-year-old, pro-Nixon viewer

These people were watching the same George McGovern, listening to the same words, and yet they were receiving vastly different impressions of the Democratic presidential nominee.

Even undecided voters are not influenced by advertising image-making. Just like partisans, the candidate images of undecided voters fluctuate with vote choice, not advertising exposure. In 1972, undecided voters' images changed very little and fit no definite pattern until *after* they had picked their candidate. Among those choosing Nixon, and only *after* they had done so, his image had a 35 percent improvement and McGovern's a 35 percent decline. This pattern of image change was the rule for those seeing many presidential ads and those seeing few or none. Likewise, for those picking McGovern, his image showed a 40 percent improvement and Nixon's a 55 percent decline. Again, there was no difference in this pattern based on the undecided voter's exposure to televised political commercials.

Spot ads do not mold presidential images because voters are not easily misled. They recognize that advertising imagery is heavily laden with something that is not intrinsically related to personal character at all—how the candidate looks on camera. This pseudocharacter, to some extent coached, posed, and created by the best media talent money can buy, is a "look" built into spots that is totally unreal. And viewers recognize its meaninglessness. Even the candid portrayals of presidential aspirants that sometimes appear in image appeals are ineffective. People's guards go up when a spot goes on. So no matter the style of presentation, when only 60 seconds are used to say that a candidate is big enough to handle the presidency, voters find the message skimpy, debatable, and unconvincing. They know that the candidate will display his strengths and mask his weaknesses and that a 60-second glimpse does not provide much of an insight into a man's fitness for the nation's highest office.

Symbolic manipulation through televised political advertising simply does not work. Perhaps the overuse of symbols and stereotypes in product advertising has built up an immunity in the television audience. Perhaps the symbols and postures used in political advertising are such patently obvious attempts at manipulation that they appear more ridiculous than reliable. Whatever the precise reason, television viewers effectively protect themselves from manipulation by staged imagery.

ADVERTISING'S ISSUE IMPACT

But where image appeals fail, issue appeals work. Through commercials, presidential candidates actually inform the electorate. In fact, the contribution of advertising campaigns to voter knowledge is truly impressive.

During the 1972 presidential election, people who were heavily exposed to political spots became more informed about the candidates' issue positions.... On every single issue emphasized in presidential commercials, persons with high exposure to television advertising showed a greater increase in knowledge than persons with low exposure. And on the typical issue, individuals who happened to see many commercials were nearly half again as likely to become more knowledgeable as people who saw few, if any, televised spots. Issue knowledge among people with considerable advertising exposure achieved a 36 percent increase compared with a 25 percent increase among those with minimal exposure. Persons heavily exposed to advertising were particularly aided in their knowledge about Nixon's position on China and military spending and about McGovern's position on military spending and taxes.

This information gain represents no small achievement. Televised political advertising has been widely maligned for saying nothing of consequence. Although the issue material contained in spots is incomplete and oversimplified, it also is abundant. So abundant in fact, that presidential advertising contributes to an informed electorate.

Advertising also educates voters because of the powerful way it transmits its issue content. Three basic advertising strategies—simplicity, repetition, and sight–sound coordination—combine to make presidential spots good communicators. Ads contain such simple messages that they leave almost no room for misunderstanding. . . .

THE EXTENT OF ADVERTISING MANIPULATION

Precise statistics on advertising's manipulative effects are hard to develop, because advertising, like other forms of media persuasion, works among and through a complex web of other influences. Seldom does a voter make his candidate choice for a single reason, whether the reason be political commercials, party loyalty, or a particular issue. Moreover, most people make up their minds about the candidates prior to the general election campaign, the time when presidential advertising saturates television programming. In 1972, as in previous elections where survey data have been gathered, about 80 percent of the electorate stayed with the choice it had decided upon before the general election began. Without doubt, some of these voters were reinforced in their initial vote choice by what they saw through television advertising. But how does one identify—among the people not changing their minds—those who would have changed their minds were it not for advertising? It is a treacherous task to assess whether people might have done something they did not do. So the effects of advertising on a voting decision are not that easily typed.

But some voters do decide their vote choice during a presidential general election and these people offer the best opportunity for understanding advertising's influence. In three interviews conducted with the same people during the 1972 general election, voters were asked which candidate they planned to support. If they changed their mind between one interview and the next, they were asked the reasons for the change and, if information about the candidates played some part in the change, where that information came from. By looking for advertising themes and sources in the reasons people gave for their vote changes, one way of estimating advertising's effects is provided. . . .

For three in every four people who arrived at their final vote choice during the 1972 general election, televised advertising had *no* discernible influence. . . . Some 42 percent cited important events, such as the Paris peace talks, as the reason why they selected their candidate; 11 percent said they decided to follow party allegiance, as did the factory worker who said, "I've always been a Democrat and McGovern is the Democrat"; 12 percent gave an old maxim, such as "not changing horses" or "it's time for a change," as their reason; 7 percent said they made their choice on the advice of their spouse or a friend or a co-worker; and 5 percent, although unable to provide a specific reason for choosing a candidate, did not watch much, if any, television during the 1972 campaign. In all of these decisions, televised advertising may have played some part, but at most, it was only a contributory influence. Additionally, 7 percent of vote changers present the situation of undetermined advertising effect. These people could give no clear reason for their candidate choice, but they were widely exposed to political ads during the campaign. Televised advertising, then, might have been the reason for their choice although other explanations, such as party loyalty or important political events, are also plausible.

So the first fact that must be recognized is that political advertising competes with other influences for the loyalties of indecisive voters. Before televised spots were used, less-informed voters were choosing candidates because they had a vague feeling that it was time for a change, because their father had pulled the same party lever years before, because an event triggered a reaction, because their spouse or union leader told them what to do. Today, most indecisive voters still select their candidate for such reasons.

Clear cases of advertising influence occurred among only 16 percent of those people making their candidate choice during the general election, or roughly 3 percent of the total electorate, since only one in five voters make up their minds during this time. But not even all these people can be labeled the victims of advertising manipulation. Indeed, the second fact about advertising influence is that simply because spot information helps people make up their minds does not mean manipulation occurs. True manipulation through advertising involves more than voters obtaining information that subsequently guides their vote choice. Spots are truly manipulative only when they convince the voter to act in the candidate's best interests and not the voter's. By this definition, of the 16 percent influenced by advertising, about half (9 percent) *were not* manipulated and about half (7 percent) *were* manipulated. To distinguish between these two types of advertising influence, here are the brief, but actual, voting histories of two people who during the 1972 general election made their vote choice from advertising information.

The first voter is a 74-year-old woman, who before she retired worked at an unskilled job. In 1972, she was deeply concerned about having enough income to live on; her social security and small savings forced her to make ends meet on only $3,000 a year. Asked at the beginning of the campaign what one political problem troubled her most, she replied: "The amount of social security. It is not enough for most people to live on." Asked the same question at the end of the campaign, she said that "taxes were too high for older people on fixed incomes."

This woman called herself an Independent, but her past voting behavior had been strongly Democratic. She claimed to have backed Kennedy, Johnson, and Humphrey in the three previous presidential elections. Her choice for the 1972 Democratic nomination was George Wallace, and when McGovern got the nod, she was undecided about whether to vote for him or Nixon. In late October, she made her choice. She selected McGovern and gave this reason:

> I've seen many commercials where George McGovern wants to help older people, to get them more social security and otherwise help them all he could. Nixon has vetoed bills for helping older people and McGovern has shown a definite interest in doing something for us. If Nixon hasn't done anything in the last four years, he probably won't do it now. He looks after big business, not the worker. Nixon's funds are from big business and they'll try to put him in again. I've no use for him.

The second voter is a 30-year-old hospital worker with two years of college. He is married and has one child. At the start of the general election, he was mainly concerned that the United States maintain a flexible foreign policy. At the campaign's end, he labeled unemployment the nation's major problem.

This man called himself a lukewarm Republican and in 1968 had not bothered to vote. But he registered to vote in 1972, and when the general election campaign began, he intended to support McGovern. By October, he had become undecided about McGovern, and just before the election day he switched to Nixon. He cited one particular commercial as the major reason:

> I saw this ad where it says McGovern keeps changing his mind. It said he had first said this and then that. He did this last year and what about next year. It put a question in my mind about whether I wanted to vote for McGovern. He doesn't seem reliable as a person. He seems to be changeable with regard to the issues. So I eliminated him. Actually I guess Nixon has done okay the last four years. I'm not crazy about either one, but I'm voting for Nixon.

Advertising did not manipulate the first voter. It did the second. The woman used the best information available to her to maximize her political values. Although McGovern was making the same arguments about the elderly in his campaign speeches and they were more fully reported and criticized in newspaper reports, the woman did not depend heavily on the news media. But she received from advertising the information she most needed. It informed her about the candidates' social security and other old-age benefits, and she chose the candidate who promised to do her the most good.

The man, on the other hand, was manipulated. He responded to the candidate's interest, not his own. Through commercials, this man's view of his stake in the political system was replaced by the candidate's view. He was concerned about America's role in world affairs and unemployment, and yet he cast his vote on the basis of an idea placed in his head by advertising and seemingly unrelated to his own political concerns. He was used. He had no strong feelings that the nation needed decisive leadership and no firm ground for assuming McGovern would not provide it. His view of politics simply came to mimic the view of a Nixon advertisement.

America can tolerate the effect that advertising has on people like this man. Counting for one or perhaps two voters in every hundred that got to the polls, this man and others like him will select a candidate for trivial reasons with or without advertising. (Before being persuaded by the Nixon commercial, the man indicated his vote for McGovern was premised on the fact that "McGovern had got a raw deal because of all the criticism about Eagleton.") And besides, since their reasons for choosing a candidate seem randomly selected, their votes distribute about equally between the candidates.

The benefits provided other voters by televised political advertising far exceed this kind of cost. Not only do more Americans, like the woman who learned which candidate was best for her, obtain information that helps them determine how their self-interest can be served, but many more people acquire information that helps them to validate a prior decision. And then there are people who simply learn a little more from ads than what they would have otherwise been able to learn. . . .

NOTES

1. Leo Bogart, *Strategy in Advertising* (New York: Harcourt Brace & World, 1967), p. 139.
2. Respondents were first asked whether they had seen a Nixon or McGovern commercial. If they indicated seeing an ad, they were then asked: "Would you tell me what you can about the Nixon (McGovern) commercial you remember best?" Those remembering nothing about the ad were classified as "unable to recall." Other replies were classified as partial or full recall depending on whether respondents stated the central message of the commercial they had seen.
3. Bogart, *Strategy in Advertising*, p. 139.

4. Raymond A. Bauer and Stephen A. Greyser, *Advertising in America* (Boston: Harvard University Press, 1968), chap. 7.
5. *Ibid.* Percentages based on a reconstruction of data contained in source.
6. Responses come from interviews conducted with potential voters during the 1972 general election. Responses have been edited to improve readability. Ages and occupations have been changed to protect identities of respondents.

CHAPTER SEVEN

ELECTIONS

At least once every four years, as we approach the election of the president, political commentators raise the issue of the electoral college method of electing the president, claiming that something ought to be done to correct the defects of that system. One such critic, Lawrence Longley, in the first of the two selections in this chapter, argues that the electoral college is both undemocratic and politically dangerous: undemocratic because voters and votes are treated unequally; dangerous because there exists the possibility that it could lead to a major disruption of the normal electoral processes.

Longley is not alone in voicing such criticisms. On the contrary, numerous public officials have offered proposals calling for a constitutional amendment that would abolish the electoral college and replace it with a system of direct popular election.

In the second selection, however, Robert Weissberg takes the view that we should retain the electoral college. While acknowledging that the present arrangement is not perfect, he maintains that the defects of the electoral college are not as serious as critics would have us believe. Moreover, he argues that there are several positive features associated with the electoral college that more than compensate for its shortcomings.

The Case Against the Electoral College

Lawrence D. Longley

The contemporary electoral college is a curious political institution.[1] Obscure and even unknown to the average citizen,[2] it serves as a crucial mechanism for transforming popular votes cast for President into electoral votes which actually elect the President. If the electoral college were only a neutral and sure means for counting and aggregating votes, it would likely be the subject of little controversy. The electoral college does not, however, just tabulate popular votes in the form of electoral votes. Instead, it is an institution that operates with noteworthy inequality—it favors some interests and hurts others. In addition, its operations are by no means certain or smooth. The electoral college can—and has—deadlocked, forcing a resort to extraordinarily awkward contingency procedures. Other flaws and difficulties with the system can also develop under various electoral situations. In short, the electoral college system has important political consequences, multiple flaws, possible grave consequences, and inherent gross inequalities. Yet, it continues to exist as a central part of our Presidential electoral machinery. . . .

THE FAITHLESS ELECTOR

The first characteristic arises out of the fact that the electoral college today is not the assembly of wise and learned elders as assumed by its creators, but is rather a state by state assembly of political hacks and fat cats.[3] Neither in the quality of the electors nor in law is there any assurance that the electors will vote as expected. Pledges, apparently unenforceable by law,[4] and party and

From Lawrence D. Longley, "The Case Against the Electoral College," paper delivered at the annual meeting of the American Political Science Association, Washington, D.C., 1977. Used with permission.

personal loyalty seem to be the only guarantee of electoral voting consistent with the will of a state's electorate.

The problem of the "faithless elector" is neither theoretical nor unimportant. Republican elector Doctor Lloyd W. Bailey of North Carolina, who decided to vote for Wallace after the 1968 election rather than for his pledged candidate Nixon, and Republican elector Roger MacBride of Virginia who likewise deserted Nixon in 1972 to vote for Libertarian Party candidate John Hospers, are two examples of "faithless electors." In the . . . 1976 election, we once again had a faithless elector—and curiously enough once again a deviant Republican elector. Washington Republican Mike Padden decided, six weeks after the November election, that he preferred not to support Republican nominee Ford, and cast his electoral vote for Ronald Reagan. Similar defections from the voter expectations also occurred in 1948, 1956, and 1960, or in other words, in six of the eight most recent presidential elections. Even more important is that the likelihood of this occurring on a multiple basis would be greatly heightened in the case of an electoral vote majority resting on one or two votes—a very real possibility in 1976 as in other recent elections.

In fact, when one looks at the election returns for the . . . 1976 election, one can observe that if about 5,560 votes had switched from Carter to Ford in Ohio, Carter would have lost that state and had only 272 electoral votes, two more than the absolute minimum needed of 270. In that case, two or three individual electors seeking personal recognition or attention to a pet cause could withhold their electoral votes, and thus make the election outcome very uncertain.

A startling reminder of the possibilities inherent in such a close electoral vote election as 1976 was provided . . . by Republican Vice President nominee Robert Dole. Testifying before the Senate Judiciary Committee on January 27, 1977, in *favor* of abolishing the electoral college, Senator Dole remarked that during the election count:

We were looking around on the theory that maybe Ohio might turn around because they had an automatic recount.

We were shopping—not shopping, excuse me. Looking around for electors. Some took a look at Missouri, some were looking at Louisiana, some in Mississippi, because their laws are a little bit different. And we might have picked up one or two in Louisiana. There were allegations of fraud maybe in Mississippi, and something else in Missouri.

We need to pick up three or four after Ohio. So that may happen in any event.

But it just seems to me that the temptation is there for that elector in a very tight race to really negotiate quite a bunch.[5]

THE WINNER-TAKE-ALL SYSTEM

The second problem of the contemporary electoral college system lies in the almost universal custom of granting all of a state's electoral votes to the winner of a state's popular vote plurality—not even a majority. This can lead to interesting results, such as in Arkansas in 1968 where Humphrey and Nixon together split slightly over 61 percent of the popular vote, while Wallace, with 38 percent, received 100 percent of the state's electoral votes. Even more significant, however, is the fact that the unit voting of state electors tends to magnify tremendously the relative voting power of residents of the larger states, since each of their voters may, by his vote, decide not just one vote, but how 41 or 45 electoral votes are cast—if electors are faithful.

As a result, the electoral college has major impact on candidate strategy—as shown by the obsession of Carter and Ford strategists, in the closing weeks of the 1976 campaign, with the nine big electoral vote states with 245 of the 270 electoral votes necessary to win. Seven of these nine states were, in fact, to be exceedingly close, with both candidates receiving at least 48 percent of the state vote.

The electoral college does not treat voters alike—a thousand voters in Scranton, Pennsylvania, are far more strategically important than a similar number of voters in Wilmington, Delaware. This also places a premium on the support of key political leaders in large electoral vote states. This could be observed in the 1976 election in the desperate wooing of Mayors Rizzo of Philadelphia and Daley of Chicago by Carter because of the major roles these political leaders might have in determining the outcome in Pennsylvania and Illinois. The electoral college treats political leaders as well as voters unequally—those in large marginal states are vigorously courted.

The electoral college also encourages fraud—or at least fear and rumor of fraud. New York, with more than enough electoral votes to elect Ford, went to Carter by 290,000 popular votes. Claims of voting irregularities and calls for a recount were made on election night, but later withdrawn because of Carter's clear national popular vote win. *If* fraud was present in New York, only 290,000 votes determined the election; under direct election, at least 1,-700,000 votes would have to have been irregular to determine the outcome.

The electoral college also provides opportunity for third-party candidates to exercise magnified political influence in the election of the President when they can gather votes in large, closely balanced states. In 1976, third-party candidate Eugene McCarthy, with less than 1 percent of the popular vote, came close to tilting the election through his strength in close pivotal states. In four states (Iowa, Maine, Oklahoma, and Oregon) totaling 26 electoral votes, McCarthy's vote exceeded the margin by which Ford defeated Carter. In those states, McCarthy's candidacy *may* have swung those states to Ford.[6] Even more significantly, had McCarthy been on the New York ballot, it is likely Ford would have carried that state with its 41 electoral votes, and with it the election—despite Carter's national vote majority.

THE CONSTANT TWO ELECTORAL VOTES

A third feature of the electoral college system lies in the apportionment of electoral votes among the states. The constitutional formula is simple: one vote per state per senator and representative. A significant distortion from equality appears here because of "the constant two" electoral votes, regardless of population, which correspond to the senators. Because of this, inhabitants of the very small states are advantaged to the extent that they "control" three electoral votes (one for each senator and one for the representative), while their population might otherwise entitle them to but one or two votes. This is weighting by states, not by population—however, the importance of this feature, as shown below, is greatly outweighed by the previously mentioned winner-take-all system.

THE CONTINGENCY ELECTION PROCEDURE

The fourth feature of the contemporary electoral college system is probably the most complex—and probably also the most dangerous in terms of the stability of the political system. This is the requirement that if no candidate receives an absolute majority of the electoral vote—in recent years, 270—the election is thrown into the House of Representatives for voting among the top three candidates. Two questions need to be asked: Is such an electoral college deadlock likely to occur in terms of contemporary politics? and, Would the consequences likely be disastrous? A simple answer to both questions is yes.

Taking some recent examples, it has been shown that, in 1960, a switch of less than 9,000 popular votes from Kennedy to Nixon in Illinois and Missouri would have prevented either man from receiving an electoral college majority.[7] Similarly, in 1968, a 53,000 vote shift in New Jersey, Missouri, and New Hampshire, would have resulted in an electoral college deadlock, with Nixon receiving 269 votes—one short of a majority. Finally, in the . . . 1976 election, if slightly less than 11,950 popular votes in Delaware and Ohio had shifted from Carter to Ford, Ford would have carried these two states. The result of the 1976 election would then have been an exact tie in electoral votes—269–269. The presidency would have been decided *not* on election night, but through deals or switches at the electoral college meetings on December 13, or the later uncertainties of the House of Representatives.

What specifically might happen in the case of an apparent electoral college nonmajority or deadlock? A first possibility, of course, is that a faithless elector or two, pledged to one candidate or another, might switch at the time of the actual meetings of the electoral college so as to create a majority for one of the candidates. This might resolve the crisis, although it is sad to think of the presidency as being mandated on such a thin reed of legitimacy.

If, however, no deals or actions at the time of the December 13 meetings of the electoral college were successful in forming a majority, then the action would shift to the House of Representatives, meeting at noon on January 6, 1977, only 14 days before the constitutionally scheduled Inauguration Day for the new President.

The House of Representatives contingency procedure which would now be followed is an unfortunate relic of the compromises of the writing of the Constitution as discussed earlier. Serious problems of equity exist, certainly, in following the constitutionally prescribed one-vote-per-state procedure. Beyond this problem of voter fairness lurks an even more serious problem— what if the House itself should deadlock and be unable to agree on a President?

In a two-candidate race, this is unlikely to be a real problem; however, in a three-candidate contest, such as 1968, there might well be enormous difficulties in getting a majority of states behind one candidate, as House members agonized over choosing between partisan labels and support for the candidate (especially Wallace) who carried their district. The result, in 1968, might well have been no immediate majority forthcoming of 26 states and political uncertainty and chaos as the nation approached Inauguration Day.

THE UNCERTAINTY OF THE WINNER WINNING

Besides the four aspects of the electoral college system so far discussed, "the faithless elector," "the winner-take-all system," "the constant two votes per state," and "the contingency election procedure," one last aspect should be described. This is that, under the present system, there is no assurance that the winner of the popular vote will win the election. This problem is a fundamental one—can an American President operate effectively in our democracy if he has received *less* votes than the loser? I suggest that the effect upon the legitimacy of a contemporary presidency would be disastrous if a president were elected by the electoral college after losing in the popular vote— yet this *can* and *has* happened two or three times, the most recent undisputable case being the election of 1888, when the 100,000 popular vote plurality of Grover Cleveland was turned into a losing 42 percent of the electoral vote.

Was there a real possibility of such a divided verdict in 1976? An analysis of the election shows that if 9,245 votes had shifted to Ford in Ohio and Hawaii, Ford would have become President with 270 electoral votes, the absolute minimum,[8] despite Carter's 51 percent of the popular vote and margin of 1.7 million votes.

One hesitates to contemplate the consequences of a nonelected President being inaugurated for four more years despite having been rejected by a majority of the American voters in his only presidential election. . . .

NOTES

1. Some of the material contained in this paper was originally prepared and presented as "Statement of Lawrence D. Longley Before the Committee on the Judiciary, United States Senate," *Hearings on the Electoral College and Direct Election*, 95th Cong., 1st sess., February 1, 1977, pp. 88–105. Earlier research drawn upon for this paper include: Lawrence D. Longley and Alan G. Braun, *The Politics of Electoral College Reform* (New Haven: Yale University Press, 1972, 2nd ed., 1975); Lawrence D. Longley, "The Electoral College," *Current History*, vol. 67 (August 1974), pp. 64–69 ff; and John H. Yunker and Lawrence D. Longley, *The Electoral College: Its Biases Newly Measured for the 1960s and 1970s* (Beverly Hills, Calif.: Sage Professional Papers in American Politics, 1976).

2. In another publication, the following "man-on-the-street" interviews are cited: "Every boy and girl should go to college, if they can't afford Yale or Harvard, why, Electoral is just as good, if you work"; "The group at the bar poor-mouth Electoral somethin' awful. Wasn't they mixed up in a basketball scandal or somethin'?" quoted in Longley and Braun, *The Politics of Electoral College Reform*, p. 1.

3. See Lawrence C. Longley, "Why the Electoral College Should be Abolished," Speech to the 1976 Electoral College, Madison, Wis., December 13, 1976. Despite being referred to as "political hacks and fat cats," the Wisconsin electors there assembled proceeded to go on record supporting the abolishment of their office.

4. Only sixteen states have laws requiring electors to vote according to their pledge, and these laws themselves are of doubtful constitutionality. See James C. Kirby, Jr., "Limitations on the Power of State Legislatures over Presidential Elections," *Law and Contemporary Problems*, vol. 27 (Spring 1962), pp. 495–509.

5. "Testimony of Honorable Robert Dole, U.S. Senator from the State of Kansas," *Hearings on Electoral College and Direct Election*, 95th Cong., 1st sess., January 27, 1977, pp. 36–37.

6. Testimony of Neal Peirce, *National Journal*, Author, February 1977 Senate Hearings, p. 248.

7. Neal R. Peirce, *The People's President: The Electoral College in American History and The Direct-Vote Alternative* (New York: Simon & Schuster, 1968), pp. 317–21. The concept of hairbreadth elections is also discussed in Longley and Braun, *The Politics of Electoral College Reform*, pp. 37–41.

8. This analysis assumes, of course, the nondefection of Republican elector Mike Padden of Washington. If he had nevertheless declined to vote for Ford, then the election would have been inconclusive and would have gone to the House in January 1977.

In Defense of the Electoral College

Robert Weissberg

Defending the electoral college is like defending sin. Almost every responsible person is against it, defenders are rare, yet it somehow survives. However, while sin may be beyond eradication, the electoral college is not deeply rooted in human nature. The electoral college can be abolished just as we abolished other archaic portions of the Constitution. Clearly, then, a defense of this system of selecting our President must be defended on grounds other than its inevitability. Our defense will be divided into two parts. We shall first show that its alleged defects are not as serious as some critics would have us believe. Second, we shall argue that there are in fact several virtues of this electoral arrangement, which the American Bar Association has characterized as "archaic, undemocratic, complex, ambiguous, and dangerous"!

CRITICISMS OF THE ELECTORAL COLLEGE

Criticisms of the electoral college basically fall into two groups. The first emphasize the unpredictable and unintended outcomes that are conceivable under the present system. In a nutshell, from the perspective of these critics, here is what *could* have happened in the 1980 presidential election: Ronald Reagan overwhelmingly wins the popular vote, but by barely winning several populous states, Jimmy Carter wins the electoral college vote and appears to have been reelected. However, several electors pledged to Carter refuse to honor this pledge, thereby depriving him of a majority in the electoral college. The contest is thus thrown into the House, and after months of deals and bitter debate, John Anderson is elected President.

Written especially for this volume by Robert Weissberg, Professor of Political Science, the University of Illinois at Urbana.

The second basic criticism accuses the electoral college of overvaluing some votes at the expense of other votes. Some disagreement occurs over just who benefits from these distortions, but most experts claim that voters in populous states, especially members of certain urban ethnic and racial groups, are overrepresented. Would-be presidents pay more attention to some New York and California voters at the expense of votes in places like North Dakota.

THE NIGHTMARE OF UNINTENDED CONSEQUENCES

These are serious charges. Let us first consider what may be called the night-mare of unintended political outcomes. Two points may be made concerning this criticism. First, the odds of any one of these events occurring is remote. Only once in U.S. history—in 1888—has the undisputed winner of the popu-lar vote lost the electoral college vote. Electors have voted contrary to their popular instructions, but this has been extremely rare, and most important, such "unfaithful electors" have never affected who won and have almost never tried to influence the election's outcome (their actions were largely symbolic in a clearly decided contest). Nor has the last 150 years seen a presi-dential election decided by the House, despite some efforts by minor-party candidates to bring this about. All in all, the odds of any one event happen-ing are low, and the odds of several such events occurring and making a dif-ference in the same election are remote.

A second rejoinder to this nightmare of unintended, undesirable conse-quences is that hypothetical catastrophes are possible under *any* electoral system. Take, for example, a direct popular election with the provision for a runoff in the event no candidate receives a majority. It is conceivable that the initial election brings forth a wide range of candidates. A large number of moderate candidates each gets 5 or 7 percent from the middle of the political spectrum, and for the runoff, the public faces a contest between two unpopu-lar extremists who together received 25 percent of the vote in the first elec-tion. *All* electoral mechanisms contain so-called time bombs waiting to go off.

MISREPRESENTATION CAUSED BY THE ELECTORAL COLLEGE

This alleged defect of misrepresentation derives from both the electoral col-lege as stated in the Constitution plus individual requirements that all of a state's electoral votes go to the candidate receiving the largest number of votes (though Maine since 1969 does allow a division of its electoral vote). The effect of this unit voting is that to win the presidency a candidate must win in several populous states. New York, California, Texas, Illinois, and a few other big states are the valuable prizes in the election and thus a few thousand New Yorkers have more electoral clout than a few thousand voters

in South Dakota. It supposedly follows, then, that the desires of these strategically placed voters are given greater attention by those seeking the presidency.

Four points can be made in response to this inequality-of-voters argument. First, it is far from self-evident just who these overadvantaged voters
are and whether these big groups can be the cornerstone of electoral victory.
It has been said, for example, that since there are many blacks in New York,
the black vote can determine who carries New York. However, New York,
like all populous states, has a varied population, so in principle the same argument can be applied to farmers, young people, white Protestants, middle-
class suburbanites—any group comprising at least 10 percent of the electorate. This "key-voting-bloc-in-a-key-state" argument is largely the creation
of statistical manipulation. Of course, it makes considerable sense for a
group *to claim* that its vote, given its strategic position, put a candidate in the
White House.

Second, it is a great exaggeration to assert that these strategically placed,
"overrepresented" voters can exert control or significantly influence the
election. Let's suppose that a candidate said that to win the presidency one
must win the big states; to win the big states one must do very well among
blacks, Jews, and union workers because these groups are overrepresented in
these big states. Not only might it be difficult to appeal to all groups simultaneously (promising jobs to blacks may anger union workers), but also, even
if one's appeals are successful, these "key" votes alone are not enough. The
idea of certain well-situated minorities running the electoral show via the
electoral college ignores the problems of creating large diverse voting coalitions and the relatively small size of these "key" groups. At best, the electoral
college may provide a disproportionate influence to voters—not a specific
group—in large states in close elections (and since World War II most national elections have been close only about half the time).

Third, the relationship between overrepresentation caused by the electoral college and disproportionate government benefits has never been demonstrated. The relationship has appeared so reasonable and been said so
often that it is now reiterated as if it were a truism. Actual evidence, however,
has never been marshaled. Obviously, presidents have endorsed some policies favorable to supposed key groups in large states, but presidents have
also opposed policies favorable to these same groups. It may be true that
presidents have occasionally taken the operation of the electoral college into
account in their policy calculations, but such action has not been sufficiently
blatant to draw widespread attention.

Finally, the electoral system embodied in the electoral college may be
biased in favor of some voters, but bias is part of *every* system of election. To
reject a system because it is somehow "unfair" makes sense only if some
perfectly fair system did exist. In fact, no such system does exist. As we did
before, let us take as an example the simple majority rule plus a runoff system commonly advocated by opponents of the electoral college. This seem-

ingly "pure" system is "unfair" for several reasons. Unlike the systems of proportional representation used by many European democracies, it provides no representation to citizens whose candidate received less than a majority—49.9 percent of all voters may get nothing. Moreover, it can be easily demonstrated that by allowing each citizen only one yes or no vote, the system does not allow citizens to rank candidates so that the candidate most acceptable to the most people is selected. In other words, a candidate who is not the first choice of a majority, but is still highly acceptable to almost everyone, is shut out under a simple majority system. In short, the issue is not one of "fair" versus "unfair," but what type of unfairness will be present.

DEFENDING THE ELECTORAL COLLEGE

Thus far we have argued that the major criticisms against the electoral college either rest on exaggerations and misunderstandings or are simply unproven. Is there, however, anything positive to be said for the frequently maligned system? At least four virtues of the electoral college seem reasonably clear and are probably advantageous to most people: (1) it is a proven, workable system; (2) it makes campaigns more manageable; (3) it discourages election fraud; and (4) it preserves a moderate two-party system.

The first virtue—*it is a proven, workable system*—is basically a conservative argument. Conservatives believe that when something works, though somewhat imperfectly, it should not be easily abandoned for the promise of perfection. That is, on paper almost every alternative to the electoral college is without defect. However, as anyone familiar with the success rates of proposed reforms knows well, political changes do not always work as intended. The nightmare and inequalities of the status quo are hypothetical and alleged; a change might bring real and consequential problems despite promises of perfection. Constitutional changes should be made only if the *real* costs of the electoral college are heavy.

The second virtue—*it makes campaigns more manageable*—derives from two facts. First, in terms of time, money, and energy, the present electoral system is already very demanding on candidates. Running for President is so exhausting physically that some have said, half jokingly, that only the mentally unbalanced are attracted to this activity. Second, the electoral college, plus the "winner-take-all" role in forty-nine of the fifty states, means that some votes are not as important as others. Swaying a few thousand uncommitted voters in a closely divided populous state is much more important than an appeal to the same number of voters in a small, one-party-dominated state. Obviously, then, without some division of voters into important and unimportant voters, campaigning for president would become even more hectic and overwhelming than ever. A rational candidate might even lock himself in a television studio rather than attempt the impossible task of trying to wage an effective nationwide personal campaign.

The third virtue—*it discourages election fraud*—also derives from the present system's division of votes into important and less important. In a state with a relatively small number of electoral votes, where the outcome is not in much doubt, little incentive exists for widespread election fraud. Such manipulation is only worthwhile in big states like New York or Illinois where presidential elections tend to be close and a large bloc of electoral votes may hinge on a few thousand votes. Under a direct popular election system, however, all votes are equally valuable and thus equally worth manipulating. Practices such as multiple voting, voting the dead, and intimidating the opposition, which were once limited to a few localities, might very well become national in scope.

The fourth and final virtue—*it preserves a moderate two-party system*—is perhaps the most important. Under the existing system, winning the presidency means winning numerous electoral votes. Since to win electoral votes you must win pluralities in many states, it takes a formidable political organization to win these big prizes. A group that won, say, 5 or 10 percent of the vote in a few states would be doomed. Even an organization that wins a few million votes usually comes up with very little where the prizes are big blocs of electoral votes. In contemporary politics, the only organizations capable of such a massive electoral undertaking are large, diverse, compromise-oriented political parties such as the Democratic and Republican parties.

To appreciate this contribution of the existing electoral college system, imagine presidential campaigns *without* the two major parties. Instead of two major candidates and a dozen or two inconsequential candidates, there would be numerous hopefuls with some reasonable chance of success. These candidates would likely draw most of their support from relatively small segments of the population. There might be an antiabortion candidate, a strong civil rights candidate, an anti–school-busing candidate, and a few others closely associated with one or two specific issues. The incentive to create broad-based coalitions to capture a majority in twenty or thirty states would be considerably reduced and thus the two major parties would virtually disappear.

This type of campaign politics would suffer from several problems. The narrow basis of candidate appeal would likely generate much sharper conflict and deepen group antagonism (for example, blacks might see for the first time in modern times an explicitly anti–civil rights candidate who could win). Perhaps most important, postelection governance would become difficult. Not only would a President have a much smaller base of popular support, but he or she would likely have to deal with a Congress composed of people with no party attachment whose primary purpose was to advance a particular group or regional interest. Of course, the present system of Democratic and Republican party politics does not eliminate the advancement of narrow interests and interbranch conflict. However, the situation would probably be even worse if numerous single-issue groups replaced the present two major political parties. In short, the electoral college, plus the winner-take-all-system, encourages the current two-party system, and this system moderates conflict and promotes effective postelection governance.

We began by noting that defending the electoral college is like defending sin. We have argued that, as some have said of sin, it is not nearly as bad as is claimed, and it may even be beneficial. We have not argued that the present system is beyond reproach. The system has been modified numerous times since its inception, and future changes are certainly possible. It is a serious mistake, however, to believe that abolishing the electoral college will be as beneficial as finally ridding ourselves of sin.

CHAPTER EIGHT

POLITICAL PARTIES

Political analysts have for years sought to make sense out of national presidential and congressional elections by classifying them on the basis of two major considerations: (1) is the party in power returned to office; and (2) do the people retain or change their party identification. Thus, an election is called a "maintaining" election if the party is continued in power and the people do not change their basic loyalties; a "deviating" election if the party in power loses the election but there continues to be no basic change in party identification; and a "realigning" election if the party in power is defeated, and, concurrently, a majority of the electorate "switch" their allegiance permanently to the other party.

With the election of President Ronald Reagan in 1980 and his landslide reelection victory in 1984, political analysts have begun to speculate that a new realignment may be occurring—that is, the old Democratic dominance is passing and a majority of the people are shifting their loyalty (and votes) to the Republican Party.

The following two articles address the question of whether or not a realignment has occurred. In the first article, syndicated columnist George Will argues that, at least at the presidential level, "realignment is a fact." Will's argument is based upon his belief that the nation has become increasingly conservative over the last three decades, which has resulted in the Republicans winning four out of the last five presidential elections.

While not disagreeing with Will, the author of the second article, William Schneider, believes that the Republican Party has not yet become the new majority party. Instead, it is his contention that the nation is divided equally among Democrats, Republicans, and independents, with the votes of independents slightly in favor of the Republicans. Thus, he predicts that should the present trend continue, and the Republicans win the presidency again in 1988, the "half a realignment of 1984" could become the complete realignment in 1988.

Realignment Is a Fact

George Will

In his 1980 concession statement, Vice President Walter Mondale said: "The people have peacefully wielded their staggering power." No one has been as blasted as Mondale by that power. Adlai Stevenson lost twice by a cumulative electoral vote total of 899 to 162. In Mondale's last two times on the national ticket, he has lost 1,014 to 62.

Often after elections the sluice gates of criticism open as leaders in the losing candidate's party say, with an air of slighted genius, "If only he had listened to me." Not this time.

Mondale might have made it slightly closer with a more plausible (and a southern) running mate, and a serious idea, such as radical tax simplification. Instead, the campaign that began with the appearance of him being bullied by women's groups ended with him promising to appoint a Hispanic to his cabinet. Ye gods.

The traditional edifice of Democratic politics has been razed, the rubble has been plowed, and salt has been sown. There should be no nonsense about the 1984 outcome being caused by tactical miscalculations. The Democratic Party is a refractory mule, but surely this third landslide in four elections will get its attention.

On election eve, Mondale told a crowd that Republicans never use the word "decent." Democrats would do well to quit using it. Mondale frequently said, "I would rather lose an election about decency than win one about self-interest." Such rhetoric, implying that Republicans are not just wrong but indecent, is the extreme moralizing of a party out of the habit of thinking and even arguing, and in the habit of asserting a moral monopoly.

The 1982 recession was bad for Democrats because it allowed them to think that they did not need to think—that they could coast, counting on the hammer blows of economic hardship to reassemble the old coalition. But by now it is bizarre, if common, for otherwise rational people to ask, "Are we on the verge of a 'realignment' in favor of the Republican Party?" Suppose Noah, in the 34th day of the 40 days of rain, had asked his wife, "Do you think we may get some rain?" At the presidential level, realignment is a fact.

Republicans have won four of the last five presidential elections. In the last four they have won 82.4 percent of the electoral votes, approaching Franklin Roosevelt's four-election achievement of 88.3 percent. And the Republicans have done it with three candidates, not just one political giant.

The nation was moderately conservative, when it chose Eisenhower over Stevenson twice. Next it barely preferred Kennedy, a moderate Democrat, over Nixon. Johnson, the only post-Truman president with a Rooseveltian, liberal domestic agenda, was an accident of assassination and the perceived radicalism of his Republican opponent, Goldwater. Two years later Republicans gained 47 House and three Senate seats.

In 1968 the combined Nixon and George Wallace vote was 57 percent. In 1972 Nixon got 61 percent against McGovern. In 1976 the Democrat perceived as the most conservative in the nomination contest, Carter, was nominated and narrowly defeated a conservative Republican, Ford. Then came two conservative landslides.

Tuesday's election buried the most ideologically uniform and liberal ticket in American history. The ticket was a quixotic offering to an electorate even more conservative than the electorate has been at any point since 1952.

Many Democrats will say that the Republican run of successes is a fluke compounded of weak Democratic nominees and the unreasonably charming Reagan personality. But in four elections the Democratic Party has tried to sell the country McGovern, Carter twice, and Mondale. Four such "aberrations" consecutively are not aberrations. They constitute a single propensity. It is the Democratic Party's propensity to disregard the public's thoughts— not thoughts about Reagan's smile, but about the issues.

Reagan has a right to feel as though he is sitting on a pink cloud over an ocean of joy with a rainbow draped around his shoulders. But Reagan will rightly insist that Democrats are deluding themselves when they say this was a rout produced by his smile rather than by his party's positions.

In the nineteenth century, an exasperated (and probably jealous) critic said: "Horatio Alger wrote the same novel 135 times and never lost his audience." In Reagan's long career he has demonstrated that in a democracy you build an audience by saying a few clear and convincing things 135,000 times. The lesson of Tuesday—a lesson so stark that it may be missed by persons in hot pursuit of subtleties—is that both Mondale and Reagan spoke clearly, but Reagan convinced.

Half a Realignment

William Schneider

> I survived.—*Abbé Sieyés, when asked what he had done during the French Revolution.*

We survived. After counting the heads that rolled into the basket, our intrepid leader, House Speaker Tip O'Neill reassured us, "There is no mandate out there." The *New York Times* backed him up with scientific evidence: POLL FINDS REAGAN FAILED TO OBTAIN A POLICY MANDATE. Even the Republicans joined in. "It was a victory for his philosophy and a victory for him personally, but I'm not sitting here claiming it's a big mandate," said White House Chief of Staff James A. Baker III. And former White House Communications Director David P. Gergen remarked, "The Republicans won the election and the Democrats are winning the interpretation."

Perhaps, but it is an interpretation that sounds suspiciously like whistling past the graveyard. The fact is, the Democratic defeat was monumental in its proportions. We lost nearly every group, nearly everywhere. President Reagan's apparent lack of coattails—the Republicans suffered a net loss of two Senate seats and gained only fourteen House seats, one governorship, and four state legislative chambers—is a fact that obscures more than it reveals. Democrats are in the same position as the French aristocracy at the time of the Bourbon Restoration. We can pretend that nothing has really happened, but the *ancien régime* is dead. Things will never be the same. The problem for the Democrats is to avoid the fate of the Bourbons, of whom Talleyrand said, "They learned nothing and they forgot nothing."

What happened is simple enough. The election was a referendum on Ronald Reagan. President Reagan's job approval ratings have been holding steady at 55 to 60 percent for the past year, which is to say that throughout the campaign most Americans felt he deserved to be reelected. Reagan's 18-

From William Schneider, "Half a Realignment," *New Republic*, December 3, 1984, pp. 19–22. Reprinted by permission of THE NEW REPUBLIC, © 1984, The New Republic, Inc.

point margin over Walter Mondale on November 6 was the same as it had been in January. Not a single poll taken during the entire campaign showed Mondale with a significant lead over Reagan. In the *Los Angeles Times'* nationwide exit poll, almost half of the voters reported that they had made up their minds about how they were going to vote before the campaign even started last February; their decision was 2 to 1 for Reagan.

Reagan had two things going for him: the economy and foreign policy. Those are very big things. The Democrats got nowhere trying to convince people that the President had failed in either area.

The voters believed that Reagan did what he was elected to do: he curbed inflation and he restored the nation's sense of military security. As it happens, many people disagreed with the way he accomplished those things. Inflation was reduced at the cost of a severe recession. Our perceived military strength was improved at the cost of a significantly higher level of international tensions. Still, after four failed presidencies in a row, it is rare enough to have a President who does what he was elected to do. As Reagan is fond of saying, "You don't quarrel with success."

Consider the economy. In the 1982 midterm election, the Democrats did very well with the fairness issue. Why didn't the issue work this year? Because in 1982, when the economy was bad, fairness meant *us*. In 1984, when the economy looked good, fairness meant *them*.

What about foreign policy? The Democrats ran ads suggesting that Reagan was going to blow us all up. A lot of people were worried about that in 1980, but not this year. Reagan has been President for almost four years, and we're still here. The polls show that this time the voters were demonstrably less concerned with Reagan's recklessness, his intellectual competence, and his age. That's what incumbency does for you. . . .

What did not happen in the election is in many ways more interesting than what did happen. Contrary to expectations, Reagan did not sweep large numbers of Republicans into office. As House Republican leader Robert H. Michel complained, "Here the son of a buck ended up with 59 percent, and you bring in only 15 seats." The explanation, in a word, is incumbency. Incumbents have a large and growing advantage in American politics because of their dominance of the media, fund-raising, communications with constitutents, and campaign technology. Americans regularly reelect over 90 percent of those members of Congress who decide to run for reelection. And most do.

Republicans actually did quite well this year in "open seats," where no incumbent was on the ballot. Open House seats were split about 50–50 before the election and ended up going 2 to 1 Republican. But they accounted for only 27 out of 435 contests. True, the Democrats gained 1 seat in the 4 open Senate races. But in the 7 open races for governor, GOP control went from 3 to 6.

The exit polls reveal that, nationwide, almost as many people voted for Republicans as for Democrats in House races this year. Democrats nevertheless retained a 3-to-2 lead in the House. One reason is that congressional district boundaries were redrawn by Democratic-controlled state legislatures after the 1980 census so as to protect incumbents of both parties by giving them districts with "safe" electoral majorities. It is significant, therefore, that more than 300 state legislative seats shifted to the Republicans this year. According to the Council of State Legislatures, "Presidential coattails tended to work best when a seat was vacant."

It was incumbency that saved the Democratic Party from ruin. If the government had passed a decree prohibiting incumbents from running for reelection, the Republican Party would probably have gained control of both houses of Congress and a substantial number of statehouses.

They would probably have held on to the White House too. Much too much has been made of the personality factor in the 1984 election. Yes, Americans tend to like Ronald Reagan, and he is an effective television performer. But Walter Mondale's complaint that he lost the election because he could not communicate effectively on television is entirely unconvincing. One can hardly imagine less effective television performers—or less congenial personalities—than Lyndon Johnson, Richard Nixon, or Jimmy Carter. The polls make it clear that if Ronald Reagan had run for reelection under the conditions prevailing in 1982 instead of 1984, he would have lost decisively, all his charm and amiability notwithstanding. . . .

As a whole, the 1984 election was not ideological. On many issues, the voters were closer to Mondale's views than to Reagan's. These included abortion, military spending, arms control, the Equal Rights Amendment, Central America, and the role of religion in politics. The same thing was true in 1980: on a left–right scale, the voters placed themselves closer to Carter than to Reagan. Then, as now, the central issue in the election was performance—not personality or philosophy. There was widespread agreement in 1980 that on the basis of his performance, Carter did not deserve to be reelected. There was widespread agreement this year that on the basis of his performance, Reagan did.

What people were voting for in 1980 was not conservatism but change. What people were voting for this year was neither conservatism nor change but continuity. The fact that both elections were decided on the basis of performance rather than ideology is surprising only because Reagan is such an ideological figure. His achievement in 1980 was to win the support (at the last minute) of many voters who did not agree with him ideologically. He did it again this year.

Which brings us to the subject of realignment. If the election was not ideological, how can anyone talk about a realignment? The answer is that, when realignment occurs, ideology is usually the last thing to change, if it changes at all.

For instance, there is little evidence that the electorate moved sharply to the left during the 1930s. In February 1936, in the midst of the Depression and only nine months before Franklin D. Roosevelt's landslide reelection, a Gallup poll found that 70 percent of the public favored cuts in government spending for the purposes of reducing the national debt. Voters did not accept FDR's New Deal philosophy until they were convinced that the New Deal worked.

A realignment occurs in two stages. First, the president has to demonstrate that his policies are effective. Only then do voters begin to convert to his vision of society. This year's election results suggest that the first stage has occurred. The second may be underway: the voters, when polled, revealed that they felt closer to Reagan than to Mondale on the issues—including many specific issues like abortion and Central America, where other evidence shows that people's positions are really closer to Mondale's.

The reason people seem to feel that they agree with President Reagan even if they really don't is that they believe his policies are working. The public's approach to the issues is pragmatic—whatever works must be right. Ideologues, on the other hand, believe that whatever is wrong cannot possibly work, even if it does work. Thus, many die-hard Republicans never admitted that the New Deal was a success, and many Democrats today refuse to believe there is a recovery. To pragmatic Americans, if big government policies worked during the New Deal, then they were probably right, at least for that time. If Reagan's antigovernment policies are working, then they are probably right, at least for now.

The exit polls also reveal a startling shift in the partisanship of American voters. In four nationwide exit polls taken on November 6, an average of 36 percent of the voters described themselves as Democrats and 32 percent as Republicans. That is a sharp change from the 42-to-28 percent margin reported in 1980. Large numbers of Democrats seem to have abandoned their party this year, some by voting Republican, some by rejecting the Democratic label, and some by staying home.

There have been marked changes in the nature of the Democratic vote as well. Compare Mondale's vote this year to the vote for Adlai Stevenson in 1956. Both were midwestern liberals, and both got about the same share of the national vote (41 percent for Mondale, 42 percent for Stevenson). But the sources of their support were very different. Mondale did significantly better than Stevenson among black voters, college graduates, women, Jews, and professionals. On the other hand, Stevenson's support was much stronger among whites, southerners, men, blue-collar workers, union members, and Catholics.

These shifts did not happen suddenly. Beginning in the mid-1960s, two streams of voters began leaving the Democratic Party—white southerners and Catholic "ethnic" voters in the North. The first stage of this realignment occurred in 1968 and 1972, when race and foreign policy were the major issues of contention. During this period, the Democrats lost most of their "social issue conservatives," primarily but not exclusively white southerners.

The second stage, 1980–84, has been much more devastating because the party has lost its credibility on economic issues. The economic issue had always held the Democratic Party together, even when race and Vietnam were tearing it apart. Since the 1930s, the Democrats have defined themselves more than anything else as the party that protects people against economic adversity. That's what kept white working-class voters in the party despite their mistrust of its racial and foreign policy liberalism.

Gallup polls show that the Democrats' long-standing advantage as the party more likely to keep the nation prosperous has vanished. In 1980, as a result of Jimmy Carter's economic failures, the voters saw no difference between the two parties on the prosperity issue. This year, as a result of Ronald Reagan's success, the Republicans hold a 17-point advantage. If the Democrats cannot offer people economic security, what reason is there to stay in the party?

The Democrats have become less of a populist party and more of a liberal party. As the party has lost moderate and conservative Catholics and southerners, it has strengthened its appeal to blacks and educated upper-middle-class liberals. Over one-quarter of the votes cast for the Democratic ticket this year came from blacks. In the South, blacks were a majority of Democratic voters.

Remember this old vaudeville routine?

DOCTOR TO PATIENT WITH MYSTERIOUS AILMENT: Sir, have you ever had this problem before?
PATIENT: Yes.
DOCTOR: Well, you've got it again.

The Democrats have had this problem before. In 1968 and 1972, to be exact. And they've got it again. Mondale's vote looks very much like the disastrous votes for Hubert Humphrey and George McGovern, both northern liberal Protestants who, like Mondale, chose northern liberal Catholics as their running mates.

The result should be clear by now: when you offer tickets like that, you write off the South. Neither Harry Truman, nor John F. Kennedy, nor Jimmy Carter would have won the presidency without southern electoral votes. Giving up the South wouldn't be so bad, except for the fact that the party is losing other constituencies as well. Catholics voted 59 percent for Humphrey in 1968, 48 percent for McGovern in 1972, and 44 percent for Mondale this year.

Essentially the national Democratic Party has lost its conservative wing, which used to be a considerable segment of the party. And its moderate support is diminishing fast. (Look at John Glenn's performance in the primaries this year.) To some extent, the party's losses on the right have been compensated by its gains among blacks and liberals, including liberal Republicans like John Anderson. Overall, however, the losses have outweighed the gains.

Which means the Democrats can no longer be called the nation's normal majority party. On the other hand, the Republicans cannot claim a natural majority of voters either. We are approaching a situation where the country is one-third Democratic, one-third Republican, and one-third independent. But keep in mind that, with the exception of 1964, independents have given the edge to the Republican candidate in every presidential election since 1952.

Can the Republican Party hold itself together? At least one issue, religion, threatens to tear the party apart. Sure, it's a problem, but remember that in the New Deal coalition, southern racists, blacks, and northern liberals managed to stick together for thirty years, mostly by avoiding the subject of race. So far President Reagan has talked a great deal about the social issues, but has avoided placing them at the top of the administration's agenda. If he decides to push the social issues in his second term, that could damage the party's future prospects.

How will we know if a realignment occurs? During the New Deal, Republicans liked to believe that Roosevelt's majorities were personal and would vanish when he left the political scene. So what happened after four straight FDR victories? Harry Truman won, and the Republicans finally had to face the fact that something fundamental had changed. If the Republicans can win without Reagan on the ticket in 1988, then we will know the same thing has happened in our time.

Can the Democrats, a party that nominated William Jennings Bryan three times, learn anything from the disasters of 1968, 1972, 1980, and 1984? Maybe, but on the other hand, many Democrats believe that they tried another approach with Jimmy Carter. And look what happened.

CHAPTER NINE

INTEREST GROUPS

One of the more significant political developments in the past decade has been the enormous growth of Political Action Committees, or PACs, as they are popularly called. The contemporary political action committee developed as a consequence of campaign finance legislation passed by Congress in 1974. This legislation permitted, and indeed encouraged, the formation of campaign finance organizations, separate from the formal Democratic and Republican parties and candidates running for office.

The primary purpose of PACs is to raise and spend money on behalf of candidates sympathetic to their causes. As a result, campaign financing has been transformed from the activity of a small number of wealthy contributors to the well-organized campaigns of literally thousands of PACs representing business, labor, professional groups, and other interest groups contributing to campaigns and spending money on their own on behalf of congressional and presidential candidates.

Some commentators have been very critical of PACs because of their alleged influence on electoral outcomes and legislation. In the first article which follows, Mark Green argues that, despite claims to the contrary, PACs have unduly influenced political campaigns and reaped the rewards of their activities by obtaining legislation favorable to their interests. As Green states in his article: "Despite the best efforts of cloistered academics and public relations aides, it is impossible to deny that the swelling volume of PAC money is distorting if not corrupting the legislative process."

Green's views are not shared by everyone, however. In the second selection, Michael J. Malbin argues that the presumed relationship between PAC money and legislation is not as direct or as strong as some contend. According to Malbin, the argument that PAC contributions influence legislation favorable to PACs suffers on at least two grounds. The first weakness has to do with the logical fallacies of the argument, such as assuming that if one finds a correlation between PAC money and votes it proves that money causes votes (it could just as logically be argued that money follows favorable votes). The second weakness has to do with the empirical evidence presuming to show a connection between PACs and legislation. According to Malbin, no such conclusion is warranted based on the empirical evidence available at this time. He suggests that a great deal more research needs to be done before it can be concluded that PACs are as influential as their critics maintain.

The Pro PAC Backlash: When Money Talks, Is It Democracy?

Mark Green

One autumn morning in 1982, I sat in the outer office of a congressman from the Midwest, waiting to interview him about political action committees. The door to his private office swung open, and the lawmaker and a half-dozen men whom I recognized as representatives of the banking lobby spilled out into the reception area. Amid guffaws and backslaps, the lobbyists kept entreating him: "Are you sure you don't want the $5,000 contribution? You sure?" When he saw me and recalled why I was there he stiffened. "You sure?" the bankers persisted. "You sure?" Forcing a wan smile, the congressman continued to demur. Receiving a campaign gift on federal property is a felony.

These days it's hard to walk around Capitol Hill without witnessing such scenes. Concern about the growing influence of political action committees has sparked a number of books and articles, including Elizabeth Drew's *Politics and Money: The New Road to Corruption*, first serialized in the *New Yorker*; sociologist Amitai Etzioni's recently published *Capital Corruption: The New Attack on American Democracy*; cover stories in *Time* and the *New Republic*; and a series in the *Wall Street Journal*, all charging that PACs are undermining the legislative process.

The attacks have generated a backlash. In the past year, numerous advocacy advertisements, Op-Ed pieces, studies, and articles have attempted to make the case for PACs. Much of the material they present is the result of a well-funded offensive by corporations and trade associations. Their arguments deserve scrutiny lest they become accepted by default. Like popcorn, they contain a kernel of truth puffed up beyond recognition. . . .

PACs account for only a small part of all political contributions. As Richard

Armstrong, head of the Public Affairs Council, a pro-business group, wrote in *Newsweek*, "The truth is that all PACs combined, including those of labor, contribute less than one-fourth of the aggregate amount spent on election campaigns."

But a PAC need not bankroll an entire campaign to be remembered by a politician after the votes are counted. Furthermore, aggregate statistics are misleading because the inclusion of candidates who get almost no PAC money pulls down the average. According to Edward Roeder, author of *PACs Americana*, the committees supplied 43 percent of the campaign treasuries of incumbents in the Ninety-seventh Congress.

Finally, PAC money, like snow in the mountains, gathers at the peaks. A large portion of it goes to committee chairs and party leaders who are most able to return favors. In 1982 the House minority leader, Robert Michel, received 68 percent of his campaign funds from PACs; House Appropriations Committee chairman Jamie Whitten filled 75 percent of his coffers with PAC money. . . .

Business isn't monolithic, so business contributions have a diffuse impact. "Business rarely takes a uniform position on *any* political issue," wrote Armstrong. PAC critics, he added, "forget the many conflicts within the business community itself—big business versus small business, industry versus industry, free trade versus protectionism, and so on."

It's true that divisions will occur within an industry on specific issues. United Airlines and Pan American Airlines favored deregulation, while other major carriers opposed it. But such examples are not typical. More frequently, business does present a united front. A broad spectrum of corporations and trade associations contributed $2.5 million to members of the House Ways and Means Committee when it was considering an across-the-board corporate tax cut during 1981 and 1982. Did any steel company lobby for a stronger Clean Air Act? Did any commodities traders' group oppose the bill that gave a tax break to commodities traders? Was there a single used-car dealer pushing for the Federal Trade Commission rule mandating disclosure of known defects by used-car dealers?

PACs on both sides of an issue cancel each other out. "These guys are getting money from all sides," one PAC director told *U.S. News & World Report.*

This is an assertion without evidence. What about the other America—the one without PACs? A hungry black child in Brooklyn doesn't have a political action committee in Washington. Nor does an unemployed teenager in Memphis, a small farmer going under in southern Illinois, a consumer paying more for a car because of protectionism in Dayton.

Indeed, on most major consumer issues—protectionism, farm subsidization, occupational health and safety, product liability, antitrust-law exceptions—the interested companies have multiple PACs, while consumer groups have none.

PAC gifts aren't inducements for future votes; they're rewards for a prior record.

According to Representative Beryl Anthony, when he gets $5,000 from a PAC it "means somebody has approved of my past service in Congress" and nothing more. If a legislator's support for the special interest group's position *preceded* the contribution, how could it have *resulted from* the contribution?

Then why do so many PACs cross-examine candidates in questionnaires and in person about their positions on pending matters? As Amitai Etzioni points out, "Unlike rocks, people can anticipate; they can act now in anticipation of payoff to follow." And according to Jay Angoff, an attorney at Public Citizen's Congress Watch: "Whether a member votes for legislation because he has received money from a certain group or receives money because he has voted for legislation sought by the group, it makes no difference to the consumer. Either way, people who vote to further the interests of the business lobbies that contribute to their campaign continue to get elected."

The average PAC gift is too small to make a difference. Since PAC gifts to candidates average $600, even a lawmaker eager to sell out would be unmoved by a typical gift. Political scientist Michael Malbin observes that while several banking PACs gave Senator John Tower a total of $90,000 when he ran for reelection in 1978, his campaign spent $4 million; so banking PACs accounted for only 2.5 percent of the total. Malbin asks, "Can anyone seriously argue that Tower's positions were influenced by his greed for that bit of money?"

Even in Senate races, which are far more expensive than House races, $90,000 is still $90,000. And for a House candidate, $10,000 out of total costs of $300,000, say, is surely memorable, especially if it comes early in the campaign, when a candidate needs to show credibility—or late, for that crucial media buy. Four years after I ran for the House I still remember who gave me $1,000 contributions and at what stage in the campaign. How many members of Congress can't?

Also, the gifts that cause problems are much greater than $600. PACs are allowed to give a candidate a total of $10,000 ($5,000 for the primary, $5,000 for the general election). And PACs run in packs, matching one another's gifts and coordinating their efforts through industry networks and teleconferencing. Hence, Tower's $90,000.

Even a $5,000 gift isn't enough to buy a member of Congress. According to a Mobil advertisement, "That's hardly enough to corrupt a legislator, even if he or she were disposed to be corrupted."

To that Representative Tom Downey quipped, "You can't buy a congressman for $5,000, but you can buy his vote." No PAC gift would sway Senator Ted Kennedy in his support of national health insurance or Representative Henry Hyde in his opposition to abortion, but most of the six hundred-odd votes a year in Congress do not involve such deep moral or philosophical commitments. As a Democratic lawmaker told *Newsday*'s Judith Bender, "If you're on the fence and it doesn't matter to you or your constituents which way you vote, but it matters to some of your biggest contributors, your mind is going to be made up very easily, because the vast majority of issues are not war and peace, equity and justice. They are really very different shades of gray."

Where's the smoking gun? Bernadette Budde, who has been associated with the Business Industry PAC for fourteen years, said heatedly in an interview with me, "No one has ever shown me one body—not one—who has sold his vote for a contribution."

In interviews with twenty-nine members of Congress, I was told about many "bodies." For example, when Representative Dan Glickman asked a colleague in 1982 to join him in opposing a measure that would forbid the FTC from regulating used-car dealers, he was told, "I'm committed. I got a $10,000 check from the auto dealers. I can't change my vote now." A New York Democrat admitted he voted for the Alaskan gas pipeline, even though he opposed it on its merits, because "I didn't want the construction unions contributing to my opponent." When Representative Claudine Schneider tried to persuade a Republican colleague to oppose more funding for the Clinch River breeder reactor, he declined, explaining, "Westinghouse is a big contributor of mine." (Westinghouse is one of the companies that will build the reactor.) Another Republican, Representative Jim Leach of Iowa, said he once suggested to an urban Democrat with no dairy constituency that it would be most politic for him to oppose a dairy price-support measure and was told, "Yeah, but their PAC gave me money; I have to support them."

Numerous studies by Common Cause and Congress Watch have shown a direct correlation between members' votes and PAC contributions. For example, 92 percent of those who received contributions of $3,000 or more from five corporations supporting the Clinch River reactor voted for it; only 29 percent of those who received nothing did so. Nineteen of the twenty-two members of the House Ways and Means Committee who received contributions from commodity industry PACs prior to a crucial 1981 vote on a measure giving traders a tax break voted in favor of it. Of the thirteen members who received no money, eight voted against the bill.

PACs sometimes lose. As Simon Lazarus wrote last year in the *Washington Post*, "Business veterans of our most recent legislative wars . . . know that the real story of the 97th Congress was how frequently the new business givers lost big battles on the Hill." . . .

PAC critics have never asserted that special interest money always wins out. Nothing *always* wins out. Occasionally a journalistic spotlight can stop a PAC in its tracks, as when the American Medical Association and its PAC unsuccessfully tried to end all FTC regulation of the medical profession. Just as obviously, PAC gifts change the odds dramatically in favor of the givers. Why else do they give? Because they believe in good government?

PACs are public. They are at least an improvement over Watergate-era practices like passing cash-filled shopping bags and making secret infusions from corporate treasuries. "The signal virtue of the 1974 election law was that it required full disclosure of who is giving how much to whom," editorialized the *New Republic* recently. Critics should "concentrate on looking through the campaign finance and congressional voting records to see who is in bed with whom."

No one is advocating a return to the days of Bobby Baker and Maurice Stans, but disclosure, however necessary, is not a sufficient step toward cleaning up the campaign financing process, for several reasons.

PAC men in bed with legislators do not receive the same media attention as, say, cohabiting movie stars. And disclosure isn't good enough if both candidates in a race are equally in hock to interest groups—a not uncommon occurrence, since almost all candidates accept PAC gifts. Finally, a Democracy Project study found that 20 percent of contributions to Republicans in close House races in the 1980 election came from business PACs that gave after the October 15 filing deadline. While legal, such quiet gifts evade the intent of campaign finance laws, for they avoid public scrutiny until after the election. . . .

PAC critics are simplistic—money is just one factor. In his review Robert Samuelson wrote: "Money is only one factor—and not always the most important factor—promoting inequality. Districts are often deliberately rigged to favor one party or the other. Well-known incumbents—with access to government contracts and power—face unknown challengers."

Of course there are other variables. Some candidates are cute; some are ugly. Some are lucky enough to run in 1974 if they're Democrats; in 1980 if they're Republicans. These are the warp and woof of politics, and they can't (and shouldn't) be regulated. But we can stop money if it is corrupting the system. That money doesn't always buy elections is no argument for PACs.

Also, money may be just one factor, but it's surely a substantial one, as any candidate running for office will vouch. A Congress Watch study found that winners of open seats outspent losers in four of five races in 1978, and that twenty-seven of thirty-three winning Senate candidates outspent their opponents that year.

Lee Atwater, former PAC coordinator in the Reagan White House, provides an insider's perspective. Atwater told Elizabeth Drew in 1982, "I think the story of this off-year election is that we've marshaled our resources and bought one or two Senate seats and fifteen to twenty House seats, and that's really good."

PAC defenders are trying to perform the political equivalent of making water run uphill. Despite the best efforts of cloistered academics and corporate public relations aides, it is impossible to deny that the swelling volume of PAC money is distorting if not corrupting the legislative process. As Representative Barney Frank has observed, politicians are the only people we allow to take thousands of dollars from perfect strangers and not expect it to influence their judgment.

Substantively, PAC apologists have lost the battle, but politically, they are winning the war. . . .

Sense and Nonsense on PACs

Michael J. Malbin

Interested money may not be new, but PACs are. . . . I want to look at the assumed connection between PAC contributors and legislative results. . . .

Logical Fallacies

The assumption that PAC contributions relate directly to policy is made not only by journalists and supporters of public finance but by many PAC representatives. In its most common form, the argument suffers from both a lack of evidence and faulty causal logic. Two simple logical errors recur frequently. The first has to do wtih what correlations mean. Common Cause regularly publishes examples of parallel contribution and voting patterns to support the claim that money influences votes. But simple correlations cannot say anything about causal direction. Therefore they cannot help one choose between Common Cause's interpretation and the opposite one offered by House Democratic Whip Thomas Foley: "Money follows votes and not the other way around."[1]

The second logical fallacy, which we learned in school as Ockham's Razor, can be found in Elizabeth Drew's book, in which she claimed that the Democratic Party was selling its soul for campaign funds. Her major example was the omnibus tax bill of 1981. In her opinion, the Democratic members of the House Committee on Ways and Means added tax breaks to the bill for independent oil producers to help the party regain campaign contributions it had lost during the 1970s.[2] From her quotations, it appears that at least one lobbyist and two Ways and Means Democrats linked campaign contributions with the party's position on the tax bills. The views of the two Demo-

From Michael J. Malbin, "Looking Back at the Future of Campaign Finance Reform: Interest Groups and American Elections," in *Money and Politics in the United States: Financing Elections in the 1980s*, edited by Michael J. Malbin (Washington, D.C.: American Enterprise Institute for Public Policy Research, 1984), pp. 247–52, 272–73. End notes have been rearranged and renumbered to conform to text—*Editors*.

crats who were central to the process were given shorter shrift. The picture they drew was a lot simpler and more persuasive. The House Democrats desperately wanted a victory on the tax bill after they were humiliated by President Reagan on the budget in May 1981. They did, as Drew said, engage in a bidding war with the Republicans. The main prizes sought were not campaign contributions in a year and a half, but the immediate floor votes of oil state members of Congress on the omnibus tax bill. Both elements may have been involved, but as Ockham might have said, the simpler and more direct explanation seems weightier.

Recent Research

Political scientists and economists who have used more sophisticated quantitative models to examine the connection between contributions and legislative floor votes have come up with a mixed picture that would lead one to dismiss Common Cause's one-dimensional view of the world, but not to dismiss the possibility that there is some connection worth examining. Two studies that looked at a large number of floor votes found that when they controlled for other factors, the members' general ideological outlooks were much better predictors of floor votes than were campaign contributions or just about anything else.[3] On the other hand, three studies that looked at individual, narrow economic regulation bills did see a relationship between contributions and votes, although a weaker one than might be expected from the popular conception.[4] The reason for the relationship was explained this way by the authors of one of the specific studies:

> Votes are linked so strongly to PAC contributions on this issue precisely because other forces are not operating as strongly as they normally do. Trucking deregulation in 1980 was not a clearly partisan or ideological issue, and for most senators it was difficult for them to calculate the issue's relevance to their constituencies. In sum, the forces that normally structure legislative voting only slightly predisposed senators in one direction or the other in this case.[5]

When supporters of stricter PAC limits are being less rhetorical, this is also the serious core of their case. Representative Dan Glickman seemed to be making essentially the same point when he testified on behalf of his own bill:

> I do not think any member of Congress votes because of how a PAC gives him money on El Salvador, or the MX missiles, or some of what I call the broader, abstract national issues. But those are not the ones I am really worried about. The ones I worry about are the specialty issues on which nobody is on the other side. . . . Where was the public last year before the dramatic rate increases that we are now seeing as a result of divestiture of the telephone company? The public

wasn't there; AT&T (The American Telephone and Telegraph Company) and CWA (Communications Workers of America) were there. Where has the public been on dairy legislation when we raise dairy price supports, which come before my committee? The public generally is not there; the dairy lobby is there. Where is the public on banking policy? On pharmaceutical legislation? Usually, when you talk about specialty legislation, the public is not there. The public doesn't know, and I think the smaller specialty issues, where no one is on the other side, are the heart of the dramatic problem of special interest contributions.[6]

Representative Glickman's argument can be supplemented, and often is, in a way that brings into question the utility of roll-call analyses for studying the role of contributions. As little as the public may not "be there" when "specialty issues" come up for votes on the House or Senate floor, still less is it there in the crucial formative stages of legislation, whether in open committee sessions or in closed private meetings that produce the agendas and bills on which committees act.

Therefore, if the correlations between floor votes and contributions are weak, they might turn out to be stronger if the focus shifted to aspects of the legislative process that are less amenable to study. No one can say for sure; the claim is worth analyzing, but the research has not been done. Before one simply assumes, however, that committees are systematically more friendly than the floor to interest groups, one should bear in mind that committees are used by members who want to sit on, and thus kill, special interest bills, as well as by members who want to advance them.

PACs and Interest Groups

Glickman does have a point. Interest groups tend to be more successful on bills that do not capture the public's attention than on ones that do. The problem is not that Glickman's argument is wrong but that it does not go far enough. Everything he has said about campaign contributions can be applied to interest groups more generally. Every one of the issues he mentioned (telephone rates, dairy price supports, banking, and pharmaceuticals), and all three specialty issues analyzed by the political scientists mentioned above (trucking deregulation, cargo preference, and dairy price supports again), involve groups that not only give campaign contributions but also maintain sophisticated Washington lobbying operations. As Eismeier and Pollock point out, most PACs do not fit this model. Even if one confines oneself to Washington-based PACs, it is difficult to separate the importance of PAC contributions from the lobbying efforts they are supposedly meant to enhance.

Some people suggest there is a connection between the growth of PACs that has occurred since the mid-1970s and the increased success of business in Congress. There are several problems with this. First, if business is so powerful, why, as President Carter's former White House aid in charge of regulatory policy pointed out, did business fail in almost every one of its major 1981–82 efforts to bring about the regulatory changes it most wanted?[7] Second, where business did have some success, it is necessary to separate the general effects of public opinion, and the messages members of Congress read into the election returns of 1978 and 1980, from the effects of interest group activity. Finally, once the issue has been narrowed to interest group activity, it is then necessary to separate out the changes in Washington lobbying before attributing too much to the role of campaign contributions.

The 1970s were years of explosive growth for the Washington lobbying community. The scope of federal regulation increased dramatically, bringing the federal government more directly into more aspects of more people's lives. (The *Federal Register* grew steadily from 20,036 pages in 1970 to 77,497 pages in 1979.)[8] As regulation grew, more corporations and associations thought it important to open Washington offices. About twice as many (or about 500) corporations had Washington offices in 1980 as in 1970; and corporate employees in Washington tripled over the same period.[9] Associations with their national headquarters in Washington also grew in number over the decade from about 1,200 to 1,739, a growth rate of about one per week.[10]

The corporate[11] and association[12] growth curves flattened in the early 1980s, during the recession, but the number of association employees continued to increase from about 40,000 in 1979 to an estimated 50,000 in 1983.[13] In addition, businesses without Washington offices tended to rely more heavily on Washington lawyers to handle their governmental affairs; membership in the D.C. bar increased from 16,800 in 1973 to 32,200 in 1980[14] and 39,212 in 1983.[15] None of this even begins to document the growth in state and local governments with offices in Washington,[16] or nonprofit and citizen groups, whose growth curves rose even more steeply during the 1970s than those for the private sector.[17]

At the same time as the number of Washington offices and employees has increased, so too has their productivity. Good lobbyists learn quickly that an argument made by a Washington representative is not nearly as effective as the same argument made by a legislator's own constituents. Washington lobbyists are important for getting early information; knowing the technical issues; knowing who are the important members of Congress, congressional staff, and agency staff on particular issues; knowing which people are most open to what kinds of arguments; knowing the real possibilities for compromise or damage control; and synthesizing all this into presentations that are appropriate for each person to be persuaded. Generally, lobbyists present their arguments directly. But on crucial issues, they have discovered it is much more effective to turn back to the grass roots. Grass-roots or indirect lobbying is "the only lobbying that counts," says Richard L. Lesher, president of the U.S. Chamber of Commerce; "the growth area of lobbying," according to Common Cause lobbyist Michael Cole.[18]

The communication revolution has helped lobbyists in almost every aspect of their work, but particularly in their ability to present technical arguments to individual members and to activate the grass roots. Computers let lobbyists tell individual members how particular options—down to the numbers used in formula grants[19]—will affect their own districts. Computers also can generate targeted mail that will stimulate a lobbying organization's members to write to their representatives or senators. (Three different commercial firms sell lists or computer tapes matching zip codes with congressional districts.[20] These lists are then further broken down by interest groups to match their members' zip codes with members of Congress arranged by subcommittee, issue area, and specific positions.)

When mail would be too slow, the changes in telecommunication—from cheap long-distance telephone rates to teleconferencing and the Chamber of Commerce's $5 million satellite television network[21]—facilitate the process. For example, when President Reagan gave a television address on July 27, 1981, two days before the House voted on his tax bill, business groups, primed by the White House, used their communication networks to stimulate an immediate flow of letters and mailgrams to Congress, often written by people who had contributed to the member's last election campaign.[22]

The amount of money spent on the new lobbying techniques dwarfs the amount given directly in campaign contributions. No reliable figures are available, but a few anecdotal stories from the press give an idea of the order of magnitude. Labor law reform was killed by a filibuster in the Senate in 1978 supported by a business and right-to-work grass-roots lobbying campaign whose cost was estimated at about $5 million.[23] On the other side of the same bill, Victor S. Kamber, who coordinated labor's efforts, said his budget for the fight was about $2.5 million.[24] That comes to $7.5 million for one bill!

More recently, AT&T reportedly spent $2 million to oppose a bill that would have overturned the antitrust and divestiture settlement it reached with the Justice Department in 1982.[25] The Health Insurance Association's advertising campaign against President Reagan's proposals to curb hospital reimbursements for Medicare reportedly cost another $2 million,[26] the Savings and Loan Foundation spent $4.5 million to publicize its industry's problems and lobby for the short-lived All-Savers' Certificates in 1981,[27] and the industry-backed Committee for Fair Insurance Rates spent about $800,000 to oppose unisex pension and life insurance rates and benefits in 1983.[28] The insurance campaign also employed a new technique that shows what money can buy these days; each of its letters contained a pretyped return letter with varying texts, complete with laser-printed personalized letterheads on different colors of stationery, for the recipient to sign and return to his or her member of Congress. The mailings, produced by the Targeted Communications Corporation for a pricey 50 to 75 cents per piece, have also been used by the Motion Picture Association on the Home Recording Act of 1982 and by AT&T on the divestiture bill.[29]

None of these examples is offered to suggest that the burden of analysis should simply shift from campaign finance to lobbying expenditures. For one thing, concentrating on lobbying expenditures may be just as problematic as concentrating on campaign finance. As James Q. Wilson has pointed out, there may be some large gaps between resources or expenditures and political power.[30] If this were not true, it would be difficult to explain the continued success environmental groups have had defending clean air and water acts from well-funded industry attacks. For another, it would be premature simply to rule out the possibility that campaign finance does have at least some independent influence over legislative decisions.

We know some lobbyists and members think that campaign finance influences legislation and some lobbyists time their contributions to coincide with crucial committee votes.[31] Others tell members that they use "report cards" of their votes on key issues to decide on their contributions.[32] On the other hand, members of Congress can and do defend themselves by taking organizational mailing lists and putting them on their own computers. When this happens, the members can turn something that started out as pressure to their own advantage, making themselves less, instead of more, dependent on a group's leaders for the group's members' electoral support.[33]

Conclusion

In summary, the view that PAC contributions influence policy can neither be fully accepted nor fully rejected out of hand. The evidence offered to support the conclusion tends to be weak or irrelevant. Common Cause's correlations defy logic, and the complicated quantitative methods used by political scientists and economists have failed to separate the financially modest role of campaign contributions from the much larger lobbying world within which they are assumed to fit. Moreover, even if you could separate the effects of lobbying and contributions, the fact that a contributor intends his money to have a certain effect does not mean that it was received in the same spirit, even if the recipient behaves as the contributor might have wished. The world is too complicated to be encapsulated by such simple analyses. Anyone who wants to say something precise about the independent effect of contributions will have to pursue a different line of research from the ones we have seen so far.

NOTES

1. Remarks before the National Capital Area Political Science Association, December 7, 1982.
2. Elizabeth Drew, *Politics and Money: The New Road to Corruption*, vol. 1 (New York:

Macmillan, 1983), pp. 38–43. First published in the *New Yorker*, December 6, 1982, p. 54.

3. Candice J. Nelson, "Counting the Cash: PAC Contributions to Members of the House of Representatives" (paper delivered at the annual meeting of the American Political Science Association, September 2–5, 1982); and James B. Kau and Paul H. Rubin, *Congressmen, Constituents and Contributors* (Boston: Nijhoff, 1982).

4. Henry W. Chappell, Jr., "Campaign Contributions and Voting on the Cargo Preference Bill: A Comparison of Simultaneous Models," *Public Choice*, vol. 36 (1981), pp. 301–12; W. P. Welch, "Campaign Contributions and Voting: Milk Money and Dairy Price Supports," *Western Political Quarterly*, vol. 35 (December 1982), pp. 478–95; and John P. Frendreis and Richard W. Waterman, "PAC Contributions and Legislative Behavior: Senate Voting on Trucking Deregulation" (paper delivered at the annual convention of the Midwest Political Science Association, April 20–22, 1983).

5. Frendreis and Waterman, "PAC Contributions and Legislative Behavior," p. 28.

6. Testimony before the Election Task Force of the House Administration Committee, June 9, 1983; not published at the time of this writing.

7. Simon Lazarus, "PAC Power? They Keep on Losing," *Washington Post*, March 27, 1983, B1–B2.

8. Timothy B. Clark, "The Public and the Private Sectors—The Old Distinctions Grow Fuzzy," *National Journal*, January 9, 1980, p. 104.

9. Atlee K. Shidler, *Local Community and National Government* (Washington, D.C.: Greater Washington Research Center, 1980), p. 19.

10. Clark, "The Public and the Private Sectors," p. 104.

11. Conversation with Raymond L. Hoewing of the Public Affairs Council, July 12, 1983.

12. *Association Trends*, July 8, 1983, sec. 2. p. 2.

13. *Ibid.*

14. Shidler, *Local Community and National Government*, p. 20, from information provided by the D.C. Bar.

15. Information provided by the D.C. Bar.

16. Shidler, in *Local Community and National Government*, p. 18, said "only a few" state governments had offices in Washington in 1970 and two-thirds had them in 1980. Over one hundred cities and towns were directly represented in 1980, two or three times the number in 1970.

17. Jack Walker, "Origins and Maintenance of Interest Groups in America," *American Political Science Review*, vol. 77, no. 2 (June 1983), pp. 390–406.

18. Both quotes are in Charles Mohr, "Grass-Roots Lobby Aids Business," *New York Times*, April 17, 1978, p. A1.

19. See R. Douglas Arnold, "The Local Roots of Domestic Policy," in *The New Congress*, eds. Thomas E. Mann and Norman J. Ornstern (Washington, D.C.: American Enterprise Institute, 1981), pp. 250–87.

20. "Grassroots Lobbying Ups Competition," *Association Trends*, July 8, 1983, sec. 2, p. 1.

21. The figure is from William J. Lanouette, "Chamber's Ponderous Decision Making Leaves It Sitting on the Sidelines," *National Journal*, July 24, 1982, pp. 1298–1301. It includes $4 million to expand the Chamber's radio and television studios and $1 million for satellite transmission equipment.

22. Elizabeth Wehr, "White House's Lobbying Apparatus Produces Impressive Tax Vote Victory," *Congressional Quarterly*, August 1, 1981, pp. 1372–73.

23. Harrison Donnelly, "Organized Labor Found 1978 a Frustrating Year, Had Few Victories in Congress," *Congressional Quarterly*, December 30, 1978, pp. 3539–42.

24. James W. Singer, "Labor and Business Heat Up the Senate Labor Law Reform Battle," *National Journal*, June 3, 1978, pp. 884–85.

25. Margaret Garrard Warner and James A. White, "AT&T Cranks Up a $2 Million Blitz to Defend Its Antitrust Settlement," *Wall Street Journal*, April 12, 1982, p. 25.

26. Robert Pear, "Critics Say Reagan Medicare Cuts Would Only Shift Hospital Costs," *New York Times*, March 3, 1982, p. A21.

27. "S & L Group Takes Some Credit for Its Ad's Effect on Congress," *Wall Street Journal*, June 25, 1981, p. 29.

28. Robert D. Hershey, Jr., "Insurance Lobbying Drive Draws Ire from 'Folks in the Boondocks,'" *New York Times*, May 20, 1983, p. A18.

29. Bill Keller, "Computers and Laser Printers Have Recast the Injunction: 'Write Your Congresssman,'" *Congressional Quarterly*, September 11, 1982, pp. 2245–47.

30. James Wilson, *Political Organizations* (New York: Basic Books, 1973), chaps. 15–16.

31. See Jerry Knight, "Commodity Trading PACs Gave to Tax Unit Members Before Vote," *Washington Post*, August 8, 1981, p. A5.

32. See James M. Perry, "How Realtors' PAC Rewards Office Seekers Helpful to the Industry," *Wall Street Journal*, August 2, 1982, pp. 1, 13; John F. Bibby, ed., *Congress off the Record: The Candid Analyses of Seven Members* (Washington, D.C.: American Enterprise Institute, 1983), pp. 33–34.

33. *Ibid.*, pp. 34, 46.

CHAPTER TEN

CONGRESS

REPRESENTATION

The three selections in this section are illustrative of a long-standing debate among both political theorists and elected officials; namely, whose views should prevail on a given issue—the constituents' or the representatives'. In the first selection, taken from an early debate in the General Assembly of the State of Virginia, the argument is made that legislators are obliged to act as instructed delegates—*that is, that they must vote in accordance with the will of their constituents. In the second selection, former Massachusetts Senator John F. Kennedy maintains that legislators should act as* trustees, *voting according to their own conscience, regardless of whether their choices reflect the sentiments of their constituents. Finally, George Galloway, a former staff assistant in Congress, contends that on some occasions legislators must follow public opinion, while on others they are obliged to vote according to their own conscience. This view, which combines both the delegate and the trustee approach, is characterized as the* politico *role.*

The Legislator as Delegate

General Assembly of Virginia

There can be no doubt that the scheme of a representative republic was derived to our forefathers from the constitution of the English House of Commons; and that that branch of the English government . . . was in its origin, and in theory always has been, purely republican. It is certain, too, that the statesmen of America, in assuming that as the model of our own institutions, designed to adopt it here in its purest form, and with its strictest republican tenets and principles. It becomes, therefore, an inquiry of yet greater utility than curiosity, to ascertain the sound doctrines of the constitution of the English House of Commons in regard to this right of the constituent to instruct the representative. For the position may safely be assumed that the wise and virtuous men who framed our constitutions designed, that, in the United States, the constituent should have at least as much, if not a great deal more, influence over the representative than was known to have existed time immemorial in England. Let us then interrogate the history of the British nation; let us consult the opinions of their wise men.

Instances abound in parliamentary history of formal instructions from the constituent to the representative, of which . . . the following may suffice: In 1640, the knights of the shire for Dorset and Kent informed the commons *that they had in charge from their constituents* seven articles of grievances, which they accordingly laid before the House, where they were received and acted on. In the 33rd year of Charles II, the citizens of London instructed their members to insist on the bill for excluding the Duke of York (afterwards King James II) from the succession to the throne; and their representative said "that his *duty* to his electors *obliged* him to vote the bill." At a subsequent election, in 1861, in many places, formal instructions were given to the members returned, to insist on the same exclusion bill; we know, from history,

From Commonwealth of Virginia, General Assembly, *Journal of the Senate*, 1812, pp. 82–89. In some instances, spelling and punctuation have been altered from the original in order to achieve greater clarity—*Editors.*

how uniformly and faithfully those instructions were obeyed. . . . In 1741, the citizens of London instructed their members to vote against standing armies, excise laws, the septennial bill, and a long train of evil measures, already felt, or anticipated; and expressly affirm their right of instruction—"We think it" (say they) "our *duty*, as it is *our undoubted right*, to acquaint you, with *what we desire and expect from you, in discharge of the great trust we repose in you*, and what we take to be *your duty as our representative*, etc." In the same year, instructions of a similar character were sent from all parts of England. In 1742, the cities of London, Bristol, Edinburgh, York, and many others, instructed their members in parliament to seek redress against certain individuals suspected to have betrayed and deserted the cause of the people. . . .

Instances also are on record of the deliberate formal knowledgement of the right of instruction by the House of Commons itself, especially in old times. Thus the commons hesitated to grant supplies to King Edward III *till they had the consent of their constituents*, and desired that a new parliament might be summoned, which might be *prepared with authority from their constituents*. . . .

"Instructions" (says a member of the House of Commons) "ought to be *followed implicitly*," after the member has *respectfully* given his constituents *his opinion* of them: *"Far be it from me to oppose my judgment to that of 6000 of my fellow citizens."* "The practice" (says another) "of consulting our constituents was good. I wish it was continued. *We can discharge our duty no better, than in the direction of those who sent us hither. What the people choose is right, because they choose it."* . . .

Without referring to the minor political authors . . . who have maintained these positions (quoted from one of them)—"that the people have a right to instruct their representatives; that no man ought to be chosen that will not receive instructions; that the people understand enough of the interests of the country to give general instructions; that it was the custom formerly to instruct all the members; and the nature of deputation shows that the custom was well grounded"—it is proper to mention that the great constitutional lawyer Coke . . . says, "It is the *custom of parliament*, when any new device is moved for on the king's behalf, for his aid and the like, that the commons may answer, *they dare not agree to it without conference with their counties."* And Sydney . . . maintains "that members derive their power from those that choose them; that those who give power do not give an unreserved power; that many members, in all ages, and sometimes the whole body of the commons have refused to vote until they consulted with those who sent them; that the houses have often adjourned to give them time to do so and if this were done more frequently, or if cities, towns and counties had on some occasions given instructions to their deputies, matters would probably have gone better in parliament than they have done." . . . The celebrated Edmund Burke, a man, it must be admitted, of profound knowledge, deep foresight, and transcendent abilities, disobeyed the instructions of his constituents; yet, by placing his excuse on the ground that the instructions were but the clamour of the day, he seems to admit the authority of instructions soberly and deliberately given; for he agrees, "he ought to look to their opinions" (which he explains to mean their permanent settled opinions) "but not to the flash of the day"; and he says elsewhere, that he could not bear to show himself "a representative, whose face did not reflect the face of his constituents—a face that did not joy in their joys and sorrow in their sorrows." It is remarkable that, notwithstanding a most splendid display of warm and touching eloquence, the people of Bristol would not reelect Mr. Burke, for this very offense of disobeying instructions. . . .

It appears, therefore, that the right of the constituent to instruct the representative, is firmly established in England, on the broad basis of the nature of representation. The existence of that right, there, has been demonstrated by the only practicable evidence, by which the principles of an unwritten constitution can be ascertained—history and precedent.

To view the subject upon principle, the right of the constituent to instruct the representative, seems to result, clearly and conclusively, from the very nature of the representative system. Through means of that noble institution, the largest nation may, almost as conveniently as the smallest, enjoy all the advantages of a government by the people, without any of the evils of democracy—precipitation, confusion, turbulence, distraction from the ordinary and useful pursuits of industry. And it is only to avoid those and the like mischiefs, that representation is substituted for the direct suffrage of the people in the office of legislation. The representative, therefore, must in the nature of things, represent his own particular constituents only. He must, indeed, look to the general good of the nation, but he must look also, and especially to the interests of his particular constituents as concerned in the commonweal; because the general good is but the aggregate of individual happiness. He must legislate for the whole nation; but laws are expressions of the general will; and the general will is only the result of individual wills fairly collected and compared. In order . . . to express the general will . . . it is plain that the representative must express the will and speak the opinions of the constituents that depute him.

It cannot be pretended that a representative is to be the organ of his own will alone; for then, he would be so far despotic. *He must be the organ of others*—of whom? Not of the nation, for the nation deputes him not; but of his constituents, who alone know, alone have trusted, and can alone displace him. And if it be his province and his duty, in general, to express the will of his constituents, to the best of his knowledge, without being particularly informed thereof, it seems impossible to contend that he is not bound to do so when he is so especially informed and instructed.

The right of the constituent to instruct the representative, therefore, is an essential principle of the representative system. It may be remarked that wherever representation has been introduced, however unfavorable the circumstances under which it existed, however short its duration, however unimportant its functions, however dimly understood, the right of instruction has always been regarded as inseparably incidental to it. . . .

A representative has indeed a wide field of discretion left to him; and great is the confidence reposed in his integrity, fidelity, wisdom, zeal; but neither is the field of discretion boundless, nor the extent of confidence infinite; and the very discretion allowed him, and the very confidence he enjoys, is grounded on the supposition that he is charged with the will, acquainted with the opinions, and devoted to the interests of his constituents. . . .

Various objections have been urged to this claim of the constituent, of a right to instruct the representative, on which it may be proper to bestow some attention.

The first objection that comes to be considered . . . is grounded on the supposed impossibility of fairly ascertaining the sense of the constituent body. The *impossibility* is denied. It may often be a matter of great *difficulty;* but then the duty of obedience resolves itself into a question, not of principle, but of fact: whether the right of instruction has been exercised or not. The representative cannot be bound by an instruction that is not given; but that is no objection to the obligation of an instruction *actually given.* . . .

It has been urged that representatives are not bound to obey the instructions of their constituents because the constituents do not hear the debates, and therefore, cannot be supposed judges of the matter to be voted. If this objection has force enough to defeat the right of instruction, it ought to take away, also, the right of rejecting the representative at the subsequent election. For it might be equally urged on that occasion, as against the right of instruction, that the people heard not the debate that enlightened the representative's mind—the reasons that convinced his judgment and governed his conduct. . . . In other words, the principle that mankind is competent to self-government should be renounced. The truth is, that our institutions suppose that although the representative ought to be, and generally will be, selected for superior virtue and intelligence, yet a greater mass of wisdom and virtue still reside in the constituent body than the utmost portion allotted to any individual. . . .

Finally, it has been objected, that the instructions of the constituent are not obligatory on the representative because the obligation insisted on is fortified with no sanction—the representative cannot be punished for his disobedience, and his vote is valid notwithstanding his disobedience. It is true that there is no mode of legal punishment provided for this . . . default of duty and that the act of disobedience will not invalidate the vote. It is true, too, that a representative may perversely advocate a measure which he knows to be ruinous to his country; and that neither his vote will be invalidated by his depravity, nor can he be punished by law for his crime, heinous as it surely is. But it does not follow that the one representative is *not bound to obey the instructions* of his constituents any more than that the other is not bound to obey the dictates of his conscience. Both duties stand upon the same foundation, with almost all the great political and moral obligations. The noblest duties of man are without any legal sanction: the great mass of social duties . . . , our duties to our parents, to our children, to our wives, to our families, to our neighbor, to our country, our duties to God, are, for the most part, without legal sanction, yet surely not without the strongest obligation. The duty of the *representative* to obey the instructions of the *constituent* body cannot be placed on higher ground.

Such are the opinions of the General Assembly of Virginia, on the subject of this great right of instruction, and such the general reasons on which those opinions are founded. . . .

The Legislator as Trustee

John F. Kennedy

The primary responsibility of a senator, most people assume, is to represent the views of his state. Ours is a federal system—a union of relatively sovereign states whose needs differ greatly—and my constitutional obligations as senator would thus appear to require me to represent the interests of my state. Who will speak for Massachusetts if her own senators do not? Her rights and even her identity become submerged. Her equal representation in Congress is lost. Her aspirations, however much they may from time to time be in the minority, are denied that equal opportunity to be heard to which all minority views are entitled.

Any senator need not look very long to realize that his colleagues are representing *their* local interests. And if such interests are ever to be abandoned in favor of the national good, let the constituents—not the senator—decide when and to what extent. For he is their agent in Washington, the protector of their rights, recognized by the vice president in the Senate Chamber as "the senator from Massachusetts" or "the senator from Texas."

But when all of this is said and admitted, we have not yet told the full story. For in Washington we are "United States senators" and members of the Senate of the United States as well as senators from Massachusetts and Texas. Our oath of office is administered by the vice president, not by the governors of our respective states; and we come to Washington, to paraphrase Edmund Burke, not as hostile ambassadors or special pleaders for our state or section, in opposition to advocates and agents of other areas, but as members of the deliberative assembly of one nation with one interest. Of course, we should not ignore the needs of our area—nor could we easily as products of that area—but none could be found to look our for the national interest if local interests wholly dominated the role of each of us.

There are other obligations in addition to those of state and region—the obligations of the party. . . . Even if I can disregard those pressures, do I not have an obligation to go along with the party that placed me in office? We believe in this country in the principle of party responsibility, and we recognize the necessity of adhering to party platforms—if the party label is to mean anything to the voters. Only in this way can our basically two-party nation avoid the pitfalls of multiple splinter parties, whose purity and rigidity of principle, I might add—if I may suggest a sort of Gresham's Law of politics—increase inversely with the size of their membership.

And yet we cannot permit the pressures of party responsibility to submerge on every issue the call of personal responsibility. For the party which, in its drive for unity, discipline and success, ever decides to exclude new ideas, independent conduct or insurgent members, is in danger. . . .

Of course, both major parties today seek to serve the national interest. They would do so in order to obtain the broadest base of support, if for no nobler reason. But when party and officeholder differ as to how the national interest is to be served, we must place first the responsibility we owe not to our party or even to our constituents but to our individual consciences.

But it is a little easier to dismiss one's obligations to local interests and party ties than to face squarely the problem of one's responsibility to the will of his constituents. A senator who avoids this responsibility would appear to be accountable to no one, and the basic safeguards of our democratic system would thus have vanished. He is no longer representative in the true sense, he has violated his public trust, he has betrayed the confidence demonstrated by those who voted for him to carry out their views. "Is the creature," as John Tyler asked the House of Representatives in his maiden speech, "to set himself in opposition to his Creator? Is the servant to disobey the wishes of his master?"

> How can he be regarded as representing the people when he speaks, not their language, but his own? He ceases to be their representative when he does so, and represents himself alone.

In short, according to this school of thought, if I am to be properly responsive to the will of my constituents, it is my duty to place their principles, not mine, above all else. This may not always be easy, but it nevertheless is the essence of democracy, faith in the wisdom of the people and their views. To be sure, the people will make mistakes—they will get no better government than they deserve—but that is far better than the representative of the people arrogating for himself the right to say he knows better than they what is good for them. Is he not chosen, the argument closes, to vote as they would vote were they in his place?

It is difficult to accept such a narrow view of the role of United States senator—a view that assumes the people of Massachusetts sent me to Washington to serve merely as a seismograph to record shifts in popular opinion. I reject this view not because I lack faith in the "wisdom of the people," but because this concept of democracy actually puts too little faith in the people. Those who would deny the obligation of the representative to be bound by every impulse of the electorate—regardless of the conclusions his own deliberations direct—do trust in the wisdom of the people. They have faith in their ultimate sense of justice, faith in their ability to honor courage and respect judgment, and faith that in the long run they will act unselfishly for the good of the nation. It is that kind of faith on which democracy is based, not simply the often frustrated hope that public opinion will at all times under all circumstances promptly identify itself with the public interest.

The voters selected us, in short, because they had confidence in our judgment and our ability to exercise that judgment from a position where we could determine what were their own best interests, as a part of the nation's interests. This may mean that we must on occasion lead, inform, correct and sometimes even ignore constituent opinion, if we are to exercise fully that judgment for which we were elected. But acting without selfish motive or private bias, those who follow the dictates of an intelligent conscience are not aristocrats, demagogues, eccentrics, or callous politicians insensitive to the feelings of the public. They expect—and not without considerable trepidation—their constituents to be the final judges of the wisdom of their course; but they have faith that those constituents—today, tomorrow, or even in another generation—will at least respect the principles that motivated their independent stand.

If their careers are temporarily or even permanently buried under an avalanche of abusive editorials, poison-pen letters, and opposition votes at the polls—as they sometimes are, for that is the risk they take—they await the future with hope and confidence, aware of the fact that the voting public frequently suffers from what ex-Congressman T. V. Smith called the lag "between our way of thought and our way of life." . . .

Moreover, I question whether any senator, before we vote on a measure, can state with certainty exactly how the majority of his constituents feel on the issue as it is presented to the Senate. All of us in the Senate live in an iron lung—the iron lung of politics, and it is no easy task to emerge from that rarefied atmosphere in order to breathe the same fresh air our constituents breathe. It is difficult, too, to see in person an appreciable number of voters besides those professional hangers-on and vocal elements who gather about the politician on a trip home. In Washington I frequently find myself believing that forty or fifty letters, six visits from professional politicians and lobbyists, and three editorials in Massachusetts newspapers constitute public opinion on a given issue. Yet in truth I rarely know how the great majority of the voters feel, or even how much they know of the issues that seem so burning in Washington.

Today the challenge of political courage looms larger than ever before.

For our everyday life is becoming so saturated with the tremendous power of mass communications that any unpopular or unorthodox course arouses a storm of protests. . . . Our political life is becoming so expensive, so mechanized, and so dominated by professional politicians and public relations men that the idealist who dreams of independent statesmanship is rudely awakened by the necessities of election and accomplishment. . . .

And thus, in the days ahead, only the very courageous will be able to take the hard and unpopular decisions necessary for our survival. . . .

The Legislator as Politico

George B. Galloway

One question which the conscientious congressman must often ask himself, especially when conflicts arise between local or regional attitudes and interests and the national welfare, is this: "As a member of Congress, am I merely a delegate from my district or state, restricted to act and vote as the majority which elected me desire, bound by the instructions of my constituents and subservient to their will? Or am I, once elected, a representative of the people of the United States, free to act as I think best for the country generally?"

In a country as large as the United States, with such diverse interests and such a heterogeneous population, the economic interests and social prejudices of particular states and regions often clash with those of other sections and with conceptions of the general interest of the whole nation. The perennial demand of the silver-mining and wool interests in certain western states for purchase and protection, the struggle over slavery, and the recent filibuster of southern senators against the attempt to outlaw racial discrimination in employment are familiar examples of recurring conflicts between local interests and prejudices and the common welfare. These political quarrels are rooted in the varying stages of cultural development attained by the different parts of the country. It is the peculiar task of the politician to compose these differences, to reconcile conflicting national and local attitudes, and to determine when public opinion is ripe for legislative action. Some conflicts will yield in time to political adjustment; others must wait for their legal sanction upon the gradual evolution of the conscience of society. No act of Congress can abolish unemployment or barking dogs or racial prejudices. . . .

TYPES OF PRESSURES ON CONGRESS

One can sympathize with the plight of the conscientious congressman who is the focal point of all these competing pressures. The district or state he represents may need and want certain roads, post offices, courthouses, or schools. Irrigation dams or projects may be needed for the development of the area's resources. If the representative is to prove himself successful in the eyes of the people back home, he must be able to show, at least occasionally, some visible and concrete results of his congressional activity. Or else he must be able to give good reasons why he has not been able to carry out his pledges. The local residence rule for congressmen multiplies the pressures that impinge upon him. Faithful party workers who have helped elect him will expect the congressman to pay his political debts by getting them jobs in the federal service. Constituents affected by proposed legislation may send him an avalanche of letters, telegrams, and petitions which must be acknowledged and followed up. The region from which he comes will expect him to protect and advance its interests in Washington. All the various organized groups will press their claims upon him and threaten him if he does not jump when they crack the whip. Party leaders may urge a congressman to support or oppose the administration program or to "trade" votes for the sake of party harmony or various sectional interests. He is also under pressure from his own conscience as to what he should do both to help the people who have elected him and to advance the best interests of the nation. Besieged by all these competing pressures, a congressman is often faced with the choice of compromising between various pressures, of trading votes, of resisting special interests of one sort or another, of staying off the floor when a vote is taken on some measure he prefers not to take a stand on, of getting support here and at the same time running the risk of losing support there. Dealing with pressure blocs is a problem in political psychology which involves a careful calculation of the power of the blocs, the reaction of the voters on election day, and the long-haul interests of the district, state, and nation. . . .

SHOULD CONGRESS LEAD OR FOLLOW PUBLIC OPINION?

It is axiomatic to say that in a democracy public opinion is the source of law. Unless legislation is sanctioned by the sense of right of the people, it becomes a dead letter on the statute books, like Prohibition and the Hatch Act. But public opinion is a mercurial force; now quiescent, now vociferous, it has various moods and qualities. It reacts to events and is often vague and hard to weigh.

Nor is public opinion infallible. Most people are naturally preoccupied with their personal problems and daily affairs; national problems and legislative decisions seem complex and remote to them, despite press and radio and occasional Capitol tours. Comparatively few adults understand the technicalities of foreign loans or reciprocal trade treaties, although congressional action on these aspects of our foreign economic policy may have far-reaching effects upon our standard of living. . . .

In practice, a congressman both leads and follows public opinion. The desires of his constituents, of his party, and of this or that pressure group all enter into his decisions on matters of major importance. The influence of these factors varies from member to member and measure to measure. Some congressmen consider it their duty to follow closely what they think is the majority opinion of their constituents, especially just before an election. Others feel that they should make their decisions without regard to their constituents' wishes in the first place, and then try to educate and convert them afterward. Some members are strong party men and follow more or less blindly the program of the party leaders. Except when they are very powerful in the home district, the pressure groups are more of a nuisance than a deciding influence on the average member. When a legislator is caught between the conflicting pressures of his constituents and his colleagues, he perforce compromises between them and follows his own judgment.

The average legislator discovers early in his career that certain interests or prejudices of his constituents are dangerous to trifle with. Some of these prejudices may not be of fundamental importance to the welfare of the nation, in which case he is justified in humoring them, even though he may disapprove. The difficult case occurs where the prejudice concerns some fundamental policy affecting the national welfare. A sound sense of values, the ability to discriminate between that which is of fundamental importance and that which is only superficial, is an indispensable qualification of a good legislator.

Senator Fulbright gives an interesting example of this distinction in his stand on the poll-tax issue and isolationism. "Regardless of how persuasive my colleagues or the national press may be about the evils of the poll tax, I do not see its fundamental importance, and I shall follow the views of the people of my state. Although it may be symbolic of conditions which many deplore, it is exceedingly doubtful that its abolition will cure any of our major problems. On the other hand, regardless of how strongly opposed my constituents may prove to be to the creation of, and participation in, an ever stronger United Nations Organization, I could not follow such a policy in that field unless it becomes clearly hopeless."[1]

A TWO-WAY JOB

As believers in democracy, probably most Americans would agree that it is the duty of congressmen to follow public opinion insofar as it expresses the desires, wants, needs, aspirations, and ideals of the people. Most Americans probably would also consider it essential for their representatives to make as careful an appraisal of these needs and desires as they can, and to consider, in connection with such an appraisal, the ways and means of accomplishing them. Legislators have at hand more information about legal structures, economic problems, productive capacities, manpower possibilities, and the like, than the average citizen they represent. They can draw upon that information to inform and lead the people—by showing the extent to which their desires can be realized.

In other words, a true representative of the people would follow the people's desires and at the same time lead the people in formulating ways of accomplishing those desires. He would lead the people in the sense of calling to their attention the difficulties of achieving those aims and the ways to overcome the difficulties. This means also that, where necessary, he would show special interest groups or even majorities how, according to his own interpretation and his own conscience, their desires need to be tempered in the common interest or for the future good of the nation.

Thus the job of a congressman is a two-way one. He represents his local area and interests in the national capital, and he also informs the people back home of the problems arising at the seat of government and how these problems affect them. It is in the nature of the congressman's job that he should determine, as far as he can, public opinion in his own constituency and in the whole nation, analyze it, measure it in terms of the practicability of turning it into public policy, and consider it in the light of his own knowledge, conscience, and convictions. Occasionally he may be obliged to go against public opinion, with the consequent task of educating or reeducating the people along lines that seem to him more sound. And finally, since he is a human being eager to succeed at his important job of statesmanship and politics, he is realistic enough to keep his eyes on the voters in terms of the next election. But he understands that a mere weather-vane following of majority public opinion is not always the path to reelection. . . .

NOTE

1. In an address on "The Legislator" delivered at the University of Chicago on February 19, 1946. *Vital Speeches*, May 15, 1946, pp. 468–72.

CONGRESSIONAL ETHICS

With the notoriety given to some celebrated cases of wrongdoing by certain members of Congress, it is no wonder that the popular perception of the average congressman is that he is at least guilty of conflict of interest, and perhaps even a crook.

Researchers for the Ralph Nader Congress Project, under the direction of Mark Green, make a strong case for the proposition that a good many, if not most, congressmen engage in activities that violate the public trust and, indeed, frequently border on the illegal. For example, the Nader group points to the widespread practice of congressmen maintaining their law practices while serving in Congress—a situation that almost inevitably invites conflict of interest problems.

If Nader and his associates are upset over this aspect of congressional ethics, the perceptions of congressmen themselves on this matter appear to be a bit different. Edmund Beard and Stephen Horn of the Brookings Institution, after conducting interviews with a sample of congressmen, conclude that what is called conflict of interest by outside observers is not always defined that way by members of Congress. And if some members of Congress view a particular action as a conflict of interest, as for example, when a congressman accepts a ride on an airplane owned by a corporation, it is not considered a conflict by other congressmen.

Given the mixed views that congressmen have, it is hardly surprising that they have had difficulty policing conflict of interest, even though the public seems to demand a higher standard of ethics and accountability today than ever before.

Lawmakers as Lawbreakers

Mark Green

> *It could probably be shown by facts and figures that there is no distinctly American criminal class except Congress.*
>
> —*Mark Twain*

When national leaders cried out for "law and order" in the late sixties and early seventies, no one thought to apply their words to themselves. Now we know better. If nothing else, Watergate—which has become as much a cliché as a lesson—should have instructed us that it is folly to assume that people of prominence and power will invariably be law-abiding. A good place to apply this wisdom is the American Congress. The most obvious reason is symbolic: if chosen people have the power to make the law, then they should respect the law. If they do not, they can scarcely expect that others will.

Corruption involving criminal conduct has shaken Congress at least since 1873, when the House censured two members for their roles in the Crédit Mobilier stock scandal. While Congress and the country have passed through fundamental metamorphoses since then, one constant theme has been the public's suspicion of the people it sends to Washington. This was not the constitutional mistrust that had plagued the Founding Fathers—the gnawing fear that people in power would become tyrants. Instead, it was the suspicion of personal venality, that those in government were somehow turning a profit.

In 1965, Gallup pollsters found that four times as many people thought that "political favoritism and corruption in Washington" were rising as thought them falling. Two years later, as Congress washed its hands of Adam Clayton Powell, Gallup asked whether the revelations about Powell had surprised the public. Sixty percent thought that Powell's offenses—which the

From *Who Runs Congress?*, 4th ed., pp. 221–34, 269–76. By Mark Green, with Michael Waldman, and an Introduction by Ralph Nader. Copyright © 1972, 1975, 1979, 1984 by Ralph Nader.

questionnaire called "misuse of government funds"—were fairly common. (Twenty-one percent disagreed.) Powell had protested, in victimized anguish, that he was only one public scapegoat among many quiet offenders. "There is no one here," he said to his accusers, "who does not have a skeleton in his closet."

The skeletons vary in size. The smallest are the personal peccadilloes—which are the stuff of public amusement, scorn, and regular exposure by Washington columnists. Outweighing these in importance are the systematic violations of Congress's own rules and laws, offenses which are not quite crimes, but which are the next biggest skeletons in congressional closets. Finally, there is the *summum malum* of congressional crime, instances of bribery, perjury, and influence-peddling. Taken together the pervasiveness of lawbreaking amounts to a grim commentary on those who govern us.

NOT QUITE A CRIME: PECCADILLOES, RULES, AND LAWS

Congressmen are people, and subject to the same temptations and flaws as other people. At times their visibility makes them suffer more for their failings than they otherwise would. An omission or mistake which would pass unnoticed in a plumber may become big news when attached to a politically important name. This does not excuse congressional misconduct. Just as the public expects higher standards of personal morality from those who instruct its children than from those who fix its pipes, so it expects high standards from those who make its laws.

In order to assure them freedom to exercise their duties free from harassment, congressmen are granted immunity from arrest for statements made, or actions taken, in Congress or while coming from or going to Congress. This desirable privilege, however, has frequently ben abused by congressmen caught in unsavory escapades. In his prepresidential days, for example, Senator Warren Harding was surprised by two New York policemen while visiting friend Nan Britton in a hotel room. As the police prepared to arrest him on charges of fornication, carnal knowledge, and drunken driving, Harding successfully argued that as a senator he could not be arrested. It was hardly what the Constitution intended for congressional immunity, but it worked well in that situation.

Several years ago Texas Representative Joe Pool rammed his car into the back of another car stopped at a red light. Pool refused to accept a traffic ticket from a policeman and, later, from his sergeant. Instead he repeated over and over, "I am a congressman and I cannot be arrested." Unimpressed, the police held him for six hours before releasing him. "He kept saying he was a congressman," said the policeman, "but he didn't look like one or sound like one." Later Pool confided to a friend, "I thought they couldn't arrest a congressman unless he'd committed a felony. But it turns out they *can* unless he's en route to or returning from a session in Congress."

They *can*, but they *don't*. On the way to a party in the summer of 1972, Mississippi Representative Jamie Whitten—who normally conducts himself with decorum—ran a stop sign in Georgetown and struck a car, an iron fence, two trees, a brick wall, and another car on the other side of the wall. Whitten said his accelerator stuck, but an investigating officer said at the scene, "The guy's been drinking; there's alcohol on his breath. I don't think he's drunk. But he's shook up." No arrest was made and no charges were filed. "The first thing [Whitten] did," said the owner of the wall, "was to get out of the car and begin shaking everyone's hand." . . .

Annoying as these cases might be, they are small potatoes. They involve single, unplanned romps, not deliberate self-enrichment or serious affairs of state. If this were the extent of congressional lawlessness, we could require a special driver's education course as a condition of entering Congress or the Oval Office and sleep a little easier at night.

But it's not. Worse is the hypocrisy of congressmen abusing their own rules. Consider, for example, junketing.

Congressmen who legislate about foreign affairs or military bases may do a better job if they've seen some of the areas for themselves. That's the theory, and it's valid for some. In practice, however, many trips are personal vacations with family rather than public fact-finding. In 1971, then Senator William Saxbe had a dismal 45 percent roll-call record because of his many excursions. "I took every free trip I could get," admitted the candid Saxbe. "I like to travel." In the same year, 51 percent of Congress—53 senators and 221 representatives—took foreign trips at public expense; the total cost to taxpayers was $1,114,386. Hong Kong and the Caribbean turned out to be favorite destinations for those supposedly seeking self-education. By 1977, 255 representatives or senators (47 percent) took a total of 415 trips costing $1,532,326. "Scratch hard in December," one congressman has joked, "and you'll come up with a quorum in Hong Kong." There may even be motives beyond the chance of a vacation. "Those who do get away," Jerry Landauer wrote in the *Wall Street Journal*, "will enjoy little-known opportunities [double-billings, for example] for lining their own pockets—opportunities that some have exploited in the past."

In August of 1981 so many members left Washington to go abroad that Congress looked like the UN at the end of a session. For example: seven members went on an eighteen-day trip to New Zealand, Australia, and Southeast Asia; five left for a week to Bermuda and Panama; eight flew off for eighteen days to four African countries; two went to visit four European capitals for three weeks; several were destined for China and Japan. Beyond such full-scale trips is the frequent use of expensive military aircraft as a kind of personal shuttle service which congressional rules say is to be used only "when travel is in the national interest and commercial travel is not available." *U.S. News & World Report* says that more than a quarter of the Congress used the Air Forces's 89th Wing for such travel—costing taxpayers

$2 million in 1982—travel, the magazine said, that occurred even though commercial flights were often available. Senator Goldwater, for example, flew on a Navy A3 from D.C. to Las Vegas and back to attend a meeting of Navy pilots; although the commercial round-trip fare was $690, the special flight cost taxpayers $13,000. When Armed Services chairman John Tower was to be a guest speaker at West Point, the 89th flew him and his wife round trip for $5,555.* . . .

Large-scale juggling of committee rules and committee staff is also widespread. It is almost impossible, for example, to separate people who work for chairman Dan Rostenkowski from those who are supposed to serve the House Ways and Means Committee. This sort of thing springs less from any special avarice in chairmen's souls than from the committee and seniority systems. The fond references that a chairman will make to "my" committee show how deep the confusion runs. When a chairman lifts a researcher from "his" committee and puts him to work on some other task, more than the committee suffers. The system of fortresslike power bases, built around the mighty chairmen, grows stronger as well. Before his downfall, Senator Tom Dodd reportedly had thirteen of the twenty-one staff members of the Juvenile Delinquency subcommittee working for Dodd's office. Occasionally voices rise in complaint. In early 1975 a seven-part series in the *Washington Post* documented the exploitation of committee staff and field hearings in painstaking detail—naming names for those who cared.

Congressmen suffer equally mild twinges of conscience about using their own staff members for political campaigns. The element of abuse is clear: staff people are paid by the government, not by the senator or representative; they are paid to serve the office, not to help the man who happens to be in office to stay there. In 1968 the two senators Kennedy admitted that twenty of their staffers were working on Robert Kennedy's presidential campaign.

But it *is* illegal: Public Law 89–90 says an assistant can't be paid "if such does not perform the services for which he receives such compensation, in the offices of such Member . . ." Because the law is so widely violated, violation becomes custom, and custom replaces law. There are many instances of this phenomenon. Nearly all congressmen violated the archaic 1925 Federal Corrupt Practices Act (replaced in 1972), which aimed to limit campaign funding and to require some disclosure of campaign finances; yet no one has ever been prosecuted for it. An 1872 law directs House and Senate officials to deduct from a member's salary a day's pay for each day's absence, except for illness; in the last hundred years this has been done exactly twice, although there are unjustified absentees daily.

Nor is Congress always attentive even to international or constitutional

---

* Both chambers do prohibit lame ducks from traveling abroad after election day and before their retirement.

law. Former Representative John Rooney, for example, for years managed to obstruct American funding of the International Labor Organization because he disliked its allegedly leftist leanings. In so doing, he violated our UN obligation to help support the ILO. And an enterprising *Fort Worth Star-Telegram* reporter in 1974 discovered that at least twenty senators and representatives had odd requirements for staff positions, like "only a white girl, prefer Floridians" (Representative James Haley, D.-Fla.): "white only" (Senator William Scott, D.-Va.): "attractive, smart, young, and no Catholics . . ." (Representative Albert Johnson, R.-Pa.). Indeed, that August the Congressional Office of Placement and Office Management had to delete discriminatory job requirements from some 80 percent of the job orders from 140 congressional offices. Senator John Glenn (D.-Ohio) calls Capitol Hill "the last plantation."

Violation of equal opportunity standards is only one of several laws members of Congress might violate—*if* they permitted the law to apply to them. But since they are the lawmakers, they have decided that they are above the following laws that private employers and citizens have to observe:

- Equal Pay Act. This law guarantees women the same pay that men receive everywhere, except on Capitol Hill.
- Age Discrimination in Employment Act. Workers between the ages of 40 and 65 are protected from discrimination by this law, except in Congress.
- The National Labor Relations Act. Congress is exempt from this law, which requires employers to recognize unions, and protects employees from unfair labor practices.
- Fair Labor Standards Act. This law, which set minimum wage, overtime pay, and child labor standards, affects all institutions except Congress.
- The Civil Rights Act of 1964. It forbids discrimination on the basis of race, color, religion, sex or national origin—but does not apply to Congress.
- Freedom of Information Act. Congress ordered the executive branch to open its files to the public, under this law, but decided to keep its own records closed to the people who pay the congressmen's salaries.
- Conflicts of interest. Federal law prohibits executive branch employees from participating in federal transactions involving companies in which they have a financial interest. Members of Congress have no such restriction.
- State and municipal taxes. Members are exempt from paying local income taxes in Maryland, Virginia, and Washington, D.C.
- Privacy Act. Congress ordered the executive branch to tightly guard the personal records of individual citizens, but exempted itself from the law.
- Occupational Safety and Health Act. This law requires all employers, except in Congress, to maintain federal health and safety standards in the workplace . . .

CONFLICTS OF INTEREST

Congress correctly demands a high standard of impartiality from those it confirms for executive and judicial appointments. In 1969, when President Nixon tried and failed to get Judge Clement Haynsworth onto the Supreme Court, the most compelling reason against the nomination was that Haynsworth had tried cases involving businesses in which he held small bits of stock. When industrialist David Packard was nominated as assistant secretary of defense, Congress required that he put $300 million of his personal fortune in a "blind trust," one which manages the money entirely out of Packard's sight. The rationale behind these requirements is biblical and clear: since no man can serve two masters, Congress insists that federal officials put their private interests aside before assuming public duties.

Unfortunately this diligence stops when it comes to the congressmen themselves. No one insists that members sell sensitive shares of stock. The only group with the power to screen the members—their voting constituency—is usually too ill informed to make any serious judgment. And such conflicts are not considered a crime. In many states they violate the law, but not in Congress, simply because Congress, which writes the laws, chooses not to call what it does illegal.

With so few barriers against it, potential conflict of interest becomes commonplace in Congress. "If everyone abstained on grounds of personal interest," former Senator Robert Kerr claimed, "I doubt if you could get a quorum in the United States Senate on any subject." Kerr's own position neatly illustrated the problem. As a multimillionaire oilman from Oklahoma, Kerr stood to lose or gain huge sums, depending on the government's tax rules for oil. As a powerful member of the Senate Finance Committee, Kerr was one of the men who decided what the tax laws would be. It does not take long to see the conflict. "Hell," Kerr bragged, "I'm in everything."

This pattern extends to other business holdings. From evidence turned up in 1976 financial disclosure forms, *Congressional Quarterly* reported that 44 representatives had holdings in one of the top 100 defense contractors, 48 had real-estate interests, 41 held oil or gas stock, and 20 were in pharmaceuticals. That year 12 representatives and 9 senators had direct or family interests in commercial radio or television stations and 81 House members reported an ownership interest in or income from banks, savings and loan associations, or bank holding companies—including 2 on the Banking Committee and 8 on Ways and Means. . . .

One of the few congressmen who have bothered to defend such self-serving behavior openly is multimillionaire Senator Russell Long of Louisiana. Like Kerr, Long is an oilman. In the five years before 1969, for example, his income from oil was $1,196,915. Of that, $329,151 was tax-free, thanks to the curious oil depletion allowance. Long was for years chairman, and is now the ranking minority member, of the Senate Finance Committee, which recommends tax plans, including oil depletion clauses, to the Senate. A conflict of interest? Not to Long. "If you have financial interests completely parallel to [those of] your state," he explained, "then you have no problem." What Long is saying is that each senator is the sufficient judge of his own propriety. Once he convinces himself that his companies are really in the best interest of his folks back home, "then you have no problem." It must ease Long's conscience to know that he is helping others when he helps himself.

Occasionally there are men for whom even these lush fringe benefits of political office are not enough. They count the moments wasted which they must spend on the tedium of bills and votes. Such a man was George Smathers. Even while serving as a Florida senator, Smathers was melancholy. "A person with my background can make more money in thirty days [as a lobbyist]," he said, "than he can in fifteen years as a senator."

In preparation for the easy days ahead Smathers spent the closing days of his Senate career collecting IOUs from private interests. According to *Newsday*, Smathers led a posse of Florida congressmen in a secret attempt to salvage a floundering Florida company, Aerodex. Because of what the Air Force called "poor quality work which was endangering the Air Force pilots and aircraft," the Defense Department wanted to cancel a several-million-dollar contract with Aerodex. After Smathers's effort the contract stood.

In 1969, when Smathers retired, he claimed some benefits. He became a director of Aerodex and got an attractive deal on stock: $435,000 worth of it for $20,000. The company also put Smathers's Washington law firm on a $25,000-a-year retainer. Smathers is now comfortably installed as a lobbyist, fulfilling his earlier exuberant prediction that "I'm going to be a Clark Clifford. That's the life for me."

A second routine conflict involves personal use of campaign funds, what the *New Republic* referred to in a seminal 1982 article as "an outright abuse of the system [that] is neither isolated nor inconsequential." "Although House rules prohibit personal use of campaign funds," said Lisa Myers in an NBC report, "they are conveniently silent on where the campaign ends and where living high on the hog begins." She went on to point out the example of Representative Robert Badham (R.–Calif.), who out of his 1982 campaign funds spent $4,758 to take his wife to Germany, Bermuda, and Panama and $1,467 for three designer dresses. He explained, "I have a pretty wife who is my first campaign asset. Anything, therefore, that puts her in a good exposure light with me . . . *is* beneficial to the campaign." Some members simply pocket surplus campaign money when they retire. The House in December 1979 prohibited future representatives from such conduct but permitted it for themselves. So when John Dent retired in 1978, he kept $44,033 to buy a Florida condominium; Mendel Davis and John Wydler in 1980 diverted $45,047 and $38,510, respectively, to personal use when they decided not to seek reelection. This self-dealing bothers Representative Andy Jacobs, who has introduced legislation to stop the practice. "Campaign contributions involve a trust they will be spent for the purpose for which they were given," he says.

A third important type of conflict of interest comes from congressmen who maintain legal practices. The moral problem here is subtler than that of the oilmen or bankers. A lawyer's business, like a doctor's or writer's, is built on reputation and skill. But when a lawyer also holds government office, his clients might conclude that he can do more for them than another person of similar talent. A widely circulated, widely respected study by the New York City Bar Association strongly condemns the lawyering congressmen. They are the fiduciaries of the public—administrators of public functions, the 1969 bar study says. Accordingly, they must administer this public trust for the public's benefit, not their own. Instead, "law practices have played a disproportionate role in the history of congressional scandals." . . .

An 1863 statute forbids congressmen-lawyers from representing clients who have claims before the federal government. To avoid embarrassing problems while keeping the business thriving, congressmen used to have an ingenious "two-door" system. On the front door of the law firm was the congressman's name; through this door came the many clients who valued his help. Another door was just the same, except the congressman's name was missing. Here entered those proscribed clients with claims before the government. The ruse was within the letter of the law, but it still irritated purists. Journalist Robert Sherrill, for example, wrote that former representative Emanuel Celler's double doors were "one of the longest-standing and most notorious embarrassments to Congress." To this, Celler had a standard reply: "Your constituents are the final arbiter of any conflicts, and I'm always re-elected."

In 1972, after fifty years in the House, Emanuel Celler lost in his Brooklyn Democratic primary to Elizabeth Holtzman.

In 1976 there were still 66 members who reported at least $1,000 in income from outside law practice. During the debate over the ethics bill in 1977 some member-lawyers warned about the impact outside earnings limits would have on their practices. "There are four guys here who have admitted to me they earn more than $130,000 from outside law practice," said Representative David Obey (D.–Wis.), head of a major House inquiry into its ethical practices, in an interview. "One of them told me, 'I don't spend any time practicing law. As my seniority and committee influence increases, these groups keep throwing more business to my firm and I get my cut.'"

As a result of this cashing in of public trust for private gain, the House in 1982 limited outside legal income to 30 percent of congressional pay, or $20,000. There is no limit, however, in the Senate. The tradition of the two-door congressmen survives. . . .

THE CONGRESSIONAL RESPONSE

Timeless customs, inherited from the night-long vigils of tribal societies, bind members of a group together. The doctors' unwritten code discourages one from testifying against another. Opposing lawyers are forbidden to criticize each other in court. Congress, too, watches out for its own. For nearly two centuries after its founding, Congress traditionally adopted a laissez-faire policy on ethics, assuming that each individual member wanted to police his own conduct. Congress, for example, has never attempted to define for its members and the public what constitutes a "conflict of interest." Senate rules have never barred a member from voting when he or she has a personal stake; across the rotunda, House rules vaguely advise representatives not to vote when they have "a direct or pecuniary interest." Only the increasing numbers of indicted legislators and the Watergate, Koreagate, and Abscam scandals provided the necessary shove for each chamber to take more formal steps toward self-regulation. In both houses the immediate response was a two-part system: the establishment of ethics committees and the requirement of financial disclosure.

If the name "Ethics Committee" is encouraging, its creation was not. The Senate Select Committee on Ethics had an almost accidental conception. Its parent was the special Senate investigating committee which dug into Bobby Baker's past.* The committee's chairman, Senator Everett Jordan, made it clear to his colleagues that the group might be questioning senators' employees, but was "not investigating senators." That satisfying setup might have lasted indefinitely, save for the Senate's absentmindedness. At a routine session in 1964 a motion came up to establish a committee to investigate senators themselves. An aide to Clifford Case recalls what happened:

> John Sherman Cooper offered the motion to set up the select committee and, to his and everybody else's amazement, it passed. I remember because I was on the floor talking with Senator Case. . . . As he talked with me he was listening to the tally and suddenly he broke off and said, "It's going to pass," and he went over to congratulate Cooper, and Cooper was looking stunned. Mansfield, who was nonplussed and didn't know what to do next, said "We'll have to consult the lawyers," and they recessed. It was one of the funniest things I've ever seen.

The Senate took to its new offspring with all the glee of a father who has found an illegitimate child dumped on his doorstep. For two years no senators were assigned to seats on the committee. Few were eager to judge their peers. Even reformer Paul Douglas (D.-Ill.) turned down an offer, his aide said, because "he didn't have the stomach for it." John Stennis of Mississippi finally stood where others had faltered; with Stennis as its first chairman the

---

* Bobby Baker, former secretary to the Senate majority leader, Lyndon Johnson, was indicted and convicted of fraud, larceny, and tax evasion in 1966—*Editors*.

Ethics Committee was ready for action in 1966. Its nominal powers were impressive: it was to take complaints, investigate alleged misconduct, and recommend disciplinary action.

Tom Dodd's case was the first to come before the committee, which, to the surprise of many, took the difficult step of recommending that Dodd be censured. Even while doing so, however, the committee shied away from some of the most serious complaints against Dodd. "How will Americans ever learn about patterns of privilege and conflict of interest," complained one of those who had exposed Dodd, "if only 10 percent of his unethical activities—and those the least important—are made public?"

Fears that the Ethics Committee might act aggressively as a partisan tool of the majority proved groundless, not because the Republicans and Democrats each were given six seats, but because the committee did relatively little. By 1975 the Senate committee had only two staff employees and a paltry budget of $54,000—almost all going to the staff.

The House Ethics Committee (officially called the Committee on Standards of Official Conduct) was established in 1967 after a 400–0 vote ("Who can vote against ethics?" a California representative asked). In its first three years of operation it conducted just two preliminary investigations—one of Representative Cornelius Gallagher and another of "ghost voting" (the trick by which members have their votes recorded at times when they are actually away from the Capitol). "If my acknowledging only two preliminary investigations makes it sound like we don't do any work," said a member of the committee's staff at that time, "then it will just have to sound that way." Indeed, in its first nine years of operation, the committee never *formally* investigated a representative. It didn't until Common Cause literally shamed it into investigating Representative Sikes's conflicts of interest.

The first major investigation the House Ethics Committee felt worth its time and money was a futile attempt to discover who leaked a secret committee report on the CIA to CBS correspondent Daniel Schorr. When it came to scandals involving possibly illegal conduct by legislators, however, the two ethics committees seemed less eager. Congress's institutional reluctance to investigate itself appeared hypocritical, coming so soon after investigations by two congressional committees forced a President to resign from office. The same Congress that investigated conflicts of interest among Nixon's staff still allowed its banking committee members to own bank stock. John Gardner, then chairman of Common Cause, called the ethics committee in the House "the worst kind of sham, giving the appearance of serving as policeman while extending a marvelous protective shield over members of Congress." . . .

While the ethics committees gave guidance and little else, the public became increasingly outraged by what seemed to be a continuing stream of revelations about congressional corruption. A Harris poll conducted in 1977 for the House Ethics Committee indicated that of eleven institutions, the public ranked Congress ninth in integrity, slightly better than large corporations and labor unions. As a result, the House established a special Commission on Administrative Review to look into possible ethics, committee, and administrative reforms. The commission, chaired by Representative David R. Obey (D.-Wis.), proposed a new more stringent code of ethics for the House, highlighted by broad financial disclosure rules, an end to office slush funds, an $8,625 ceiling on annual outside earned income by members, and limitations on the franking privilege and foreign travel. . . .

The cornerstone of these recommendations is the sweeping requirement of disclosure. The financial disclosure provisions for the House, and a similar version for the Senate, require that congressmen report the source and amount of all income and gifts over $100; any gifts of transportation, food, entertainment, or reimbursement totaling more than $250; the approximate value of any financial holding having a fair market value of at least $1,000; and the identity of any debt of more than $2,500, unless it is a mortgage. Most controversial by far, though, was the proposed limitation on outside earned income to 15 percent of salary. Earned income includes money generated by work that requires a substantial investment of time and effort (law practice, speechmaking), but does not include dividends, capital gains, and family business income. This standard presumes that members of Congress should be full-time public officials.

In the 96th and 97th Congresses, Abscam has had one strongly positive result: the de facto adoption of a "felony rule" by Congress. Every congressman convicted of a felony in Abscam was expelled, forced to resign, or retired by the voters. This is a good precedent, but it is still too informal. Congress should codify what it now appears to (and should) believe: that a felon should not sit in Congress. This aside, the trends have not been hopeful.

As memories of Watergate began to fade and the so-called Koreagate scandal began to bore even the guilty, the push for ethics and reform on Capitol Hill rapidly lost momentum in the 95th Congress. Its members were already taking for granted a pay raise nearly equal to the median family income in America and were regretting all the outside income they had sacrificed to what many saw as a temporary hysteria for ethics.

A backlash spread. Suddenly, by 1978, "ethics" and "reform" became dirty words in the halls of Congress. A package of reforms developed by the Obey Commission, to improve administration of the House and establish a grievance procedure for Capitol employees, was defeated. The House voted against the public financing of congressional elections. Congress did pass an ethics bill dealing largely with the executive and judicial branches—only after House leaders quelled an attempt to repeal the 15 percent limitation on outside earned income.

Even Representative Obey, author of several frustrated reforms, observed that Congress "just got so damn fed up seeing the House broad-brushed by every damn demagogue in the country and nobody back home is being told how much we've reformed. . . . If you've got a bum the people to blame are the people who elected him, not the people who have to work with him." According to Illinois Democrat Morgan Murphy, "The whole atmosphere here—with all these investigations—is that a majority of the members of Congress are crooks or have something to hide. There's a suspicion every time you call someone in the bureaucracy on behalf of a constituent that you're doing someone a favor because you owe him something. The pendulum has swung too far since Watergate."

Obey and Murphy each have a piece of the truth. The House has adopted several important reforms; and most members of Congress aren't crooks. Indeed, many are models of probity, independent of the existence or extent of any ethics code. Former senators Wayne Morse and Paul Douglas began publicly disclosing their financial holdings years ago. Senator Charles Percy put his $6 million fortune in the hands of a blind trust in the 1960s. His predecessor, Paul Douglas, also refused all contributions for personal expenses or from people with a financial interest in matters before the Senate. Former Representative Ken Hechler (D.-W.Va.) gave up his commission as an Army reserve colonel—one year short of a guaranteed $220-per-month pension—when the House considered a military pay bill which would have boosted his pension about 10 percent.

But such exemplars are measures of how far their colleagues have to go. It is difficult to ignore that the 1970s saw the greatest documentation of congressional corruption in this century. True, the people of a district may elect a "bum," but this individual influences policies that affect 434 other districts and 49 other states. If the scandals of the past decade were not enough to motivate Congress to prohibit convicted members from serving as chairmen, prohibit members with substantial commercial interests from chairing committees with jurisdiction over such interests, require the public funding of campaigns, insist that its ethics committees investigate charges of corruption and censure rather than wrist-slap those guilty of corruption, then one wonders what will be necessary to spur Congress to complete its cleanup.

Few, if any, people run for public office with the secret intent of profit by illegal means. Rather, there is something in the congressional environment which raises this temptation and then lowers resistance—a something that may well inhere in the legislative process itself. Laws can seriously affect important people; politicians need money to stay in office; important people can give money to politicians in order to influence them. Thus there are two sides to the coin of the congressional power: there is the potential to improve the lot of all Americans and there is the potential of corruption.

It would be polite to end a discussion of congressional lawlessness by intoning that, while there are a few rotten apples, the overwhelming majority of congressmen are honest. This appears true, but how would we know? Existing public financial disclosures do not tell us enough, nor are the ethics committees vigilant enough to make us sanguine. By failing to police itself adequately, Congress—especially given the cynicism inspired by Watergate and other scandals—has failed to elevate itself above suspicion. A critical observer can hardly take heart at the number of congressmen and staff who have been caught. There are no cops regularly patrolling Capitol Hill corridors, and law enforcement agencies usually do not devote resources to congressional crime. The luckless few are exposed more by fluke than by investigation, which predictably leads friends and cynics alike to wonder not so much what congressmen do as how many of them get away with it. . . .

Conflict of Interest: The View From the House

Edmund Beard and Stephen Horn

Any congressional behavior that is not designed to advance the common interests of constituents and country might be termed conflict of interest. But this generalization is not useful, neglecting as it does the many complexities and ambiguities of congressional service. At one extreme, conflict of interest becomes corruption; at the other, it merges with the legitimate representation of constituents.

A congressman is approached by many people other than the residents of his district—his own or the opposing party's leadership, colleagues, the President or his agents, and a host of representatives of private interests seeking the congressman's voice and vote. These groups can create divided loyalties for the congressman, and they can also offer a variety of material and nonmaterial rewards for his cooperation.

Congressmen lament about the special burdens and contradictions that characterize their responsibilities—problems they feel the public and the media do not recognize. A legislator is simultaneously expected to represent the interests of his constituency and of the nation as a whole, but these interests may not always be identical, and, even when they are substantially complementary, other claims to limited federal resources may be more valid. This ambiguity of role creates some of the most intense ethical dilemmas faced by congressmen.

The problem of conflicting national and constituent interests is complicated because most legislators feel that if they consistently oppose the interests of the constituency, even when those interests are quite narrowly conceived, their prospects for continued tenure are bleak, and they are likely to be replaced by more compliant representatives. This situation forces a pattern of ad hoc compromise whereby competing images of constituency interests and national interests are held in tandem while the representative sometimes attempts to "educate" his district and at other times works wholeheartedly for narrow constituent benefits. Some legislators see their role merely as that of a promoter of constituency interests and never confront such conflicts. For a great many legislators, however, such dilemmas are a real part of congressional life.

Related problems arise over the meaning of "constituency." Is a constituency simply a majority of the population or of the voting-age population? Is it the members of one's own party since the other party would have elected someone else and in many cases worked actively in opposition? Is the constituency composed primarily of those who contributed the major part of one's campaign expenses and without whom one might not have been elected? Is the district characterized by its largest employers? These are questions that confront all legislators and that touch in one way or another on many of the unresolved issues discussed in this study. . . .

FIVE POSSIBLE CONFLICTS

One analyst of the executive branch conflict of interest law passed in 1961 has defined five areas of possible conflict: self-dealing by a public official, discretionary transfer of economic value to a public official from a private source, assistance by public officials to private parties dealing with the government, postemployment assistance by former public officials to private parties dealing with the government, and private gain derived from information acquired in an official capacity.[1] Using this list as a guide, we will illustrate the distinction claimed . . . between the executive and congressional situations and the difficulty in defining congressional conflict of interest.

Self-Dealing by a Public Official

The implication of "self-dealing by a public official" is that public officials ought to disqualify themselves when a particular course of government action might significantly affect their personal economic interest. The difficulty with this notion when applied to the House of Representatives is that, unless congressmen are to have no source of income other than their salaries, it may be difficult for them to avoid situations that affect their own interests. A member of the executive branch charged with overseeing only one policy area may without undue hardship avoid personal holdings in that field. Congressmen cannot handle the problem that easily. As the late Senator Robert Kerr said, "If everyone abstained from voting on grounds of personal interest, I doubt if you could get a quorum in the United States Senate on any subject."[2]

In a recent study two researchers attempted to examine "associations between the personal financial holdings of members of the Ninetieth Congress and their roll-call responses on votes relevant to those holdings."[3] They analyzed eleven fields of interest: finance, defense, the antiballistic missile system, farming, transportation, broadcasting, electrical power, law, airlines, petroleum, and capital gains. Although the authors found apparent correlations between personal holdings in an industry and proindustry voting patterns in the case of electrical power and airlines, they found the opposite pattern in the case of farming, transportation, capital gains, and petroleum. In general, they discovered "few if any examples of self-serving in the U.S. House of Representatives."

The authors of the study did find differences between interested and disinterested members (those with or without relevant financial holdings) with respect to the size of winning coalitions. Members with relevant financial holdings showed a tendency to favor those holdings in close votes and were more likely than others to change their votes when a compromise alternative was offered. The authors pointed out in addition that "record votes on the floor are but a small part of the total legislative process" and that there may be errors in their findings because overly stringent standards may have caused them to overlook potentially interesting results. Furthermore, there may have been shortcomings in the financial data available or in the nature of the inquiry itself.

On the other hand, the findings may be accurate. As another observer has commented: "In the ordinary ranges of stock ownership the rewards from favoritism or worse are simply inadequate. The official runs all the risks of detection and obloquy but receives only one-thousandth or one-millionth of the proceeds. Even a narrow, grasping man will find this disproportion between risks and profits uninviting."[4] The benefits a congressman might get from favoring his stock holdings are not worth the risks he runs. A congressman risks less if he favors an interest for other deferred compensation such as future employment, which we will discuss later. In addition, a legislator's vote in favor of a certain stock holding may also benefit his constituents (depending on how they are defined). . . .

Congressmen believe that it is a common practice for their colleagues to promote personal interests that coincide with constituent interests [see Table 1]. Item 3, for example, in which a legislator owning $100,000 worth of savings and loan stock votes for a tax amendment favoring the savings and loan industry, was the most disapproved item in this group, presumably because of the size of the stock holding, yet the respondents did not believe that disapproval would prevent such behavior on the part of their colleagues. In general, these questionnaire responses support the interview conclusions that congressmen are not particularly worried about promoting personal interests that coincide with constituent interest. . . .

Outside business interests do present unnecessary and avoidable conflicts, but congressmen disagree widely about their legitimacy. There are three distinct opinions in Congress about such interests: that any time spent away from congressional business is improper; that although outside income is desirable, law practice is very conflict prone; and that outside business is acceptable, including law practice, which is no different from any other business and should not be discriminated against.

One northeastern Republican put the first case forcefully.

People invariably think of a conflict of financial interest, but the conflict in time is more important. Unless you give to the job all your time and energy, I think you have a conflict of interest. When I see it, it bothers me as I know I need between seventy and seventy-five hours a week to do this job. I just don't think a member should have outside professional and business interests.

A western Democrat exemplified the second position.

I have to maintain outside interests. What if I'm defeated tomorrow? What do I do? My business might be a fiction, but I keep it like a security blanket. It's something that I might have to use. I think the big problem is the lawyer/legislator. If I did what they do, I could be put in prison.

This critique was echoed by a southern Democrat.

The biggest criticism I can see is those attorneys who maintain an active law practice. A large percentage of that practice is generated because of their position in Congress. They are also the active members of the Tuesday-to-Thursday Club. If we could get them to come down here and work a five-day week, why we would be done with our work three months earlier.

Despite what several lawyer members saw as an apparent injustice in condemning law practice while allowing other business interests, many other members felt quite strongly that law ties presented special difficulties. As one western Democrat said bluntly: "The similarity of legal practice and congressional behavior is so close that it is an obvious channel for sanitized bribery and influence-peddling. Every major bribery effort of a public official goes through a law firm." "Double door" law firms with one "door" listing a congressman's name as a partner (for the nonfederal business) and another eliminating the name (for federal business) were often unfavorably mentioned.

Both of the positions above—that of abstaining totally from outside occupations and that of prohibiting only law practice—were disputed by several lawyer members. As a southern Democrat put it:

I think a member should have an outside interest. The worst single mistake I made, besides probably running for Congress, was to give up my law practice. I think you need—at least I need—an adequate income to support a family when you have several children in college at one time as I do.

Table 1
Mean scores on questionnaire items, group 6:
promoting personal interests that coincide with constituent interests

Questionnaire item	Mean Score	
	Judgment of practice*	Extent of practice**
(3) A legislator owns $100,000 worth of stock in a home-town savings and loan association and votes in favor of an amendment to a tax bill that benefits the savings and loan industry as a whole.	2.28	2.24
(37) A legislator owns 2,000 acres of cotton-producing land. He represents a constituency in which cotton is the major agricultural crop. He receives an assignment to the Committee on Agriculture where he actively works for higher price supports for cotton.	2.48	2.23
(38) A legislator is president of a local labor union. He wins election to Congress and is granted a two-year leave by his union executive board, which continues his pension and retirement rights. He is appointed to the committee with jurisdiction over labor matters. He works actively for repeal of the right-to-work laws and less restrictive federal controls over labor organizations.	2.56	2.20
(2) A legislator owns $5,000 worth of stock in a home-town savings and loan association and votes in favor of an amendment to a tax bill that benefits the savings and loan industry as a whole.	2.65	1.74

* Scoring for judgment of practice:
   1 = clearly unethical   3 = probably ethical
   2 = probably unethical 4 = clearly ethical

** Scoring for extent of practice:
   1 = most congressmen   3 = few
   2 = many   4 = none

Other members cited another important reason for maintaining an outside occupation and income. "I could survive without having a law firm partnership," one said, "but I think having the partnership gives me a feeling of independence as to what I do here. Otherwise my future will be up to the whims of local party officials." This argument also applies to independence from special interests. As a northern Republican noted:

I think that if you have a business or income connection, you can be very much more independent as a member of Congress. If you're defeated, you can go back

*to your profession. If you're a professor, you can get a job in a university. If you
have nothing to go back to, why you may become more dependent and less independent.*

Several members said that a legislator from a rural area may have more
time to pursue an outside interest than one from an active urban district may
have. The time conflict was not seen as much of a problem if, in fact, a member's district did not put time demands on him. This position overlooks the
possibility that a member less pressed by constituent demands could spend
more time on substantive legislative business. Nevertheless, several members did make the distinction. . . .

In their responses to questions about ties with law firms, congressmen
recognized the ethical problems an active law practice can entail, or even encourage. They also recognized, however, that a junior congressman who may
not be reelected should not have to cut himself off from his legal career. The
respondents saw a difference between a congressman who simply maintains
ties with his law firm and one who allows his law firm to profit from his congressional service. . . .

Judging from the responses to the questions in this study, congressmen
are unlikely to voluntarily limit the range of outside activities open to them.
There is a widespread feeling in Congress that outside business interests
(with the possible exception of a law practice) are legitimate and necessary,
either for personal financial security or for legislative independence. Coupled
with the unwillingness of congressmen to interfere with their colleagues'
personal habits or relations with their constituents, these attitudes protect
even law affiliation. The difficulty of regulating one particular activity, which
will certainly be considered unfair discrimination by those most affected,
makes it unlikely that outside law practice will be formally prohibited. . . .

Discretionary Transfer of Economic Value

The most extreme form of discretionary transfer of economic value from a
private source to a public official—the second area of possible conflict—is
bribery, which is illegal. There are many less extreme forms, however, that
also raise questions.

Even in cases of demonstrated bribery, the congressional situation is
unique. Congressmen are protected under the Constitution from arrests in
civil suits and for words written or spoken in the execution of their office.
Former Congressman John Dowdy of Texas was convicted of bribery, conspiracy, and perjury in a case involving the protection of a home improvement firm accused of fraud. In April 1973 an appeals court overturned the
bribery and conspiracy convictions. The court did not find that Dowdy was
innocent of the acts charged; rather, it ruled that his acts could be interpreted

as being in the line of his duty on a subcommittee and as such would be protected legislative acts, even if he was being bribed to so act.[5] The perjury conviction was left standing.

In 1963 the conviction of Congressman Thomas L. Johnson of Maryland on charges of receiving a bribe in exchange for giving a speech on the House floor was also overturned on these constitutional grounds. Johnson's speech, extolling savings and loan institutions, was reprinted and distributed by officers of a Maryland savings and loan company then under indictment. . . . Congressman Johnson was later convicted for a second time on federal conflict of interest charges and was sentenced to six months in prison.

The difficulties of trying to regulate behavior such as Johnson's floor speech are enormous. To be able to convict Johnson on the basis of his speech would jeopardize, for example, a member from an urban district who received large campaign contributions from labor interests and subsequently gave a speech in the House favorable to those interests. The latter is an example of legitimate political behavior and the promotion of constituency interests, as well as a common method of rewarding contributors. . . .

Many other unique circumstances surrounding congressional rewards from private sources blur the charge of conflict of interest. Just as no laws forbid congressmen to engage in outside business activity, none forbid them to accept honorariums, although legislation in 1974 limited payments for each speech or article to $1,000 and the total annual income from such activities to $15,000. Legislators commonly receive stipends for speaking before private groups, including those concerned with legislation before their committees. Two questionnaire items addressed this issue. One asked about a member who accepted a $1,000 honorarium from a group with which he had long been identified. The other asked about a member who accepted the same sum from a group, new to him, that was interested in upcoming legislation, while he was undecided how to vote on the issue. The respondents deemed the first situation probably ethical and widely practiced. They considered the second more unethical . . . but also fairly likely to be practiced. . . .

Honorariums can be treated as direct income. They are an obvious, and for many a very lucrative, discretionary transfer of economic value to a public official. Campaign contributions are a different matter. Nevertheless, they fall in the same category and may present many of the same conflicts.

Members of the House of Representatives must run for reelection every two years. In a closely contested district the costs of a primary and general campaign may run over $100,000. A congressman earning less than half that sum a year could not hope to manage such expenses on his own, and he is not expected to. He can use his salary and associated allowances to partially support his campaign, but he must raise a campaign fund to meet the bulk of his expenses. Although the amounts of money needed in an election campaign and the methods employed for raising funds vary greatly among members, the funds all come from the private sector.

Campaign funds and personal finances may complement each other, with an unclear line between expenses that should be charged to one or the other. Unexpended campaign funds can be used for political as opposed to personal expenses between campaigns. However, if a congressman does not have unused campaign funds, he pays for political expenses vital to his performance (or continuance) in office out of his own pocket. Many respondents reported that they used considerable amounts of their own funds to run their offices and to serve their constituents.

In addition to the trips that congressmen are authorized to take to their districts at government expense each year, they can use unexpended campaign funds to pay for additional trips home by including one political function. By visiting the district office, meeting with supporters, or addressing a local organization, a congressman can claim that the trip was political and charge it to excess funds, whether he spends most of the time at leisure with his family or not.

The respondents agreed that the use of campaign funds for activities that bear little relation to any campaign is improper.... The responses clearly reveal congressional disapproval of improper diversion of campaign money. When the activity in question has more to do with constituency service, congressmen approve it more. This pattern appeared often in this study and indicates distinctions that should be considered in reform proposals....

In the interviews, we asked questions about the extent to which congressmen would accept special favors from lobbyists. Specific questions referred to lobbyists paying the entertainment costs of legislators or lending them planes for personal travel or campaign purposes. Other questions dealt with the leasing or selling of automobiles to legislators at substantial discounts and the provision of free hotel rooms in the legislators' districts.

Overall, the congressmen saw very little wrong in most of these practices. Many reported that lobbyists had never paid for entertainment for groups of constituents or for political gatherings; others mentioned that it happened once in a while or that they had been to parties that were probably paid for by private interests. Those who recognize the practice were not particularly upset by it, believing it to be a legitimate campaign-associated activity.

The practice of using private planes for personal travel or campaigning also raised few eyebrows. Slightly less than half of the sample admitted to using planes that had been put at their disposal, although the majority stated that they did so occasionally rather than frequently. More than 10 percent of the sample, however, said that they used such planes often. Only a small number of congressmen said such activity was wrong. A western Republican said he was "wary of the practice," and a midwestern Republican said he considered it "questionable," but many others who did not report using private planes said this practice was inconvenient or unnecessary. (One southern legislator reported simply, "I don't go home.")

A midwestern Republican gave a typical response to a question about using airplanes belonging to others: "I think these planes come in handy. Nobody ever tried to collect from me because they hauled me around to a speech. Firms in my area do it for the Democratic senator and the national committeeman as well as myself." Another Republican from a border state agreed. "I don't think there is any real problem on this. I don't think anybody really expects anything. You are just one person on a committee, and unless you are the chairman I don't see how you can be too much help to them."

Most congressmen in the sample looked upon the provision of planes as a convenience that they would be foolish to ignore and as the sort of activity that does not create difficult bonds or debts. One eastern Republican who did not engage in the practice said, "I really can't think why I haven't done it, since I would do anything for the company anyhow because they're in my constituency." He added, however, "I guess it would look bad if I did take a ride on the plane." A large proportion of his colleagues did not agree. Much more common were comments such as this one from a western Democrat: "I was offered a trip on a DC-6, but it would take a week across the country in a DC-6. Both [major air frame companies] that have plants in my district made the offer. I turned it down for inconvenience. I don't think it's any problem."

Scarcely any congressmen thought it was wrong to accept free hotel rooms in their districts. Many reported that they enjoyed such benefits and considered it perfectly legitimate behavior. Many others said they did not receive such treatment and wished they did. A number of congressmen mentioned that it was possible to offend a constituent by refusing the offer of a hotel room or a complimentary dinner in a restaurant.

Many members thought that it was improper to accept discounts on car leases. One reported that he used to get the free use of a car from one of the major auto companies but that he "certainly cut it out once the Dodd case happened." Even though they disapproved, members knew of such arrangements, indicating that the practice was not completely rejected. In several cases the main complaint was that the discounts were a privilege reserved only for committee chairmen. "I told a friend of mine in Congress who has such an arrangement to send the person around, but he never came by. I'd certainly like to take advantage of it," one legislator said.

We asked the congressmen if they participated in inaugural airline trips. (An inaugural trip takes place when an airline opens service to a new location. The airline invites dignitaries on the initial flight. This can constitute a free vacation.) Very few saw anything wrong with accepting the trip. On the contrary, most members believed that travel helped them in their work by contributing to their understanding of world conditions. No one was offended by the junketing aspect of the trips, although several admitted to that dimension. A typical comment was:

I don't think it's a problem. I found it very helpful. I went to India on a TWA flight. I had never been there. We spent ten days there and I learned much more about India than I had ever known before. TWA has never asked me for a thing, and I have a better understanding of the country.

Others stated that they had not taken trips, but in the words of one: "It's been a matter of time, not ethics. I think it would be a good thing." Another noted: "I've never been invited on any and I regret it. It's all very disillusioning never to have been asked."

In a general discussion of government-paid travel by congressmen that grew out of the inaugural flight questions, most respondents said that much work did get done on the trips and that the diligent members on study/work trips well outnumbered those along for pleasure. Work and relaxation may enjoy a peaceful coexistence, however, as one comment demonstrates:

I can remember when I was on the Agriculture Committee, and the committee was going to Europe to investigate Public Law 480, and I found out they were taking two of the best-looking secretaries along who weren't necessarily the most competent. I protested to the chairman and told him that either they stayed home or I did. The result was that I stayed home.

Despite such reports, most of the congressmen resented the "junketing" label given to congressional travel and the skeptical attitude taken by many journalists. They felt that press stories often create unfair public bias against travel that damages hard-working members who seriously need to learn the effects of American policies abroad or to witness firsthand the practices and conditions in other nations. Former Speaker Sam Rayburn's boast that he had never been outside the United States was often cited by the congressmen as indicative of an unfortunate parochialism, not far removed from xenophobia. . . .

A common although initially surprising finding was that lobbyists paid little or no attention to many members. "As I said, I have never had a lobbyist take me to lunch and I'm frankly amazed, because it is different in my state legislature," was a common refrain. Those members who had served in state legislatures before being elected to Congress believed that standards of conduct were much lower in the state capitals than in Washington.

The apparently higher standard at the national level is not simply due to the fact that the greater responsibility or the year-round term of a national legislature brings out the best in its members or to the fact that there is much more probing and sophisticated journalistic coverage of Washington politics.

One reason for the higher level of conduct may be that the average member of Congress is ordinarily not worth as much to a lobbyist as the average member of a state legislature is. The House is a large and in many ways unwieldy body. The division of labor into committees and subcommittees that takes place in all legislatures is much greater in the 435-member House of Representatives than in, say, the 100-member Senate. House members usually serve on only one major committee, but in the U.S. Senate and in many state legislatures it is normal to serve on two, three, or even more committees. As a consequence, House members feel more remote from much of the legislation and from even the daily operations of Congress. . . .

The Other Potential Conflicts

With respect to the third possible conflict under consideration—public officials giving assistance to private parties dealing with the government—the dilemma caused by the demands of the legislator's role is immediately apparent. Constituents expect most congressmen to offer assistance in dealing with a huge and seemingly unresponsive government, and legislators view such service as vital to reelection.

The fourth possible conflict can occur when former public officials give assistance to private parties dealing with the government. Again the situations of congressmen and executive branch personnel are different. The latter presumably could offer special access to government deliberations only in the field (and indeed perhaps only in the bureau) in which they had been previously employed. Thus, to legislate a required period during which they could not deal with the bureau that had formerly employed them would be neither difficult nor excessively discriminatory. Congress, however, is not a bureau. A comparable prohibition would debar former members from lobbying Congress itself. Yet to prohibit retired or defeated members from such practice might be discriminatory. Moreover, the potential for the misuse of an executive official's knowledge of contemplated administrative actions has few parallels on the legislative side.

In any case, members are unlikely to vote such a restriction. Some of them look upon the possibility of service as a Washington representative as a form of insurance. The legislative process is what they know best. To preclude congressmen from this field would be unfair in their view.

In a related area, members of Congress were asked about the extent and effectiveness of former legislators serving as lobbyists, particularly because of their access to the House floor. The general response was that, with certain exceptions, ex-legislator lobbyists did not abuse their privileges. Several members noted that the floor is not a good place to lobby because members often leave the floor quickly when they are not needed so that they can attend to other responsibilities. . . .

Only in the last of the five suggested conflicts of interest—deriving private gain from the use of information acquired in an official capacity—is the situation of a congressman similar to that of a nonelected official. Clearly congressmen should refrain from using inside information. It is as improper for them to use information gained from executive sessions of a committee as it is for a member of a regulatory commission to do so. Because congressmen deal with many issues, however, they might consider themselves a special case and believe that they should not be prohibited from using inside information. But the organization of Congress, with its division of labor through the committee system, generally limits a congressman's access to useful inside information to those activities that come under the jurisdiction of his committee. Requesting a congressman to refrain from dealing in those specific matters would not constitute the same penalty as a more generalized prohibition. This might also prove a satisfactory way of limiting lobbying by ex-congressmen.

When we questioned congressmen about using information obtained in executive sessions of a committee for private gain, few of them cited evidence of members benefiting from such information. The responses were quite uniform: "There isn't much opportunity really—if you read the *Washington Post* you know as much as we do," or "You'd have to really hustle out of the committee room to have it work," or "There are a lot easier ways of getting rich around here if you really want to cheat." Congressmen generally suggest that rewards from committee assignments, if there are any, come in other forms. As one said, "I think you get a lot more of this in terms of campaign contributions.". . .

The range of possible congressional conflicts of interest is considerable. At one extreme are the unavoidable conflicts. As one member observed:

> *Obviously I have conflicts of interest in terms of Medicare, since I have a mother who is very old. I have a conflict of interest on education legislation since I have a little boy six months old. I have a conflict of interest on social security, since my mother is on it, and I'll eventually be on it.*

Most Americans recognize the inevitability of such conflicts and do not expect congressmen to disqualify themselves from votes on these issues. In a representative system conflicts of this kind are bound to appear since the legislators are selected from the population they represent. But the other extreme, of course, is outright bribery.

Once outside the boundaries of bribery and overt self-dealing, there is very little consensus, at least among our respondents, about what constitutes a legitimate or an illegitimate business or political transaction. . . .

NOTES

1. Roswell Perkins, "The New Federal Conflict of Interest Law," *Harvard Law Review*, vol. 26 (April 1963), pp. 1118–19.
2. Cited in Laurence Stern and Edwin Knoll, "Congress: When the Private Life of a Lawmaker Becomes a Public Affair," *Esquire*, April 1964, pp. 82–84.
3. James W. Lindeen and Shirley A. Lindeen, "Conflict of Interest in the U.S. House of Representatives: Some Preliminary Findings" (paper delivered at the Annual Meeting of the Midwest Political Science Association in Chicago, May 1973).
4. George Stigler, "The Economics of Conflict of Interest," *Journal of Political Economy*, vol. 75 (February 1967), pp. 100–101.
5. Article 1, Section 6 of the Constitution protects legislators against being "questioned in any other place" for legislative acts. This is commonly referred to as the "speech or debate" clause.

CHAPTER ELEVEN

THE PRESIDENCY

PRESIDENTIAL POWER

The first of the following selections is written by George Reedy, who served for a time as President Lyndon Johnson's press secretary. He maintains that the office of the presidency has evolved into something substantially more than the rather narrowly confined manage-rial role that the Founding Fathers intended for it. The net result of this evolution, ac-cording to Reedy, is that the President now dominates the federal establishment.

John Kenneth Galbraith, while willing to acknowledge that considerable power at-taches to the office of the presidency, nevertheless contends that a president's power is something less than is commonly perceived. According to him, this gap between the per-ception and the reality of presidential power results from several factors: the tendency to judge power in terms of actions rather than results; the inclination of those around the President to exaggerate his power because it serves to exaggerate their own; the attribu-tion, to the President alone, of power that in fact resides in the vast bureaucracy over which he presides; and finally, the failure to fully appreciate how circumstances and events in the real world severely constrain his ability to get his way.

The Presidential Advantage

George E. Reedy

...The theory of democracy is that power shall reside in the people and that they shall have an opportunity to register their desires at periodic intervals. But since the mood of the people is subject to repeated and unforeseen changes, the great problem has always been to combine the necessary continuing authority to rule with the necessary checks to prevent that rule from becoming despotic. The contribution of the men who wrote the American Constitution was the thesis that power could be divided and lodged in different institutions—the executive, the legislative, the judiciary—in such a way that no one of these institutions could ever gain a monopoly. The success of this thesis has been little short of amazing in that the United States has remained a reasonably democratic nation since 1789. But it is equally interesting that, in the process of history, the American government has undergone changes which have taken it far from the concepts set forth by the men of Philadelphia. The most interesting change has been in the power and the authority of the President.

The men who wrote the Constitution very obviously ascribed to the President a lesser role than the legislative in the field of policy. It was clear that he would manage the affairs of the government, both military and civil, and that he would represent the United States in its dealings with other nations. But his management was assumed to be within limits laid down by legislation; and in dealing with other nations what he represented was supposed to be determined by Congress. There was little realization that his role as an activist would place the President in an advantageous position from which his domination of the federal establishment became an inevitability.

In our managerial-oriented society, where administrative techniques have been raised to the status of an intellectual discipline in leading universities, we are all conscious of the direct relationship between the capacity to launch action and the control over the instruments and resources which make the action possible. To us it is self-evident that the chief executive officer, who administers payrolls, the collection and disbursement of funds, and the activities of production and sales, will determine the policies of a corporation until he is replaced by a successor. He can be harassed by stockholders, his life can be made difficult by an unfriendly board of directors. But even though the stockholders, and their representatives on the board of directors, can cause a shift in policy by firing their chief executive officer and bringing in a replacement, it is still *the new man* who will make corporate policy. Presumably, he will take into account the forces that placed him in office. But the extent to which he *must* do so is determined only by his political skill. And he is in a position almost daily to make commitments for the corporation of such a nature that the stockholders and directors have little alternative other than to acquiesce. They can, of course, get rid of him but this is a step that is usually taken only when provocation is extreme. Once he has his basic budget approved, he has the power of initiative—the power to initiate lawsuits, specific expenditures, sales campaigns, and new production models, and all these steps have self-perpetuating forces built into them. It is entirely possible for any corporate manager to lead his firm in a direction diametrically opposite from that intended by his stockholders without abusing any of his authority or usurping any undue prerogatives. He can do it merely by day-to-day decisions which *must* be made by someone and which *cannot* be made by a committee.

This concept was not very clear to the Founding Fathers. They thought of usurpation of power only in terms of bad law, ignored law, or violated law. They felt that the capacity of human reasoning to determine or alter human destiny was limited only by the quality of the intellects that could be brought to bear, by the physical environment, and by the relative balance of coercive powers in a society. As sophisticated men, they had little faith in human wisdom but thought it was perfectible through discussion. They accepted the physical environment philosophically as having both advantages and disadvantages (difficult trade routes from Europe to the New World were also difficult invasion routes). And they sought to create a balance of coercive powers which would cancel each other out. Their reaction was both rational and adequate to the times. No one then could have foreseen the rise of our interdependent society with its almost minute division of labor creating social forces that have a life of their own.

They made the President commander-in-chief of the armed forces. But they counterbalanced his power by lodging in the Congress the authority to raise and support those forces and by guaranteeing the people the inviolable right to bear arms.

They made the President the sole spokesman in the field of foreign affairs. But they counterbalanced this power by lodging in the Senate the sole right to pass upon the validity of treaties.

They made the President responsible for staffing the executive agencies which would administer the nation's business. But they counterbalanced this power by lodging in the Senate the right to approve or disapprove his key appointees and in the House of Representatives the right to initiate appropriation of the funds needed to run the government.

They made the President (of course, acting through an agent) the prosecutor of offenses against the government. But they specified that adjudication of the charges would be handled through an independent judiciary.

When to all this was added the power of impeachment (carefully structured so it could not be managed in a frivolous fashion), it would appear that the Founding Fathers had performed a superb job of employing reason to devise safeguards for freedom. What they had not reckoned with was the ability of the "manager" to make commitments which could not easily be revoked.

The clearest example in our history was presented by Theodore Roosevelt, who in 1907 wanted to send America's navy around the world on a "goodwill" tour. The proposal engendered a considerable amount of heat. Roosevelt's propensity for extravagant and somewhat overly masculine language had aroused fears as to his intentions. It was felt that he was uncomfortably enamored of foreign adventures and might be preparing to annex foreign territory in accordance with the traditions already established by the great imperialistic powers of Western Europe. The debate raged in Congress. Roosevelt could not send the navy (then known as the "Great White Fleet") completely around the world because he did not have the necessary money. Unfortunately for the opposition, the President did have enough funds to send the navy halfway around the world. He did so. Congress suddenly, and without warning, found itself confronted not with the choice of sending or not sending the navy but with the choice of leaving it somewhere in Asia or bringing it home. There were loud cries of "arrogance" and "bully-boy tactics." But they were futile cries and the opposition knew it. Congress dutifully voted the necessary funds and the Great White Fleet completed its round-the-world tour. The influence of this trip on America's position in world affairs may have been questionable, but its influence on Roosevelt's position domestically was clear. He was a hero simply because he had been able to act decisively, and it is a good general rule that people prefer decisive leaders. The most that Congress could do was to grumble—and grumbling has yet to win a single election.

Theodore Roosevelt, of course, was not the first President to use the power of the initiative to extend the scope of the office far beyond anything that was conceivable by the Founding Fathers. From the very beginning of the Republic, presidents have found that it is a relatively simple matter to place Congress in a position where it has no alternative other than to back the President. This was the case in the punitive expeditions against the Barbary pirates; in the Louisiana Purchase; in the Indian wars in southern Georgia and Florida; and, more recently, in the landing of troops in the Dominican Republic and the escalation of the undeclared war in Vietnam. The President has the capacity to order troops into any area of the world, and as long as the troops are loyal, the orders will be obeyed. And once Americans are placed in a position of difficulty or peril by such orders, Congress has no alternative other than to bail them out. . . .

The President's power of initiative, of course, is subject to certain checks. But in the field of foreign affairs and defense, these checks are almost entirely in the nature of a review. Theoretically, Congress can always hamper his activities by refusing to grant the necessary appropriations to pay for the acts taken by the executive. It is inconceivable though that Congress would refuse appropriations to support men who are fighting in the name of their country's freedom. It is also inconceivable that Congress would withhold appropriations that are essential to sustain the nation's prestige. And it is even more inconceivable that Congress would fail to approve a President's action against an avowed enemy.

The war in Vietnam . . . rested for years on the Gulf of Tonkin resolution, which gave carte blanche to President Johnson to take virtually unprecedented steps in Southeast Asia. Some senators have since stated that had they known what was to follow, they would not have voted for it. This, of course, is not only hindsight but nonsense. The resolution was passed following an effort to torpedo an American naval vessel in the Gulf of Tonkin and after strong U.S. air retaliation against North Vietnamese torpedo boats in Haiphong. It is unthinkable that very many members of Congress would have been willing under such circumstances to tell the world that the United States would not support its leader in a moment of national peril (actually, only two senators took that course).

In domestic affairs, however, the President's power of initiative is far less effective. This is simply because there are very few domestic crises which require an immediate affirmation of national unity. In the domestic field, Congress is willing to repudiate a President because this is something that rests within the family. It does not assume that catastrophe will follow clear evidence of division. Even here, presidents have developed techniques which give them an initiative over the legislative branch of the government. These include preparation of the budget, at which Congress can only nitpick; the establishment of revolving funds, which go a long way toward negating the appropriation authority; and the use of executive orders which have limited force of law but which can completely bypass Congress.

A most dramatic example of the latter was the executive order by which President Kennedy set up an Equal Employment Opportunity Commission that had far more drastic authority to enforce nondiscrimination than could possibly have been accorded to a legally established Fair Employment Practices Commission. This was done by the simple device of permitting the commission to cancel any government contracts if the contractor was held guilty of bigotry in his hiring practices. Congress has no adequate countermeasures to such an act. It can only react, and while the reaction can be violent, that is not equivalent to having the edge that comes with the initiative.

Almost, but not quite, as important as the power of the initiative is the ability of the chief executive to place his views before the public. This is one arena in which he has no equal from the standpoint of opportunity. When he has a point of view, that point of view can be communicated instantly to the American people, and it has behind it all the power of the nation speaking through the voice of one individual. Furthermore, the President has the capability of shaping his words as he wants them without the necessity of sifting them through a "committee" process, which hampers any similar expression of views on the part of the Congress or the courts.

The President's ability to place his views before the public is important primarily because he can usually set the terms of the national debate—and anyone who can set the terms of a debate can win it. An outstanding example was the manner in which Harry S Truman converted certain defeat into unexpected victory in 1948.

At the beginning of the year, no one conceded Mr. Truman any chance for reelection. He had been plagued by deep divisions within the Democratic Party and by the strains placed upon the economy by the postwar readjustment. In 1946 the voters had signaled their disapproval by the election of the first Republican Congress in fourteen years, and there was no reason to believe that they were dissatisfied with their decision. The situation was so serious that leading Democrats debated the almost unheard-of possibility of denying renomination to Mr. Truman. Important leaders of the party had even proposed that General Eisenhower be asked to be the Democratic standard bearer (at that time no one had any idea of General Eisenhower's politics). The Democratic convention in Philadelphia was dispirited and lackluster, with the only heartening note a remarkable speech by Senator Alben W. Barkley, of Kentucky—a speech which secured for him the vice presidential nomination. There was, of course, no real alternative to Mr. Truman's renomination and the delegates went along reluctantly.

But Mr. Truman was a fighter. He startled the convention and the country by declaring immediate war on the "do-nothing, good-for-nothing, Republican-controlled, Eightieth Congress." He whistle-stopped the nation, lambasting the Republican Congress at every crossroads and every train station. The issue became the Congress itself, and the Republican candidate, who considered his victory a foregone conclusion, made the mistake of not rallying to its defense. The outcome was Mr. Truman's election, a result so unexpected that one American newspaper found itself on the stands with a banner headline ("Dewey Wins Election") which had been set in advance and released before the results were in. Mr. Truman had taken advantage of an important power of the presidency and had proved its effectiveness. . . .

The third source of presidential power is basically the ability to place others in a position of authority or prestige. This is something more than the power of appointment. A lawyer who is known to dine privately with the President (for example, Clark Clifford before he became secretary of defense) is raised to a position of eminence in the legal profession. An author who is known to be favored by the President or his family (for example, Truman Capote) finds that his readership increases overnight. A businessman who is seen at the President's elbow on more than one occasion (for example, banker Arthur Krim) finds his place in the business community enhanced. And all three are quite likely to use their newfound prestige to promote the cause of the President. By careful manipulation of such favors, a President can establish a network of Americans from coast to coast ready and anxious at any hour of the day or night to explain his cause, form supporting committees, or raise the money without which politics would be impossible. It may well be that an early sign in the decline of presidential power is the decline in the caliber of the people immediately around him.

All these powers added together are truly formidable. It is unlikely that any president could be defeated for reelection if he exercised them wisely. Franklin D. Roosevelt secured four terms in office, and it is not adequate to explain his dominance solely on the fact that he was a wartime president. Basically, he was a man who maintained his grip on reality and knew how to recover quickly from such mistakes as the Supreme Court packing bill. A president who suffers a defeat or a loss does so because he has made the wrong decisions and has not acted to recover from his errors.

The trend is clear. Over the passage of the years, what was little more than managerial authority has become power over the life of the nation itself. The right to check this power still rests in Congress and the courts. But the ability to check assumes the capacity to offer alternatives, to explain them to the public, and to manage a structure that carries them out. In the modern age, when action with little time for reflection becomes increasingly urgent, these capabilities are lessened with each passing day for every arm of the government except the presidency.

How Powerful Is the President?

John Kenneth Galbraith

As the presidential campaigns continue, some things are predictable:

Several dozen commentators will speak of the U.S. presidency as the most powerful position in the free world. Quite a few will refer to the President as the leader of the free world, and none can doubt that such leadership implies power. A few, with no great gift for novelty, will note that the President has his finger on the Button that, if pressed, would extinguish us all. This, too, is an awesome manifestation of power, though with negligible opportunity for a repeat performance.

As this is written, three Democrats and Ronald Reagan are running for President. The pay is good but by corporate standards not spectacular. The perquisites—residence, jets, servants, incomparable telephone service and Camp David—are, indeed, special. But none of this is what has attracted these candidates. All are running because they yearn for the power—including, all will say, the power to do good.

I come to my present point: Presidential power is no slight thing. But it does not quite conform to the vision that the aspirants or most of the rest of us hold.

Max Weber, the great German social scientist (some would say the greatest of the past century), defined power as the ability of an individual or group to win the subordination of others—if necessary, against *their* will. Not even from the White House is such subordination easily won.

From John Kenneth Galbraith, "How Powerful Is the President?," *Parade Magazine*, May 13, 1984, pp. 12–13.

The tendency to misjudge the power of the Presidency begins with what may be called the illusion of power. This, a matter of prime importance, takes several forms. A politician, and notably a President, goes before a thoughtfully chosen audience and makes a speech that is written, as a matter of course, to express what the audience already believes. The resulting applause is deafening. Everyone, and notably the reporters covering the scene, see this oratory as a decisive exercise of power. It is so described. At best, those addressed have been confirmed a little more deeply in their previously held beliefs—or prejudices.

Radio and television lend themselves further to the illusion of power. When at a loss as to what else to do, the President all but automatically takes his case to the public. Much toil goes into the speech; eventually, it emerges in acceptable English, and the President is said to have expressed himself extremely well. No one reflects that, in a day or two, most people will have forgotten what they heard. There is simply too much these days to remember. The presumption of power lies in the *act* of speaking, not the result. Let the reader try to recall a presidential speech that changed his or her mind.

Next, there is what may be called the sycophancy of power. If the President is held to have power, a very large number of other people can believe that they have power too. This is highly agreeable, and they will be sought out and celebrated by those who are similarly misled. I speak here of the presidential staff, the cabinet members and, most important of all, the newspaper and television reporters who cover the White House. All are freeloaders on the presumed power of the presidency. All, by enhancing the impression of presidential power, enhance the impression of their own.

This impulse is especially the tendency of the media. All have seen it in the faces and manner of the television news commentators covering the White House. Here are men and women whose responsibility is a heavy burden. None allows himself or herself a trace of humor; there is that special gravity in those closing words: "Joseph Zilch *at the White House.*" Joe is there sharing that power; not for him to do anything to minimize it. Someday, he will tell of his burdens and responsibilities and how he discharged them in a very serious book with a slightly offhand title, *The White House Beat.*

Then there is the question of how presidential decisions are actually made—the matter of the large organization and the related role of what may be called the synthetic personality. This requires a word of explanation:

We live in an age of very large organizations—large public bureaucracies (the Pentagon, Department of Health and Human Services), large corporate bureaucracies (Exxon, General Motors, General Dynamics). In each, the process of decision-making begins deep within the organization—with the shared knowledge of experts and specialists working in a hierarchy of committees and task forces from which comes the best or least bad course of action or, as often happens, the only available compromise. In such fashion, decisions emerge at the top from General Motors and similarly from the

Pentagon, the State Department, the Department of Agriculture—and from the President's own large staff around the Oval Office.

In other words, the power in the great number of everyday presidential decisions lies not with the President but with the organization. This is not publicly admitted; it is regularly concealed even from the President himself. Everyone with White House experience knows the design: The President is presented with alternative courses of action called options. One is possible; the others range from the politically disastrous to the overtly insane. The President chooses the only possible one; those seeking the decision express their agreement and nod with approval when he announces it to the press. The decision should, of course, be attributed to the organization. But there is no glamour in that. So wherever decision is by organization, personal power is emphasized—personality is synthesized. It is not the Pentagon but Caspar Weinberger. It is not the Presidential staff but the President.

How we attribute to individuals much that really belongs to organization is demonstrated by what happens to the Cabinet officer or corporation president when he leaves office. A curtain descends; nothing is heard of him again until the few fulsome paragraphs in the obituary columns. Past Presidents do better, but not much. Ford and Carter have passed largely from sight, although, perhaps with some effort, Richard Nixon does keep himself in the news. Calvin Coolidge was a considerable figure when in office; when word came of his death, the writer Dorothy Parker asked, "How can they tell?"

In considering the role of organization, we must reflect in a somber way on the possibility that such organization can, in our time, become stronger than the President himself. President Dwight D. Eisenhower, in his best-remembered speech, given in his last days in office, warned against the power, sought or unsought, of the military-industrial complex—of the hundreds of thousands of people, reinforced by hundreds of billions of dollars, that now comprise the civilian staff of the Pentagon, the armed services, the weapons industry, the serving scientists and engineers and the captive politicians. It will not be said, even by his most devout defenders, that President Reagan has been much motivated to control this complex; he has contributed notably to its power. But the greater question arises as to whether any President can control it. It is a question on which all should reflect and on which all Presidential candidates should be warned and pressed.

The final limitation on the President's power is the restraining force of circumstance. Our most marked political error lies in exaggerating the role of political ideology and minimizing that of hard, insouciant reality. Conservatives, with their hope of recovering a simple, idealized past, are the most vulnerable, but those with glowing utopian visions of the left are far from exempt. Mr. Reagan, to cite one striking example, came to the Presidency with the belief that environmental regulation was the product of liberal ideology, extensively unnecessary, a burden on industry. His appointees, Anne

Gorsuch Burford and James Watt, strongly reflected this doctrine. The hard opposing facts were the existence of dioxin and PCBs, the waste sites and the acid rain. By these was the Presidential power curtailed, as were the public careers of those immediately involved.

A modestly more sophisticated matter was the wonderfully seductive economic policy of monetarism. It promised that inflation could be arrested with no great hardship or cost by stern control of the money supply. Money in the modern economy is created by bank lending; from such lending come bank deposits, the everyday form of money. High interest rates are the instrument by which bank lending and borrowing are curbed and controlled. Control bank lending with high interest rates, and you control the money supply. There were a few other details, but this was the essence. The policy involved no bureaucracy and left all economic management to the Federal Reserve System. President Reagan was ideologically committed to this policy, an obvious area for the firm exercise of Presidential power.

The harsh circumstance is that monetarism works against inflation only as it causes massive unemployment, much idle plant capacity, much small business and farm distress. Only then do the unions give up on wage increases, corporations forgo price increases, and are food and farm commodity prices pressed down. So it was in the first Reagan years. And given this painful reality, the policy had to be abandoned. The hold on bank lending and the money supply was relaxed, interest rates were allowed to fall, the money supply was allowed to increase substantially (and, as always, somewhat erratically), and Professor Milton Friedman—the proponent of the policy and the most influential economic voice of our time—was led to say sadly, "If this be monetarism, I am not a monetarist." Once again, the President's power did not extend to policy that was in conflict with the world as it is.

The controlling role of circumstance is strong as regards foreign policy. It is within the power of the President to deploy advisers and ships to Central America; were the revolutions there the work of bands of foot-loose subversives, they could quickly be squelched. The hard circumstance is that the people in those unhappy precincts are in revolt against a regressive social, economic and political structure going back to colonial times, one that we would not tolerate here in the United States—one which, in our own Revolution, the Civil War and the great civil rights movement of our own time, we moved, not without bloodshed, to correct.

Reality not only intervenes in Central America, it also governs our relations with the Russians. The alternative to coexistence as a policy is no existence at all.

In seeking to put presidential power in perspective, I do not suggest that those of the Democratic Party now announced for the post should stand down on the discovery that it is not worth their while. Or that Ronald Reagan, having experienced the truth here offered, should immediately give way to George Bush. My thought is that we should understand better presidential power and be aware of the extraordinary influences that are on the side of misunderstanding it and that contribute to public bamboozlement. There will still be enough power left—enough capacity to bend others to one's will—to reward amply the individual who achieves the office this autumn. And, even on the worst days, there *is* the telephone system I mentioned. Once, many years ago, I spent a few months on the White House staff. Nothing in life was so wonderful and to my vanity so rewarding as the way people got on the line when the operator said, "The White House calling."

PRESIDENTIAL TENURE

In constructing the office of the presidency, the Founding Fathers provided that, among other things, the President would serve a four-year term and be eligible to seek as many additional terms as he wished. The wisdom of this provision was not seriously challenged until the presidency of Franklin Roosevelt. Our first president to seek more than two terms, he occupied the White House for nearly twelve and a half years. The merits of having a President serve so long became the subject of considerable public debate and ultimately culminated in a proposed constitutional amendment limiting the President to two terms in office. Ratified by three-fourths of the states in 1951, it became the Twenty-second Amendment to our Constitution.

In recent years, the issue of presidential tenure has once again surfaced as a subject of public discussion. More specifically, from several quarters has come the suggestion that the President be given a single six-year term. While this is not the first time in our history that the six-year term has been proposed, it is now being debated more seriously if only because its supporters include our three past presidents—Nixon, Ford, and Carter. President Carter, for example, observed, "I have begun to realize lately that if I could just, by the stroke of a pen, change the Constitution, I think one six-year term would be preferable."

The two selections that follow consider the merits of a single six-year term. In the first selection, the Foundation for the Study of Presidential and Congressional Terms favors the proposal, arguing that it would encourage presidential candor, improve the presidential selection process, and provide the President with a greater opportunity to realize his goals. In the second selection, Thomas Cronin contends that neither the President nor the public would be well served by a proposal that, in effect, removes the presidency from the realm of politics.

A Single
Six-Year Term
for the President?

Foundation for the Study of Presidential and Congressional Terms

Arguments for and against a single term for the President of the United States are like the ribbons that dangle from a maypole. The presidency is the pole and those who debate the issue dance around it, wrapping the pole in the ribbon of their choice. The presidency means many things to different people, so there are many ribbons and, at the end of the dance, the pole is wound in a confusion of colors. . . .

The growth of government has so multiplied the burdens and extended the reach of the President that he can no longer focus his attentions on getting reelected without affecting in various negative ways his broader obligations to the national interest.

Proponents of term limitation point out that the presidency has changed. The type of problems our nation faces today are monstrously complex. Government has grown larger and harder to manage. World changes require tough decisions that ride on the brink of possible catastrophe. To deal with our national problems, proponents argue that a President must be able to focus his complete attention on the tasks and duties of his office, without being concerned about reelection. Senator Thurmond, in introducing an amendment to the Constitution to limit the President to a single term of six years, said of the presidency:

> . . . *We cannot be certain that it is possible for a President of the United States to meet the responsibilities which come with the office while he is involved with*

Excerpted from Foundation for the Study of Presidential and Congressional Terms, *Presidential and Congressional Term Limitation: The Issue That Stays Alive* (Washington, D.C.: Foundation for the Study of Presidential and Congressional Terms, 1980), pp. 16–23, 33. Reprinted with permission.

all aspects of mounting a national campaign for reelection. The pressures of campaigning bend an incumbent President physically just as they bend his policies. And if it were not enough to preside over the departments and agencies of the executive branch, to be commander in chief of the armed forces and ceremonial head of state, we ask our presidents to defend their policies in a heavy schedule of state primaries, and exercise their powers of incumbency in a long struggle for renomination and reelection.[1]

The education of the public on the complex issues of the time is best accomplished by a straight-talking President. But presidents bent on reelection do not always talk straight and the people's trust in their leadership is weakened by a dialogue that seems more political than educational.

The presidency, as Theodore Roosevelt said, is a "bully pulpit" and the President has an obligation to use it to inform the people. Much of the breakdown of faith in government has developed from a popular suspicion that the public is being deceived by elected officials whose concern is reelection. Just as Mr. Carter complained that his motivations are always construed as political, many of his predecessors have seen their credibility erode under these suspicions. Lyndon Johnson's access to the public's ear was badly impaired by his attempts to put a bright face on the developments in Vietnam. Richard Nixon acknowledged in *The Real War* that he inflated the illusion of peace, for political reasons, after his 1972 summit meetings. "During my administration," he wrote, "excessive euphoria built up around the 1972 Peking and Moscow summit meetings. I must assume a substantial part of the responsibility for this. It was an election year, and I wanted the political credit for what I believed were genuinely major advances toward a stable peace."[2]

A six-year term is a reasonable compromise. It gives a President time to learn his duties and accomplish his goals without declining into a stale and fatigued condition.

A President's first term goes quickly. He spends his first year learning the job and developing his working relationships, his second year governing, and the next two years working to get reelected. After the midterm elections, public attention quickly swings to the upcoming presidential race. Foreign leaders complain it is difficult to do business with the United States government because its top officials are continually involved in campaigns.

Under the present system an administration operates for only two years under its best budget calculations. Federal budgets are prepared nine months in advance so, in its first year, an administration operates on the budget of its predecessor. In its second year it operates on the budget which reflects its early aspirations. Only the budgets for the third and fourth years are prepared on the basis of solid experience.

Henry Clay put the first term problem succinctly in a Senate speech . . . : "Much observation and deliberate reflection have satisfied me," he said, "that too much of the time, the thoughts, the exertions of the incumbent are occupied during the first term in securing his reelection. The public business consequently suffers."

Another Senate leader, Mike Mansfield, told the Senate on May 22, 1973 that it is "intolerable" for any President to be compelled to devote time, energy, and talents to political campaign tasks. He said a President pursuing reelection faces "a host of demands that range from attending the needs of political office-holders, office-seekers, financial backers and all the rest to riding herd on the day-to-day developments within the pedestrian partisan arena."

Lyndon Johnson wrote in his memoirs, "The old belief that a President can carry out the responsibilities of his office and at the same time undergo the rigors of campaigning is, in my opinion, no longer valid."[3] In an interview after he left office, Johnson alluded to the tendency of a first-term President to put off dealing with prickly problems until his second term. John Kennedy talked often with his cabinet officials of the prospect that his administration's significant accomplishments would not come until the second term. This was because the major focus of the first term was on getting reelected. Several weeks before he was assassinated, Kennedy remarked to a friend that he did not plan to build a library to house his papers if he did not win a second term. "If I only have one term," he said, "nobody will give a damn."

Most recent presidents have shared this inclination to wait for the leverage of a second term to deal with problems that only lend themselves to long-term solutions. One consequence of this practice, particularly in times like this when the White House is occupied by a series of presidents who do not win reelection, is that a great deal of important work is swept into the corner and ignored.

A single-term President will not be insulated from politics nor consider himself any longer accountable to the people.

A great many political scientists echo the contention of Thomas E. Cronin that it is naive to think of turning the job of President into a managerial or strictly executive post. As Cronin writes: "The presidency is a highly political office and it cannot be otherwise. Moreover, its political character is for the most part desirable. A President separated from or somehow above politics might easily become a President who doesn't listen to the people, doesn't respond to majority sentiment, or pay attention to views that may be diverse, intense, and at variance with his own."[4]

By the nature of his office and his need to deal with two coequal branches of government along with the press and public, a President is inextricably immersed in politics. His pursuit of support for his programs is politics; his leadership within his administration is politics; and his instinctive effort to command popular esteem is politics. His success or failure as President will be a political assessment made first by contemporary opinion and later by historians. He will be judged first and last as a political leader because, as Harry Truman observed, "A politician is a man who understands government and it takes a politician to run a government."[5]

Professional politicians did not exist in anything like their present numbers when the Constitution was drafted. For most of the delegates at Philadelphia, politics was a sideline, a patriotic exertion to launch the young republic. They inevitably anticipated that the powers of the new government would mainly be lodged in the hands of people like themselves. They did not envision a government dominated by careerists for whom political survival was an ultimate aim. The evolution of a professional class of politicians has led to changes which sometimes seem to make the campaigns more important than the government. As politics has become more and more an end in itself, candidates have begun running for the presidency many years in advance. The day is not far off when the presidential election process will be continual.

The single-term amendment will curb the concerns of presidents for their own political survival and it will hold them somewhat above the political levels at which competitors are elbowing for advantage. But it will not remove them from the broad sweep of political play which constantly works to shape the nation's destiny.

If presidential elections were held every six years instead of every four, citizens eligible to vote might be persuaded to take them more seriously, to give closer scrutiny to the qualifications of the contenders, and to turn out to vote in large numbers on election day.

The testimony of recent presidential elections is that an increasing number of eligible American citizens are following the example of the lady who declared, "I never vote. It just gives them encouragement." The turnout has been declining toward a prospect that at some point less than half the eligible voters will participate in the choice of the President.

What is this voting malaise? Registration procedures have been simplified in most states and television gives the public a fuller view of the candidates than ever before. Politicians spend more money to make more of a splash and the contests get harder to ignore. But good citizens continue to turn their backs on the democratic process.

Part of the cause is the individual's sense of political impotence in the face of the organized pressure groups. Part of it is boredom with politics fostered by diversions and duties closer at hand. Part of it is the fact that the looming problems are too complex to be widely understood by those reluctant to take the time to study them. Part of it is a rampant cynicism fed by the tendency of politicians to make their appeals in TV spots, to speak in vague, ambivalent terms, and to create a general impression that they are not sincere. A big part of it is the decline of the party system and the party disciplines that once brought voters out.

A six-year term will not rectify all this but it will give disenchanted voters more of an incentive to focus on the issues and candidates. It will alleviate the impression that elections are always in process and make the choice of the President more of a high point in the national life.

A single-term President would be less tempted to use his incumbency and the resources of government to court voting blocs and win elections.

A President's political use of his incumbency, in a government spending over $600 billion a year, is an election factor that no one is inclined to minimize. It becomes controversial when the incumbency is used in ways that waste public funds or seem to affect the national interest adversely. It causes frictions between the White House and the executive departments when a President's political advisers perceive that cabinet officers are not giving top priority to their campaign objectives. Maximum use of the incumbency, as practiced in the Nixon and Carter campaigns of 1972 and 1976, politicizes and ultimately distorts the functioning of government.

Nevertheless, a President's use of the incumbency to improve his prospects in presidential primaries and general elections is widely accepted as a fact of life. He is rarely criticized when he bends his policies to meet the demands of powerful voting blocs, targets an array of grants into states on the eve of their primary contests, and uses his powers to build illusions of prosperity as election day approaches. A Princeton professor, Edward Tufte, has documented a thesis that most presidents have been so adept at manipulating the economy to their political advantage that election years are frequently the peak of the economic cycle.[6]

But while the criticisms are muted, blatantly political use of presidential power is clearly a factor in the decline of respect for the office. It stirs cynicism that limits the reach of presidential leadership. It has inspired members of Congress to make the most of their incumbency potential and thus expand the politicization of government. It renders the government less efficient by putting political priorities ahead of administrative objectives. It contributes to a disproportionate allocation of the government's outlays because groups organized to make the most of their political weight invariably get the most attention.

It is argued that a single-term President will still use his powers to guide the selection of his successor. This may be true to a degree but the all-out mobilization of an administration to win elections and the distortion of government priorities will be unlikely to occur because it is the nature of political leaders to think first of their own reputations. It is most unlikely that single-term presidents will be willing to risk damage to their records for the sake of those who aspire to succeed them.

The Twenty-second Amendment already imposes the restraints envisioned as potentially harmful by those who oppose the single-term presidency.

Congress and the state legislatures, in adding the Twenty-second Amendment to the Constitution, have already done most of the so-called damage which some see as negative aspects of the single-term limitation. The lame-duck question is, for example, widely raised against the single-term reform. Some political scientists contend that a President deprived of the right to seek reelection will suffer a loss of influence that will diminish his effectiveness. As noted earlier, the second-term successes of Dwight Eisenhower, the only President who has so far served two full terms under the twenty-second Amendment, offer one reassuring answer to this concern.

But the essential fact is that any President who manages to secure reelection under the Constitution as it stands will confront what is described as lame-duck status for his final four years in office. To the extent that it is an infringement on people's rights to limit their options in choosing a President, that infringement has already occurred. If there are risks in the arbitrary termination of the services of a President who may have capabilities particularly suited to the situation in which the nation finds itself, those risks already exist.

Most of those who oppose the single-term reform would like to repeal the Twenty-second Amendment. But this seems now to be a disposition mainly confined to the political science fraternity. There is no sign of broad popular support for the removal of a limitation widely seen as a barrier to the usurpation of power.

So the realistic choice is between the present system, in which presidents use their first terms to win second terms in which they hope to retrieve their promises, and the single-term proposition. The augury of the arguments is that the latter offers a better prospect of political leadership that will face problems promptly, address the public candidly, and inspire the faith and optimism needed to close the spreading gap between the governed and their government.

NOTES

1. Strom Thurmond, *Congressional Record*, September 10, 1979, p. S12309.
2. Richard M. Nixon, *The Real War* (New York: Warner Books, 1980).
3. Lyndon B. Johnson, *The Vantage Point* (New York: Holt, Rinehart and Winston, 1971).

4. Thomas E. Cronin, "The Presidency and Its Paradoxes," in Harry A. Bailey, Jr., *Classics of the American Presidency* (Oak Park, Ill.: Moore, 1980), p. 116.
5. Quoted by William Safire in *The Language of Politics* (New York: Random House, 1968).
6. Edward R. Tufte, *Political Control of the Economy* (Princeton, N.J.: Princeton University Press, 1978).

Taking the Presidency out of Politics: The Six-Year Term

Thomas E. Cronin

Despite some attractive features, the six-year term would cause more problems than it would solve. The required reelection after four years is one of the most democratic aspects of the presidency. It affords an opportunity for assessment. It enhances the likelihood that a President will carefully weigh the effects of whatever he does on his reelection chances. At the core of our system is the belief that our President should have to worry about reelection and be subject to all the same vicissitudes of politics as other elected officials. Moreover, a political party should retain the threat of dumping a President as a check upon the incumbent and the office, especially upon a President who refuses to honor his party's pledges.

When the U.S. Senate in 1913 passed a resolution in favor of the single six-year term, Woodrow Wilson argued against it and his reasoning still seems valid: "The argument is not that it is clearly known now just how long each President should remain in office. Four years is too long a term for a President who is not the true spokesman of the people, who is imposed upon and does not lead. It is too short a term for a President who is doing, or attempting, a great work of reform, and who has not had time to finish it." Wilson also contended that "to change the term to six years would be to increase the likelihood of its being too long without any assurance that it would, in happy cases, be long enough. A fixed constitutional limitation to a single term of office is highly arbitrary and unsatisfactory from any point of view."[1.]

From Thomas E. Cronin, *The State of the Presidency*, 2nd ed., pp. 336–61. Copyright © 1980 by Thomas E. Cronin, © 1975 by Little, Brown and Company (Inc.). Reprinted by permission of Little, Brown and Company.

The proposed divorce between the presidency and politics presupposes a significantly different kind of political system from that of the United States, which is glued together largely by ambiguity, compromise, and the extensive sharing of powers. In light of the requisites of democracy, the presidency must be a highly political office, and the President an expert practitioner of the art of politics. Quite simply, there is no other way for presidents to negotiate favorable coalitions within the country, Congress, and the executive branch and to gather the authority needed to translate ideas into accomplishments. A President who remains aloof from politics, campaigns, and partisan alliances does so at the risk of becoming the prisoner of events, special interests, or his own whims.

The very means for bringing a President in touch with reality is the process of political debate and political bargaining, with all of the necessary changes of course, arguments, and listening to other points of view. What makes domestic politics so distasteful to presidents, that it is full of groups to persuade and committees to inform, is precisely its virtue; indeed, it is the major hope for maintaining an open presidency, one neither bound by its own sources of information nor aloof to the point that it will no longer listen.

By calling the President "more presidential" whenever he ignores partisan politics, citizens encourage him to even greater isolation. By turning up their noses at politics in the White House and urging the President to get on with his real business of guiding the nation, they also help to establish the two important conditions for secrecy and duplicity, with which the nation has become so familiar. First, with all the apparatus and technology for secret statesmanship at hand, a President can more easily call upon aides when something needs fixing than persuade the public or Congress to his point of view. Second, because the President will look unpresidential if he participates in normal party politics, his aides must go through grotesque contortions to prove that their boss has never thought about anything except being President of all the people. The tactic of secrecy, so tempting to those who have it within their grasp, amounts to insulating the President from the normal checks and balances of the political system. New bait will be needed to lure presidents out of this comfortable sanctuary and into the morass of open politics, for the present enticements are small.

The premise that politics stops at the water's edge must also be rejected. To bring too little politics and partisanship to bear on foreign-policy matters often means that political parties are not responding to critical issues or are not debating worthwhile alternative policies and deep-seated differences of opinion. Neither of the major American political parties is constituted along neat liberal and conservative lines. A realignment, even a moderate realignment, surely would help to create more effective opposition parties and, hence, the politics of opposition that is so vital on any occasion.

One way to prevent future abuses of presidential power, as others have noted, is to make the White House more open; and one way to do that, as has not been suggested so often, is to begin regarding a President as a politician once again. Politics, in the best sense of that term, is the art of making decisions in the context of debate, dialogue, and open two-way conversations, the art of making the difficult and desirable possible. This kind of politics at the White House should not be diminished. Indeed, as pointed out above, it is highly desirable that presidents be great practitioners of the craft of politics. They, as well as Congress and our parties, would profit from more politics, not less.

Most of the effective presidents have also been highly political. They knew how to stretch the limited resources of the office, and they loved politics and enjoyed the responsibilities of party leadership. The nation has been well served by sensitive politicians disciplined by the general thrust of partisan and public thinking. Many of the least political presidents were also the least successful and seemingly the least suited temperamentally to the rigors of the office. The best have been those who listened to people, who responded to majority as well as to intense minority sentiment, who saw that political parties are often the most important vehicle for communicating voter preferences to those in public office, and who were attentive to the diversity and intensity of public attitudes even as they attempted to educate and to influence the direction of opinion.

President Nixon told the nation during his Watergate crisis that the presidency had to come first and politics second. This, he said, is why he did not involve himself in the 1972 election campaign. So too, Presidents Kennedy and Ford tried on occasion to argue that the problems facing the nation were so technical and administrative in character that they did not lend themselves to the clash of partisan and ideological debate. In essence, they appealed to the belief that highly political decisions must now be placed in the hands of dispassionate bipartisan experts, a notion that is certainly as dangerous as it is blatantly undemocratic.

Everything a President does has political consequences, and every political act by a President has implications for the state of the presidency. The nation must fully recognize that presidents will and must be political, that they ought to be vigorous partisan leaders. Bipartisanship rarely has served the nation well. James MacGregor Burns aptly noted that "almost as many crimes have been committed in the name of mindless bipartisanship as in the name of mindless patriotism."[2] If patriotism in an autocratic system implies blind loyalty to the regime, then patriotism in a democracy must include a responsibility and even obligation to speak out as a citizen whenever one believes that the government is following an unjust or misguided course of action. (Recognizing presidents as partisan political leaders also underscores our lack of an opposition party. Such a party could challenge a President's program and the presidential establishment and would be eager and able to proclaim alternative national priorities.) Decision-making processes in a democracy will be messier and often more confusing than in alternative systems, but if the dreams of Jackson and Van Buren are to be taken seriously, then the real secret and strength of democracy rests in encouraging regular elections and vigorous opposition politics.

If national leaders do become isolated or insulated from the mood of the public, then electing presidents for longer terms would only encourage this tendency.[3] Frequent elections necessarily remain a major means of motivating responsive and responsible behavior. An apolitical President, disinterested in reelection, motivated by personal principle or moralistic abstractions, and aloof from the concerns of our political parties, could become a highly irresponsible President. Elections customarily force an assessment of presidential performance. They are welcomed when promises have been kept and feared when performance has been unsatisfactory. Was it, for example, a mere coincidence, or were President Nixon's troop-withdrawal rates calculated with the election of 1972 in mind? Was the Johnson–Humphrey bombing halt of 1968 aimed toward that year's election? Nixon's economic game-plan reversal in 1971 and Johnson's vain efforts at peace negotiations in 1967 and 1968 were unmistakably related to the positive, constructive, and dynamic character of American elections.

Although change in important national policy is a slow process, a six-year term is not necessarily an appropriate remedy for this. Frequently, policy changes whose pace has frustrated the White House have come slowly because they have been highly controversial and adequate support had not yet been assembled. Mobilizing support is just as much a presidential responsibility as proclaiming the need, and support would be no less crucial with a seven-year or a seventeen-year term. Only a shrewdly political President who is also his party's leader, who is sensitive to political moods, and who is allied with dozens of the political party elite, can build those coalitions able to bridge the separation of powers in Washington and to offset the strong forces bent on thwarting progress.

Often, when the White House is frustrated in attempting reform, the proposed changes have not been adequately planned or tested. In the case of the Johnson administration, as has been noted earlier, too many policies were pronounced prematurely—sometimes policy was "made" by press release—and the administration acted as though bill-signing ceremonies were the culmination of the policymaking process. The administration also was frustrated in its attempt to implement sweeping domestic policy changes precisely because too much emphasis was placed on getting the laws on the books, to the neglect of developing the managerial and bureaucratic organizations necessary for imaginative administration of these laws. A White House that becomes overly transfixed with a legislative box score, or that succumbs to the unquenchable thirst for quick political credit, may appear, at least for a while, to be accomplishing great innovations. But translating paper victories into genuine policy accomplishments requires far more than monopolizing the legislative process.

The President who cannot be reelected after four years is unlikely to accomplish anything of value if he is given a free ride for another two. What was true in the past remains true today: effective national leadership requires what the Constitution actually tried to discourage, that a party or faction disperse its members or its influence across the branches of government. Under normal circumstances, a President who ignores this maxim or retreats from these partisan and political responsibilities is unlikely to achieve much in the way of substantive policy innovation. Further, as one former counselor to three presidents put it: "A President who can never again be a candidate is a president whose coattails are permanently in mothballs."[4] A President elected to a single six-year term would be a President inescapably confronted with a bureaucracy as well as senior political appointees even less responsive to him than now. Even when presidents are both popular and eligible for reelection, they depend on senior and mid-career civil servants, a situation summed up in the wry Washington saying that "the bureaucracy eats presidents for lunch." When it is known that a chief executive is to leave by a certain date, bureaucratic entrepreneurs suddenly enjoy wider degrees of discretion and independence. Reeligibility, used or not, is a potentially significant political resource in the hands of a President; and denying that resource, even in the more limited way that the Twenty-second Amendment has done, will diminish the leadership discretion of future presidents who desire to be activist initiators of policy. President Truman spoke to this point, "You do not have to be very smart to know that an officeholder who is not eligible for reelection loses a lot of influence. . . . It makes no sense to treat a President this way—no matter who he is—Republican or Democrat. He is still President of the whole country and all of us are dependent on him; and we ought to give him the tools to do his job."[5]

Political analyst Stephen Hess calls our attention to another practical consideration about the six-year term: If we elect a truly outstanding President under this proposed reform we have him or her in the White House for two years less than under the present practice that would have provided them eight years. If we elect a really bad President we are stuck for two years more than under the present system which provides for getting rid of such types at the end of four years.[6]

The single-term proposal has a comforting ring of good, old-time government and nonpartisanship to it. Yet it represents the last gasp of those who cling to the hope that we can separate national leadership from the crucible of politics and of those who contend that our presidency is too beholden to the workings of a patronage or spoils system. Neither is the case: the former remains an impossibility—it is impossible to take the politics out of public leadership in a democracy—whereas the latter is a problem whose time largely has passed. Equally undesirable is the notion that intense conflict over policy choices, that is, intense political activity, somehow can be removed from the presidency. The conflicts that surround the presidency require a President to act as a public mediator to mirror those existing and potential conflicts over values that exist within the American society at large. If presidents were not required to resolve political conflicts by making political choices, they would not be fulfilling those responsibilities we rightly associate with democratic leadership.

NOTES

1. Woodrow Wilson, letter placed in the *Congressional Record,* 64th Cong., 2d sess., August 15, 1916, 53, pt. 13:12620.
2. James MacGregor Burns, "Keeping the President in Line," *New York Times,* April 8, 1973, p. E-15.
3. The possibility also exists that a six-year term, or "a term-and-a-half" as some call it, with reelection precluded, would intensify the presidential selection process. Certainly in such a winner-take-more situation, there is the likelihood that ideological competition would be more aggressive and perhaps more bitter than at present. Conflict would assuredly be heightened. How harmful this would be is difficult to assess, but judging from how corrupt the 1972 reelection campaign became this factor must be considered.
4. Clark Clifford, in hearings before the Subcommittee on Constitutional Amendments of the U.S. Senate, Committee on the Judiciary, October 1971; processed, 92nd Cong., 1st sess.
5. Harry S Truman, testimony before the Subcommittee on Constitutional Amendments of the U.S. Senate, Committee on the Judiciary, Hearings on S.J. Resolution II: "Presidential Term of Office," 86th Cong., 1st sess., 1959, Part I, p. 7.
6. Stephen Hess, "Espousing a Six-Year Presidency," *Rocky Mountain News,* March 11, 1979, p. 73.

CHAPTER TWELVE

BUREAUCRACY

It has become commonplace among business leaders, politicians, and the public alike to criticize government for its waste and inefficiency. U.S. Senator William Proxmire (D.-Wis.), for example, periodically presents the "Golden Fleece" award to some bureaucrat or government agency for wasting the taxpayers' money. And President Reagan made one of his major campaign themes the discovery and elimination of government waste. So it was not surprising that, shortly after taking office, the President took the lead in establishing a commission charged with finding ways to reduce government spending and eliminate bureaucratic waste and mismanagement. Known as the Grace Commission (for its chairman, Peter Grace, one of America's top corporate executives), the commission issued a massive report outlining ways to make the government more efficient.

In the first of the articles in this chapter, Edward Meadows reviews the work of the Grace Commission and concurs with its conclusion that "the government is the worst-run enterprise in America." Citing example after example from the report, Meadows paints a dismal picture of typical bureaucratic waste. According to Meadows, the government overly indulges its workers, tolerates the spending of the taxpayers' money to an excessively high degree, and is blind to the need to get government out of doing what the free market itself should be doing.

In the second selection, authors H. Brinton Milward and Hal G. Rainey, although recognizing the problem of government waste and inefficiency, argue at once for a more balanced view of the bureaucracy and for a greater understanding of the problems the government encounters. For example, they argue that the government should not be faulted for being inefficient when, as is often the case, it is asked to do things which no private business is willing or able to do; nor should it be condemned for not being efficient when, as a matter of fact, the lack of efficiency is the result of conflicting values in society. In short, unlike some critics of government, Milward and Rainey are unwilling to "blame the bureaucracy" for things over which it has no control.

The Government Is the Worst-Run Enterprise in America

Edward Meadows

. . . When President Reagan named Peter Grace chairman of his new budget-study commission, back on February 18, 1982, the President bade him and his men go forth like tireless bloodhounds. The President asked Mr. Grace to command troops of corporate volunteers—accountants, staff officers, management experts—who would stalk the government's red-tape jungle, sniffing out inefficiency. In order not to add to the problem it was investigating, the commission would be funded privately, the President decreed, by corporate donations of time and money. Such a scheme had worked in California under his governorship, and it would work again in Washington. . . .

Bloodcurdling pig screams echoed down the Washington Mall as the Grace Commission began to release its findings in 1983. One task force proposed, for instance, that military commissaries be shut down. The military press ranted, and Defense Secretary Weinberger agreed that the matter needed "more study." This was typical and predictable.

A listing of the commission's executive committee reads like an honor roll of blue-chip corporate America, names like Frank Cary, chairman of IBM; William Agee, chairman of Bendix; John W. Hanley, chairman of Monsanto; and 157 other top-ranking executives. They remanded some two thousand of their employees to root in government files for evidences of mismanagement. The volunteer inspectors ended up writing 47 hefty blue-bound reports, many of them two inches thick, all chock-full of fascinating detail. They wrote 23,000 pages in all, suggesting budget cuts ranging from half a million dollars to $59 billion. All the work was done at a cost of $75 million in donated manpower, equipment, and materials, plus $3.3 million in

From Edward Meadows, "Peter Grace Knows 2,478 Ways to Cut the Deficit," *National Review,* March 9, 1984, pp. 26–36.

cash contributions. Corporations footed the entire bill. Not a cent of the money came from the federal government. . . .

. . . The government is the worst-run enterprise in America. Thus it is the thesis of the Grace Commission that the country can save that $454 billion simply by curbing outright, blatant, casebook mismanagement, without ripping the social safety net, or even cutting some government services that many people, libertarians especially, would deem unwarranted on principle.

To begin, here is a random sampler of this mismanagement. Read and be outraged:

- The Health and Human Services Department has been paying Medicare benefits to 8,500 dead people.
- A Mississippi supplier bought a gravity timer from the sole manufacturer for $11 and sold it to the Navy for $256—a 2,227 percent markup.
- The Minority Business Development Agency didn't notice when a management consulting firm used part of its $4 million MBDA grant to rent a townhouse and two cars for its executives, buy unauthorized gifts for its employees, and promote "questionable activities." The firm also neglected to pay some $315,000 in federal and state taxes, consulting fees, and salaries.
- It costs the Veterans Administration from $100 to $140 just to process a single medical claim, while the average for private insurance companies is $3 to $6 per claim.
- But the VA is a paragon of efficiency in letter-writing. It requires only twenty days to finish a letter. Compare with Health and Human Services, where a single piece of correspondence needing the signature of the Secretary takes 47 days to get done and involves about sixty people.
- The Army spends $4.20 to issue each payroll check, compared to the private-sector cost of $1. This wastes $40 million a year.
- Some unsuspecting citizens open their mailboxes to find 29 or more copies of pamphlets with titles like *How to Serve Nuts*, because the Government Printing Office uses out-of-date, duplicate, and incorrect mailing lists to post its myriad free publications. The lack of centralized correct mailing lists costs an estimated $96 million a year.

Say, is this Ubanga or the Central Banana Republic we're talking about? No, it's glittering Washington, and you're paying the tab. How does one get a firm hold on such maddeningly diverse ways of wasting taxpayers' money? The Grace Commission has broken down the inefficiencies by government agency and by function. For simplicity's sake, here are some specific categories of inefficiency, and what the Grace Commission thinks ought to be done to get things in shape.

INFORMATION PROCESSING

The federal government uses 17,000 computers, operated by 250,000 employees. But they are mostly obsolete—on average, they are twice as old as computers in private business. Half of them are so old they can no longer be supported by the manufacturer. And these ancient computers can't tie in with each other. Beyond that, government decision-makers mostly don't know what information they need, where to get it, or how to analyze it. Witness the results:

- The Social Security Administration's computers stay four to six weeks behind in issuing new Social Security cards, and the agency has a three-year backlog in posting retirement contributions. It is unable to process the 7.5 million new claims each year on time or correctly.
- Some 20 percent of all tax returns for 1978, that's right, 1978—have yet to be entered into the IRS computer system, a twenty-year-old dinosaur that predates most modern computer technology. Delinquent accounts are therefore at $23.2 billion and growing.
- Though the Urban Mass Transportation Administration spent $10 million to buy new computers to keep track of the $25 billion in grants it hands out, the agency has been unable to close its accounting books since 1979. No account reconciliations have been possible since 1977. The UMTA has no central ledger showing who owes what to whom. Despite the computers, the agency must do its financial data by hand.
- The cost of the Army's business computer systems can only be estimated (at $1.5 billion), because the Army simply doesn't know how much it has spent on these computers, what kinds of computers it has, where they are, how many there are, or whether they should be replaced.

The Grace Commission argues that, for starters, some $20 billion can be saved over a three-year period by straightening out the computer mess. The commission recommends naming a manager to oversee computer operations throughout the government; hiring competent professionals; upgrading the obsolete systems; and using common payroll, personnel, property-management, and other such systems throughout the government. And if the government went even further in closing its information gap, by such means as figuring out what information it needs and then setting up mechanisms to get it, some $78 billion could be saved.

ASSET MANAGEMENT

Any businessman worth his P&L statement knows how to manage financial assets, mainly by putting idle money in interest-bearing accounts, and timing his own payments to avoid costing himself interest. Another way is to cut down the "float" that offers free credit as a payment takes its time getting to its destination. The federal government, however, is ignorant of these common techniques. Because of this, it loses millions of your dollars a year. Consider the evidence:

- In 1982 the Justice Department seized $317 million in the form of cash and of property, such as dope-smuggling planes. But the captured cash, $79 million of the total, wasn't put into interest-bearing bank accounts. Instead, the Justice Department just let it sit. Noncash assets are allowed to depreciate to as little as 65 percent of their value before they are sold off.
- At the Transportation Department, some $473 million in recent grants was paid to contractors an average of 13 days sooner than necessary, costing the government $13 million in interest payments. If payments were made only when due, and bills collected promptly, the department could save $144 million per year.
- The State Department squandered some $17 million over a three-year period by failing to acquire foreign currency before it was actually needed. (And when the dollar weakens, State should delay buying foreign currency.)
- Some $635 million could be saved over three years if the government used direct deposit for the 48.3 million payments it makes each month. This would allow the money to remain on deposit longer.
- The Education Department could generate some $4.68 billion in cash-flow improvements and $1 billion in interest savings over three years merely by making loans to students in increments rather than in lump sums. Consolidating the student-loan programs could return at least $290 million per year to the Treasury.

In spite of a daily cash flow of $6.8 billion, the federal government obviously hasn't got a handle on the management of its financial assets. The Grace Commission says the government could save up to $79 billion if it ran its asset management as business does.

PERSONNEL

The federal government employs nearly three times the number of high-grade white-collar workers found in the private sector. They tend to be overpaid and underworked, given to absenteeism and job-hopping. They get 35 percent more vacation time than private-industry workers and health benefits that cost $134 a month per family, versus the private-sector average of $93. They like to file such things as on-the-job injury claims (6.3 percent of federal employees filed in 1980, versus 1.7 percent of private-industry employees).

- In 1981, a typical year, Postal Service workers took an average of nearly nine sick days each, versus the 5.3-day average in private enterprise. This lost 21.734 workweeks, at a cost to the taxpayers of $652 million.

■ The Department of Energy has one supervisor for every three employees, twice the number of supervisors in the rest of the federal government, not to mention the private sector. Just bringing the Energy Department into line with the rest of government would save a tidy $19 million over three years.

■ The Education Department overpays nearly 30 percent of its workers, since that many are "overclassified" and there hasn't been a classification audit since the department was formed in 1980. Education Department employees don't mind. Nor do they complain about cost-of-living raises. The average increase was 17.3 percent in 1980 and 27.3 percent in 1981.

■ Government pensions are twice as generous as private ones, and military pensions are 600 percent higher than those in the private sector. These pensions are sweetened by lavish cost-of-living increases, such that between 1977 and 1981, civil-service pension pay rose by 50 percent. Between 1973 and 1982, the government handed out more than $200 billion in pension checks to civil-service and military retirees. These costs will more than double over the next decade, rising to $500 billion, not including an unfunded pension liability of a trillion dollars over that period. (For example, there are a million retired railroad workers and only 450,000 active workers in the Railroad Retirement System—that is, 2.2 retirees per worker. The system already has an unfunded liability of $30 billion and will run out of funds sometime before next year.)

■ To decide how much to pay its workers, the government surveys salaries in the private sector. But this "comparability survey" covers only a quarter of federal jobs and excludes 95 percent of companies in major industries. Thus the survey is biased toward high salaries. The average blue-collar salary is 8 percent higher in government enterprises than in private industry. In any case, about half of all federal job-classification standards are more than ten years out of date, with excessively detailed requirements and time-consuming procedures.

■ One government study determined that word-processing operators weren't as skilled as regular secretaries, so it cut word-processing pay by $3,000 a year. The predictable result was that word-processing operators disappeared from federal word-processing pools, only to turn up as secretaries. Some word-processing centers went idle for lack of operators. Productivity fell.

■ The VA has a hospital construction staff of eight hundred, while the Hospital Corporation of America does the same work with a staff of fifty. As a result of overstaffing, it takes the VA seven years to finish a project, versus two years at the HCA. Administrative costs are 8 percent, versus 2 percent in the private sector.

The Grace Commission says the government could save a neat $58 billion over three years by such things as raising the retirement age to 62 (it now can be as low as 55 for civil service and 40 for the military), imposing early-retirement penalties, offering more reasonable cost-of-living adjustments, and redesigning the job-comparability surveys and the job-classification system. More savings would come just from bringing government pay and work customs into line with those in private business.

PROCUREMENT

One-fifth of the federal budget goes for buying equipment and supplies. In fiscal 1982, for instance, procurement totaled nearly $160 billion, with more than three-fourths of that sum going for Defense Department purchases. Add to the total some $88 billion in inventories that government agencies hold stored all over the country in hundreds of locations.

To do all the federal shopping, some 130,000 federal procurement officers take part in about 18 million "procurement actions" per year. They do all this while entangled in more than eighty thousand pages of regulations, plus twenty thousand new pages of revisions each year.

Here are some examples of what federal procurement has wrought:

- The Navy's Training Equipment Center in Orlando paid $511 for bulbs that cost 60 cents in the grocery store.
- The Navy paid $100 last year for aircraft simulator parts that cost a nickel at the hardware store.
- Costs for 25 major weapons systems that were started between 1971 and 1978 have risen an average of 323 percent. One reason is that defense contractors typically underbid on contracts—sometimes as much as 80 percent below true costs—to get government work. Then, as they proceed, they double and even triple the cost estimates. But by then it is too late to do anything about it.
- The government compounds the cost-overrun problem by allowing a defense contractor that underbids to become the government's monopoly supplier of a system or product for up to twenty years. During that time, the contractor has a free hand to raise and re-raise the price as much as he pleases. Costs are typically doubled and tripled again by these monopoly contractors.
- When the Agency for International Development bought 399 cars and trucks for projects in the Middle East, an audit found that five were missing, 93 had been diverted to personal or nonproject use; 84 had been sitting idle in parking lots, some for two years; and many of the remaining vehicles had been commandeered by host-country government officials for their private use.
- The U.S. Coast Guard pays $100 per week for the use of an office trailer, while the Environmental Protection Agency pays $100 per day to the same supplier for the identical trailer. The EPA's unwitting generosity is blamed on the way the agency deals with its suppliers, and on the fact that the contractor forgot to mention that the $100 was a weekly rate, not a daily one.

More than $28 billion could be saved in procurement over a three-year span, says the Grace Commission, if the government would tighten up its procedures. It could cure cost overruns by using two competing contractors for production of things like weapons systems; by spreading procurement funding over several years to allow better monitoring; and by purchasing spare parts from a source other than the manufacturer (who tends to mark up spare parts outrageously). Federal agencies should also hold smaller inventories, in line with the practice in private business, and they should consider past performance when deciding on a bid award, and ride herd on bidders' cost estimates.

PRIVATIZATION

The federal government is the world's largest (and worst-run) conglomerate. It is at once the nation's largest insurer, lender, borrower, hospital-system operator, power producer, landowner, tenant, holder of grazing land and timberland, grain owner, warehouse operator, ship owner, and truck-fleet operator.

This unnatural situation evolved from the assumption that only government can provide some services. That might have been true years ago when the feds got into most of the businesses they run today. But now it is often nonsensical:

▪ In the 1860s the government decided to provide cheap food for soldiers in isolated frontier outposts by setting up government grocery stores, the military commissaries. Nowadays, a wild frontier town like Washington, D.C., has six commissaries; San Francisco and San Antonio have five each; there are four each in San Diego and in Norfolk. The government has 358 commissary stores, 238 of them in the continental United States, duplicating private supermarkets, but without the profit motive. The result is an uncompetitive and inefficient government grocery chain with annual sales of $4.2 billion, at an annual cost to taxpayers of $597 million.
▪ Europe and Japan are beginning to cut into the U.S. monopoly on outer space, because semiprivate companies like Arianespace can undercut NASA. If the United States is to compete in this growing high-tech business, it should let private companies in on space launches, especially since, by the government's own estimates, it won't be able to meet the commercial demand for space launches in this decade.
▪ The Department of Energy operates 123 hydroelectric dams and 622 substations, supplying 45 percent of the nation's hydroelectric power. But revenues aren't enough to cover the federal investment, the pricing doesn't make sense, and the account books are a mess.
▪ Federal agencies try to do everything in-house. The Defense Department has 11,700 employees doing such things as providing food service, mainte-

nance, laundry service, firefighting, etc. Contracting out this kind of work would save $70 million a year at the Department of Defense.

The Grace Commission has found $28.4 billion of potential savings over three years through privatization. Of these savings, $20 billion would come from selling off the government's hydroelectric dams and substations, some $2.5 billion would come from selling off military commissaries, and the rest would come from contracting out services like VA hospital management and turning over redundant operations to the private sector.

SUBSIDIES

The federal government handed out nearly $500 billion in 1983 to individuals, businesses, and other government agencies. The Department of Health and Human Services alone gives away two out of every five tax dollars—$269 billion last year. Not counting such earned entitlements as Social Security and VA benefits, the federal government offers 64 different welfare programs, costing close to $100 billion a year. In 1983, there were an estimated 22 million Medicaid recipients, 19 million food-stamp recipients, 4.1 million Supplemental Security Income recipients, and 11 million recipients of Aid to Families with Dependent Children. Aside from welfare, there are billions more in subsidies paid to industry and even foreign governments. Without debating the basic validity of some of those programs, here are a few of the obvious abuses:

- Food-stamp cheating amounted to $1 billion in 1981, 10 percent of the whole program. It happens largely because recipients lie about their income and the government never checks.
- An estimated 206,100 aliens living abroad collect U.S. Social Security benefits. The average alien family gets $24 in benefits for every dollar paid in FICA taxes.
- Most of the subsidized mortgage loans made by the government in 1982 went to folks who could have bought homes without help. The typical mortgage revenue bond buyer had an income between $20,000 and $40,-000. Some 53 percent were among the more affluent families in their states, with several making over $50,000 a year.
- An audit revealed nearly $1 billion in rail-modernization money lying idle at the Urban Mass Transportation Administration because the agency has no system for awarding urban discretionary grants.

Some $59 billion could be saved over three years, according to the Grace Commission, by better management of subsidy programs. One recommendation is to tax subsidy payments above a certain income level or corporate tax bracket. Benefit programs ought to be consolidated, and agency accounting systems need to be improved to provide accurate, up-to-date information. The commission says poverty statistics should be redefined to include in-kind transfer payments such as food stamps and Medicaid.

These broad management categories account for some $330 billion in savings over three years, 78 percent of the total. The rest comes from applying the principles of good business management in diverse cases; for example, the Agriculture Department could save an extra $7 billion over three years by cutting out the overlap and duplication in its services; by shifting the FHA's activities from direct loans to loan guarantees and transferring its housing functions to HUD; by charging for such things as maps, soil survey reports, and firewood, all of which are now given away free; and by increasing user fees for grazing, recreation, and the like.

The Grace Commission calls for an Office of Federal Management to be set up in the executive office of the President. Such an office would guide and coordinate management of the government's $800 billion conglomerate. It would institute the kind of budgeting and strategic planning that large corporations practice, and develop common government-wide software for standardized receivables, payroll, pension-plan, and fixed-asset accounting.

After Peter Grace presented the final report to the President in a White House cermony on January 16 [1984,] the networks dutifully ran stories on the evening news, usually ending with the remark that here is another commission report to be filed away. Who, in an election year, was going to propose serious budgetary pigsticking? The *New York Times* wanly editorialized that the Grace Commission was "wishful, but worthwhile, on waste." Some of the Grace Commission's recommendations are already being carried out, but three-quarters of them need congressional approval. Hence, the question lingers: Can it really be done? And we are led to the crux of the issue: psychology.

News that the government pays $30 million in Medicare checks to the deceased, and loses track of $10 billion in block-grant money, seems almost beyond reality, somewhere in the realm of the absurd. It makes neat newspaper filler material, American black humor, good for a chuckle over coffee. It's another little confirmation of what most Americans have suspected of the government since the time of Thomas Jefferson.

Upon reflection, the unreality of the abuses becomes as overwhelming and unimaginable as the sheer size of the expenditures. More discouraging still is the realization that this sort of thing has obviously been going on for ages. So one shakes one's head and flips the page. What's to be done? *Nada, niente, rien du tout.*

The irony is that something can indeed be done, if enough citizens believe it can be, and make their wish known in Washington. Only by the force of widespread dissatisfaction can Congress find the courage to stick some pigs. In this sense, Peter Grace's work has only begun.

Don't Blame the Bureaucracy!

H. Brinton Milward
Hal G. Rainey

1. THE DENIGRATION OF BUREAUCRACY

For over a decade, there has been increasing skepticism about the performance of the public bureaucracy in the United States. The problem has been a
major theme in the last several presidential administrations, and has reached
a high point in the Reagan administration. President Reagan's contempt for
the bureaucracy is no secret. Ed Meese, one of the President's major counsel-
ors, came to a cabinet meeting with a rotund, faceless, large-bottomed doll.
He announced that it was a bureaucrat doll; you put it on a stack of papers
and it just sits there! (Raines, 1981).

    If presidents and their aides are acting this way, you can predict that
they feel that most of the voters approve. Public opinion polls have in fact
been detecting a widespread conviction that government is wasteful, meddle-
some, and ineffective, and much of this concern focuses on public agencies
and their employees as a major part of the problem. A Roper poll asked respondents to estimate how much of each $100 spent by the Social Security
Administration goes for administrative costs. The median estimate was about
$52.10. The acutal cost is $1.30 (Germond and Witcover, 1981). In May of
1981 a Lou Harris poll found that 88 percent of the 1,207 respondents felt
that too much tax money is wasted by an inefficient bureaucracy.[1] . . .

    A great many people assume we have gone too far in the political and
bureaucratic direction, and need to move back towards heavier reliance on
private markets. We do not claim to be certain that they are wrong, but we
feel strongly that such decisions should not be made without considering

From H. Brinton Milward and Hal G. Rainey, "Don't Blame the Bureaucracy," *Journal of Public
Policy*, vol. 3, no. 2 (1983), 149–68. Notes and references have been edited to conform to the
text—*Editors*.

some points about the performance and value of the public bureaucracy which we want to raise in this paper. Some of these points stress that the public bureaucracy may be more effective and valuable than often supposed. Other points emphasize that, if the bureaucracy performs badly in certain ways, the source of the problem may not be in the organizations and employees themselves. Blaming the bureaucracy, then, may be a very bad way of trying to improve things.

2. THE CRY FOR EFFICIENCY: "RUN GOVERNMENT LIKE A BUSINESS"

The most popular current charge against the government bureaucracy is that government at all levels is inefficient and ineffective because of bad management. The solution proposed in Washington and in many state capitals and city halls is to "run government more like a business." Government's ship must be made tighter and more efficient, through centralization of power in the executive's hands, and elimination of waste, duplication, and overlap. This theme is nothing new in American public administration, but has been heavily emphasized recently. For example, President Reagan once said that many of his budget cuts could be accomplished simply through the elimination of waste and mismanagement. Certain governors have made the call for more businesslike procedures into a theme for their administrations.

No one opposes efficiency in government, and many business practices should be used more frequently in government, but the call for "running government more like a business" is often badly misconceived. It overlooks several serious points. One of these points is that heavy emphasis on operating efficiency may distort the role, purpose, and value of government in our society. The United States government, with its sharing of executive power between Congress and the President, was originally designed with less emphasis on simple efficiency than on avoiding concentrated power and centralized administration of the type European monarchies possessed. Indeed, the same emphasis exists today. . . .

A second misconception in the calls for more businesslike efficiency in government is their underestimation of the actual value that can be attached to government, if it really were viewed in businesslike fashion. Former Governor Dan Evans of Washington provided an excellent example of this when he grew tired of the constant calls for "running government more like a business." He had a document prepared titled *Report to the Shareholders of the State of Washington* (1976). In it he applied the corporate model to the state to show the inappropriate nature of the comparison. Imagine, he said, trying to run a company whose "stockholders," the electorate, only gave you a razor thin vote of confidence; where the "board of directors," the legislature, was often controlled by a rival group; and where your "management team," the cabinet, was in part separately elected and partly picked by you. How would you like to manage this "company" knowing you were limited by law to either one or two four-year terms? Evans went on to apply the accounting system used by Boeing, the largest company in Washington, to the assets and liabilities of the state. In spite of these constraints on management of the state, the analysis showed it to be far from a precarious financial position. Accepted accounting standards showed that the net worth of the state worked out to $1,800 per citizen. The reason was that capital investments like buildings and highways previously had been treated as expenditures and were assumed to have no worth after construction.

Some observers even argue that the immense value of government assets and services are part of the problem in managing our economy. Lindblom (1976) points out that a great deal of government activity in the USA, now and in the past, has actually been devoted to the support and promotion of private business. James O'Connor, in *The Fiscal Crisis of the State* (1973), similarly argues that a major problem for our public finances is that private corporations, especially in certain noncompetitive industries, force major costs of their operations onto government. The taxpayers pick up the tab for roads, schools, cultural and entertainment facilities, police, public transportation, and numerous other assets and services which benefit business enterprises far more than they cost those enterprises. Yet public agencies usually receive the blame for the high costs. As one example, much has been made of the regulatory costs imposed on the automobile industry. Those costs may well be excessive, but the critics seldom note that the automobile industry's development has been directly linked to the hundreds of billions spent by taxpayers and government for roadbuilding. The huge costs of maintaining those roads and highways is emerging as a major issue, and government will have to take the heat and solve the problem. Is government a burden on the auto industry, or is it really the other way around?

Another shortsighted aspect of the cries for business efficiency in government is that they often overestimate business efficiency and actually underestimate the efficiency with which government operates. It is commonly assumed that business is more efficient, but this is more easily assumed than proven. There is plenty of evidence of immense waste and inefficiency in business organization, which makes it hard to say whether they are any better or worse than government organizations on that score.

Among many examples of this evidence of poor performance by some American business organizations is the current attack on them in two recent books (Ouchi, 1981; Pascale and Althos, 1981) and numerous articles which compare American management practices very unfavorably with those of the Germans and Japanese. These criticisms make one wonder whether American business organizations are really an ideal model for government to copy, and they point up an irony in some of the calls for more businesslike efficiency in government. The observers of Japanese industrial success say it results in large part from willingness to forego the short-term profit which comes at the expense of maintenance, capital investment in the plant, and humane management practices. Ironically, the changes urged on the public sector often involve financial techniques and control systems which focus on short-term efficiency and tightened control with little attention to long-term investment in the organization and commitment to it. One clear instance of this is the effort to remove civil service protections at many levels of government. While many successful business organizations here and abroad make long-term commitments to employees and emphasize their personal development, critics of government assume that government will become more productive if we make employees more afraid they will be fired.

That last point brings us to the ultimate jibe at the "run the government like a business" argument. It is usually unclear, if not simply meaningless. It is a simple minded proposal that merits a simple response; should we run it like W. T. Grant, Penn Central, and the fifty thousand businesses that go bankrupt every year; or should we run it like successful companies like IBM or Delta Airlines, both of which practice "inefficient" practices like not laying off employees during cyclical downturns in business conditions? The simple proposal contains no clear advice as to what we should do. . . .

3. VALUE COMPLEXITY: MULTIPLE, CONFLICTING, HARD-TO-MEASURE GOALS

We have made the point that government serves values more complex than operating efficiency. It is important to recognize the true variety and complexity of those additional values, the ways in which they complicate evaluation of the public bureaucracy, and most of all, to recognize that attention to them is simply inescapable. If the functions of government could be easily packaged for exchange on markets, then the private sector would normally get the jobs. Governments gets the messy jobs, and government agencies have many goals imposed upon them. This naturally makes it harder to achieve all of them.

One reason for this is that the goals are often contradictory. Pursuit of one detracts from achievement of others. Wilson and Rachel (1977) provide a vivid illustration of this problem. Imagine, they say, a state highway department. It is largely composed of engineers who have been told by the legislature and governor to build a highway between two cities at the lowest cost, given accepted engineering standards. Here we have a public agency with a goal which is actually clear and unambiguous compared to the goals of many public programs. Construction begins, however, and immediately efficient achievement of the goal is frustrated. The engineers are forced to pay the prevailing union wage, whether the workforce is union or not, because of the Davis-Bacon Act. Next, minority groups complain that the contractors have not given enough of the subcontract work to minority owned firms. The contractors claim that the minority subcontractors had higher bids and/or were less experienced than competing subcontractors. Nevertheless the law is clear and they must be given a piece of the action. Construction finally begins, and costs have already risen substantially, but the end appears to be in sight. Then the Sierra Club threatens to sue the contractors and the state if an alternate route is not chosen which avoids a swamp which is also a wildlife refuge. Again the law is clear and the state reroutes the highway at a cost of millions of dollars. The road is finally completed several years late and millions over budget. Those groups who along the way pressed additional goals are happy but the public at large views the late completion and excessive cost as just another example of bureaucratic bungling.

The clear lesson from this example is that efficiency is a very important value but there are other values such as equity and protection of the environment which by law must be observed, and which compete with simple operating efficiency. If the road had been built efficiently the state would have been pilloried for spoiling the environment, supporting the vestiges of discrimination and being antiunion. Public agencies are often put in a no-win situation where the achievement of one goal insures poor performance on another.

The government agency may be seen as inefficient, but is actually incorporating into its own operations the value conflicts which must somehow be worked out in a complex society. Equity (defined as equal treatment of citizens) and governmental responsiveness and accountability are also very important values in our political life.

These values mean that there are multiple criteria for judging success or failure. A program can be run very efficiently and still be accused of being unresponsive, because to be efficient means that you cannot continually respond to this or that request or you will no longer be judged efficient. It is the ability of business to deflect many intrusions into how they operate that often makes them better able to perform on the efficiency criterion than government. Thus GM does not have to hold "citizen participation" hearings before every major decision they make. Having to manage in a fishbowl and to have your files constantly open for public inspection—as the Freedom of Information Act allows—may be wonderful if judged from the criterion of accountability but it makes it very difficult to be efficient.

Equity is another value that is difficult to reconcile with efficiency. From an efficiency standpoint, it was economic madness to spend millions upon millions of dollars making public transportation accessible to the handicapped. Not only did it direct large amounts of money to a small proportion of the population but there were less costly ways to achieve the same goal of making public transportation available to the handicapped. Rather than retrofitting old buses, buying new ones with wider aisles and wheelchair lifts or putting elevators in subway stations (which then break down because of lack of use), cities could have more cheaply provided a system of wheelchair accessible minibuses that could be available on demand to take the handicapped person where he wanted to go. This alternative was rejected by organized groups representing the handicapped because handicapped people would not have the same access to the same facilities as nonhandicapped people. Thus a great amount of money was spent complying with this interpretation of the law which said that federal funds must not be spent on facilities that are not accessible to the handicapped. The courts decreed that the money was to be spent to insure equity with no thought given to economic efficiency.

There is no better example of these difficulties of considering multiple values and avoiding stereotypes than that most frequent choice as the quintessential government giveaway program, "welfare." Public opinion polls and other sources consistently show that high percentages of Americans see "welfare" as one of the major forms of government waste and a major reason for higher taxes. Yet in the 1982 budget proposed by the Reagan administration, these programs normally considered welfare programs (AFDC, Medicaid, and several others) accounted for about $50 billion of the total of approximately $650 billion (Pechman,1981, p. 55). Fifty billion dollars is a huge amount, and the programs may have huge problems, but it is clear that even if we eliminated them completely and passed all the money directly back to taxpayers, tax bills would not go down as much as 10 percent. There is really not nearly that much which can be cut, of course, because we cannot let the poor starve in the streets, and most welfare recipients are not chiselers, but persons who work when they can or who simply are unable to work. It is clear that "welfare" as a source of high taxes and bureaucratic waste is exaggerated in the minds of a great many Americans.

Still, some critics argue that we would do better to return the money to the private sector, and let business expand to absorb the welfare recipients. The private sector is assumed to be more efficient, so the money would be better used. But is this argument not a good example of the oversimplification about complex systems which plagues our public debate? One of the ways in which industry has made its impressive gains in productivity is by displacing workers with machines. Industry has required higher and higher levels of skill from workers, and has less and less demand for the unskilled labor which most welfare recipients can provide. Government is given the task of providing for the persons least useful to industry, and is also saddled with the blame for the problem.

Complaints about the wasteful welfare system usually overlook the more general societal issues which are so complicated to resolve. Do we really know the social costs we are saving through the welfare system, even if it is riddled with waste, mismanagement, and disincentives? One could observe that the society is getting a perverse bargain, by buying off the impoverished lower end of the income scale with small payments, while the rest of us, including the much-pitied middle class, live in a state of comfort never dreamed of, even by the aristocrats of a century or two ago. Another perspective is to view the system of welfare programs with a certain degree of pride, as a system which is flawed, but which has largely eradicated acute malnutrition and other aspects of abject poverty in a country not particularly inclined to address those problems. These arguments are oversimplifications themselves, but show how complicated the evaluation of even a widely pilloried program can be. . . .

4. PUBLIC SECTOR STANDARDS ARE HIGHER

The value complexity involved in evaluating public bureaucracy is also due to the higher performance standards which are applied to government. We feel a sense of ownership of government, and a caution about its powers. We demand that, in addition to being efficient, government must be fair, open, honest, accountable, consistent, and responsive.

A good example of these particularly high standards for government, ironically, is the matter of efficiency, where business is often assumed to be superior. What organization, public or private, doesn't waste 5 to 10 percent of its revenue? This "waste" takes many forms—theft, breakage, spoilage, unnecessary perks for managers, poor decisions about projected demand, and slack resources to meet peak demand. All of these factors exist in both sectors, but they cause much more concern in the public sector. The federal government at the request of Congress is now requiring that Prime Sponsors under the CETA program account for and be responsible for every dollar spent by the autonomous training programs that they fund. No waste at all is allowed in a program which is supposed to be flexible and responsive to the needs of those who need job training. Most of the training programs which are storefront community organizations cannot afford accountants or trained financial managers, but the Prime Sponsor is held completely responsible for every dollar they spend (Barnes, 1980).

The same pattern holds in the matter of ethics. If Labor Secretary Raymond Donovan had still been a New Jersey contractor instead of Secretary of Labor, no one would bat an eye over his being accused of giving a union official with ties to the Mafia several thousand dollars to ensure labor peace at a construction site. In many northeastern states, this is part of the cost of doing business. Against a Secretary of Labor, however, this becomes a serious charge and, if proven, grounds for dismissal. Thus in ethics as in performance we seem to have created a double standard.

To this point, we have suggested that public bureaucracy has more value than is commonly recognized. As we have said, however, there are plenty of indications that government agencies often do perform poorly. Here again, it can be harmful simply to berate the bureaucracy, because the real source of the problem often lies outside it.

5. THE SPECIAL INTEREST STATE

. . . John Gardner, the founder of Common Cause, describes the special interest state this way:

> *Imagine a checkers player confronted by a bystander who puts a thumb on one checker and says, "Go ahead and play just don't touch this one," and then another bystander puts a thumb on another checker with the same warning, and then another and another. Pretty soon all thumbs and no moves. The irony is that the owners of the thumbs—the special interests—don't want to make the game unwinnable; they just don't want you to touch their checker. The result is they paralyze the policymaking process* (Gardner, 1979, p. 32).

In addition to the immobility that comes from the checker game, another aspect of the special interest state is that the pervasiveness of bureaucratic rules and regulations (the proverbial "red tape") is caused by special interests and Congress, not rule-bound bureaucrats. What Samuel Halperin says of education can be applied to any policy arena:

> *Much of the prescriptive language that occurs in federal statutes does not come from congressmen who are trying to oppress educators. Much of it comes from one group in society that doesn't trust or agree with another group in society* (Halperin, 1978, pp. 14–15).

The last special interest state argument concerns the fragmentation of policy and the lack of policy consistency one finds in federal programs. Joe Califano conducted an antismoking crusade at HEW while the Department of Agriculture was supporting price supports and acreage allotments for tobacco farmers and the Department of Commerce was not requiring manufacturers of tobacco to put the Surgeon General's health warning on cigarettes to be exported. The reason this occurs is not bureaucratic stupidity. Fragmentation arises precisely from a key function of democratic government—to respond to diverse demands from interests which are mutually incompatible. This leads directly to policies which tend to be directly contradictory. . . .

6. CONGRESS ASKS BUREAUCRACIES TO DO THINGS WHICH NO ONE KNOWS HOW TO DO

This approach to the "bureaucracy problem" locates the problem squarely in the Congress. Congress, due to the pressure of interest groups (some of them organizations of professionals who work for government), will pass laws calling for government agencies to do things that they or anyone else simply do not know how to do. Or if the technology is known, the Congress may be very reluctant to provide the necessary funds to perform the task adequately.

Problems of this nature usually occur in organizations that are charged with changing the behavior of individual clients. Whether it is the prisons which are supposed to rehabilitate criminals or social workers who are supposed to change pathological behavior of some welfare clients involving spouse abuse, civil servants are being asked to do things that our society does not know how to do. If we do know how to do these things, it is usually possible only in an individualistic setting where massive amounts of human and monetary resources are brought to bear on the client. This can hardly be the case in a resource-tight public sector that runs programs that must of necessity be geared to large numbers of clients and diffused over fifty states and ten thousand cities.

Congress and the American peole have been unwilling to accept some harsh realities . . . There are few if any comprehensive solutions to problems like moral decay, declining cities, or welfare. Such matters are either unknowable or, for a variety of reasons, not achievable. While Congress can pass laws on any topic and spend money for any public purpose, implementing policies depends on bureaucracies being able to translate legislative intent into an implementable program. If there is no known cause-and-effect relationship between the theory underlying the program and what an agency is asked to do then the bureaucracy will once again become a scapegoat.

The most ridiculous current example comes not from the Democrats or social work do-gooders but from ultraconservative Senator Jeremiah Denton (R.–Ala.). He introduced a bill in Congress to create a program to "study the causes of teenage pregnancy" and develop ways of promoting chastity among teenagers. While the *causes* of teenage pregnancy are obvious the solutions are not and even if they were, the imposition of chastity belts in a democratic society would not be looked upon with great favor. . . .

7. GOVERNMENTAL OVERLOAD

This view of the problem is similar to the above argument concerning doing things we do not know how to do. It holds that because all issues become political and the special interest state has no criteria for refusing any request, the state will try to do everything (see King, 1975). Some things will be within its capacity, some will not, but all will be attempted. The result is that the carrying capacity of the government will become overloaded and because resources will be spread too thin the system will overload and falter. . . .

8. MACROECONOMIC MANAGEMENT HINDERS PROGRAM PERFORMANCE

The President and Congress live and die not on whether CETA is perceived as being an efficiently run program but rather on the rates of inflation and unemployment. These two summary statistics are far more important to political survival than any government program; because of this the management of the economy has become the single most important single task of government.

In Maryland an aide to Governor Harry R. Hughes points out that

the energy assistance program is designed to keep people warm in winter. But they (OMB) want to give you the money in equal amounts every quarter. We don't need the money in July, we need it now, and these guys in Washington are sitting on the money. You know why? They want to keep it in the bank and draw interest on it, and we've got people freezing (Herbers, 1982).

Steps designed to better manage or "fine tune" the economy (across-the-board budget cuts, personnel reductions in force which lay off good workers and bad, and personnel ceilings unrelated to the magnitude of the job to be done) can cripple the effectiveness of government programs. The U.S. Office of Surface Mining issued 800 fewer mine violations in 1980 than in 1979. They attributed the decrease, rightly or wrongly, not to a change in policy from Carter to Reagan; rather, they attributed it to not being able to replace mine inspectors who resigned during the federal hiring freeze.

9. STEREOTYPES OF BUREAUCRACY: TWO COGNITIVE LEVELS

The preceding points show how hard it is to say whether we are simply underestimating public bureaucracy or whether bureaucracy actually is doing badly because of burdens imposed on it. A problem in resolving the issue is that there are widely held unfavorable stereotypes of public bureaucracy. It is hard to separate accurate evaluation from invidious myth. The views of public bureaucracy are also paradoxical, making it hard to say what people really want to do about bureaucracy.

In one of the most careful and interesting studies of such views ever done, Daniel Katz and associates (1975) reported that the public's general evaluation of government agencies is not particularly favorable. They asked respondents to rate how well government agencies meet a number of performance criteria, such as solving clients' problems, prompt service, fair treatment, and others. About 25 to 35 percent of the respondents gave generally unfavorable ratings of public agencies, and only small percentages gave highly favorable ratings. When asked to say whether business or government meets the standards better, about half of the respondents saw no difference, but of those who did, more than twice as many felt that business does better.

Strikingly, however, respondents' ratings of their own specific encounters with public agencies were much more favorable than their impressions of public agencies in general. Katz et al. concluded that their respondents' attitudes tended to be organized along two levels. The attitudes on specific matters—the way particular agencies have actually treated you—tended to be favorable. When the referent is less specific—public agencies in general—negative stereotypes have a greater influence and ratings become less favorable. There are also similar survey findings of unfavorable ratings of Congress as an institution by respondents who at the same time are pleased with their own Congressman. Only 20 percent of the respondents in a University of Michigan poll taken in 1978 said Congress was doing a good job. In contrast, 65 percent of those responding gave their congressman a high rating on job performance. Polls consistently report similarly paradoxical views. People will say that they want less government and lower taxes, but more public services.

The problem of destructive stereotyping brings us back to the Ed Meese joke with which we started. The public employee is probably the easiest target for cheap shots in our political and economic system, and the criticisms have a very tangible impact. As we said earlier, there are many reports of demoralization, and of departure of good people from the public service in the first year of the Reagan presidency. An official working in Washington commented to one of us, only partly in jest, that the rhetoric there made him feel that as a public employee he had never earned an honest dollar. . . .

10. CONCLUSION

We have argued two main points which it is dangerous to overlook. First, the public bureaucracy in the United States is more valuable, and is performing more effectively, than many people assume. We noted that its performance and value cannot be evaluated only in terms of simple operating efficiency, because of the need for complex controls of the public bureaucracy and the need to assess its impact on complex societal objectives. We pointed out the immense and often underestimated value of the functions and services provided by public agencies, and argued that those agencies are not as wasteful and inept as is often casually assumed. Among the reasons that they may seem to be performing badly are that we assign them particularly complex, multiple, hard-to-measure goals, which often conflict with each other, and at the same time we hold their performance up to particularly high standards.

The second main point is that when public bureaucracies do perform badly, the problem is often due to external factors rather than internal laziness, incompetence, or mismanagement. Public agencies must respond to demands of multiple special interests within the society. They are asked to do things which are immensely difficult or sometimes impossible, and are often overloaded with responsibilities relative to the resources they have for carrying out those responsibilities. Chief executives and legislatures emphasize macroeconomic management in a way that hinders internal program management and efficiency. We also pointed out that public agencies and officials must operate in an environment of crude, contradictory stereotypes, where berating bureaucrats and the bureaucracy are favorite pastimes. These stereotypes can be self-fulfilling, and in themselves create performance problems.

. . . The outcomes of the current emphasis on cutback and fiscal constraint are uncertain at this writing, but it is clear that no one is going to dismantle government. The United States—and other industrialized countries—will continue to need effective large-scale management. The public services which discharge those functions must be subject to public criticism, so a certain degree of blaming the bureaucracy is inevitable. More of our citizens and leaders, however, need to begin to think like managers themselves. We must respond to problems with clear thinking and an intelligent search for solutions, and deny ourselves the luxury of easy excuses, oversimplifications, scapegoating, myths, and damaging stereotypes. Only if we do so can we successfully address the challenges of governing a complex, advanced society.

NOTE

1. "Why the Middle Class Supports Reagan," *Business Week*, May 18, 1981. The Institute for Social Research at the University of Michigan has been finding that very high percentages of the respondents to their polls feel that the government wastes a lot of money. See Smith, Taylor, and Mathiowetz (1980).

REFERENCES

Barnes, P. W. (1980) CETA audits of local funds spark protest, *Wall Street Journal*, 26 August 1980.
Evans, D. J. (1976) *Report to the Stockholders of the State of Washington*, Olympia, Washington.
Gardner, J. (1979) The special interest state, *Encounter*, vol. 52, no. 1.
Germond, J., and J. Witcover (1981) GOP playing numbers, *Tallahassee Democrat*, 19 July 1981.
Halperin, S. (1978) Emerging education policy issues in the federal city. Occasional paper No. 42, National Center for Research in Vocational Education, Ohio State University.
Herbers, J. (1982) Budget cuts, tax hikes confront many states, *Lexington Herald Leader*, 3 January 1982.
Katz, D., B. A. Gutek, R. L. Kahn, and E. Barton (1975) *Bureaucratic Encounters: A Pilot Study in the Evaluation of Government Services*. Ann Arbor: Survey Research Center, Institute for Social Research, University of Michigan.
King, A. (1975) Overload: problems of governing in the 1970s, *Political Studies*, 23, 162-74.
Lindblom, C. (1976) *Politics and Markets*. New York: Basic Books.
O'Connor, J. (1973) *The Fiscal Crisis of the State*. New York: St. Martin's Press.
Ouchi, W. (1981) *Theory Z, How America Can Meet the Japanese Challenge*. Reading, Mass.: Addison-Wesley.

Pascale, R. T., and A. G. Althos (1981) *The Art of Japanese Management.* New York: Simon and Schuster.

Pechman, J. A. (ed.) (1981) *Setting National Priorities: The 1982 Budget.* Washington, D.C.: Brookings Institution.

Raines, H. (1981) Bureaucrats: The scapegoats again for Reagan and staff, *Louisville Courier Journal,* 23 October 1981.

Smith, T. W., D. G. Taylor, and N. A. Mathiowetz (1980) Public opinion and public regard for the Federal government. In A. Barton and C. Weiss (eds.), *Making Bureaucracies Work,* Beverly Hills, Calif.: Sage.

Wilson, J. Q., and P. Rachel (1977) Can government regulate itself? *Public Interest,* 46 (Winter, 1977), 3-14.

CHAPTER THIRTEEN

THE SUPREME COURT

While few would contend that the Supreme Court should not have the power to interpret the Constitution, there is considerable disagreement over how the nine justices should approach this awesome responsibility. On one side of this debate are those who advocate "judicial restraint," while on the other are those who favor "judicial activism."

Sam Ervin, a former U.S. Senator from North Carolina and for a time a member of that state's Supreme Court, comes down hard on the side of judicial restraint. He argues that the justices of the Supreme Court are obligated to interpret the Constitution solely on the basis of the language contained therein. Where the language is ambiguous, the justices must put themselves in the place of the framers of that document and interpret such language as they believe the framers would have. If provisions of the Constitution are inadequate and require change, then it must come solely through a constitutional amendment, and not through judicial fiat. In this connection, Ervin is highly critical of the Warren Court, which he feels substituted its own ideological preferences for the true meaning of the Constitution.

Ramsey Clark, the U.S. Attorney General during the Johnson administration, sides with those who would take a more activist approach to interpreting the Constitution. Noting that the Founding Fathers could not have anticipated the fundamental political, social, and economic alterations which have occurred in our society, Clark argues that interpretation of the Constitution must be made in light of these changes. To this extent, the Constitution may be viewed as an evolving document. To interpret the Constitution literally is to wed us to the past, thereby denying us the ability to cope with the present.

259

In Support of
Judicial Restraint

Sam J. Ervin, Jr.

In discussing the question whether the role of the Supreme Court is that of policymaker or that of adjudicator, I will use the term "Founding Fathers" to designate the men who drafted and ratified the Constitution.

The Constitution answers this question with unmistakable clarity. There is not a syllable in it which gives the Supreme Court any discretionary power to fashion policies based on such considerations as expediency or prudence to guide the course of action of the government of our country. On the contrary, the Constitution provides in plain and positive terms that the role of the Supreme Court is that of an adjudicator, which determines judicially legal controversies between adverse litigants.

In assigning this role to the Supreme Court, the Founding Fathers were faithful to the dream which inspired them to draft and ratify the Constitution, and to their action in rejecting in the Constitutional Convention repeated proposals that the Supreme Court should act as a council of revision as well as a court and, in its capacity as a council of revision, possess discretionary power to veto all acts of Congress the justices deemed unwise, no matter how much those acts harmonized with the Constitution.[1]

These things do not gainsay that some Supreme Court justices have been unhappy with the role assigned them by the Constitution and have undertaken to usurp and exercise policymaking power. But their usurpations have not altered the rightful role of the Supreme Court. Murder and larceny have been committed in every generation, but that fact has not made murder meritorious or larceny legal. . . .

From Sam J. Ervin, Jr., "First Lecture," in *Role of the Supreme Court: Policymaker or Adjudicator?*, pp. 1–16 (Washington, D. C.: American Enterprise Institute for Public Policy Research, 1970). © American Enterprise Institute, 1970. Reprinted with permission.

THE CONSTITUTION

Let me indicate what the Founding Fathers did in the Constitution to give our nation a government of laws and to preserve for themselves and their posterity the blessings of liberty.

To make our nation "an indestructible union composed of indestructible states,"[2] they delegated enumerated governmental powers to the federal government, and reserved all other governmental powers to the states. To further fragmentize political power, they allocated federal legislative power to the Congress, federal executive power to the President, and federal judicial power to the Supreme Court and "such inferior courts as the Congress may from time to time ordain and establish."[3]

To further forestall tyranny, they forbade federal and state governments to do specified things inimical to freedom, and conferred upon individuals enumerated liberties enforceable against government itself. And, finally, to make government by law secure, they made the Constitution and laws enacted by Congress pursuant to it the supreme law of the land, and imposed upon all public officials, both federal and state, as well as upon the people the duty to obey them.[4]

While they intended the Constitution to endure throughout the ages as the nation's basic instrument of government, the Founding Fathers realized that useful alterations of the Constitution would be suggested by experience. Consequently they made provision for its amendment in one way, and one way only, i.e., by concurrent action of Congress and the states as set forth in Article V.[5] By so doing, they ordained that "nothing new can be put into the Constitution except through the amendatory process" and "nothing old can be taken out without the same process."[6]

THE ROLE OF THE SUPREME COURT

A policy is a definite or settled course of action adopted and followed by government. The power to make policy is discretionary in nature. It involves the making of choices on the basis of expediency or prudence among alternative ways of action.

The power to make policy in a government of laws resides with those who are authorized to participate in the lawmaking process.

The Founding Fathers made policy when they ordained and established the Constitution, which determines the fundamental policies of our country.

Since Article I of the Constitution grants Congress the power to make laws and requires every bill passed by it to be presented to the President for his approval or disapproval before it takes effect, the Congress and the President have policymaking power. Moreover, Article V confers upon the Congress and the states, acting in conjunction, limited policymaking power, i.e., the power to amend the Constitution.

Article III denies the Supreme Court policymaking power in plain and positive terms. It does this by making the Supreme Court a court of law and equity and by granting to it "judicial power" only. Under this article, the Supreme Court has no power whatever except the power to hear and determine cases between adverse litigants, which are within the scope of its original or appellate jurisdiction.

Article III denies the Supreme Court policymaking power in another way. When it is read in conjunction with the supremacy clause of Article VI, Article III obligates Supreme Court justices to base their decisions in the cases they hear upon the Constitution, the laws, and the treaties of the United States, and thus forbids them to take their personal notions as to what is desirable into account in making their rulings.

For this reason, Supreme Court justices are endowed with power to interpret any provision of the Constitution or any law or treaty which is determinative of the issue arising in a case coming before them.

THE POWER TO INTERPRET THE CONSTITUTION

The power to interpret the Constitution is an awesome power. This is so because, in truth, constitutional government cannot exist in our land unless this power is exercised aright.

Chief Justice Stone had this thought in mind when he stated this truth concerning Supreme Court justices:

> While unconstitutional exercise of power by the executive and legislative branches of the government is subject to judicial restraint, the only check upon our exercise of power is our own sense of self-restraint.[7]

The power to interpret the Constitution, which is allotted to the Supreme Court, and the power to amend the Constitution, which is assigned to Congress and the states acting in conjunction, are quite different. The power to interpret the Constitution is the power to ascertain its meaning, and the power to amend the Constitution is the power to change its meaning.

Justice Cardozo put the distinction between the two powers tersely when he said:

> We are not at liberty to revise while professing to construe.[8]

Justice Sutherland elaborated upon the distinction in this way:

> The judicial function is that of interpretation: it does not include the power of amendment under the guise of interpretation. To miss the point of difference between the two is to miss all that the phrase "supreme law of the land" stands for and to convert what were intended as inescapable and enduring mandates into mere moral reflections.[9]

America's geatest jurist of all times, Chief Justice John Marshall, established these landmarks of constitutional interpretation:

1. That the principles of the Constitution "are designed to be permanent."[10]

2. That "the enlightened patriots who framed our Constitution, and the people who adopted it, must be understood . . . to have intended what they have said."[11]

3. That the Constitution constitutes a rule for the government of Supreme Court justices in their official action.[12]

Since it is a court of law and equity, the Supreme Court acts as the interpreter of the Constitution only in a litigated case whose decision of necessity turns on some provision of that instrument. As a consequence, the function of the Court is simply to ascertain and give effect to the intent of those who framed and ratified the provision in issue. If the provision is plain, the Court must gather the intent solely from its language, but if the provision is ambiguous, the Court must place itself as nearly as possible in that condition of those who framed and ratified it, and in that way determine the intent the language was used to express. For these reasons, the Supreme Court is duty bound to interpret the Constitution according to its language and history.[13] . . .

THE WARREN COURT

During most of our history, Supreme Court justices were faithful to the dream of the Founding Fathers. They accepted the Constitution as the rule for their official action, and decided constitutional issues in accordance with its precepts.

Unfortunately, however, this has not been true during recent years. Shortly before 1953, Supreme Court justices began to substitute their personal notions for constitutional provisions under the guise of interpreting them, and provoked one of their colleagues, Justice Robert H. Jackson, into making this righteous outcry:

> Rightly or wrongly, the belief is widely held by the practicing profession that this Court no longer respects impersonal rules of law but is guided in these matters by personal impressions which from time to time may be shared by a majority of the Justices. Whatever has been intended, this Court also has generated an impression in much of the judiciary that regard for precedents and authorities is obsolete, that words no longer mean what they have always meant to the profession, that the law knows no fixed principles.[14]

With the advent of the Warren Court, this practice increased in frequency and intensity; and the Supreme Court decisions irreconcilable with the Constitution became in Milton's colorful phrase as "thick as autumnal leaves that strow the brooks in Vallombrosa."

I use the terms "Warren Court" and "justices of the Warren Court" to designate Chief Justice Warren and Justices Douglas, Brennan, Goldberg, Fortas, and Marshall who repeatedly undertook to revise the Constitution while professing to interpret it. Candor compels the confession that despite his eloquent protests against their misuse of the due process clauses of the Fifth and Fourteenth Amendments, Justice Black often aligned himself with the justices of the Warren Court; and that although the other justices who served at various times during the incumbency of Chief Justice Warren, namely, Justices Reed, Frankfurter, Jackson, Burton, Clark, Minton, Harlan, Stewart, and White, were rather steadfast in their adherence to the Constitution, some of them joined the Warren Court on some occasions in handing down revolutionary decisions inconsistent with the words and history of that instrument.[15]

The tragic truth is that, under the guise of interpreting them, the Warren Court repeatedly assigned to constitutional provisions meanings incompatible with their language and history.

By so doing, it has impeded the President and his subordinates in the performance of their constitutional duty to execute the laws.

At times it has undertaken to abridge the constitutional powers of Congress as the nation's lawmaker, and at other times it has undertaken to stretch the legislative powers of Congress far beyond their constitutional limits. And sometimes it has thwarted the will of Congress by imputing to congressional acts constructions which cannot be harmonized with their words.

What the Warren Court has done to the power allotted or reserved to the states by the Constitution beggars description. It has invoked the due process and equal protection clauses of the Fourteenth Amendment as *carte blanche* to invalidate all state action which Supreme Court justices think undesirable.

This is tragic, indeed, because nothing is truer than this observation attributed to Justice Brandeis by Judge Learned Hand:

> *The states are the only breakwater against the ever pounding surf which threatens to submerge the individual and destroy the only kind of society in which personality can survive.*

Besides, the Warren Court twisted some constitutional provisions awry to deny individuals basic personal and property rights.

All of the decisions of which I complain have tended to concentrate power in the federal government in general and the Supreme Court in particular.

The time presently allotted to me does not permit me to analyze or even enumerate these decisions.

These things mean little or nothing to those who would as soon have our country ruled by the arbitrary, uncertain, and inconstant wills of judges as by the certain and constant precepts of the Constitution. But they mean everything to those of us who love the Constitution and believe it evil to twist its precepts out of shape even to accomplish ends which may be desirable.

If desirable ends are not attainable under the Constitution as written, they should be attained in a forthright manner by an amendment under Article V, and not by judicial alchemy which transmutes words into things they do not say. Otherwise, the Constitution is a meaningless scrap of paper.

Nobody questions the good intentions of the justices of the Warren Court. They undoubtedly were motivated by a determination to improve and update the Constitution by substituting their personal notions for its principles. But candor compels the confession that their usurpations call to mind these trenchant observations of Daniel Webster:

> Good intentions will always be pleaded for every assumption of power. It is hardly too strong to say that the Constitution was made to guard the people against the dangers of good intentions. There are men in all ages who mean to govern well, but they mean to govern. They promise to be good masters, but they mean to be masters.

Those who champion or seek to justify the activism of the Warren Court assert with glibness that the Constitution is a living document which the Court must interpret with flexibility.

When they say the Constitution is a living document, they really mean that the Constitution is dead, and that activist justices as its executors may dispose of its remains as they please. I submit that if the Constitution is, indeed, a living document, its words are binding on those who pledge themselves by oath or affirmation to support it.

What of the cliché that the Supreme Court should interpret the Constitution with flexibility? If those who employ this cliché mean by it that a provision of the Constitution should be interpreted with liberality to accomplish its intended purpose, they would find me in hearty agreement with them. But they do not employ the cliché to mean this. On the contrary, they use the cliché to mean that the Supreme Court should bend the words of a constitutional provision to one side or the other to accomplish an objective the provision does not sanction. Hence, they use the cliché to thwart what the Founding Fathers had in mind when they fashioned the Constitution.

The genius of the Constitution is this: the grants of power it makes and the limitations it imposes are inflexible, but the powers it grants extend into the future and are exercisable with liberality on all occasions by the departments in which they are vested.

SAVING THE CONSTITUTION

As the result of the assumptions of power of the Warren Court, the people of our nation are now ruled in substantial areas of their lives by the partial wills of Supreme Court justices rather than by the impartial precepts of the Constitution. . . .

It is obvious to those who love the Constitution and are willing to face naked reality that the Warren Court took giant strides down the road of usurpation, and that if the course set by it is not reversed, the dream of the Founding Fathers will vanish and the most precious liberty of the people—the right to constitutional government—will perish.

Despite their perilous state, the dreams of the Founding Fathers can be rekindled and the precious right of the people to constitutional government can be preserved if those who possess the power will stretch forth saving hands while there is yet time.

Who are they that possess this saving power?

They are Supreme Court justices, who are able and willing to exercise self-restraint and make the Constitution the rule for the government of their official action; presidents, who will nominate for membership on the Supreme Court persons who are able and willing to exercise self-restraint and make the Constitution the rule for the government of their official action; and senators, who will reject for Supreme Court membership nominees who are either unable or unwilling to exercise self-restraint and make the Constitution the rule for the government of their official action.

And, finally, if Supreme Court justices, presidents, and senators fail them, the people may employ their own saving power. Through Congress and the states, they may adopt a constitutional amendment similar to my proposal which would compel presidents and senators to make appointments to the Supreme Court from among persons recommended to them by the chief justices of the states. The people can rely upon the chief justices of the states to restrict their recommendations to persons who revere the federal system ordained by the Constitution and who will not sanction the concentration of power which always precedes the destruction of human liberties.

Let me add that lawyers who love the Constitution can aid the cause by practicing this preachment of Chief Justice Stone:

> Where the courts deal, as ours do, with great public questions, the only protection against unwise decisions, and even judicial usurpations, is careful scrutiny of their action, and fearless comment upon it.

In closing I make a conditional prophesy. If those who possess the power to rekindle the dream of the Founding Fathers and to preserve the right of the people to constitutional government do not act, Americans will learn with agonizing sorrow the tragic truth taught by Justice Sutherland:

The saddest epitaph which can be carved in memory of a vanished liberty is that it was lost because its possessors failed to stretch forth a saving hand while yet there was time.

NOTES

1. *United States: Formation of the Union,* pp. 147, 152, 165, 167, 422, 429, 548, 752, 753, 756, 848, 849, 852.
2. *Texas v. White,* 7 Wall. 700.
3. Article III, sec. 1.
4. Article VI.
5. James Madison: *The Federalist,* No. 43.
6. *Ullman v. U.S.,* 350 U.S. 422.
7. *U.S. v. Butler,* 297 U.S. 1, 78–79.
8. *Sun Printing and Publishing Association v. Remington Paper and Power Co.,* 235 N.Y. 338, 139 N.E. 470.
9. *West Coast Hotel Co. v. Parrish,* 300 U.S. 379, 404, 81 L.ed. 703, 715.
10. *Marbury v. Madison,* 1 Cranch. 137, 175.
11. *Gibbons v. Ogden,* 9 Wheat. 1, 188.
12. *Marbury v. Madison,* 1 Cranch. 137.
13. *Gibbons v. Ogden,* 9 Wheat. 213, Ex Parte Bain, 121 U.S. 1; *Lake County v. Rollins,* 130 U.S. 662.
14. *Brown v. Allen,* 334 U.S. 443, 535.
15. See, e.g., Justice White in *Reitman v. Mulkey,* 387 U.S. 369 (1967); and Justice Stewart in *Jones v. Mayer Co.,* 392 U.S. 409 (1968).

In Support of
Judicial Activism

Ramsey Clark

We demean the Constitution of the United States by this endless metaphysical debate over "strict construction." There are real constitutional issues to be faced, perhaps even constitutional crises. They will require all the vision and courage we can muster. The false notion that men who wrote those words 183 years ago—distant age—could foresee the unforeseeable, or that we can look back and in words alone, or from their intent in the context of 1787, divine the authors' precise meaning as applied to current facts is contrary to all human experience. Our problems, actual and immense, cannot be solved by such conjury. We are fortunate that nature spares us from the foresight that would be required to give truth to the doctrine of strict construction, because the only thing worse than such an impossibility would be its possibility.

Change is the dominant fact of our times. Population and technology, the major dynamics, create more change in a decade than centuries witnessed heretofore. Life changes, the meanings of words change, the needs of man change. The Constitution, born in a fundamentally different epoch, must have the durability and wisdom to grow, to encompass essentially new situations, to meet new needs. It can.

To invoke the Founding Fathers against change is to charge them with seeking to deny subsequent generations that to which they were wholly committed for their own. To vest the Supreme Law of the Land with some religious attachment to the status quo is to deny its very meaning and disable the Ship of State in the turbulent seas of change. The purpose behind the doctrine of strict construction as utilized today is not to find specific guidance where none can exist. It is to resist change: to stay where we are, do as we have done and offer no hope. We can no longer afford this.

From Ramsey Clark, "Second Lecture," in *Role of the Supreme Court: Policymaker or Adjudicator?*, pp. 19–28 (Washington, D. C.: American Enterprise Institute for Public Policy Research, 1970). © American Enterprise Institute, 1970. Reprinted with permission.

The results of efforts to invoke the doctrine of strict construction dot our legal history. Their consequences have often been disastrous.

A high water mark came in *Scott v. Sandford*, the "Dred Scott" decision, in 1857. There, the Supreme Court held that it lacked jurisdiction to determine whether Congress had power to ban slavery in the territories north of Missouri, or whether a slave voluntarily taken into a free state by his master thereby became free, because on a narrow and technical reading of some of the words of the Constitution, it concluded that no slave could be a "citizen" for purposes of federal jurisdiction. The language of the Constitution as readily read otherwise. Having disclaimed jurisdiction, the Court then proceeded, because strict constructionists are human and have their purposes, to answer these nation-shattering questions in the negative, ruling out not only a judicial, but a legislative, solution to the slavery issue and thereby failing to do what it could to prevent the most calamitous war in our history. The majority sought to justify these tragic rulings by pleading obedience to strict construction, saying:

> *No one, we presume supposes that any change in public opinion or feeling, in relation to this unfortunate race . . . shall induce the court to give to the words of the Constitution a more liberal construction in their favor than they were intended to bear when the instrument was framed and adopted.*

In 1918, a bare majority of the Supreme Court again showed what strict construction can mean. Reading the Commerce Clause alone, it said the federal government is powerless to prevent interstate shipment of the products of child labor. *Hammer v. Dagenhart*, 247 U.S. 251 (1918). The Constitution by that construction—unsupported incidentally in the language of the charter— did not empower the Congress to prevent virtual slave labor of 10- and 12- year-old children working in sweatshops 70 hours or more a week for subsistence wages. These men were not deciding issues on the basis of some clear understanding of intentions from 1787. The men in the Hall at Philadelphia could not foresee such questions, much less their answers. They were cruelly used by justices who would decide by fiat what words meant to them, then grace themselves in the mantle of the Founding Fathers. The experience and sympathies of the Court's majority were closer to the cotton mill owners who destroyed children than to justice and humane concerns, and they resisted change. If the majority opinion in *Hammer v. Dagenhart* prevailed today, the union would be a shambles. Can the commerce of 1787 be equated with the commerce of 1970? . . .

. . . The words of the Constitution matter greatly, but they do not suffice to solve the problems of another day. They are the place of beginning, not of ending. To begin and end, poring over words to find meanings they do not contain denies us the benefits of experience, the strength of growth, and the wisdom of the spirit of the Constitution.

Strict construction is at best a convenient argument with which to support or attack particular judicial decisions. How many of us are really prepared to have our Constitution construed solely by its words and their intention when written? There is, after all, not a word in the Constitution about many of our most important protections. The hallowed presumption of innocence, and the requirement that guilt in criminal cases be proven beyond a reasonable doubt are not found in the words of the Constitution. Nor does the Constitution say that state governments may not trample upon freedom of speech or press or religion, that state legislatures must be fairly apportioned, or that any of us have any "right to privacy."

Even the most distinguished advocates of strict construction do not interpret the Constitution from its words when they address principles where words fail. Thus the Supreme Court's most prominent advocate of strict construction has fought tirelessly to preserve our First Amendment freedoms against interference by state governments and to require fair apportionment of state legislatures. The Constitution does not say this. And our foremost senatorial spokesman for strict construction champions the cause of the "right to privacy," believing that the Constitution itself prevents intrusion into the private lives of government employees by government snoopers armed with wiretaps, bugs, or computers. On these crucial issues, even the strict constructionists must look to the spirit of the Constitution and to the requirements of a free society.

It is hardly surprising that the words of the Constitution, even supplemented by their historical context, do not resolve the great questions of our time. In 1791, when the ink on the Constitution was hardly dry, President Washington, who had chaired the Convention, Thomas Jefferson, and Alexander Hamilton were unable to agree among themselves on whether the "necessary and proper clause" authorized the federal government to charter a national bank. Eventually the matter was resolved not on the basis of some nonexistent "plain meaning" of the constitutional language, but on the best judgment the statement of the day could make as to what was an appropriate rule for a constitutional federal government considering the general powers delegated to it. The crises which we face today, the great constitutional questions which are put to the Supreme Court for resolution, are far more difficult. Mass society, urban poverty, racism, vast industry, huge labor unions, tall skyscrapers, automobiles, jet aircraft, television, nuclear energy, environmental pollution, mass assemblies and protests, the interdependence of nations and individuals create issues undreamed of in the philosophies of the Founding Fathers.

The Constitution guides by general principle—a light that recognizes the existence of change. By its very nature it must embody a whole theory in a quick phrase—to regulate commerce—the general welfare—due process of law—the equal protection of the laws. Hundreds, thousands of cases are required to give the phrase a growing content, but the Constitution sets the tone. If it were to be specific, it could not be a Constitution or hope to maintain a theory and framework of government with general powers and limitations.

The nature of the Constitution and the decisional process by which its principles are extended to new conditions have been recognized from the beginning.

Perhaps the most famous and profound expression was by Chief Justice John Marshall in *McCulloch v. Maryland*, 4 Wheat. 316 (1819): ". . . we must never forget that it is a Constitution we are expounding . . . [a] Constitution intended to endure for ages to come, and consequently, to be adapted to the various crises of human affairs." Words of immutable meaning cannot be adapted to crises, and nations bound to them fail. But in truth there are no immutable words. To say there are is only to place the power to divine their meaning in some high priest. This has never led to truth. As Benjamin Cardozo observed in *The Truth of Law*, "Magic words and incantation are fatal to our science (law) as they are to any other." Learned Hand, a blunt man, said "There is no surer way to misread any document than to read it literally." *Guiseppe v. Walling*, 144 F.2d 608, 624 (2d Cir., 1944).

Cardozo demonstrated in *The Nature of the Judicial Process* that "the great generalities of the Constitution have a content and significance that vary from age to age . . . A *Constitution* states . . . principles for an expanding future," pp. 17, 83. . . .

The essential qualities to give integrity, force, and vitality to the Constitution are deep commitment to its spirit, stern self-discipline in relating that spirit to present facts, understanding of the history and function of law in society, and sensitivity to the expanding future. A dictionary, smallness of spirit, and fear of change will not empower an old piece of parchment to curtail conduct of people that new conditions compel.

Perhaps the major question of our times is whether institutions can change to cope with the vast dynamics of mass urban population and burgeoning technology. The answer is far from clear. Can government be responsive to the needs of its people? Will technology master man? Can violence as an international and interpersonal problem solver be conditioned from human capability? Can we assure human dignity? Will racism divide people who must live together with dignity, respect, and love?. . .

The United States Supreme Court, inherently the most conservative institution within our system of government, has addressed itself to the present and future more effectively than any other agent of our society. Somehow, these last twenty years, it has detected the greatest needs of our times in the cases that have found their way to its forum and has acted to meet those needs.

The reapportionment cases, beginning with *Baker v. Carr*, 369 U.S. 186 (1962), in essence liberate government from the nineteenth century. Without that liberation, legislative bodies could not possibly address themselves meaningfully to the crushing problems of the people. The decisions were constitutional necessities. To have held otherwise would have crippled the spirit of a constitution that serves the people.

In *Brown v. Board of Education*, 347 U.S. 483 (1954), and a multitude of other civil rights cases, the Court addressed itself to the one huge wrong of the American nation—racism—and caused us to begin to do what decency and justice require. The spirit of the Constitution was clear on this subject. What other meaning can the Thirteenth, Fourteenth, and Fifteenth Amendments have? The failure was in the people. To now blame the Court for upholding the Constitution is hardly to respect that document or to seek fulfillment of its word.

Finally, in a whole series of cases we sometimes describe under the heading of civil liberties, the Supreme Court, enforcing the Constitution, recognized the great crisis in the meaning of the individual in our times—in human dignity. It said things we should have known all along. If we are to have equal justice, the poor, the ignorant, the sick, and despised as well as the rich and powerful must have "the assistance of counsel for his defense." *Gideon v. Wainwright*, 372 U.S. 335 (1963). No longer can police question persons in their custody without advising them of their rights. *Miranda v. Arizona*, 384 U.S. 436 (1966). Fullfillment of constitutional rights is no mere game. We insist on them. Government has an obligation to give them vitality, not seek their waiver. The educated know their rights, the rich have their lawyers; the powerful, however capable of crime, will be protected. So must the poor, the ignorant, and the powerless. So Danny Escobedo and Ernest Miranda could not be convicted by their own confessions when they were denied constitutional rights.

If we care for the future, our concern must not be that the Supreme Court had the wisdom and courage to face the central issues of our times, but that other institutions have done so little not only to seek solutions but to fulfill the critically important constitutional rights decreed by the Court. . . .

CHAPTER FOURTEEN

CIVIL LIBERTIES

FREE SPEECH

At what point does it become necessary for society to restrict the freedoms granted to us in the First Amendment to the Constitution? Of the many questions that the Supreme Court has had to confront over the course of our history, this one has surely proved to be one of the most vexing. This question last became the subject of national debate in 1978 when the city of Skokie, Illinois, 60 percent of whose residents are Jewish, passed an ordinance prohibiting members of the American Nazi Party from marching through its community. The American Nazi Party contended that this ordinance represented an unconstitutional infringement upon its right to freedom of speech. This view was shared by the American Civil Liberties Union (ACLU), an organization long reluctant to see any restrictions imposed upon freedom of expression. In this particular instance, however, the ACLU's position came under such heavy fire from within its own ranks that the organization decided to issue a pamphlet explaining why it felt compelled to defend the right of the American Nazi Party to parade through Skokie. The contents of this pamphlet appear as the first selection in this section.

In the second selection, George Will makes clear that he is not persuaded by those who contend that all manner of free expression is guaranteed by the First Amendment. On the contrary, he insists that the Constitution does not and should not provide any protection for the expression of views antithetical to the values upon which our Republic is based. To argue otherwise is not only imprudent but also inconsistent with the intent of those who formulated the First Amendment.

Why Free Speech for Racists and Totalitarians

American Civil Liberties Union

Why does the ACLU defend free speech for Nazis, KKK members, and others who advocate racist or totalitarian doctrines?

Because we believe that the constitutional guarantees of freedom of speech and press would be meaningless if the government could pick and choose the persons to whom they apply. The ACLU's responsibility—since its founding in 1920—has been to make sure that all are free to speak, no matter what their ideas.

In what circumstances does the ACLU defend such people?

The ACLU defends the right of such persons to make speeches in which they express their beliefs; to print and distribute written material; to hold peaceful marches and rallies; to display their symbols; and to be members of groups which promote their doctrines.

Has the ACLU always defended such people?

Yes. Always. The ACLU's very first annual report describes a case in which the ACLU defended free speech for the KKK. We have been defending free speech for these groups—and all others—ever since.

ACLU defense is needed when the views of some people are unpopular and the government interferes with their ability to express their views peacefully. In times and places where the views of civil rights activists, pacifists, religious and political dissenters, labor organizers, and others have been unpopular, the ACLU has insisted on their right to speak.

From *Why the American Civil Liberties Union Defends Free Speech for Racists and Totalitarians* (New York: American Civil Liberties Union). Used with permission.

Throughout the history of the ACLU, we have adhered to Voltaire's principle that "I may disapprove of what you say, but I will defend to the death your right to say it."

But does the First Amendment protect even those who urge the destruction of freedom? Does it extend to those who advocate the overthrow of our democratic form of government or who espouse violence?

In 1969, in an ACLU case involving a KKK leader who had urged at a rally in Hamilton County, Ohio, that black Americans be sent back to Africa, the United States Supreme Court unanimously established the principle that speech may not be restrained or punished unless it "is directed to inciting or producing imminent lawless action and is likely to incite or produce such action." (*Brandenburg v. Ohio*)

In this, and in earlier cases involving advocates of draft resistance in World War I and leaders of the Communist Party during and following World War II, the Supreme Court made it clear that before a speaker can be suppressed there must be a clear and present danger that the audience will *act illegally and do what the speaker urges*—not just *believe* in what is advocated.

When Nazis or others like them choose to demonstrate in places like Skokie, Illinois, where hundreds of survivors of the concentration camps live, are they not creating a clear and present danger of violent reactions?

Speaking or marching before a *hostile* audience is not the same as inciting a *sympathetic* crowd to engage in illegal acts. The audience is not being urged to become violent and do bodily harm to the demonstrators. Hostile crowds must not be allowed to exercise a veto power over the speech of others by themselves creating a clear and present danger of disorder. Otherwise, any of us could be silenced if people who did not like our ideas decided to start a riot.

It is common practice for speakers and demonstrators to carry their messages to hostile audiences—perhaps in the hope of making conversions, perhaps to attract attention, or perhaps to test the potential for restraint or for ugliness in their adversaries.

In hundreds of cases, the ACLU has defended the right to speak even when the speakers were so unpopular that opponents reacted violently. The Wobblies carried their unionization message to western mining towns. That message was so unpopular that some of them were lynched. Jehovah's Witnesses distributed their tracts in Roman Catholic neighborhoods. They were stoned. Norman Thomas spoke in Mayor Frank Hague's Jersey City. He was pelted with eggs and narrowly escaped serious violence. Paul Robeson sang at a concert in Peekskill, New York. There was a riot. Civil rights activists in

the 1960s chose to demonstrate in Mississippi and Alabama. Some of them
were murdered. Opponents of the Vietnam war picketed military bases.
Many of them were beaten. Martin Luther King, Jr., marched in the most racist neighborhoods of Chicago. And there was racial violence.

The duty of government is to permit speech and to restrain those who
would disrupt it violently. Opponents of a point of view must be free to have
their say, but not to make any public place off-limits for speech they don't
like.

*But isn't a demonstration in an intensely hostile area the same as falsely shouting "fire"
in a crowded theater?*

Speaking or marching with offensive messages in public places is not at all
the same as falsely shouting "fire" in a crowded theater. The members of the
crowd are not in a tightly enclosed arena where a panic would almost certainly follow by a sudden and unexpected cry of danger before any contrary
view could be heard. They have come to the scene freely, probably knowing
what to expect, and they may freely turn away if they are upset by what they
see or hear. Just as speakers have a right to express themselves, listeners have
a right to ignore them or, if they choose, to hold peaceful counterdemonstra-
tions.

*Hasn't the Supreme Court said that certain kinds of communication—like hurling epi-
thets at another person—are so likely to lead to fighting that the speaker, and not the
audience, is responsible? Isn't the display of a swastika or the burning of a cross the same
as such "fighting words"?*

The Supreme Court has made it clear that speech can be punished as "fighting words" only if it is directed at another person in an *individual, face-to-face
encounter.* The Court has never applied this "fighting words" concept to non-
verbal symbols displayed before a *general* audience (like the display of a
swastika or a peace symbol or the burning of a cross or of an effigy of a political leader).

*Why do the ACLU and the courts believe that prior restraints on free speech are so
much worse than punishments after a speech has been made?*

Prior restraints not only prevent *entirely* the expression of the would-be
speaker, but they also deprive the public of its *right to know* what the speaker
would have said.

When the Nixon administration tried to impose a prior restraint on the
Pentagon Papers, they told us that publication would injure the national secu-

rity. When the *Pentagon Papers* were published, we discovered that they exposed misdeeds by the government, but did no damage to national security.

If the purpose of the First Amendment is to insure a free flow of ideas, of what value to that process are utterances which defame people because of their race or religion? Can't we prohibit group libel that merely stirs up hatred between peoples?

Legal philosopher Edmond Cahn dealt with this subject in a notable address delivered at the Hebrew University in Jerusalem in 1962. If there were a prohibition against group defamation, said Cahn:

> *The officials could begin by prosecuting anyone who distributed the Christian Gospels, because they contain many defamatory statements not only about Jews but also about Christians; they show Christians failing Jesus in his hour of deepest tragedy. Then the officials could ban Greek literature for calling the rest of the world "barbarians." Roman authors would be suppressed because when they were not defaming the Gallic and Teutonic tribes they were disparaging the Italians. For obvious reasons, all Christian writers of the Middle Ages and quite a few modern ones could meet a similar fate. Even if an exceptional Catholic should fail to mention the Jews, the officials would have to proceed against his works for what he said about the Protestants and, of course, the same would apply to Protestant views on the subject of Catholics. Then there is Shakespeare who openly affronted the French, the Welsh, the Danes. . . . Dozens of British writers from Sheridan and Dickens to Shaw and Joyce insulted the Irish. Finally, almost every worthwhile item of prose and poetry published by an American Negro would fall under the ban because it either whispered, spoke, or shouted unkind statements about the group called "white." Literally applied, a group-libel law would leave our bookshelves empty and us without desire to fill them.*

History teaches us that group libel laws are used to *oppress* racial and religious minorities, not to protect them. For example, none of the anti-Semites who were responsible for arousing France against Captain Alfred Dreyfus was ever prosecuted for group libel. But Emile Zola was prosecuted for libeling the military establishment and the clergy of France in his magnificent *J'Accuse* and had to flee to England to escape punishment.

Didn't Weimar Germany's tolerance for free speech allow Hitler to achieve power?

No. The Weimar government did not uphold free speech. When Hitler and the Nazis violently interfered with the speech of their opponents, the Weimar government took no effective action to protect speech and restrain violence. Even murder of political opponents by the Nazis—where the murderers were known—went unpunished or virtually unpunished.

Why should someone who detests the Nazis and the KKK support defense of their right to speak?

In a society of laws, the principles established in dealing with racist views necessarily apply to all. The ACLU defended the right of Father Terminiello, a suspended Catholic priest, to give a racist speech in Chicago. In 1949, the U.S. Supreme Court agreed with our position in a decision that is a landmark in the history of free speech. Time and again, the ACLU was able to rely on the decision in *Terminiello v. Chicago* in defending free speech for civil rights demonstrators in the deep South. The Supreme Court cited its own decision in *Terminiello* in its leading decisions on behalf of civil rights demonstrators, *Cox v. Louisiana* and *Edwards v. South Carolina.* Similarly, the Supreme Court's decision in 1969 in *Brandenburg v. Ohio* upholding free speech for the KKK was the principal decision relied upon by a lower court the following year in overturning the conviction of Benjamin Spock for opposing the draft.

The principles of the First Amendment are indivisible. Extend them on behalf of one group, and they protect all groups. Deny them to one group, and all groups suffer.

Doesn't providing racists and totalitarians with a legal defense give publicity to their cause and their ideas that they would otherwise not receive?

It is the attempts by communities to *prevent* such people from expressing themselves that gives them the press coverage they would ordinarily not receive. If providing a legal defense for their constitutional rights results in a continuation of the publicity, that is an unavoidable consequence of the events that were set in motion by the original denial of First Amendment guarantees. A fact that seems little understood by those who take a restrictive view toward speech they do not like is that attempts at suppression ordinarily increase public interest in the ideas they are trying to stamp out.

But doesn't the ACLU have more important things to do with its limited resources than to defend racists and totalitarians?

The ACLU has many important jobs to do and it devotes its resources to a wide range of civil liberties concerns—sexual equality; racial justice; religious freedom; the freedom to control one's own body; the constitutional rights of students, prisoners, mental patients, service personnel, juveniles, the elderly; and the rights of privacy for all of us. More than six thousand court cases are undertaken each year by the ACLU to protect these rights.

But first among the freedoms we are dedicated to defending are those of speech, press, and assembly, for they are the bedrock on which all other rights rest. We are involved in only five or six cases each year to defend free speech for racists or totalitarians. Even though this is only a tiny fraction of the ACLU's work, we think it is important.

We cannot remain faithful to the First Amendment by turning our backs when it is put to its severest test—the right to freedom of speech for those whose views we despise the most.

Nazis: Outside the Constitution

George F. Will

During World War II, Sol Goldstein lived in Lithuania, where Nazis threw his mother down a well with fifty other women and buried them alive in gravel. Today he lives in Skokie, Illinois, where on April 20 Nazis wearing brown shirts and swastikas may demonstrate to celebrate Hitler's birthday.

Sixty percent of Skokie residents are Jewish, including thousands of survivors of the Holocaust. Aided by the American Civil Liberties Union, the Nazis have successfully challenged an injunction against demonstrations with swastikas, and almost certainly will succeed in challenging ordinances banning demonstrations involving military-style uniforms and incitements of hatred. After sixty years of liberal construction of the First Amendment, almost anything counts as "speech"; almost nothing justifies restriction.

The Nazis say they want to demonstrate in Skokie because "where one finds the most Jews, one finds the most Jew-haters." Beyond inciting hatred, the Nazis' aim is to lacerate the feelings of Jews. Liberals say the Skokie ordinances place unconstitutional restrictions on the Nazis' "speech." But Skokie's ordinances do not prohibit "persuasion," in any meaningful sense. The ordinances prohibit defamatory verbal and symbolic assault. What constitutional values do such ordinances violate?

The *Washington Post* says the rationale for striking down restrictions on advocacy of genocide is that "public policy will develop best through the open clash of ideas, evil ideas as well as benign ones." A typical Nazi idea is expressed on the poster depicting three rabbis—the Nazis call then "loose-lipped Hebes"—conducting the ritual sacrifice of a child. The *Post* does not suggest exactly how it expects the development of policy to be improved by "clashes" over ideas like that, or like the idea that Jews favor the "niggerization" of America.

Liberals quote Oliver Wendell Holmes's maxim that "the best test of truth is the power of the thought to get itself accepted in the competition of the market." Liberalism is a philosophy that yields the essential task of philosophy—distinguishing truth from error—to the "market," which measures preferences (popularity), not truth. Liberals say all ideas have an equal "right" to compete in the market. But the right to compete implies the right to win. So the logic of liberalism is that it is better to be ruled by Nazis than to restrict them.

Liberals seem to believe that all speech—any clash between any ideas—*necessarily* contributes to the political ends the First Amendment is supposed to serve. But they must believe that the amendment was not intended to promote particular political ends—that there is no connection between the rationale for free speech and the particular purposes of republican government.

A wiser theory is in "The First Amendment and the Future of American Democracy," in which Professor Walter Berns argues that the First Amendment is part of a political document. There are political purposes for protecting free speech, and some speech is incompatible with those purposes.

The purpose of the Constitution, he argues, is to establish a government faithful to the "self-evident" truths of the Declaration of Independence. Holmes said the Constitution was written for people of "fundamentally differing views." That would be an absurd idea about any constitutional community and is especially absurd about this one. The Founders thought rational persons could hardly avoid agreeing about "self-evident" fundamentals. The Founders believed in freedom for all speech that does not injure the health of the self-evidently proper kind of polity, a republic.

So the distinction between liberty and license, between permissible and proscribable speech, is implicit in the Constitution's purposes. Hence restraint can be based on the substance as well as the time, place, and manner of speech.

Berns argues it is bizarre to say that the Constitution—a document designed to promote particular political ends—asserts the equality of ideas. There is no such thing as an amoral Constitution, neutral regarding all possible political outcomes.

American Nazis are weak, so liberals favor protecting Nazi swastikas and other "speech." Liberals say the pain to Jews is outweighed by the usefulness of the "clash of ideas" about "loose-lipped Hebes." Were the Nazis becoming stronger, liberals would favor protecting Nazi speech because "market"—the best of truth—would be affirming Nazi truth. Besides, restricting speech can be dangerous.

But it is not more dangerous than national confusion about fundamental values. Evidence of such confusion is the idea that restrictions on Nazi taunts and defamations are impermissible because the Constitution's fundamental value is political competition open equally to those who, if they win, will destroy the Constitution and then throw people down wells.

SCHOOL PRAYER

In one of its most controversial decisions of this century, the Supreme Court in 1962 ruled that school-sponsored prayer in the public schools was unconstitutional. The Court reasoned that such activity constituted an unwarranted intrusion by the state into religion and was therefore in violation of the "wall of separation doctrine." Since 1962, there have been numerous attempts in Congress—all unsuccessful—to propose a constitutional amendment providing for a restoration of school prayer. Moreover, in the last four years such efforts have taken on a special urgency in light of President Reagan's strong endorsement of voluntary school prayer.

The following two selections are taken from a debate on the floor of the Senate in March 1984. The subject of this debate was Senate Joint Resolution 73, which called for proposing an amendment to the Constitution allowing voluntary, school sponsored, spoken *prayer in our public schools. In the first selection, Senator Warren Rudman (R.–N.H.) calls for defeat of the resolution, arguing that it not only runs contrary to the views of the Founding Fathers and the framers of the First Amendment, but that it would also impose severe social pressures on those not wishing to take part. Senator Jeremiah Denton (R.–Ala.), on the other hand, vigorously endorses the resolution. His reading of the Founding Fathers and the framers of the First Amendment is quite different from Rudman's. In his view, these men believed that the state should encourage religious activity, as long as no preference was shown toward any particular religion. Moreover, the restoration of prayers in schools, he contends, would foster among our children a sense of mutual toleration and sensitize them to an important dimension of our cultural heritage.*

On the Dangers of School Prayer

Warren Rudman, Republican Member of the U.S. Senate from the State of New Hampshire

Mr. RUDMAN. . . . Mr. President, I rise today in opposition to Senate Joint Resolution 73, not because I am opposed to prayer, or even because I am opposed to religious activity in public schools if properly structured. I am opposed to the resolution because rather than embracing the precepts of our political and religious heritages, it rejects them in a simplistic manner that ignores the delicate balance between secular authority and personal freedom which is the cornerstone of our nation. I can only liken Senate Joint Resolution 73 to an attempt to carve a facet in a precious gem by use of a battering ram: The attempt most surely will fail in its primary objective and may destroy the gem itself in the process.

To begin, I ask the following question: What is it that we are really discussing? We are certainly not talking about the right of children to pray in public school. That right exists today just as it has existed throughout the history of our country. Subject only to the necessity to maintain classroom structure and discipline, children are free to pray during many periods of the school day. Admittedly, many of those periods would dictate silent prayer as the preferred choice, but I know of no religion that maintains that communication with its deity requires vocalization.

Nor are we discussing a proposal which reflects the views of the framers of the Constitution and the First Amendment. At that time there were no public schools in this country. More to the point, even had there been public schools, there is every reason to believe that language such as that before us today would have been rejected. In explaining the First Amendment provision that "Congress shall make no law respecting establishment of religion or prohibiting the free exercise thereof," Thomas Jefferson provided the following insight in an 1802 letter:

From U.S. *Congressional Record*, 98th Cong., 2nd sess., vol. 130, no. 29 (March 13, 1984), pp. S2551–2.

Believing . . . that religion is a matter which lies solely between man and his god, that he owes account to none other for his faith or his worship, that the legislative powers of government reach actions only, and not opinions, I contemplate with sovereign reverence the act of the whole American people which declared that their legislature should "make no law respecting an establishment of religion, or prohibiting the free exercise thereof," thus building a wall of separation between church and state.

James Madison also gives us insight concerning the collective state of mind which led to the adoption of the First Amendment separation clause. In his 1785 "A Memorial and Remonstrance Against Religious Assessments," a statement in opposition to a bill which would have subsidized the teaching of Christianity in Virginia schools of the time, Madison observed that the bill under consideration implied—

. . . either that the Civil Magistrate is a competent Judge of Religious truth; or that he may employ Religion as an engine of social policy. The first is an arrogant pretention falsified by the contradictory opinions of Rules in all ages, and throughout the world; the second an unhallowed perversion of the means of salvation.

The "wall of separation" defended so eloquently by Madison and Jefferson, born of the religious persecution which was their heritage, was built at a time when the population of the United States was at least 95 percent Protestant. To suggest today, at a time when within our borders can be found 89 distinct religions with 50,000 or more celebrants, that the language of Senate Joint Resolution 73 is what our forefathers "really meant to say," is either the height of arrogance suggested by Madison or a deductive leap unsupported by the evidence.

No; what we are really talking about is whether or not we will mandate a period of spoken *prayer* in our public schools. I italicize the word prayer because I do not know what it means in the context of the resolution. Of the 89 religions that I referred to above, the prayers of only one or two would be meaningful to any one individual. The rest would fall between meaningless at best and offensive at the other end of the spectrum. To require of children a meaningless act is, quite simply, a waste of precious time in an educational system already under fire. To require of children something that is offensive to others threatens the fabric of society.

Do we learn nothing from history? In 1854, a Jesuit priest in Maine advised his parishioners to defy a school committee regulation requiring children to read the King James version of the Bible and, subsequently, as chronicled in "Church, State and Freedom" by Leo Pfeffer: "A mob broke into his house, dragged him out, tore off his clothing, tarred and feathered him, and after two hours of cruel treatment, finally released him." Mr.

Pfeffer also chronicles an 1843 event in which a Catholic bishop petitioned the Philadelphia School Board to allow Catholic children to use the Catholic version of the Bible, a petition that resulted in months of controversy, riots, the destruction of churches, convents, and homes, and the murder of both participants in the controversy and innocent bystanders.

Likewise, the result of a 1949 appeal by two Jewish mothers in Chelsea, Mass., then 45 percent Jewish, to appear before the school committee to present their views against the singing of Christmas carols and the presentation of Christmas pageants led to threatening letters, threatening telephone calls, and threats of boycott against all Jewish merchants. Finally, for those of you who think that we in America are now beyond such action: In 1982 an Oklahoma resident and member of the Church of the Nazarene who initiated the filing of a suit against religious activities in her child's school was assaulted on school grounds and was forced to move to another school district to avoid harassment. I ask my colleagues: Is this the type of activity that we in Congress wish to encourage by adopting Senate Joint Resolution 73?

Our Supreme Court has long recognized the danger in what we argue here today. In a line of cases dating back to 1947, the Court has held that the promoting of certain religious exercises in public schools is unconstitutional. In Everson against the Board of Education (1947) the Court held that "no tax in any amount, large or small, can be levied to support any religious activities or institutions, whatever they may be called, or whatever form they may adopt to teach or practice religion."

That landmark decision formed the basis for the 1962 decision in Engel against Vitale prohibiting the recitation of a prayer composed by the State, and the 1963 decision in Abington School District against Schempp prohibiting the recitation of religious passages not composed by the State. In both these cases, schoolchildren had been granted permission to remain silent or to excuse themselves from the room. The Engel court correctly observed that:

> The . . . argument . . . that the program does not require all pupils to recite the prayer, but permits those who wish to do so to remain silent or be excused from the room, ignores the essential nature of the program's constitutional defects . . . When the power, prestige, and financial support of government is placed behind a particular religious belief, the indirect coercive pressure upon religious minorities to conform to the prevailing officially approved religion is plain.

The Supreme Court's view has been supported by a number of noted conservatives. Columnist James Kilpatrick has observed:

> We are talking about state-sanctioned prayer in public schools where attendance is compulsory. It is pure sham to contend that in such circumstances that "prayer" can be "voluntary."

Likewise, it is interesting that the Moral Majority recognizes the divisiveness of what we would do today. Reverend Jerry Falwell has said: "If we ever opened a Moral Majority meeting with prayer, silent or otherwise, we would disintegrate."

Mr. Cal Thomas, Director of Communications for Moral Majority, amplified on the statement by explaining that meetings were not opened with prayer because, "It is a political organization which includes Jews, Catholics, Mormons, Protestants, and even 'nonreligious' members."

Mr. Thomas' rhetorical question was: "What kind of prayer would we use?" I commend Reverend Falwell for his insight in this regard, and can only wonder why it is that he supports Senate Joint Resolution 73. Does not his logic extend to our public school system as well?

Finally, it has been suggested that schools might choose a nondenominational prayer in order to avoid the problems I have cataloged. Although there is nothing in this proposed amendment which would require nondenominational prayer, if that were my only objection, I am sure that I could be brought around by some creative amendment to the resolution. This is not the case. Our distinguished colleague, Senator DANFORTH, an ordained Episcopalian minister, has put his finger on the real problem with nondenominational prayer. As he stated in one of his recent speeches:

> Prayer that is so general and so diluted as not to offend those of most faiths is not prayer at all. True prayer is robust prayer. It is bold prayer. It is almost by definition sectarian prayer. Yet such genuine prayer would offend children of other faiths.

Even so neutral a prayer as, "Almighty God, we acknowledge our dependence on Thee, and we beg Thy blessings upon us, our parents, our teachers, and our country"—the prayer which was the subject of the Engel decision—was found to be blasphemous by leaders of certain Christian churches.

To reiterate, the adoption of such an amendment either would require of children a meaningless act or would create a situation in which divisiveness would be the outcome. We dare not pass such legislation. In this regard, I am struck by the fact that approximately 25 religious organizations have taken a position opposing Senate Joint Resolution 73. These include the following denominations: Presbyterian, Seventh Day Adventist, Episcopal, Church of the Brethren, Church of Christ, Baptist—admittedly, with some dissent—Methodist, Quaker, Hebrew, Unitarian, Congregational, and Lutheran. The Roman Catholic Church is neutral on the issue. With this united opposition to Senate Joint Resolution 73 among religious leaders, one might properly ask, "Why are we debating it at all?"

Having said that, I also reiterate my original statement that I am not opposed to religious activity in public schools if properly structured. I am proud to be a cosponsor of Senate bill 815, introduced by the senior Senator from Oregon, Mr. HATFIELD. That measure would establish, as a matter of law, the principle that schoolchildren have the same rights to engage in voluntary, extracurricular activity for religious purposes as they do to engage in any other voluntary, extracurricular activity. Although the Supreme Court has never held otherwise, some misguided and poorly conceived lower court rulings have cast doubt on that question.

In addition, I intend to support Senate Joint Resolution 212, a proposed constitutional amendment offered by the junior senator from Utah, Mr. HATCH. That bill, which may be offered either as a substitute for Senate Joint Resolution 73 or considered as a separate measure, addresses both the right to engage in voluntary, extracurricular religious activity and would permit as well the establishment of required periods for meditation or silent prayer during the school day.

Correctly structured, religious activity has a place in our public schools. Periods of silence would allow children to communicate with the God of their choice or to reflect on matters otherwise important to them. I see no harm and much to be gained by such periods of reflection. Much of what is wrong with our society today, from individual actions to the often muddled actions of our government, can be traced directly to lack of reflection on our priorities and how they might best be achieved.

Yet, the activity must be voluntary, truly voluntary. We dare not risk the consequences of having the State or representatives of the State promoting or sponsoring specific forms of oral religious activity. To do so would be to violate our traditions, ignore the teachings of history, and risk the harmony that we all hope defines our society.

Unfortunately, the debate . . . has underscored the many religious differences which exist in our society, differences which, to date we have kept out of government and the realm of public policy. Why we seek to transfer the problem of dealing with these differences to the backs of 7- and 8-year-old children in public school is, quite frankly, beyond me.

In Defense of School Prayer

Jeremiah Denton, Republican Member of the U.S. Senate from the State of Alabama

Mr. DENTON . . . Mr. President, I have listened with respect and care to speeches on this subject from many senators. . . .

This is a delicate subject. It is one which I have approached with a great deal of caution myself and about which I have learned a great deal by holding four hearings on the subject. I have come to some conclusions which I should like to share with my colleagues.

As we continue to debate religious liberty in our nation's schools, I remind my colleagues that we in this chamber are considering perhaps the most special, the most sacred of our liberties: the freedoms of expression, association in a public forum, religion, and equal treatment under law. Each of those liberties is in a very real sense a component of the right of our citizens to communicate their thoughts, ideas, and beliefs free from the threat of censorship or official reprisal.

It was the sacredness of those liberties that kept alive the quest for freedom in the hearts and souls of our nation's early colonists. For example, the Pilgrims, who faced religious persecution in England, exiled themselves to Holland for seven hard years as a mere preliminary to the effort to travel to America and live free according to the dictates of conscience.

The only problem was that the early colonists were sometimes mutually intolerant of one another, so much so that Roger Williams left Massachusetts, fled to Rhode Island, and tried to set up a system that was more tolerant.

I studied Maryland and the Maryland Toleration Act as a Catholic kid, and I was proud of the act. It said that any citizen in the state of Maryland could feel free to practice his Christian religion in any manner he saw fit, without fear of persecution. Maryland was the only colony that was to be-

From U.S. *Congressional Record*, 98th Cong., 2nd sess., vol. 130, no. 31 (March 15, 1984), pp. S2775–8.

come one of the United States which had such a liberal policy. I was proud of it, because I grew up in Alabama, a state that at that time was not particularly tolerant of Catholics.

I did not learn until later that the footnotes said, of course, that anyone who did not study or practice the Christian religion would be summarily executed. . . .

God is acknowledged in four separate places in the Declaration of Independence, signed in 1776. By the spring of 1777, every colony had organized an independent government and, without exception, the constitution of each state recognized God and his preeminence. At the start of the Revolution, at least nine colonies had state-supported churches. Four of those established churches were still in existence when the Constitution of the United States was adopted.

When, on March 2, 1781, the Continental Congress adopted the Articles of Confederation, under which our new nation was to be governed, it included in them a statement of respect for "the great Governor of the world." Article III provided for the common defense of the several states against all attacks made upon them because of "religion, sovereignty, trade, or any other pretence whatever." The drafters of the articles clearly were aware of the dangers of conflict arising from religious intolerance, and they believed that the defense of the religious preferences of the people of each state was an important part of their "firm league of friendship."

The debates in the House and Senate leading to the passage of the First Amendment to the Constitution in 1789 do not give the slightest indication that the authors of the amendment intended to prohibit all governmentally sponsored prayer and acknowledgment of God. In reality, the first Congress simply desired to prevent the establishment of a national church or the preferential treatment of one sect over another. Today, however, we are told that any law permitting governmental recognition of God is a law respecting the establishment of theistic religion, to the exclusion of religions that do not acknowledge God.

The Constitution, and the First Amendment, were part of, not alien to, the stream of American thought and tradition. An important part of that tradition is the religious affirmation found in the Declaration of Independence. The references to God in the Declaration were theistic in their recognition of God and His providence.

Thomas Jefferson mentioned God in his draft of the Declaration of Independence, but he also espoused a philosophy of religious tolerance. In 1789, he wrote,

> *The legitimate powers of government extend to such acts only as are injurious to others. But it does me no injury for my neighbor to say there are twenty Gods, or no God.*

I do not believe that the purpose of the First Amendment to our Constitution is to deny the validity of all faiths and religions in expectation of the dawn of some newer or truer faith. The recognition that the laws of this nation and the actions of all men are influenced by God motivated our founders and has sustained our freedoms. Our forefathers never intended that the Supreme Court should prohibit all public and common prayer.

The framers of the Constitution could never have anticipated the current hostility toward religion, although they also recognized that some people would not choose any religion at all and must not be coerced by a national or state church.

The key to understanding the intent of the framers is in a twofold analysis of the meaning that they thought the word "establishment" had in the First Amendment, and of the politica! practices of the people who were involved in drafting the First Amendment, based on their experiences in their own states and then in national government following the adoption of the Articles of Confederation in 1781 and the approval of the Constitution in 1789.

James Madison, who was a member of the House–Senate conference on the First Amendment, believed that the word "establishment" was commonly understood to mean that no national church would be set up by the federal government. Indeed, earlier drafts of the amendment, and the debates on them by the Senate, show that all understood that the term meant that no national state religion should be established. . . .

Several early actions by Congress, the President, and the judiciary give us an understanding of the scope of the establishment clause as our early leaders interpreted and applied it.

The first Congress authorized the President to appoint a chaplain for the military.

Congress approved regulations requiring church attendance and prayer at military academies.

On the same day that the House adopted the final version of the First Amendment, it also adopted a request that the President declare a day of prayer and thanksgiving.

Accordingly, President Washington, President Adams, and President Madison all issued thanksgiving proclamations.

Congress passed legislation on August 7, 1789, appropriating funds for religious proselytization and education among the Indians. . . .

The list of examples goes on and on. It is inconceivable to me that the framers of the First Amendment, and those who acted under its structures, could ever countenance that the word "establishment" meant that school children could not pray or read the Bible in school.

The glue that binds families, societies, and ultimately civilizations, is the belief in God. As a Christian, I believe that all the faiths that acknowledge

God can produce a commonality of understanding that draws this country together. Accordingly, I believe that, in our well-meant effort to accommodate religious diversity, we need not and dare not abandon the principle that ultimate authority rests with God, not with the state or individuals.

In this nation's colonial history, there was strong religious intolerance. That fact is worthy of consideration.

We are not yet perfect but we have moved a long way, and I do not believe that the permission of vocal prayer in schools, prayers made up by children, will be a regression but, rather, a contribution to that progress.

Today a Protestant senator from Iowa rises in support of school prayer; a Mormon senator from Utah is the floor manager of the President's version of the constitutional amendment. Our members of the Jewish faith will vote for the amendment or against it according to their beliefs and their conscience.

I have listened to rabbis who were for or against, depending on how they saw the issue of embarrassment or intolerance. I want to proceed in the vein of our progress toward tolerance and the need for it.

This senator, the only Catholic ever elected to the Senate from Alabama, whose election was another example of increasing religious tolerance, also supports school prayer.

Religious toleration in our country has greatly improved, as the composition of this body demonstrates. We still begin each day with a prayer. I have seen no indication that any member of this body has been adversely affected by that practice. Yet, we cannot agree that our children in their schools should have the same right as do we and our colleagues in the other chamber.

Given our devotion to free communication in this chamber, which depends for its very existence upon free speech, I am saddened that some of my colleagues, some members of the judiciary, and some educators believe that a particular kind of speech, religious speech, is not legitimate; is dangerous and has no place in one particular marketplace of ideas, the public schools. . . .

School administrators sometimes go to extreme lengths to avoid even the appearance of religious activity in the programs or on the premises of their institutions. In a New England high school, students are denied the privilege of meeting after school hours to discuss Scripture and to pray. In the Midwest, a university refused a group of Christian students the use of a campus room for similar purposes. In that instance, it required action by the Supreme Court to reverse the university's policy, and even then the Court did so only on the ground that the university was restricting freedom of speech rather than freedom of worship.

Mr. President, our public school students come from a plurality of national and religious backgrounds. They associate with each other in the classroom not as mere intellectual entities but as total persons with deep and overlapping emotional, social, spiritual, and intellectual facets to their characters. Each student must learn, through a wide assortment of experiences, to cooperate, tolerate, and understand persons from other backgrounds.

That is what America is all about, and none of the freedom we have is more important than the freedom to practice our religion, and the freedom of speech has no more important outlet than the one dealing with that subject.

To declare that prayer or other religious expression is not a part of that great pluralism is to practice a myopic censorship that tramples true liberty underfoot. We need to appreciate the rich and varied cultural heritage within the classroom as well as without. To regard schools as helping to shape the world view of our children and then to censor religion and prayer cannot help but bring about a would without religion. Our children in their most important formative years are in essence being instructed that God is not relevant, or that religion is a lie.

I believe that our public school students perceive the banning of prayer on the school ground as state hostility toward religion. Consider the comment made about her high school by Bonnie Bailey in recent testimony before the Judiciary Committee:

> We have been taught that the Constitution guarantees us freedom of speech. But we feel that here we have been discriminated against, because we can picket, we can demonstrate, we can curse, we can take God's name in vain, but we cannot voluntarily get together and talk about God on any part of our campus, inside or out of the school.
>
> We just feel frustrated because we don't feel like we are being treated equally.

Another young person, Judith Jankowski, a high school student of Polish descent, compared the policies of two nations on religious liberty:

> A few years ago, I visited Poland with my family. We stayed with a family that has five children in school. I observed how restricted they were to express themselves politically and religiously, and I was thankful that I lived in the United States and that I had the freedom to express myself and share political and religious beliefs with others.
>
> Now, just a few years later, I see the same restrictions put on me and my fellow classmates that are on the students in Poland, and I find this very disturbing.

It is ironic that, while we debate whether our children should be allowed to pray in schools, students in Poland are willing to take to the streets to protest their government's decision to remove crucifixes from classrooms. The Polish government argues that the schools are secular institutions, an argument that is remarkably like some of the arguments presented in this chamber. . . .

In 1965, fifteen parents, of varying religious faiths, and with a total of twenty-one young children attending a public school, asked a district court to prevent the principal of the school from ordering his teachers to stop the young children from reciting, before they ate their cookies and drank milk in the morning session, the simple and ancient prayer:

God is Great, God is Good and we thank Him for our food. Amen!

He also ordered the teachers who were instructing the afternoon kindergarten classes to stop the young children from reciting the simple and ancient prayer:

Thank You for the world so sweet,
Thank You for the food we eat,
Thank You for the birds that sing—
Thank You God for everything.

When asked to review the district court's decision, the Second Circuit Court of Appeals held that:

The constitutional provisions relating to free exercise of religion and to freedom of speech do not require a State to permit persons to engage in public prayer in State-owned facilities wherever and whenever they desire.

Mr. President, that decision flies in the face of the principles upon which our country was founded, of the practice of its founders, and indeed of the practices of the Senate of the United States.

In 1970, a group of students from Herbert Hoover High School in Kanawha County, W. Va., began holding a preschool prayer meeting each morning. The meetings were initiated by the students. The principal of the school told the students that their meetings were in violation of a Supreme Court decision. The federal district of West Virginia agreed. The students were banned from voluntarily and privately praying together before the start of classes.

Mr. President, I think that it is time for the Congress to acknowledge that the federal courts have distorted the meaning of the First Amendment and that civil liberties organizations have used the federal courts to whipsaw both students and school administrators. Moreover, we need to realize that the several states have long and honorable histories of protecting the religious liberties of their citizens. . . .

I confess to my colleagues that I am intensely motivated personally by situations in which individuals are deprived of the right of prayer. When I was a prisoner of war in North Vietnam, prayer was what sustained my life and that of my fellow prisoners. Silent prayer was important, group prayer was especially important, and vocal prayer was most important. And we fought for it, and their people fought for it, and they died for it, and we abandoned them. Tens of millions of them now are now not free to exercise their religion, and we are about the same kind of thing in what we are talking about today. But when we were able to pray aloud together, we viewed that as a major victory over our captors, and indeed it was, and we drew great strength from it. And our prayers were answered. Silent prayer is what is allowed in totalitarian nations. They cannot stop it. It was what the North Vietnamese tried to limit us to. Those people in our country who say "pray silently only," "pray to yourself," do not understand what it means to be prevented from praying out loud. I have had that experience, and I do not wish it on anyone else, least of all our children.

If we adopt silent prayer, and only silent prayer, as the constitutional standard, we will in effect equate our Constitution and our practices to the paper constitutions of totalitarian regimes that find abhorrent all expressions of freedom. We will by implication rule out all other forms of expressions, such as invocations, benedictions, Christmas carols, and the like.

I have attended many Jewish ceremonies. When we opened a big hotel in Mobile, the man who had contributed the most to it in the way of investment had a Jewish ceremony with the candles and we all, Christians and Jews alike, prayed there. I have addressed so many Christian and Jewish congregations and meetings that I could not count them. I do not see any problem with listening to someone who is of another faith pray. I respect his right to his faith or her right to her faith, and I expect them to respect mine. I think children can understand that and I believe that the word "God" said in schools will cure much more than it will harm. . . .

CHAPTER FIFTEEN

CIVIL RIGHTS

RACIAL QUOTAS

In the case of Bakke v. Regents of the University of California *(1978), the United States Supreme Court ruled that the special admissions program for minorities at the Davis Medical School violated the Civil Rights Act of 1964. The Court ordered Davis officials to admit 38-year-old Allan Bakke, a white engineer who had scored higher on the entrance examination than any black applicant and yet was denied entrance because of the University's racial quota system. The ruling of the Court was widely acclaimed by some whites as a victory against "reverse discrimination."*

While the Supreme Court did not completely disallow the use of racial criteria in university admissions, it strongly discouraged use of racial quotas or other such preferential systems for minorities.

The Court was not unanimous in its opinion, however, and one of those who dissented was Justice Thurgood Marshall, a long-time civil rights advocate. In Justice Marshall's opinion, a portion of which is presented here, medical schools and other types of professional schools must give preferential treatment to blacks because of our past history of discrimination against blacks in this country. Without such a policy, blacks will continue to suffer the consequences of inequality.

Taking issue with racial quotas is Thomas Sowell, a professor of economics. He argues that a policy of racial quotas is unwarranted for a number of reasons. One is the assumption that the absence of blacks in professional positions is due solely to past discrimination. According to Sowell, this is not necessarily the case. He also argues that a policy of racial quotas may actually be unfair to blacks because it places black students at a disadvantage in many colleges and universities. Finally, Sowell suggests that racial quotas are not even desired by a majority of blacks and may well lead to an increase, rather than a decrease, in racial tensions.

The Case for Racial Quotas

Thurgood Marshall

Mr. Justice MARSHALL.

... I do not agree that petitioner's admissions program violates the Constitution. For it must be remembered that, during most of the past two hundred years, the Constitution as interpreted by this Court did not prohibit the most ingenious and pervasive forms of discrimination against the Negro. Now, when a state acts to remedy the effects of that legacy of discrimination, I cannot believe that this same Constitution stands as a barrier. ...

I

The status of the Negro as property was officially erased by his emancipation at the end of the Civil War. But the long awaited emancipation, while freeing the Negro from slavery, did not bring him citizenship or equality in any meaningful way. Slavery was replaced by a system of "laws which imposed upon the colored race onerous disabilities and burdens, and curtailed their rights in the pursuit of life, liberty, and property to such an extent that their freedom was of little value." *Slaughter-House Cases*, 16 Wall. 36, 70, 21 L.Ed. 394 (1873). Despite the passage of the Thirteenth, Fourteenth, and Fifteenth Amendments, the Negro was systematically denied the rights those amendments were supposed to secure. The combined actions and inactions of the state and federal government maintained Negroes in a position of legal inferiority for another century after the Civil War.

The southern states took the first steps to reenslave the Negroes. Immediately following the end of the Civil War, many of the provisional legislatures passed Black Codes, similar to the Slave Codes, which, among other things, limited the rights of Negroes to own or rent property and permitted

From *Regents of University of California v. Bakke*, 98 S. Ct. 2733 (1978).

imprisonment for breach of employment contracts. Over the next several decades, the South managed to disenfranchise the Negroes in spite of the Fifteenth Amendment by various techniques, including poll taxes, deliberately complicated balloting processes, property and literacy qualifications, and finally the white primary.

Congress responded to the legal disabilities being imposed in the southern states by passing the Reconstruction Acts and the Civil Rights Acts. Congress also responded to the needs of the Negroes at the end of the Civil War by establishing the Bureau of Refugees, Freedmen, and Abandoned Lands, better known as the Freedmen's Bureau, to supply food, hospitals, land and education to the newly freed slaves. Thus for a time it seemed as if the Negro might be protected from the continued denial of his civil rights and might be relieved of the disabilities that prevented him from taking his place as a free and equal citizen.

This time, however, was short-lived. Reconstruction came to a close, and, with the assistance of this Court, the Negro was rapidly stripped of his new civil rights . . . .

The Court began by interpreting the Civil War Amendments in a manner that sharply curtailed their substantive protections. See, e.g., *Slaughter-House Cases, supra; United States v. Reese*, 92 U.S. 214, 23 L.Ed. 563 (1876); *United States v. Cruikshank*, 92 U.S. 542, 23 L.Ed. 588 (1876). Then in the notorious *Civil Rights Cases*, 109 U.S. 3, 3 S.Ct. 18, 27 L.Ed. 835 (1883), the Court strangled Congress's efforts to use its power to promote racial equality. In those cases the Court invalidated sections of the Civil Rights Act of 1875 that made it a crime to deny equal access to "inns, public conveyances . . . , theatres, and other places of public amusement." According to the Court, the Fourteenth Amendment gave Congress the power to proscribe only discriminatory action by the state. The Court ruled that the Negroes who were excluded from public places suffered only an invasion of their social rights at the hands of private individuals, and Congress had no power to remedy that. *Id.*, at 24–25, 3 S. Ct., at 31. "When a man has emerged from slavery, and by the aid of beneficent legislation has shaken off the inseparable concomitants of that state," the Court concluded, "there must be some stage in the progress of his elevation when he takes the rank of a mere citizen, and ceases to be the special favorite of the laws. . . ." *Id.*, at 25, 3 S. Ct., at 31. As Justice Harlan noted in dissent, however, the Civil War Amendments and Civil Rights Acts did not make the Negroes the "special favorite" of the laws but instead "sought to accomplish in reference to that race . . .—what had already been done in every State of the Union for the White race—to secure and protect rights belonging to them as freemen and citizens; nothing more." *Id.*, at 61, 3 S.Ct., at 57.

The Court's ultimate blow to the Civil War Amendments and to the equality of Negroes came in *Plessy v. Ferguson*, 163 U.S. 537, 16 S.Ct. 1138, 41 L.Ed. 256 (1896). In upholding a Louisiana law that required railway com-

panies to provide "equal but separate" accommodations for whites and Negroes, the Court held that the Fourteenth Amendment was not intended "to
abolish distinctions based upon color, or to enforce social, as distinguished
from political equality, or a commingling of the two races upon terms unsatisfactory to either." Id., at 544, 16 S.Ct., at 1140. Ignoring totally the realities
of the positions of the two races, the Court remarked:

> We consider the underlying fallacy of the plaintiff's argument to consist in the
> assumption that the enforced separation of the two races stamps the colored race
> with a badge of inferiority. If this be so, it is not by reason of anything found in
> the act, but solely because the colored race chooses to put that construction upon
> it. Id., at 511, 16 S.Ct., at 1143.

Mr. Justice Harlan's dissenting opinion recognized the bankruptcy of
the Court's reasoning. He noted that the "real meaning" of the legislation
was "that colored citizens are so inferior and degraded that they cannot be
allowed to sit in public coaches occupied by white citizens." Id., at 560, 16
S.Ct., at 1147. He expressed his fear that if like laws were enacted in other
states, "the effect would be in the highest degree mischievous." Id., at 563, 16
S.Ct., at 1148. Although slavery would have disappeared, the state would retain the power "to interfere with the full enjoyment of the blessings of freedom; to regulate civil rights, common to all citizens, upon the basis of race;
and to place in a condition of legal inferiority a large body of American citizens. . . . " Id., at 563, 16 S.Ct., at 1148.

The fears of Mr. Justice Harlan were soon to be realized. In the wake of
Plessy, many states expanded their Jim Crow laws, which had up until that
time been limited primarily to passenger trains and schools. The segregation
of the races was extended to residential areas, parks, hospitals, theaters,
waiting rooms, and bathrooms. There were even statutes and ordinances
which authorized separate phone booths for Negroes and whites, which required that textbooks used by children of one race be kept separate from
those used by the other, and which required that Negro and white prostitutes
be kept in separate districts. . . .

Nor were the laws restricting the rights of Negroes limited solely to the
southern states. In many of the northern states, the Negro was denied the
right to vote, prevented from serving on juries and excluded from theaters,
restaurants, hotels, and inns. Under President Wilson, the federal government began to require segregation in government buildings; desks of Negro
employees were curtained off; separate bathrooms and separate tables in the
cafeterias were provided; and even the galleries of the Congress were segre-
gated. . . .

The enforced segregation of the races continued into the middle of the
twentieth century. In both world wars, Negroes were for the most part confined to separate military units; it was not until 1948 that an end to segrega-

tion in the military was ordered by President Truman. And the history of the exclusion of Negro children from white public schools is too well known and recent to require repeating here. That Negroes were deliberately excluded from public graduate and professional schools—and thereby denied the opportunity to become doctors, lawyers, engineers, and the like—is also well established. It is of course true that some of the Jim Crow laws (which the decisions of this Court had helped to foster) were struck down by this Court in a series of decisions leading up to *Brown v. Board of Education of Topeka*, 347 U.S. 483, 74 S.Ct. 686, 93 L.Ed. 873 (1954). See, e.g., *Morgan v. Virginia*, 328 U.S. 373, 66 S.Ct. 1050, 90 L.Ed. 1317 (1946); *Sweatt v. Painter*, 339 U.S. 629, 70 S.Ct. 848, 94 L.Ed. 1114 (1950); *McLaurin v. Oklahoma State Regents*, 339 U.S. 637, 70 S.Ct. 851, 94 L.Ed. 1149 (1950). Those decisions, however, did not automatically end segregation, nor did they move Negroes from a position of legal inferiority to one of equality. The legacy of years of slavery and of years of second-class citizenship in the wake of emancipation could not be so easily eliminated.

II

The position of the Negro today in America is the tragic but inevitable consequence of centuries of unequal treatment. Measured by any benchmark of comfort or achievement, meaningful equality remains a distant dream for the Negro. . . .

When the Negro child reaches working age, he finds that America offers him significantly less than it offers his white counterpart. For Negro adults, the unemployment rate is twice that of whites,[1] and the unemployment rate for Negro teenagers is nearly three times that of white teenagers.[2] A Negro male who completes four years of college can expect a median annual income of merely $110 more than a white male who has only a high school diploma.[3] Although Negroes represent 11.5 percent of the population,[4] they are only 1.2 percent of the lawyers, and judges, 2 percent of the physicians, 2.3 percent of the dentists, 1.1 percent of the engineers, and 2.6 percent of the college and university professors.[5]

The relationship between those figures and the history of unequal treatment afforded to the Negro cannot be denied. At every point from birth to death the impact of the past is reflected in the still disfavored position of the Negro.

In light of the history of discrimination and its devastating impact on the lives of Negroes, bringing the Negro into the mainstream of American life should be a state interest of the highest order. To fail to do so is to ensure that America will forever remain a divided society.

III

... It is plain that the Fourteenth Amendment was not intended to prohibit measures designed to remedy the effects of the nation's past treatment of Negroes. The Congress that passed the Fourteenth Amendment is the same Congress that passed the 1866 Freedmen's Bureau Act, an act that provided many of its benefits only to Negroes: Act of July 16, 1866, ch. 200, 14 Stat. 173. ...

Since the Congress that considered and rejected the objections to the 1866 Freedmen's Bureau Act concerning special relief to Negroes also proposed the Fourteenth Amendment, it is inconceivable that the Fourteenth Amendment was intended to prohibit all race-conscious relief measures. It "would be a distortion of the policy manifested in that amendment, which was adopted to prevent state legislation designed to perpetuate discrimination on the basis of race or color." *Railway Mail Association v. Corsi*, 326 U.S. 88, 94, 65 S.Ct. 1483, 1487, 89 L.Ed. 2072 (1945), to hold that it barred state action to remedy the effects of that discrimination. Such a result would pervert the intent of the framers by substituting abstract equality for the genuine equality the amendment was intended to achieve.

As has been demonstrated in our joint opinion, this Court's past cases establish the constitutionality of race-conscious remedial measures. Beginning with the school desegregation cases, we recognized that, even absent a judicial or legislative finding of constitutional violation, a school board constitutionally could consider the race of students in making school assignment decisions. See *Swann v. Charlotte-Mecklenburg Board of Education*, 402 U.S. 1, 16 ... (1971); *McDaniel v. Barresi*, 402 U.S. 39, 41, ... (1971). ...

> ... As we have held in Swann, *the Constitution does not compel any particular degree of racial balance or mixing, but when past and continuing constitutional violations are found, some ratios are likely to be useful as starting points in shaping a remedy.* ...

As we have observed, "[a]ny other approach would freeze the status quo that is the very target of all desegregation processes." *McDaniel v. Barresi, supra,* 402 U.S. at 41, 91 S.Ct. at 1289.

Only last term, in *United Jewish Organization v. Carey*, 430 U.S. 144, 97 S.Ct. 996, 61 L.Ed. 229 (1977), we upheld a New York reapportionment plan that was deliberately drawn on the basis of race to enhance the electoral power of Negroes and Puerto Ricans; the plan had the effect of diluting the electoral strength of the Hasidic Jewish community. We were willing in *UJO* to sanction the remedial use of a racial classification even though it disadvantaged otherwise "innocent" individuals. In another case last term, *Califano v. Webster*, 430 U.S. 313, 97 S.Ct. 1192, 51 L.Ed.2d 360 (1977), the Court upheld a provision in the Social Security laws that discriminated against men because its purpose was "'the permissible one of redressing our society's long standing disparate treatment of women.'" *Id.*, at 317, 97 S.Ct. at 1195, quoting *Califano v. Goldfarb*, 430 U.S. 199, 209n. 8, 97 S.Ct. 1021, 1028, 51 L.Ed.2d 270 (1977) (plurality opinion). We thus recognized the permissibility of remedying past societal discrimination through the use of otherwise disfavored classifications.

Nothing in those cases suggests that a university cannot similarly act to remedy past discrimination.[6] It is true that in both *UJO* and *Webster* the use of the disfavored classification was predicated on legislative or administrative action, but in neither case had those bodies made findings that there had been constitutional violations or that the specific individuals to be benefited had actually been the victims of discrimination. Rather, the classification in each of those cases was based on a determination that the group was in need of the remedy because of some type of past discrimination. There is thus ample support for the conclusion that a university can employ race-conscious measures to remedy past societal discrimination, without the need for a finding that those benefited were actually victims of that discrimination.

IV

While I applaud the judgment of the Court that a university may consider race in its admissions process, it is more than a little ironic that, after several hundred years of class-based discrimination against Negroes, the Court is unwilling to hold that a class-based remedy for that discrimination is permissible. In declining to so hold, today's judgment ignores the fact that for several hundred years Negroes have been discriminated against, not as individuals, but rather solely because of the color of their skins. It is unnecessary in twentieth-century America to have individual Negroes demonstrate that they have been victims of racial discrimination; the racism of our society has been so pervasive that none, regardless of wealth or position, has managed to escape its impact. The experience of Negroes in America has been different in kind, not just in degree, from that of other ethnic groups. It is not merely the history of slavery alone but also that a whole people were marked as inferior by the law. And that mark has endured. The dream of America as the great melting pot has not been realized for the Negro; because of his skin color he never even made it into the pot.

These differences in the experience of the Negro make it difficult for me to accept that Negroes cannot be afforded greater protection under the Fourteenth Amendment where it is necessary to remedy the effects of past discrimination. . . .

It is because of a legacy of unequal treatment that we now must permit the institutions of this society to give consideration to race in making decisions about who will hold the positions of influence, affluence, and prestige in America. For far too long, the doors to those positions have been shut to Negroes. If we are ever to become a fully integrated society, one in which the color of a person's skin will not determine the opportunities available to him or her, we must be willing to take steps to open those doors. I do not believe that anyone can truly look into America's past and still find that a remedy for the effects of that past is impermissible.

It has been said that this case involves only the individual, Bakke, and this university. I doubt, however, that there is a computer capable of determining the number of persons and institutions that may be affected by the decision in this case. For example, we are told by the attorney general of the United States that at least 27 federal agencies have adopted regulations requiring recipients of federal funds to take *"affirmative action* to overcome the effects of conditions which resulted in limiting participation . . . by persons of a particular race, color, or national origin." Supplemental Brief for the United States as *Amicus Curiae* 16 (emphasis added). I cannot even guess the number of state and local governments that have set up affirmative action programs, which may be affected by today's decision.

I fear that we have come full circle. After the Civil War our government started several "affirmative action" programs. This Court in the *Civil Rights Cases* and *Plessy v. Ferguson* destroyed the movement toward complete equality. For almost a century no action was taken, and this nonaction was with the tacit approval of the courts. Then we had *Brown v. Board of Education* and the Civil Rights Acts of Congress, followed by numerous affirmative action programs. *Now*, we have this Court again stepping in, this time to stop affirmative action programs of the type used by the University of California. . . .

NOTES

1. U.S. Dept. of Labor, Bureau of Labor Statistics, Employment and Earnings, January 1978, at 170 (table 44).
2. *Ibid.*
3. U.S. Dept. of Commerce, Bureau of the Census, Current Population Reports, Series P-60, No. 105, at 198 (1977) (table 47).
4. U.S. Dept. of Commerce, Bureau of the Census, Statistical Abstract of the United States 25 (table 24).
5. *Id.*, at 407–8 (table 622) (based on 1970 census).
6. Indeed, the action of the university finds support in the regulations promulgated under Title VI by the Department of Health, Education, and Welfare and approved by the President, which authorize a federally funded institution to take affirmative steps to overcome past discrimination against groups even where the institution was not guilty of prior discrimination. 45 CRF sec. 80.3(b)(6)(ii).

Are Quotas Good
for Blacks?

Thomas Sowell

Race has never been an area noted for rationality of thought or action. Almost every conceivable form of nonsense has been believed about racial or ethnic groups at one time or another. Theologians used to debate whether black people had souls (today's terminology might suggest that *only* black people have souls). As late as the 1920s, a leading authority on mental tests claimed that test results disproved the popular belief that Jews are intelligent. Since then, Jewish IQs have risen above the national average and more than one-fourth of all American Nobel Prize winners have been Jewish.

Today's grand fallacy about race and ethnicity is that the statistical "representation" of a group—in jobs, schools, etc—shows and measures discrimination. This notion is at the center of such controversial policies as affirmative-action hiring, preferential admissions to college, and public-school busing. But despite the fact that far-reaching judicial rulings, political crusades, and bureaucratic empires owe their existence to that belief, it remains an unexamined assumption. Tons of statistics have been collected, but only to be interpreted in the light of that assumption, never to test the assumption itself. Glaring facts to the contrary are routinely ignored. Questioning the "representation" theory is stigmatized as not only inexpedient but immoral. It is the noble lie of our time.

AFFIRMATIVE-ACTION HIRING

"Representation" or "underrepresentation" is based on comparisons of a given group's percentage in the population with its percentage in some occupation, institution, or activity. This might make sense if the various ethnic

Reprinted from *Commentary* 65 (June 1978): 39–43, by permission; all rights reserved.

groups were even approximately similar in age distribution, education, and other crucial variables. But they are not.

Some ethnic groups are a whole decade younger than others. Some are two decades younger. The average age of Mexican Americans and Puerto Ricans is under twenty, while the average age of Irish Americans or Italian Americans is over thirty—and the average age of Jewish Americans is over forty. This is because of large differences in the number of children per family from one group to another. Some ethnic groups have more than twice as many children per family as others. Over half of the Mexican American and Puerto Rican population consists of teenagers, children, and infants. These two groups are likely to be underrepresented in any adult activity, whether work or recreation, whether controlled by others or entirely by themselves, and whether there is discrimination or not.

Educational contrasts are also great. More than half of all Americans over thirty-five of German, Irish, Jewish, or Oriental ancestry have completed at least four years of high school. Less than 20 percent of all Mexican Americans in the same age bracket have done so. The disparities become even greater when you consider quality of school, field of specialization, postgraduate study, and other factors that are important in the kind of high-level jobs on which special attention is focused by those emphasizing representation. Those groups with the most education—Jews and Orientals—also have the highest quality education, as measured by the rankings of the institutions from which they receive their college degrees and specialize in the more difficult and remunerative fields, such as science and medicine. Orientals in the United States are so heavily concentrated in the scientific area that there are more Oriental scientists than there are black scientists in absolute numbers, even though the black population of the United States is more than twenty times the size of the Oriental population.

Attention has been focused most on high-level positions—the kind of jobs people reach after years of experience or education, or both. There is no way to get the experience or education without also growing older in the process, so when we are talking about top-level jobs, we are talking about the kind of positions people reach in their forties and fifties rather than in their teens and twenties. Representation in such jobs cannot be compared to representation in a population that includes many five-year-olds—yet it is.

The general ethnic differences in age become extreme in some of the older age brackets. Half of the Jewish population of the United States is forty-five years old or older, but only 12 percent of the Puerto Rican population is that old. Even if Jews and Puerto Ricans were identical in every other respect, and even if no employer ever had a speck of prejudice, there would still be huge disparities between the two groups in top-level positions, just from age differences alone.

Virtually every underrepresented racial or ethnic group in the United States has a lower than average age and consists disproportionately of children and inexperienced young adults. Almost invariably these groups also have less education, both quantitatively and qualitatively. The point here is not that we should "blame the victim" or "blame society." The point is that we should, first of all, *talk sense!* "Representation" talk is cheap, easy, and misleading; discrimination and opportunity are too serious to be discussed in gobbledygook.

The idea that preferential treatment is going to "compensate" people for past wrongs flies in the face of two hard facts:

1. Public opinion polls have repeatedly shown most blacks opposed to preferential treatment either in jobs or college admissions. A Gallup poll in March 1977, for example, found only 27 percent of non-whites favoring "preferential" over "ability as determined by test scores," while 64 percent preferred the latter and 9 percent were undecided. (The Gallup breakdown of the U.S. population by race, sex, income, education, etc. found that "not a single population group supports affirmative action."[1])

    How can you compensate people by giving them something they have explicitly rejected?

2. The income of blacks relative to whites reached its peak *before* affirmative-action hiring and has *declined* since. The median income of blacks reached a peak of 60.9 percent of the median income of whites in 1970—the year before "goals" and "timetables" became part of the affirmative-action concept. "In only one year of the last six years," writes Andrew Brimmer, "has the proportion been as high as 60 percent."[2]

    Before something can be a "compensation," it must first be a benefit.

The repudiation of the numerical or preferential approach by the very people it is supposed to benefit points out the large gap between illusion and reality that is characteristic of affirmative action. So does the cold fact that there are few, if any, benefits to offset all the bitterness generated by this heavy-handed program. The bitterness is largely a result of a deeply resented principle, galling bureaucratic processes, and individual horror stories. Overall, the program has changed little for minorities or women. Supporters of the program try to cover up its ineffectiveness by comparing the position of minorities today with their position many years ago. This ignores all the progress that took place under straight equal-treatment laws in the 1960s— progress that has not continued at anywhere near the same pace under affirmative action.

Among the reasons for such disappointing results is that hiring someone to fill a quota gets the government off the employer's back for the moment, but buys more trouble down the road whenever a disgruntled employee chooses to go to an administrative agency or a court with a complaint based on nothing but numbers. Regardless of the merits, or the end result, a very costly process for the employer must be endured, and the threat of this is an incentive *not* to hire from the groups designated as special by the government. The affirmative-action program has meant mutually canceling incentives to hire and not to hire—and great bitterness and cost from the process, either way.

If blacks are opposed to preferential treatment and whites are opposed to it, who then is in favor of it, and how does it go on? The implications of these questions are even more far-reaching and more disturbing than the policy itself. They show how vulnerable our democratic and constitutional safeguards are to a relative handful of determined people. Some of those people promoting preferential treatment and numerical goals are so convinced of the rightness of what they are doing that they are prepared to sacrifice whatever needs to be sacrificed—whether it be other people, the law, or simply honesty in discussing what they are doing (note "goals," "desegregation," and similar euphemisms). Other supporters of numerical policies have the powerful drive of self-interest as well as self-righteousness. Bureaucratic empires have grown up to administer these programs, reaching into virtually every business, school, hospital, or other organization. The rules and agents of this empire can order employers around, make college presidents bow and scrape, assign schoolteachers by race, or otherwise gain power, publicity, and career advancement—regardless of whether minorities are benefited or not.

While self-righteousness and self-interest are powerful drives for those who have them, they can succeed only insofar as other people can be persuaded, swept along by feelings, or neutralized. Rhetoric has accomplished this with images of historic wrongs, visions of social atonement, and a horror of being classed with bigots. These tactics have worked best with those most affected by words and least required to pay a price personally: nonelected judges, the media, and the intellectual establishment.

The "color-blind" words of the Civil Rights Act of 1964, or even the protections of the Constitution, mean little when judges can creatively reinterpret them out of existence. It is hard to achieve the goal of an informed public when the mass media show only selective indignation about power grabs and a sense of pious virtue in covering up the failures of school integration. Even civil libertarians—who insist that the Fifth Amendment protection against self-incrimination is a sacred right that cannot be denied Nazis, Communists, or criminals—show no concern when the government routinely forces employers to confess "deficiencies" in their hiring processes, without a speck of evidence other than a numerical pattern different from the government's preconception.

PREFERENTIAL ADMISSIONS

Preferential admissions to colleges and universities are "justified" by similar rhetoric and the similar assumption that statistical underrepresentation means institutional exclusion. Sometimes this assumption is buttressed by notions of "compensation" and a theory that (1) black communities need more black practitioners in various fields; and that (2) black students will ultimately supply that need. The idea that the black community's doctors, lawyers, etc. should be black is an idea held by white liberals, but no such demand has come from the black community, which has rejected preferential admissions in poll after poll. Moreover, the idea that an admissions committee can predict what a youth is going to do with his life years later is even more incredible—even if the youth is one's own son or daughter, much less someone from a wholly different background.

These moral or ideological reasons for special minority programs are by no means the whole story. The public image of a college or university is often its chief financial asset. Bending a few rules here and there to get the right body count of minority students seems a small price to pay for maintaining an image that will keep money coming in from the government and the foundations. When a few thousand dollars in financial aid to students can keep millions of tax dollars rolling in, it is clearly a profitable investment for the institution. For the young people brought in under false pretense, it can turn out to be a disastrous and permanently scarring experience.

The most urgent concern over image and over government subsidies, foundation grants, and other donations is at those institutions which have the most of all these things to maintain—that is, at prestigious colleges and universities at the top of the academic pecking order. The Ivy League schools and the leading state and private institutions have the scholarship money and the brand-name visibility to draw in enough minority youngsters to look good statistically. The extremely high admissions standards of these institutions usually cannot be met by the minority students—just as most students in general cannot meet them. But in order to have a certain minority body count, the schools bend (or disregard) their usual standards. The net result is that thousands of minority students who would normally qualify for good, nonprestigious colleges where they could succeed, are instead enrolled in famous institutions where they fail. For example, at Cornell during the guns-on-campus crisis, fully half of the black students were on academic probation, despite easier grading standards for them in many courses. Yet these students were by no means unqualified. Their average test scores put them in the top quarter of all American college students—but the other Cornell students ranked in the top 1 percent. In other words, minority students with every prospect of success in a normal college environment were artificially turned into failures by being mismatched with an institution with standards too severe for them.

When the top institutions reach further down to get minority students, then academic institutions at the next level are forced to reach still further down, so that they too will end up with a minority body count high enough to escape criticism and avoid trouble with the government and other donors. Each academic level, therefore, ends up with minority students underqualified for that level, though usually perfectly qualified for some other level. The end result is a systematic mismatching of minority students and the institutions they attend, even though the wide range of American colleges and universities is easily capable of accommodating those same students under their normal standards.

Proponents of "special" (lower) admissions standards argue that without such standards no increase in minority enrollment would have been possible. But this blithely disregards the fact that when more *money* is available to finance college, more low-income people go to college. The GI Bill after World War II caused an even more dramatic increase in the number of people going to college who could never have gone otherwise—and without lowering admissions standards. The growth of special minority programs in recent times has meant both a greater availability of money and lower admissions standards for black and other designated students. It is as ridiculous to ignore the role of money in increasing the numbers of minority students in the system as a whole as it is to ignore the effect of double standards on their maldistribution among institutions. It is the double standards that are the problem, and they can be ended without driving minority students out of the system. Of course, many academic hustlers who administer special programs might lose their jobs, but that would hardly be a loss to anyone else.

As long as admission to colleges and universities is not unlimited, someone's opportunity to attend has to be sacrificed as the price of preferential admission for others. No amount of verbal sleight-of-hand can get around this fact. None of those sacrificed is old enough to have had anything to do with historic injustices that are supposedly being compensated. Moreover, it is not the offspring of the privileged who are likely to pay the price. It is not a Rockefeller or a Kennedy who will be dropped to make room for quotas; it is a De Funis or a Bakke. Even aside from personal influence on admissions decisions, the rich can give their children the kind of private schooling that will virtually assure them test scores far above the cutoff level at which sacrifices are made.

Just as the students who are sacrificed are likely to come from the bottom of the white distribution, so the minority students chosen are likely to be from the top of the minority distribution. In short, it is a forced transfer of benefits from those least able to afford it to those least in need of it. In some cases, the loose term "minority" is used to include individuals who are personally from more fortunate backgrounds than the average American. Sometimes it includes whole groups, such as Chinese or Japanese Americans, who have higher incomes than whites. One-fourth of all employed Chinese in this country are in professional occupations—nearly double the national average. No amount of favoritism to the son or daughter of a Chinese doctor or mathematician today is going to compensate some Chinese of the past who was excluded from virtually every kind of work except washing clothes or washing dishes.

The past is a great unchangeable fact. *Nothing* is going to undo its sufferings and injustices, whatever their magnitude. Statistical categories and historic labels may seem real to those inspired by words, but only living flesh-and-blood people can feel joy or pain. Neither the sins nor the sufferings of those dead are within our power to change. Being honest and honorable with the people living in our own time is more than enough moral challenge, without indulging in illusions about rewriting moral history with numbers and categories. . . .

However futile the various numerical approaches have been in their avowed goal of advancing minorities, their impact has been strongly felt in other ways. The message that comes through loud and clear is that minorities are losers who will never have anything unless someone gives it to them. The destructiveness of this message—on society in general and minority youth in particular—outweighs any trivial gains that may occur here and there. The falseness of the message is shown by the great economic achievements of minorities during the period of equal-rights legislation before numerical goals and timetables muddied the waters. By and large, the numerical approach has achieved nothing, and has achieved it at great cost.

Underlying the attempt to move people around and treat them like chess pieces on a board is a profound contempt for other human beings. To ignore or resent people's resistance—on behalf of their children or their livelihoods—is to deny our common humanity. To persist dogmatically in pursuit of some abstract goal, without regard to how it is reached, is to despise freedom and reduce three-dimensional life to cardboard pictures of numerical results. The false practicality of results-oriented people ignores the fact that the ultimate results are in the minds and hearts of human beings. Once personal choice becomes a mere inconvenience to be brushed aside by bureaucrats or judges, something precious will have been lost by all people from all backgrounds.

A multiethnic society like the United States can ill afford continually to build up stores of intergroup resentments about such powerful concerns as one's livelihood and one's children. It is a special madness when tensions are escalated between groups who are basically in accord in their opposition to numbers games, but whose legal establishments and "spokesmen" keep the fires fueled. We must never think that the disintegration and disaster that has hit other multiethnic societies "can't happen here." The mass internment of Japanese Americans just a generation ago is a sobering reminder of the tragic idiocy that stress can bring on. We are not made of different clay from the Germans, who were historically more enlightened and humane toward Jews

than many other Europeans—until the generation of Hitler and the Holocaust.

The situation in America today is, of course, not like that of the Pearl
Harbor period, nor of the Weimar republic. History does not literally repeat,
but it can warn us of what people are capable of, when the stage has been set
for tragedy. We certainly do not need to let emotionally combustible materials accumulate from ill-conceived social experiments.

NOTES

1. Gallup Opinion Index, June 1977, Report 143, p. 23.
2. *Black Enterprise*, April 1978, p. 62. A newly released RAND study similarly concludes that very little credit should be given to government affirmative-action
   programs for any narrowing of the income gap between white and black workers.
   The RAND researchers write, "Our results suggest that the effect of government
   on the aggregate black-white wage ratio is quite small and that the popular notion
   that . . . recent changes are being driven by government pressure has little empirical support" (*New York Times*, May 8, 1978).

COMPARABLE WORTH

Under existing law, men and women must be paid equally for performing the same job, for the same employer, at the same workplace. Despite the fact that this law has been in place for many years, women continue to earn substantially less than men. This is so largely because women tend to be concentrated in occupations which have traditionally paid less.

In the judgment of women's rights advocates, the income differential between the sexes provides clear evidence of wage discrimination against women. Accordingly, as a remedy to this problem, they have proposed adoption of a principle known as "comparable worth." Briefly stated, this principle asserts that people performing different jobs should receive equal pay if those jobs are comparable in skills and responsibilities. In the state of Washington, for example, one study found that the job of laundry workers (dominated by females) was comparable to that of lower-level truckdrivers (dominated by men); yet the laundry workers were in fact earning 41 percent less than truckdrivers.

As the following two selections will reveal, there is considerable disagreement over the desirability of implementing the comparable worth principle. Former U.S. Attorney General William French Smith, a critic, maintains that comparable worth would become an administrative nightmare. What standards would one use to compare occupations, and how would these standards be kept up-to-date? In addition, he argues that such a principle would constitute an unwarranted interference with free market forces; would be enormously costly to implement; and, finally, would actually make it more difficult for women to move out of jobs which have traditionally been dominated by females. Nancy Reder, on the other hand, rejects the contention that one cannot assess the comparable worth of various occupations. According to her, employers have been making these kinds of judgments for years. Moreover, she also insists that the importance of market forces in determining wages has been greatly exaggerated.

Forcing Equal Pay for Different Work Is a Bad Idea

William French Smith

Comparable worth, or equal pay for *different* work, is emerging as one of the most controversial labor issues of the 1980s. On January 3, [1985,] legislation was introduced in Congress to authorize a study of alleged pay disparities between civil service jobs held mainly by men and ones primarily performed by women. A similar bill was passed last year by the House.

Legislatures in several states, including Minnesota and Iowa, have recently passed measures seeking the adoption of comparable worth in state pay practices. Legislatures in a number of other states including Nevada, Rhode Island, and Virginia have either authorized or passed resolutions calling for comparable worth studies of state employment. In California, Connecticut, Hawaii, and Illinois, public employes are in federal court, charging their employers (in most cases, the states) with violations of federal law that they believe already requires equal pay for jobs of allegedly comparable value.

Meanwhile, in New Haven, Connecticut, the comparable worth movement has made its most publicized stand in the private sector. Seeking more pay in contract negotiations with Yale University, the school's clerical and technical workers, who are predominantly female, have publicly couched their demands in terms of the equal pay for different work debate. For example, it was said that Yale's administrative assistants, who are mostly female and make on average $13,424, do work at least as valuable to the university as its truckdrivers, who are mostly men and make on average $18,470.

Comparable worth has gained a degree of popularity in some circles.

From William French Smith, "Forcing Equal Pay for Different Work Is a Bad Idea," *Washington Post*, January 27, 1985, pp. C1, C4. © 1985, The Washington Post Company. Reprinted with permission.

But in our view comparable worth cannot be justified on any gound—legal, economic, or policy. It does not merit adoption by the public sector, and one can be sure of this: It would enter the private sector only by government mandate.

What is comparable worth, and why is it said that we need it? Contrary to what its advocates say, comparable worth is *not* the same as equal pay for equal work. Equal pay for equal work means that two printers, one male and one female, who do the same work for the same employer, should be paid the same. The Equal Pay Act of 1963 affirms this principle of basic fairness. No one questions its validity, and this administration wholeheartedly supports it.

Comparable worth incarnates a far different principle—that two jobs, one performed mostly by women, the other mostly by men, which are not identical but are alleged to be "comparable" in value to employers or society, should pay the same wage.

In a case pending in the federal district court in Michigan, for example, secretaries, almost all of whom are female and are paid $12,882 to $16,432 annually, are said to perform jobs of as much worth as those held by maintenance mechanics, who are all male and earn from $15,868 to $19,961 a year. Not equal pay for equal work but equal pay for work of allegedly comparable worth—indeed, different work—that is the idea involved.

Comparable worth proponents note that jobs traditionally held by women—nursing, secretarial, and other office jobs, for example—have paid less than those traditionally performed by men, such as plumbing, engineering, and maintenance.

They argue that the "female" jobs are worth at least as much to employers or society as the "male" ones. The explanation for the difference in pay, they assert, must be sex-based discrimination. Ratcheting salary schedules upward so that the female jobs are paid as much as the male ones is the remedy proposed by advocates of comparable worth.

Thus, in a case pending in the U.S. District Court for the District of Oregon, it has been alleged that university teachers in the "female" fields of nursing, dental hygiene, secretarial science, business education, and teacher education should be paid as well as those in the "male" fields of medicine, dentistry, business administration, and education administration.

Congress had never passed a law mandating comparable worth in any form or fashion, yet the federal judiciary, as in the Michigan and Oregon examples, is being invited to read comparable worth into Title VII of the Civil Rights Act of 1964, which states that it is unlawful for an employer "to discriminate against any individual with respect to his compensation . . . because of such individual's sex." A comparable worth interpretation of Title VII, however, does not square with the intent of the law.

Title VII can be understood only in light of the Equal Pay Act of 1963. In passing that law, Congress thoroughly considered and specifically *rejected* proposals covering jobs of a "comparable" character. Instead, Congress drew a circle around the one area where discriminatory treatment could reasonably be presumed—men and women doing the same work but receiving unequal pay—and outlawed such differentials.

The Equal Pay Act was just that—a guarantee that equal work would be equally compensated. There is nothing in the record to suggest that this sense of Congress changed during the subsequent months as it debated and passed into law Title VII.

So far, only one federal court, in the Western District of Washington, has gone beyond the intent of Title VII by adopting a comparable worth interpretation. Last year, in a much-discussed case brought by the American Federation of State, County and Municipal Employees against the state of Washington, that court found the state liable for sex-biased pay discrimination against women under Title VII. The court ordered the state to increase the salaries of all employees, male and female, in jobs held mostly by women, to levels commensurate with their rating in a state-sponsored comparable worth study conducted in 1973.

The AFSCME case is now pending before the U.S. Court of Appeals for the Ninth Circuit, which in 1984 rejected a comparable worth claim by the predominantly female nursing faculty of the University of Washington. The Supreme Court decided not to review this decision, thus leaving interpretation of the law, for the moment, in the hands of the circuit courts of appeals. To date, the six courts of appeals to rule on comparable worth claims have unanimously rejected them.

Not only is comparable worth not the law, it plainly shouldn't be. Comparable worth would reverse the long overdue trend toward more cost-efficient government and freer labor markets. In the public sector, comparable worth would only further reduce, if not eliminate altogether, the influence of the marketplace on determining the pay of civil servants. Applied to the private sector, comparable worth would dramatically increase government influence upon the workings of the marketplace by disrupting the current mixed system of supply and demand (including the effects of competition from abroad), collective bargaining contracts, and state and federal rules (such as the minimum-wage law) that determine private sector pay.

Comparable worth is plainly a very bureaucratic and most expensive proposition. At the federal level no existing bureaucracy has the time or manpower even to attempt an implementation of comparable worth. A new agency would have to be created, and it would dictate "comparability" standards, order subsequent adjustments and oversee the implementation of every jot and tittle of its various commands. The regulation comparable worth implies for the private sector would exceed the scope and influence of any it currently experiences.

In the public sector, comparable worth costs would be passed on to the already overburdened taxpayers; if the decision in the AFSCME case is not reversed, the cost to the state of Washington (read: Washington taxpayers) is reliably estimated to be $400 million in the first year of implementation and $60 million every year thereafter. In the private sector, comparable worth costs also would be passed on to the taxpayers in the form of higher prices.

This might not be the only cost. With the price of certain types of labor increased by government fiat, employers might well decide to buy less of that labor. Employment in areas affected by comparable worth decisions would then decline, as would total output. The darkness one sees at the end of the comparable worth tunnel is economic decline.

No one can seriously consider comparable worth without reflecting on the practical problems it would raise. A comparable worth bureaucracy—made up of government officials, lawyers, and judges—would determine which jobs are, in effect, "male" and which "female." But is a "male" or "female" job one in which 70 percent of those performing the job are men or women, as one comparable worth proponent has said? Why not 80 percent, as another comparable worth study concludes? For that matter, why not 90? Why not 60? Or 69 or 71? And what happens when, whatever percentage is chosen, it begins to slip? Is the job in question still a "male" or "female" job?

Further, there is the problem of figuring out the "worth" of each job. How does one say which job is worth more or less than another one? Obviously, one person's criteria for job "worthiness" may not be another's. And it is hardly clear how the criteria of any person who has the task of determining the value of jobs should be evaluated. Not only the criteria, but also the weight assigned to each criterion, are subjective matters.

Most fundamentally, there is the question of who is to make all of these determinations. Who is to say which jobs are "male" or "female," which jobs are "worth" more than others, how many points to assign to this job as opposed to that one and how then to evaluate the points assigned? And why should anyone want to give these arbitrary tasks to government bureaucracies? Who is government to say that administrative assistants and truck-drivers, or nurses and mechanics, should be paid the same? It is not clear that government would determine pay scales in a more competent manner than now exists. Moreover, only the naive could suppose that comparable worth bureaucracies would be unaffected by political considerations as they assign points and evaluate jobs.

Comparable worth is an idea rich in irony. Advanced in the name of women's equality, it would require government's labeling some jobs as "male" and others as "female." Furthermore, those who would benefit from comparable worth would be, as the Washington state case illustrates, not only the females who fill "female" jobs, but also the males in those jobs. Comparable worth, whatever else may be said against it, is overinclusive in terms of those who would benefit from it.

There is also the irony that comparable worth, if implemented, would reduce the incentives for women to move out of jobs traditionally held by their sex into those long held by men.

The increased pay in traditionally female jobs would encourage women to stay in those jobs and could lead to an oversupply of workers for certain occupations.

A case pending in federal court in Illinois demonstrates the far-from-unreasonable fear of some women that comparable worth could even reduce the salaries paid to women who move into "male" occupations. In a complaint brought by the American Nurses Association and others against the state of Illinois, it is alleged that the state uses "a sex-biased system of pay and classification which results in and perpetuates discrimination in compensation" against those employed in occupations historically held mostly by women, such as nursing, health technician, switchboard operator, and clerk typist. The complaint cites an official study commissioned by the state concluding that "female" jobs possess greater value than certain "male" jobs and are paid less. For example, the study rated nurse IV above electrician, but the nursing job pays an average monthly salary of $2,104 and the electrician job paid $2,826.

It is obvious, however, that many women in Illinois disagree with this study and indeed with the whole idea of comparable worth. Fifteen women, all of whom hold jobs traditionally performed by men, have recently asked the court for permission to join the state as *defendants*. According to the state's comparable worth study, the jobs these women hold—as correctional officers, a security officer, an accountant, and an office manager—should be, in effect, devalued. These women believe that if the decision in this case requires the implementation of the comparable worth study, their pay checks will be smaller.

In their filing with the court these fifteen women deny "that they are beneficiaries of sex discrimination, or are overpaid. On the contrary, any favorable salary positions they enjoy relative to [the plaintiffs] are the result of special skill, hard work, and the nondiscriminatory forces of supply and demand."

The group of women also states "a direct interest" in preserving the present system of compensation, which "rewards them for their special skills; their performance of particularly difficult, dangerous, or unpleasant work, and their willingness to challenge stereotypes and perform jobs traditionally occupied by males."

These Illinois women represent the healthy trend of the past two decades, during which the work force has become more and more integrated, with women making dramatic inroads into jobs traditionally held by men.

One reason for this trend, no doubt, is the very willingness of many women to "challenge stereotypes and perform jobs traditionally occupied by males."

Surely there is no reason to change this trend by jettisoning current public policy in favor of comparable worth. Aggressive enforcement of Title VII to ensure women equal employment opportunities, combined with vigorous enforcement of the Equal Pay Act, remains the best means of securing the great goal of equal employment opportunity and equitable employer treatment for all Americans, regardless of sex.

Pay Equity: Putting an End to Wage Discrimination

Nancy D. Reder

THE WAGE GAP

The wage gap between women and men is not new. It is one of the oldest and most persistent symptoms of sexual inequality in the United States. Today, women who work full time year round earn approximately 62 cents for every dollar earned by their male counterparts in the United States; a woman with a college degree earns an average of $2,000 *less* per year than a male high school dropout.

The single biggest reason for this wage gap is that women, overwhelmingly, do not work in the same jobs as men but are instead concentrated in a small number of sex-segregated occupations. Fifty percent of employed women work in only 20 occupations.* The incidence of job segregation among minority women is even higher than that for white women.

In 1981, the National Academy of Sciences released a landmark study, *Women, Work and Wages: Equal Pay for Work of Equal Value,* that concluded: "Not only do women do different work than men, but also the work women do is paid less, and the more an occupation is dominated by women, the less it pays." The study added that "only a small part of the earnings differences between men and women can be accounted for by differences in education, labor force experience, labor force commitment, or other human capital factors believed to contribute to productivity differences among workers."

Twenty years of wage corrections required by the Equal Pay Act—which mandated equal wages for men and women performing the same

---

* In 1982, 98 percent of all secretaries were women, but only 1.6 percent of electricians and 1.7 percent of carpenters were women. Women were 96 percent of all registered nurses, but only 15 percent of all doctors. Minority women were heavily concentrated in low-paying clerical and health-related jobs.

Prepared especially for this volume by Nancy D. Reder, director, Social Policy League of Women Voters Education Fund, and former chair, National Committee on Pay Equity.

work for the same employer in the same workplace—have brought higher wages to thousands of women. But these adjustments have not reduced the wage gap because relatively few women hold the same jobs as men. Similarly, although affirmative-action measures have created many new job opportunities for women, they, too, have not reduced the wage gap because the movement of women into what are considered to be "nontraditional" jobs has not matched the growing numbers of women workers in traditionally female occupations.

THE CONCEPT OF PAY EQUITY

The principle of pay equity* requires the elimination of wage discrimination among jobs that, although not identical, are comparable, based on the skill, effort, responsibility, and working conditions required. Although many of the pay equity initiatives that have occurred to date have focused on sex-based wage discrimination, the principle of pay equity is equally applicable in those workplaces where job segregation and low wages are associated with race or ethnicity, rather than gender. In other words, pay equity advocates assert that workers should be paid on the basis of the value of their work to their employers, and not on the basis of the sex or race of the job occupant.

HOW JOB WORTH IS DETERMINED

Many opponents argue that it is impossible to value jobs or to compare dissimilar jobs. This is frequently referred to as "the apples and oranges" argument. However, employers—both public and private—have always compared dissimilar jobs for purposes of establishing salaries. All employers—large or small—have to make determinations about how to pay their employees. Small employers may use an informal approach. ("I'm the boss so I get the most. You're the delivery person so you make the least. Everyone else makes something in-between.") Large employers use more formal systems.

Modern job evaluation systems were developed almost fifty years ago to evaluate managerial jobs. With some revisions, they have been adapted to evaluate blue-collar, service, and clerical jobs as well. Almost every large employer uses some method to evaluate the internal relationships of different jobs based on an objective evaluation of certain prerequisites or characteristics of the job relating to skill, effort, responsibility, and working

* The terms "pay equity," "comparable worth," and "sex- and race-based wage discrimination" are frequently, but not always, used interchangeably. For purposes of this discussion, these terms are synonymous.

conditions. The federal civil service (GS) system operates on such a system, as do many state civil service systems, including the system in place in the state of Washington (see below).

It is interesting, therefore, that employers, who have been happily comparing dissimilar jobs for years suddenly are saying that job evaluation systems cannot be used to compare male-dominated and female-dominated jobs. Many pay equity opponents appear to have accepted this argument without question.

Pay equity advocates, on the other hand, emphasize the need to design job evaluation systems that are free from sex or race bias. One way of accomplishing this goal is to question some of the assumptions that have linked certain jobs together for job evaluation purposes or that have discounted certain aspects of female-dominated jobs. Some examples may serve to clarify these points:

1. In one lawsuit, *Gerlach v. Michigan Bell Telephone Co.*, the employer linked the female-dominated engineering layout clerk position to clerical jobs, instead of to the higher-paying (and more similar) male-dominated craft jobs. The engineering layout clerks sued, claiming that these jobs were undervalued. By early 1985, attorneys for both sides were trying to work out a negotiated settlement.

2. Job requirements or work conditions in female-dominated jobs are frequently overlooked for purposes of compensation. For example, skills required by receptionists—such as the ability to deal with many people while remaining pleasant—have rarely been recognized as being worthy of compensation. Aides who work in mental hospitals (another female-dominated job) may be subjected to abuse and/or assault by patients, yet this factor may not be considered a negative working condition for which the employee should be compensated.

The job evaluation study performed by Willis & Associates in Washington state was an effort to examine the assumptions upon which the existing system was built, to see if those assumptions were still valid.

THE USE OF MARKET WAGE RATES

Another argument frequently raised against pay equity is that salaries are based purely on what the marketplace will bear. However, this argument exaggerates the reliance that many employers place on what other employers are paying for similar jobs.

In the first place, employers have to take into account both internal and external equities in setting salaries. An employer may determine that the market rate for a senior secretary is $20,000 per year, but if this is more money than the employer is paying an employee with an MBA (Masters of Business Administration) to run a company division, it is highly unlikely that the secretary will earn the market rate.

Second, market rates may well reflect prior discrimination that is built into society as a whole. Reliance solely upon the market is one way in which the depression of wages of women and minorities is transferred from employer to employer. It is no defense to a charge of discrimination that everyone is doing it.

Third, experience shows that employers respond differently to market situations depending on the sex or race composition of the jobs for which they are setting wages. According to market theory, when there are shortages in occupations, the salaries of those occupations should rise. There is a great deal of evidence, however, to suggest that this often does not happen when the occupation is female- or minority-dominated. The well-known and long-time shortage of nurses—a vastly underpaid profession—vividly illustrates that supply and demand can have little effect on the wages of female-dominated professions. Some employers went to the extreme of recruiting nurses from the Philippines rather than increasing salaries in order to attract nurses from other parts of this country.

The history of the female-dominated nursing profession provides a sharp contrast to the male-dominated engineering profession, where shortages over the past ten years have dramatically increased entry-level salaries as well as those for more experienced engineers.

THE COST FACTOR

Opponents of pay equity maintain that increasing women's salaries in order to achieve pay equity would lead to economic chaos, and they point to cost estimates exceeding $500 million that have been bandied about in the lawsuit against the state of Washington as an example. Pay equity advocates are concerned about cost, but to date, no one has developed a reliable or accurate method for projecting the cost of implementing pay equity nationwide. The state of Minnesota, which has moved ahead to implement pay equity for its state employees, estimated that it would cost 4 percent of the state payroll. In January 1983, the legislature allocated $21.7 million for the first two years of a planned four-year phase-in of pay equity. It has been estimated that it would have cost the state of Washington only 5 percent of its payroll had it moved ahead to implement pay equity in the mid-1970s. What has escalated the projected costs in the lawsuit against Washington state is a back-pay award that the state will be required to pay should the employees prevail in their legal action against the state. Clearly, these are costs that employers can avoid if they move voluntarily to implement pay equity instead of waiting to be sued.

It is critical to remember that the cost of correcting discrimination is no justification for violating the law. In 1978, the Supreme Court ruled in the case of *Los Angeles Department of Water and Power v. Manhart* that the cost of correcting discriminatory practices is no justification for violating Title VII of the Civil Rights Act of 1964, which prohibits discrimination in employment.

It also is interesting to note that charges that economic chaos would result have been raised every time labor reforms have been proposed or enacted in this country—reforms that have included passage of the Fair Labor Standards Act, the abolition of child labor, the institution of the eight-hour workday, and passage of the Equal Pay Act and the Pregnancy Discrimination Act.*

A LANDMARK CASE

In July 1982, the American Federation of State, County, and Municipal Employees (AFSCME) filed a lawsuit in federal district court on behalf of its members—Washington state public employees—against the state of Washington alleging that the state was guilty of sex-based wage discrimination. The U.S. Supreme Court had held, in 1981 in the case of *County of Washington (OR) v. Gunther*, that such discrimination is prohibited by Title VII, whether or not the jobs involved are equal.

In its December 1983 ruling, the district court found that the state had engaged in a policy and practice of discrimination on the basis of sex in compensating occupants of jobs performed by women. An essential element of the court's finding was the substantial sex segregation in job classifications in state employment. (More than 86 percent of 1,783 job classifications were filled predominantly by either men or women; more than 67 percent were filled *exclusively* by either men or women.) Another major component of AFSCME's evidence included documentation that the state did not pay according to market rates, as it had claimed. Although the state did conduct salary surveys, it never implemented the results of those surveys. In fact, 97 percent of the classified jobs were never surveyed.

These key factors—job segregation and the employer's failure to rely on market rates as it had claimed—coupled with sex-based wage discrimination, are found throughout the labor force in the United States today. They provide the basis of other lawsuits being brought around the country.

PAY EQUITY AS AN EMERGING FACT OF LIFE

Pay equity has become more than a theoretical concept. In the last several years, a variety of approaches have been undertaken to identify and elimi-

---

* The Pregnancy Discrimination Act, passed by Congress in 1978 as an amendment to Title VII of the Civil Rights Act, prohibits discrimination in employment due to pregnancy.

nate sex- and race-based wage discrimination involving jobs that are not identical. Women's groups, labor unions, and civil rights organizations all have undertaken education campaigns to inform their members and the general public about this issue.

Forty-one states and many local jurisdictions either are considering or already have begun studies of their job classification systems. A survey published in the fall of 1984 by the National Committee on Pay Equity, a coalition of groups and individuals working to accomplish comparable worth, identified over one hundred such initiatives, and the number is increasing.

At the federal level, legislation introduced by U.S. Representative Mary Rose Oakar (D.-Ohio) calling for a job evaluation study of federal employees was passed overwhelmingly by the House of Representatives in the summer of 1984, but it never came up for a vote in the Senate.* A compromise worked out by key members of the House and Senate asked the General Accounting Office (GAO) to prepare a feasibility study of federal employees. The GAO report was due to Congress March 1, 1985.

Labor unions, among the leaders of the movement for pay equity, are actively pursuing these issues through negotiated joint labor–management job evaluation studies, negotiated wage equity increases, joint labor–management conducted job studies, and, if necessary, litigation.

The use of pay equity as a means to eliminate long-entrenched wage discrimination has become a fact of life. In fact, developments show that Eleanor Holmes Norton, former Chair of the Equal Employment Opportunity Commission, was right on target when she called pay equity "*the* civil rights issue of the 1980s."

---

* This bill, and other pay equity legislation, was reintroduced during the 1985 legislative session of Congress.

CHAPTER SIXTEEN

CHARACTERIZATIONS OF THE AMERICAN POLITICAL SYSTEM

Up to this point, the selections in this reader have focused narrowly upon various political institutions and processes. These final two selections, however, examine our political system at a more general level. Specifically, they attempt to characterize the structure of power in our political system. C. Wright Mills' book The Power Elite *respresents one of the most ambitious treatments of this subject. In it, he argues that all decisions of at least national consequence are determined by a power elite—a group of individuals who occupy the top positions in* three *different sectors of our national life. The members of this power elite can move with relative ease from the top of one sector to another. While Mills is not prepared to say that these individuals conspire with one another, he contends that they quite naturally hold similar views of the world because of common interests and backgrounds. Mills expresses concern about this power elite because many of them are not held accountable to the electorate for the exercise of their power. Also, in his judgment, the interests of this elite do not necessarily coincide with the public interest.*

Arnold Rose, author of the second selection, contends that the structure of power in the American political system is not as monolithic as Mills would have us believe. He notes that the group which Mills designates as power elite is not unified in its views and goals and that the evidence does not suggest this group is all that successful in bringing about the adoption of policies favoring its own interests. This is so because our society is in fact composed of a multiplicity of competing interests, no one of which is able to call the tune all of the time.

The Power Elite

C. Wright Mills

2

. . . We study history, it has been said, to rid ourselves of it, and the history of the power elite is a clear case for which this maxim is correct. Like the tempo of American life in general, the long-term trends of the power structure have been greatly speeded up since World War II, and certain newer trends within and between the dominant institutions have also set the shape of the power elite and given historically specific meaning to its fifth epoch:

I. Insofar as the structural clue to the power elite today lies in the political order, that clue is the decline of politics as genuine and public debate of alternative decisions—with nationally responsible and policy-coherent parties and with autonomous organizations connecting the lower and middle levels of power with the top levels of decision. America is now in considerable part more a formal political democracy than a democratic social structure, and even the formal political mechanics are weak.

The long-time tendency of business and government to become more intricately and deeply involved with each other has, in the fifth epoch, reached a new point of explicitness. The two cannot now be seen clearly as two distinct worlds. It is in terms of the executive agencies of the state that the rapprochement has proceeded most decisively. The growth of the executive branch of the government, with its agencies that patrol the complex economy, does not mean merely the "enlargement of government" as some sort of autonomous bureaucracy: it has meant the ascendancy of the corporation's man as a political eminence.

During the New Deal the corporate chieftains joined the political directorate; as of World War II they have come to dominate it. Long interlocked with government, now they have moved into quite full direction of the economy of the war effort and of the postwar era. This shift of the corporation executives into the political directorate has accelerated the long-term relegation of the professional politicians in the Congress to the middle levels of power.

II. Insofar as the structural clue to the power elite today lies in the enlarged and military state, that clue becomes evident in the military ascendancy. The warlords have gained decisive political relevance, and the military structure of America is now in considerable part a political structure. The seemingly permanent military threat places a premium on the military and upon their control of men, material, money, and power; virtually all political and economic actions are now judged in terms of military definitions of reality: the higher warlords have ascended to a firm position within the power elite of the fifth epoch.

In part at least this has resulted from one simple historical fact, pivotal for the years since 1939: the focus of elite attention has been shifted from domestic problems, centered in the thirties around slump, to international problems, centered in the forties and fifties around war. Since the governing apparatus of the United States has by long historic usage been adapted to and shaped by domestic clash and balance, it has not, from any angle, had suitable agencies and traditions for the handling of international problems. Such formal democratic mechanics as had arisen in the century and a half of national development prior to 1941, had not been extended to the American handling of international affairs. It is, in considerable part, in this vacuum that the power elite has grown.

III. Insofar as the structural clue to the power elite today lies in the economic order, that clue is the fact that the economy is at once a permanent-war economy and a private-corporation economy. American capitalism is now in considerable part a military capitalism, and the most important relation of the big corporation to the state rests on the coincidence of interests between military and corporate needs, as defined by warlords and corporate rich. Within the elite as a whole, this coincidence of interest between the high military and the corporate chieftains strengthens both of them and further subordinates the role of the merely political men. Not politicians, but corporate executives, sit with the military and plan the organization of war effort.

The shape and meaning of the power elite today can be understood only when these three sets of structural trends are seen at their point of coincidence: the military capitalism of private corporations exists in a weakened and formal democratic system containing a military order already quite political in outlook and demeanor. Accordingly, at the top of this structure, the power elite has been shaped by the coincidence of interest between those who control the major means of production and those who control the newly enlarged means of violence; from the decline of the professional politician and the rise to explicit political command of the corporate chieftains and the professional warlords; from the absence of any genuine civil service of skill and integrity, independent of vested interests.

The power elite is composed of political, economic, and military men, but this instituted elite is frequently in some tension: it comes together only on certain coinciding points and only on certain occasions of "crisis." In the long peace of the nineteenth century, the military men were not in the high councils of state, not of the political directorate, and neither were the economic men—they made raids upon the state but they did not join its directorate. During the thirties, the political man was ascendant. Now the military and the corporate men are in top positions.

Of the three types of circle that compose the power elite today, it is the military that has benefited the most in its enhanced power, although the corporate circles have also become more explicitly intrenched in the more public decision-making circles. It is the professional politician that has lost the most, so much that in examining the events and decisions, one is tempted to speak of a political vacuum in which the corporate rich and the high warlord, in their coinciding interests, rule.

It should not be said that the three "take turns" in carrying the initiative, for the mechanics of the power elite are not often as deliberate as that would imply. At times, of course, it is—as when political men, thinking they can borrow the prestige of generals, find that they must pay for it, or, as when during big slumps, economic men feel the need of a politician at once safe and possessing vote appeal. Today all three are involved in virtually all widely ramifying decisions. Which of the three types seems to lead depends upon "the tasks of the period" as they, the elite, define them. Just now these tasks center upon "defense" and international affairs. Accordingly, as we have seen, the military are ascendant in two senses: as personnel and as justifying ideology. That is why, just now, we can most easily specify the unity and the shape of the power elite in terms of the military ascendancy.

But we must always be historically specific and open to complexities. The simple Marxian view makes the big economic man the *real* holder of power; the simple liberal view makes the big political man the chief of the power system; and there are some who would view the warlords as virtual dictators. Each of these is an oversimplified view. It is to avoid them that we use the term "power elite" rather then, for example, "ruling class."*

* "Ruling class" is a badly loaded phrase. "Class" is an economic term; "rule" a political one. The phrase, "ruling class," thus contains the theory that an economic class rules politically. That short-cut theory may or may not at times be true, but we do not want to carry that one rather simple theory about in the terms that we use to define our problems; we wish to state the theories explicitly, using terms of more precise and unilateral meaning. Specifically, the phrase "ruling class," in its common political connotations, does not allow enough autonomy to the political order

Insofar as the power elite has come to wide public attention, it has done so in terms of the "military clique." The power elite does, in fact, take its current shape from the decisive entrance into it of the military. Their presence and their ideology are its major legitimations, whenever the power elite feels the need to provide any. But what is called the "Washington military clique" is not composed merely of military men, and it does not prevail merely in Washington. Its members exist all over the country, and it is a coalition of generals in the roles of corporation executives, of politicians masquerading as admirals, or corporation executives acting like politicians, of civil servants who become majors, of vice admirals who are also the assistants to a cabinet officer, who is himself, by the way, really a member of the managerial elite.

Neither the idea of a "ruling class" nor of a simple monolithic rise of "bureaucratic politicians" nor of a "military clique" is adequate. The power elite today involves the often uneasy coincidence of economic, military, and political power.

3

Even if our understanding were limited to these structural trends, we should have grounds for believing the power elite a useful, indeed indispensable, concept for the interpretation of what is going on at the topside of modern American society. But we are not, of course, so limited: our conception of the power elite does not need to rest only upon the correspondence of the institutional hierarchies involved, or upon the many points at which their shifting interests coincide. The power elite, as we conceive it, also rests upon the similarity of its personnel, and their personal and official relations with one another, upon their social and psychological affinities. In order to grasp the personal and social basis of the power elite's unity, we have first to remind ourselves of the facts of origin, career, and style of life of each of the types of circle whose members compose the power elite.

The power elite is *not* an aristocracy, which is to say that it is not a political ruling group based upon a nobility of hereditary origin. It has no compact basis in a small circle of great families whose members can and do consis-

---

and its agents, and it says nothing about the military as such. It should be clear to the reader by now that we do not accept as adequate the simple view that high economic men unilaterally make all decisions of national consequence. We hold that such a simple view of "economic determinism" must be elaborated by "political determinism" and "military determinism"; that the higher agents of each of these three domains now often have a noticeable degree of autonomy; and that only in the often intricate ways of coalition do they make up and carry through the most important decisions. Those are the major reasons we prefer "power elite" to "ruling class" as a characterizing phrase for the higher circles when we consider them in terms of power.

tently occupy the top positions in the several higher circles which overlap as the power elite. But such nobility is only one possible basis of common origin. That it does not exist for the American elite does not mean that members of this elite derive socially from the full range of strata composing American society. They derive in substantial proportions from the upper classes, both new and old, of local society and the metropolitan 400. The bulk of the very rich, the corporate executives, the political outsiders, the high military, derive from, at most, the upper third of the income and occupational pyramids. Their fathers were at least of the professional and business strata, and very frequently higher than that. They are native-born Americans of native parents, primarily from urban areas, and, with the exceptions of the politicians among them, overwhelmingly from the East. They are mainly Protestants, especially Episcopalian or Presbyterian. In general, the higher the position, the greater the proportion of men within it who have derived from and who maintain connections with the upper classes. The generally similar origins of the members of the power elite are underlined and carried further by the fact of their increasingly common educational routine. Overwhelmingly college graduates, substantial proportions have attended Ivy League colleges, although the education of the higher military, of course, differs from that of other members of the power elite.

But what do these apparently simple facts about the social composition of the higher circles really mean? In particular, what do they mean for any attempt to understand the degree of unity, and the direction of policy and interest that may prevail among these several circles? Perhaps it is best to put this question in a deceptively simple way: in terms of origin and career, who or what do these men at the top represent?

Of course, if they are elected politicians, they are supposed to represent those who elected them; and, if they are appointed, they are supposed to represent, indirectly, those who elected their appointers. But this is recognized as something of an abstraction, as a rhetorical formula by which all men of power in almost all systems of government nowadays justify their power of decision. At times it may be true, both in the sense of their motives and in the sense of who benefits from their decisions. Yet it would not be wise in any power system merely to assume it.

The fact that members of the power elite come from near the top of the nation's class and status levels does not mean that they are necessarily "representative" of the top levels only. And if they were, as social types, representative of a cross-section of the population, that would not mean that a balanced democracy of interest and power would automatically be the going political fact.

We cannot infer the direction of policy merely from the social origins and careers of the policymakers. The social and economic backgrounds of the men of power do not tell us all that we need to know in order to understand the distribution of social power. For: (1) Men from high places may be ideological representatives of the poor and humble. (2) Men of humble origin, brightly self-made, may energetically serve the most vested and inherited interests. Moreover (3), not all men who effectively represent the interests of a stratum need in any way belong to it or personally benefit by policies that further its interests. Among the politicians, in short, there are sympathetic *agents* of given groups, conscious and unconscious, paid and unpaid. Finally (4), among the top decision-makers we find men who have been chosen for their positions because of their "expert knowledge." These are some of the obvious reasons why the social origins and careers of the power elite do not enable us to infer the class interests and policy directions of a modern system of power.

Do the high social origin and careers of the top men mean nothing, then, about the distribution of power? By no means. They simply remind us that we must be careful of any simple and direct inference from origin and career to political character and policy, not that we must ignore them in our attempt at political understanding. They simply mean that we must analyze the political psychology and the actual decisions of the political directorate as well as its social composition. And they mean, above all, that we should control, as we have done here, any inference we make from the origin and careers of the political actors by close understanding of the institutional landscape in which they act out their drama. Otherwise we should be guilty of a rather simple-minded biographical theory of society and history.

Just as we cannot rest the notion of the power elite solely upon the institutional mechanics that lead to its formation, so we cannot rest the notion solely upon the facts of the origin and career of its personnel. We need both, and we have both—as well as other bases, among them that of the status intermingling.

But it is not only the similarities of social origin, religious affiliation, nativity, and education that are important to the psychological and social affinities of the members of the power elite. Even if their recruitment and formal training were more heterogeneous than they are, these men would still be of quite homogeneous social type. For the most important set of facts about a circle of men is the criteria of admission, of praise, of honor, of promotion that prevails among them; if these are similar within a circle, then they will tend as personalities to become similar. The circles that compose the power elite do tend to have such codes and criteria in common. The cooptation of the social types to which these common values lead is often more important than any statistics of common origin and career that we might have at hand.

There is a kind of reciprocal attraction among the fraternity of the successful—not between each and every member of the circles of the high and mighty, but between enough of them to insure a certain unity. On the slight side, it is a sort of tacit, mutual admiration; in the strongest tie-ins, it proceeds by intermarriage. And there are all grades and types of connection between these extremes. Some overlaps certainly occur by means of cliques and clubs, churches and schools.

If social origin and formal education in common tend to make the members of the power elite more readily understood and trusted by one another, their continued association further cements what they feel they have in common. Members of the several higher circles know one another as personal friends and even as neighbors; they mingle with one another on the golf course, in the gentleman's clubs, at resorts, on transcontinental airplanes, and on ocean liners. They meet at the estates of mutual friends, face each other in front of the TV camera, or serve on the same philanthropic committee; and many are sure to cross one another's path in the columns of newspapers, if not the exact cafés from which many of these columns originate. As we have seen, of "The New 400" of café society, one chronicler has named forty-one members of the very rich, ninety-three political leaders, and seventy-nine chief executives of corporations.

"I did not know, I could not have dreamed," Whittaker Chambers has written,

> of the immense scope and power of Hiss' political alliances and his social connections, which cut across all party lines and ran from the Supreme Court to the Religious Society of Friends, from governors of state and instructors in college faculties to the staff members of liberal magazines. In the decade since I had last seen him, he had used his career, and, in particular, his identification with the cause of peace through his part in organizing the United Nations, to put down roots that made him one with the matted forest floor of American upper class, enlightened middle class, liberal and official life. His roots could not be disturbed without disturbing all the roots on all sides of him.[1]

The sphere of status has reflected the epochs of the power elite. In the third epoch, for example, who could compete with big money? And in the fourth, with big politicians, or even the bright young men of the New Deal? And in the fifth, who can compete with the generals and the admirals and the corporate officials now so sympathetically portrayed on the stage, in the novel, and on the screen? Can one imagine *Executive Suite* as a successful motion picture in 1935? Or *The Caine Mutiny*?

The multiplicity of high-prestige organizations to which the elite usually belong is revealed by even casual examination of the obituaries of the big businessman, the high-prestige lawyer, the top general and admiral, the key senator: usually, high-prestige church, business associations, plus high-prestige clubs, and often plus military rank. In the course of their lifetimes, the university president, the New York Stock Exchange chairman, the head of the bank, the old West Pointer—mingle in the status sphere, within which they easily renew old friendships and draw upon them in an effort to understand through the experience of trusted others those contexts of power and decision in which they have not personally moved.

In these diverse contexts, prestige accumulates in each of the higher circles, and the members of each borrow status from one another. Their self-images are fed by these accumulations and these borrowings, and accordingly, however segmental a given man's role may seem, he comes to feel himself a "diffuse"or "generalized" man of the higher circles, a "broad-gauge" man. Perhaps such inside experience is one feature of what is meant by "judgment."

The key organizations, perhaps, are the major corporations themselves, for on the boards of directors we find a heavy overlapping among the members of these several elites. On the lighter side, again in the summer and winter resorts, we find that, in an intricate serious of overlapping circles; in the course of time, each meets each or knows somebody who knows somebody who knows that one.

The higher members of the military, economic, and political orders are able readily to take over one another's point of view, always in a sympathetic way, and often in a knowledgeable way as well. They define one another as among those who count, and who, accordingly, must be taken into account. Each of them as a member of the power elite comes to incorporate into his own integrity, his own honor, his own conscience, the viewpoints, the expectations, the values of the others. If there are no common ideals and standards among them that are based upon an explicitly aristocratic culture, that does not mean that they do not feel responsibility to one another.

All the structural coincidence of their interests as well as the intricate, psychological facts of their origins and their education, their careers and their associations make possible the psychological affinities that prevail among them, affinities that make it possible for them to say of one another: He is, of course, one of us. And all this points to the basic, psychological meaning of class consciousness: nowhere in America is there as great a "class consciousness" as among the elite; nowhere is it organized as effectively as among the power elite. For by class consciousness, as a psychological fact, one means that the individual member of a "class" accepts only those accepted by his circle as among those who are significant to his own image of self.

Within the higher circles of the power elite, factions do exist; there are conflicts of policy; individual ambitions do clash. There are still enough divisions of importance within the Republican Party, and even between Republicans and Democrats, to make for different methods of operations. But more powerful than these divisions are the internal discipline and the community of interests that bind the power elite together, even across the boundaries of nations at war.[2]

4

Yet we must give due weight to the other side of the case which may not question the facts but only our interpretation of them. There is a set of objections that will inevitably be made to our whole conception of the power elite, but which has essentially to do with only the psychology of its members. It might well be put by liberals or by conservatives in some such way as this:

"To talk of power elite—isn't this to characterize men by their origins and associations? Isn't such characterization both unfair and untrue? Don't men modify themselves, especially Americans such as these, as they rise in stature to meet the demands of their jobs? Don't they arrive at a view and a line of policy that represents, so far as they in their human weaknesses can know, the interests of the nation as a whole? Aren't they merely honorable men who are doing their duty?"

What are we to reply to these objections?

I. We are sure that they are honorable men. But what is honor? Honor can only mean living up to a code that one believes to be honorable. There is no one code upon which we are all agreed. That is why, if we are civilized men, we do not kill off all of those with whom we disagree. The question is not: Are these honorable men? The question is: What are their codes of honor? The answer to that question is that they are the codes of their circles, of those to whose opinions they defer. How could it be otherwise? That is one meaning of the important truism that all men are human and that all men are social creatures. As for sincerity, it can only be disproved, never proved.

II. To the question of their adaptability—which means their capacity to transcend the codes of conduct which, in their life's work and experience, they have acquired—we must answer: Simply no, they cannot, at least not in the handful of years most of them have left. To expect that is to assume that they are indeed strange and expedient: such flexibility would in fact involve a violation of what we may rightly call their character and their integrity. By the way, may it not be precisely because of the lack of such character and integrity that earlier types of American politicians have not represented as great a threat as do these men of character?

It would be an insult to the effective training of the military, and to their indoctrination as well, to suppose that military officials shed their military character and outlook upon changing from uniform to mufti. This background is more important perhaps in the military case than in that of the corporate executives, for the training of the career is deeper and more total.

"Lack of imagination," Gerald W. Johnson has noted,

> is not to be confused with lack of principle. On the contrary, an unimaginative man is often a man of the highest principles. The trouble is that his principles conform to Cornford's famous definition: "A principle is a rule of inaction giving valid general reasons for not doing in a specific instance what to unprincipled instinct would seem to be right."[3]

Would it not be ridiculous, for example, to believe seriously that, in psychological fact, Charles Erwin Wilson represented anyone or any interest other than those of the corporate world? This is not because he is dishonest; on the contrary, it is because he is probably a man of solid integrity—as sound as a dollar. He is what he is and he cannot very well be anything else. He is a member of the professional corporation elite, just as are his colleagues, in the government and out of it; he represents the wealth of the higher corporate world; he represents its power; and he believes sincerely in his oft-quoted remark that "what is good for the United States is good for the General Motors Corporation and vice versa."

The revealing point about the pitiful hearings on the confirmation of such men for political posts is not the cynicism toward the law and toward the lawmakers on the middle levels of power which they display, nor their reluctance to dispose of their personal stock.[4] The interesting point is how impossible it is for such men to divest themselves of their engagement with the corporate world in general and with their own corporations in particular. Not only their money, but their friends, their interests, their training—their lives, in short—are deeply involved in this world. The disposal of stock is, of course, merely a purifying ritual. The point is not so much financial or personal interests in a given corporation, but identification with the corporate world. To ask a man suddenly to divest himself of these interests and sensibilities is almost like asking a man to become a woman.

III. To the question of their patriotism, of their desire to serve the nation as a whole, we must answer first that, like codes of honor, feelings of patriotism and views of what is to the whole nation's good, are not ultimate facts but matters upon which there exists a great variety of opinion. Furthermore, patriotic opinions too are rooted in and are sustained by what a man has become by virtue of how and with whom he has lived. This is no simple mechanical determination of individual character by social conditions; it is an intricate process, well established in the major tradition of modern social study. One can only wonder why more social scientists do not use it systematically in speculating about politics.

IV. The elite cannot be truly thought of as men who are merely doing their duty. They are the ones who determine their duty, as well as the duties of those beneath them. They are not merely following orders: they give the orders. They are not merely "bureaucrats": they command bureaucracies. They may try to disguise these facts from others and from themselves by appeals to traditions of which they imagine themselves the instruments, but there are many traditions, and they must choose which ones they will serve. They face decisions for which there simply are no traditions.

Now, to what do these several answers add up? To the fact that we cannot reason about public events and historical trends merely from knowledge about the motives and character of the men or the small groups who sit in the seats of the high and mighty. This fact, in turn, does not mean that we should be intimidated by accusations that in taking up our problem in the way we have, we are impugning the honor, the integrity, or the ability of those who are in high office. For it is not, in the first instance, a question of individual character; and if, in further instances, we find that it is, we should not hesitate to say so plainly. In the meantime, we must judge men of power by the standards of power, by what they do as decision-makers, and not by who they are or what they may do in private life. Our interest is not in that: we are interested in their policies and in the *consequences* of their conduct of office. We must remember that these men of the power elite now occupy the strategic places in the structure of American society; that they command the dominant institutions of a dominant nation; that, as a set of men, they are in a position to make decisions with terrible consequences for the underlying populations of the world.

5

Despite their social similarity and psychological affinities, the members of the power elite do not constitute a club having a permanent membership with fixed and formal boundaries. It is of the nature of the power elite that within it there is a good deal of shifting about, and that it thus does not consist of one small set of the same men in the same positions in the same hierarchies. Because men know each other personally does not mean that among them there is unity of policy; and because they do not know each other personally does not mean that among them there is a disunity. The conception of the power elite does not rest, as I have repeatedly said, primarily upon personal friendship.

As the requirements of the top places in each of the major hierarchies become similar, the types of men occupying these roles at the top—by selection and by training in the jobs—become similar. This is not mere deduction from structure to personnel. That it is a fact is revealed by the heavy traffic that has been going on between the three structures, often in very intricate patterns. The chief executives, the warlords, and selected politicians came into contact with one another in an intimate, working way during World War II; after that war ended, they continued their associations, out of common beliefs, social congeniality, and coinciding interests. Noticeable proportions of top men from the military, the economic, and the political worlds have during the last fifteen years occupied positions in one or both of the other worlds: between these higher circles there is an interchangeability of position, based formally upon the supposed transferability of "executive ability," based in substance upon the cooptation by cliques of insiders. As members of a power elite, many of those busy in this traffic have come to look upon "the government" as an umbrella under whose authority they do their work.

As the business between the big three increases in volume and importance, so does the traffic in personnel. The very criteria for selecting men who will rise come to embody this fact. The corporate commissar, dealing with the state and its military, is wiser to choose a young man who has experienced the state and its military than one who has not. The political director, often dependent for his own political success upon corporate decisions and corporations, is also wiser to choose a man with corporate experience. Thus, by virtue of the very criterion of success, the interchange of personnel and the unity of the power elite is increased.

Given the formal similarity of the three hierarchies in which the several members of the elite spend their working lives, given the ramifications of the decisions made in each upon the others, given the coincidence of interest that prevails among them at many points, and given the administrative vacuum of the American civilian state along with its enlargement of tasks—given these trends of structure, and adding to them the psychological affinities we have noted—we should indeed be surprised were we to find that men said to be skilled in administrative contacts and full of organizing ability would fail to do more than get in touch with one another. They have, of course, done much more than that: increasingly, they assume positions in one another's domains.

The unity revealed by the interchangeability of top roles rests upon the parallel development of the top jobs in each of the big three domains. The interchange occurs most frequently at the points of their coinciding interest, as between regulatory agency and the regulated industry; contracting agency and contractor. And, as we shall see, it leads to coordinations that are more explicit, and even formal.

The inner core of the power elite consists, first, of those who interchange commanding roles at the top of one dominant institutional order with those in another: the admiral who is also a banker and a lawyer and who heads up an important federal commission; the corporation executive whose company was one of the two or three leading war materiel producers who is now the secretary of defense; the wartime general who dons civilian clothes to sit on the political directorate and then becomes a member of the board of directors of a leading economic corporation.

Although the executive who becomes a general, the general who becomes a statesman, the statesman who becomes a banker, see much more than ordinary men in their ordinary environments, still the perspectives of even such men often remain tied to their dominant locales. In their very career, however, they interchange roles with the big three and thus readily transcend the particularity of interest in any one of these institutional milieux. By their very careers and activities, they lace the three types of milieux together. They are, accordingly, the core members of the power elite.

These men are not necessarily familiar with every major arena of power. We refer to one man who moves in and between perhaps two circles—say, the industrial and the military—and to another man who moves in the military and the political, and to a third who moves in the political as well as among opinion-makers. These in-between types most closely display our image of the power elite's structure and operation, even of behind-the-scenes operations. To the extent that there is any "invisible elite," these advisory and liaison types are its core. Even if—as I believe to be very likely—many of them are, at least in the first part of their careers, "agents" of the various elites rather than themselves elite, it is they who are most active in organizing the several top milieux into a structure of power and maintaining it.

The inner core of the power elite also includes men of the higher legal and financial type from the great law factories and investment firms, who are almost professional go-betweens of economic, political, and military affairs, and who thus act to unify the power elite. The corporation lawyer and the investment banker perform the functions of the "go-between" effectively and powerfully. By the nature of their work, they transcend the narrower milieu of any one industry, and accordingly are in a position to speak and act for the corporate world or at least sizable sectors of it. The corporation lawyer is a key link between the economic and military and political areas; the investment banker is a key organizer and unifier of the corporate world and a person well versed in spending the huge amounts of money the American military establishment now ponders. When you get a lawyer who handles the legal work of investment bankers you get a key member of the power elite.

During the Democratic era, one link between private corporate organizations and governmental institutions was the investment house of Dillon, Read. From it came such men as James Forrestal and Charles F. Detmar, Jr.; Ferdinand Eberstadt had once been a partner in it before he branched out into his own investment house from which came other men to political and military circles. Republican administrations seem to favor the investment firm of Kuhn, Loeb and the advertising firm of Batten, Barton, Durstine and Osborn.

Regardless of administrations, there is always the law firm of Sullivan and Cromwell. Midwest investment banker Cyrus Eaton has said that:

> *Arthur H. Dean, a senior partner of Sullivan & Cromwell of No. 48 Wall Street, was one of those who assisted in the drafting of the Securities Act of 1933, the first of the series of bills passed to regulate the capital market. He and his firm, which is reputed to be the largest in the United States, have maintained close relations with the SEC since its creation, and theirs is the dominating influence on the commission.*[5]

There is also the third largest bank in the United States: the Chase National Bank of New York (now Chase-Manhattan). Regardless of political administration, executives of this bank and those of the International Bank of

Reconstruction and Development have changed positions: John J. McCloy, who became chairman of the Chase National in 1953, is a former president of the World Bank; and his successor to the presidency of the World Bank was a former senior vice president of the Chase National Bank.[6] And in 1953, the president of the Chase National Bank, Winthrop W. Aldrich, had left to become ambassador to Great Britain.

The outermost fringes of the power elite—which change more than its core—consist of "those who count" even though they may not be "in" on given decisions of consequence nor in their career move between the hierarchies. Each member of the power elite need not be a man who personally decides every decision that is to be ascribed to the power elite. Each member, in the decisions that he does make, takes the others seriously into account. They not only make decisions in the several major areas of war and peace; they are the men who, in decisions in which they take no direct part, are taken into decisive account by those who are directly in charge.

On the fringes and below them, somewhat to the side of the lower echelons, the power elite fades off into the middle levels of power, into the rank and file of the Congress, the pressure groups that are not vested in the power elite itself, as well as a multiplicity of regional and state and local interests. If all the men on the middle levels are not among those who count, they sometimes must be taken into account, handled, cajoled, broken, or raised to higher circles.

When the power elite find that in order to get things done they must reach below their own realms—as is the case when it is necessary to get bills passed through Congress—they themselves must exert some pressure. But among the power elite, the name for such high-level lobbying is "liaison work." There are "liaison" military men with Congress, with certain wayward sections of industry, with practically every important element not directly concerned with the power elite. The two men on the White House staff who are *named* liaison men are both experienced in military matters; one of them is a former investment banker and lawyer as well as a general.

Not the trade associations but the higher cliques of lawyers and investment bankers are the active political heads of the corporate rich and the members of the power elite.

While it is generally assumed that the national associations carry tremendous weight in formulating public opinion and directing the course of national policy, there is some evidence to indicate that interaction between associations on a formal level is not a very tight-knit affair. The general tendency within associations seems to be to stimulate activities around the specific interests of the organization, and more effort is made to educate its members rather than to spend much time in trying to influence other associations on the issue at hand.

. . . As media for stating and re-stating the over-all value structure of the nation they (the trade associations) are important. . . . But when issues are

firmly drawn, individuals related to the larger corporate interests are called upon to exert pressure in the proper places at the strategic time. The national associations may act as media for coordinating such pressures, but a great volume of intercommunication between members at the apex of power of the larger corporate interests seems to be the decisive factor in final policy determination.[7]

Conventional "lobbying," carried on by trade associations, still exists, although it usually concerns the middle levels of power—usually being targeted at Congress, and, of course, its own rank-and-file members. The important function of the National Association of Manufacturers, for example, is less directly to influence policy than to reveal to small businessmen that their interests are the same as those of larger businesses. But there is also "high-level lobbying." All over the country the corporate leaders are drawn into the circle of the high military and political through personal friendship, trade and professional associations and their various subcommittees, prestige clubs, open political affiliation, and customer relationships. "There is . . . an awareness among these power leaders," one firsthand investigator of such executive cliques has asserted, "of many of the current major policy issues before the nation such as keeping taxes down, turning all productive operations over to private enterprises, increasing foreign trade, keeping governmental welfare and other domestic activities to a minimum, and strengthening and maintaining the hold of the current party in power nationally."[8]

There are, in fact, cliques of corporate executives who are more important as informal opinion leaders in the top echelons of corporate, military, and political power than as actual participants in military and political organizations. Inside military circles and inside political circles and "on the sidelines" in the economic area, these circles and cliques of corporation executives are in on most all major decisions regardless of topic. And what is important about all this high-level lobbying is that it is done within the confines of that elite.

6

The conception of the power elite and of its unity rests upon the corresponding developments and the coincidence of interests among economic, political, and military organizations. It also rests upon the similarity of origin and outlook, and the social and personal intermingling of the top circles from each of these dominant hierarchies. This conjunction of institutional and psychological forces, in turn, is revealed by the heavy personnel traffic within and between the big three institutional orders, as well as by the rise of go-betweens as in the high-level lobbying. The conception of the power elite, accordingly, does *not* rest upon the assumption that American history since the origins of World War II must be understood as a secret plot, or as a great and coordinated conspiracy of the members of this elite. The conception rests upon quite impersonal grounds.

There is, however, little doubt that the American power elite—which contains, we are told, some of "the greatest organizers in the world"—has also planned and has plotted. The rise of the elite, as we have already made clear, was not and could not have been caused by a plot; and the tenability of the conception does not rest upon the existence of any secret or any publicly known organization. But, once the conjunction of structural trend and of the personal will to utilize it gave rise to the power elite, then plans and programs did occur to its members and indeed it is not possible to interpret many events and official policies of the fifth epoch without reference to the power elite. "There is a great difference," Richard Hofstadter has remarked, "between locating conspiracies *in* history and saying that history *is*, in effect, a conspiracy. . . ."[9]

The structural trends of institutions become defined as opportunities by those who occupy their command posts. Once such opportunities are recognized, men may avail themselves of them. Certain types of men from each of the dominant institutional areas, more far-sighted than others, have actively promoted the liaison before it took its truly modern shape. They have often done so for reasons not shared by their partners, although not objected to by them either; and often the outcome of their liaison has had consequences which none of them foresaw, much less shaped, and which only later in the course of development came under explicit control. Only after it was well under way did most of its members find themselves part of it and become gladdened, although sometimes also worried, by this fact. But once the coordination is a going concern, new men come readily into it and assume its existence without question.

So far as explicit organization—conspiratorial or not—is concerned, the power elite, by its very nature, is more likely to use existing organizations, working within and between them, than to set up explicit organizations whose membership is strictly limited to its own members. But if there is no machinery in existence to ensure, for example, that military and political factors will be balanced in decisions made, they will invent such machinery and use it, as with the National Security Council. Moreover, in a formally democratic polity, the aims and the powers of the various elements of this elite are further supported by an aspect of the permanent war economy: the assumption that the security of the nation supposedly rests upon great secrecy of plan and intent. Many higher events that would reveal the working of the power elite can be withheld from public knowledge under the guise of secrecy. With the wide secrecy covering their operations and decisions, the power elite can mask their intentions, operations, and further consolidation. Any secrecy that is imposed upon those in positions to observe high decision-makers clearly works for and not against the operations of the power elite.

There is accordingly reason to suspect—but by the nature of the case, no proof—that the power elite is not altogether "surfaced." There is nothing hidden about it, although its activities are not publicized. As an elite, it is not organized, although its members often know one another, seem quite naturally to work together, and share many organizations in common. There is nothing conspiratorial about it, although its decisions are often publicly unknown and its mode of operations manipulative rather than explicit.

It is not that the elite "believe in" a compact elite behind the scenes and a mass down below. It is not put in that language. It is just that the people are of necessity confused and must, like trusting children, place all the new world of foreign policy and strategy and executive action in the hands of experts. It is just that everyone knows somebody has got to run the show, and that somebody usually does. Other do not really care anyway, and besides, they do not know how. So the gap between the two types gets wider.

When crises are defined as total, and as seemingly permanent, the consequences of decision become total, and the decisions in each major area of life come to be integrated and total. Up to a point, these consequences for other institutional orders can be assessed; beyond such points, chances have to be taken. It is then that the felt scarcity of trained and imaginative judgment leads to plaintive feelings among executives about the shortage of qualified successors in political, military, and economic life. This feeling, in turn, leads to an increasing concern with the training of successors who could take over as older men of power retire.[10] In each area, there slowly arises a new generation which has grown up in an age of coordinated decisions.

In each of the elite circles, we have noticed this concern to recruit and to train successors as "broad-gauge" men, that is, as men capable of making decisions that involve institutional areas other than their own. The chief executives have set up formal recruitment and training programs to man the corporate world as virtually a state within a state. Recruitment and training for the military elite has long been rigidly professionalized, but has now come to include educational routines of a sort which the remnants of older generals and admirals consider quite nonsensical.

Only the political order, with its absence of a genuine civil service, has lagged behind, creating an administrative vacuum into which military bureaucrats and corporate outsiders have been drawn. But even in this domain, since World War II, there have been repeated attempts, by elite men of such vision as the late James Forrestal's, to inaugurate a career service that would include periods in the corporate world as well as in the governmental.[11]

What is lacking is a truly common elite program of recruitment and training; for the prep school, Ivy League College, and law school sequence of the metropolitan 400 is not up to the demands now made upon members of the power elite.[12] Britishers, such as Field Marshal Viscount Montgomery, well aware of this lack, recently urged for adoption of a system "under which a minority of high-caliber young students could be separated from the mediocre and given the best education possible to supply the country with leadership." His proposal is echoed, in various forms, by many who accept his criticism of "the American theory of public education on the ground that it is ill suited to produce the 'elite' group of leaders . . . this country needs to fulfill its obligations of world leadership."[13]

In part these demands reflect the unstated need to transcend recruitment on the sole basis of economic success, especially since it is suspect as often involving the higher immorality; in part it reflects the stated need to have men who, as Viscount Montgomery says, know "the meaning of discipline." But above all these demands reflect the at least vague consciousness on the part of the power elite themselves that the age of coordinated decisions, entailing a newly enormous range of consequences, requires a power elite that is of a new caliber. Insofar as the sweep of matters which go into the making of decisions is vast and interrelated, the information needed for judgments complex and requiring particularized knowledge,[14] the men in charge will not only call upon one another; they will try to train their successors for the work at hand. These new men will grow up as men of power within the coordination of economic and political and military decision.

7

The idea of the power elite rests upon and enables us to make sense of (1) the decisive institutional trends that characterize the structure of our epoch, in particular, the military ascendancy in a privately incorporated economy, and more broadly, the several coincidences of objective interests between economic, military, and political institutions; (2) the social similarities and the psychological affinities of the men who occupy the command posts of these structures, in particular the increased interchangeability of the top positions in each of them and the increased traffic between these orders in the careers of men of power; (3) the ramifications, to the point of virtual totality, of the kind of decisions that are made at the top, and the rise to power of a set of men who, by training and bent, are professional organizers of considerable force and who are unrestrained by democratic party training.

Negatively, the formation of the power elite rests upon (1) the relegation of the professional party politician to the middle levels of power, (2) the semiorganized stalemate of the interests of sovereign localities into which the legislative function has fallen, (3) the virtually complete absence of a civil service that constitutes a politically neutral, but politically relevant, depository of brainpower and executive skill, and (4) the increased official secrecy behind which great decisions are made without benefit of public or even congressional debate.

As a result, the political directorate, the corporate rich, and the ascendant military have come together as the power elite, and the expanded and centralized hierarchies which they head have encroached upon the old balances and have now relegated them to the middle levels of power. Now the balancing society is a conception that pertains accurately to the middle levels, and on that level the balance has become more often an affair of intrenched provincial and nationally irresponsible forces and demands than a center of power and national decision.

But how about the bottom? As all these trends have become visible at the top and on the middle, what has been happening to the great American public? If the top is unprecedentedly powerful and increasingly unified and willful; if the middle zones are increasingly a semiorganized stalemate—in what shape is the bottom, in what condition is the public at large? The rise of the power elite, we shall now see, rests upon, and in some ways is part of, the transformation of the publics of America into a mass society.

NOTES

1. Whittaker Chambers, *Witness* (New York: Random House, 1952), p. 550.
2. For an excellent introduction to the international unity of corporate interests, see James Stewart Martin, *All Honorable Men* (Boston: Little, Brown, 1950).
3. Gerald W. Johnson, "The Superficial Aspect," *New Republic*, October 25, 1954, p. 7.
4. See the Hearings before the Committee on Armed Services, U.S. Senate, 83rd Cong., 1st sess., on Nominees Designate Charles E. Wilson, Roger M. Keyes, Robert T. Stevens, Robert B. Anderson, and Harold E. Talbott, 15, 16, and 23 January 1953 (Washington, D.C.: U.S. Government Printing Office, 1953).
5. Hearings before the Subcommittee on Study of Monopoly Power of the Committee on the Judiciary, House of Representatives, 81st Cong., 1st sess., Serial No. 14, Part 2-A (Washington, D.C.: U.S. Government Printing Office, 1950), p. 468.
6. Cf. *New York Times*, December 6, 1952, p. 1.
7. Floyd Hunter, "Pilot Study of National Power and Policy Structures," Institute for Research in Social Science, University of North Carolina, Research Previews, vol. 2, no. 2, March 1954 (mimeo), p. 8.
8. *Ibid.*, p. 9.
9. Richard Hofstadter, *The Age of Reform* (New York: Knopf, 1955), pp. 71–72.
10. Cf. Hans Gerth and C. Wright Mills, *Character and Social Structure* (New York: Harcourt, Brace, 1953).
11. Cf. Mills, "The Conscription of America," *Common Sense*, April 1945, pp. 15 ff.
12. Cf. "Twelve of the Best American Schools," *Fortune*, January 1936, p. 48.
13. Speech of Field Marshal Viscount Montgomery at Columbia University as reported in *New York Times*, November 24, 1954, p. 25.
14. Cf. Dean Acheson, "What a Secretary of State Really Does," *Harper's*, December 1954, p. 48.

Power Is Pluralistic

Arnold M. Rose

The belief that an "economic elite" controls governmental and community affairs, by means kept hidden from the public, is one that can be traced at least as far back in American history as the political attacks of some Jeffersonians on some Hamiltonians at the end of the eighteenth century. Scarcely any lower-class political movement in the United States has failed to express the theme that the upper classes successfully used nondemocratic means to thwart democratic processes. Perhaps the widest popular use of the theme was achieved by the Populist movement in the decades following 1890. Anarchism and Marxism were imports from Europe that accepted the theme as one of the essential elements of their ideologies. The history of the United States also provides ample factual examples to strengthen credence in the theme. The literature of exposure, especially that of the "muckrakers" in the first decade of the twentieth century, provides details as to how economically privileged individuals and groups illegally bought and bribed legislators, judges, and executive heads of government to serve their own desires for increased wealth and power.

The belief is not entirely wrong. But it presents only a portion of relevant reality and creates a significant misimpression that in itself has political repercussions. A more balanced analysis of the historical facts would probably arrive at something like the following conclusion: segments of the economic elite have violated democratic political and legal processes, with differing degrees of effort and success in the various periods of American history, but in no recent period could they correctly be said to have controlled the elected and appointed political authorities in large measure. The relationship between the economic elite and the political authorities has been a constantly varying one of strong influence, cooperation, division of labor, and conflict, with each influencing the other in changing proportion to some extent and each operating independently of the other to a large extent. Today there is significant political control and limitation of certain activities over the economic elite, and there are also some significant processes by which the economic elite uses its wealth to help elect some political candidates and to influence other political authorities in ways which are not available to the average citizen. Further, neither the economic elite nor the political authorities are monolithic units which act with internal consensus and coordinated action with regard to each other (or probably in any other way). In fact there are several economic elites which only very rarely act as units within themselves and among themselves, and there are at least two political parties which have significantly differing programs with regard to their actions toward any economic elite, and each of them has only a partial degree of internal cohesion.[1] On domestic issues, at least, it is appropriate to observe that there are actually four political parties, two liberal ones and two conservative ones, the largest currently being the national Democratic Party, which generally has a domestic policy that frustrates the special interests of the economic elite. This paragraph states our general hypothesis, and we shall seek to substantiate it with facts that leave no significant areas of omission. Merely to provide it with a shorthand label, we shall call it the "multi-influence hypothesis," as distinguished from the "economic-elite-dominance" hypothesis.

. . .

. . . Specifically, this study presents evidence against the following statements of Mills:

> There is no effective countervailing power against the coalition of the big businessmen—who, as political outsiders, now occupy the command posts—and the ascendant military men—who with such grave voices now speak so frequently in the higher councils.
> While the professional party politicians may still, at times, be brokers of power, compromisers of interests, negotiators of issues, they are no longer at the top of the state.
> The executive bureaucracy becomes not only the center of power but also the arena within which all conflicts of power are resolved or denied resolution. Administration replaces electoral politics. . . .

Implicit in these and other remarks are Mills's political assumptions that (1) voting means little or nothing; (2) there is no significant difference between the two major political parties; (3) the economic-military elite has an interest in all major political issues against the interest of the masses, and that the former interest is always victorious over the latter; (4) the legislative branch of government is subordinate to the executive branch. . . .

Mills adopts an economic determinism which we cannot accept. He points to the fact that most congressmen are of upper-class or middle-class origin . . . , and assumes that they must therefore reflect the economic interests of businessmen and other members of the economic elite. Even when a congressman does not have an upper-class or middle-class background, he is assumed to take orders from the economic elite. These assumptions neglect the vast amount of social welfare legislation, particularly since the 1930s, and of other legislation designed to protect the interests of the working classes. They neglect the fact that some of the wealthiest of elected government officials have been among those leading in the fight for such legislation. The aristocratic Franklin Roosevelt doubtless represented the interests of the working masses better then his "average man" political opponent of 1936, Alfred Landon; and a similar comparison could be made between the wealthy John Kennedy and his opponent of more nearly average wealth, Richard Nixon. Of course, Mills can consider Landon and Nixon as "lieutenants" of the economic elite, but he cannot get around the fact that Roosevelt, Kennedy, and such other liberal politicians as W. Averill Harriman, Joseph Clark, Herbert Lehman, Stuart Symington, and G. Mennen Williams are members of the upper economic class. It may be true that military leaders have growing power in government circles, but they have not succeeded in getting much of the legislation they have asked for, nor has any President allowed them to speak freely in public. It is not illuminating to be told by Mills that "a small group of men are now in charge of the executive decisions" . . . , for there has always been, and must continue to be, leadership in a democracy; this is even part of the definition of "executive." The significant question is in whose interests the political elite acts and whether it is checked by the mass of voters and of interest groups. There is every evidence that the masses of the American people today are better off economically, both absolutely and relatively, than they were in the past, and that this has been largely due to government intervention, supported by the majority of the voters.

It is explicit in Mills's . . . analyses that the elected legislators have no power in and of themselves. At most, they are "lieutenants" who carry out the orders of the economic elite, who—Mills claims—have taken over the direction of the government through appointment to the top policymaking offices in the federal executive. In fact, a considerable number of statutes originate in the Congress rather than in the executive branch—more than in European parliamentary regimes—and many of these are responses to the wishes of private pressure groups, including those of the economic elite. Yet, there are also some bills that are originated by the congressmen themselves, sometimes in opposition to the wishes of both the executive branch and the pressure groups. Congress also controls the purse strings, and the areas of taxation and appropriations involve far more creative opportunities than is generally understood.

Administrations since 1933 have been diligent in efforts to solve social problems, and have sought enabling statutes and appropriations from the Congress, a large number with success, some after a delay, and others with failure. In most cases Congress has "improved" the bills submitted to it by the executive before passing them, and that has been its chief role. But in some outstanding instances, it has initiated or expanded legislation on its own when it felt the executive branch was evasive or dilatory. The Civil Rights Act of 1964 and the Medicare Act of 1965 provide examples of liberal legislation enacted by Congress with provisions that went much beyond what the administration requested. Congress's annual allocation of funds for medical research and often for medical facilities is usually greater than that requested by the President, and in 1965 Congress doubled the educational program for veterans that the President requested, and made a special allocation, that the President did not request, for schools in areas of high federal employment.[2]

There are a number of other general points to be made against the Mills thesis:

1. The important facts of political power and political influence are not "secret" or "hidden" or "behind the scenes" most of the time. Pressure groups—of which many represent economic interests—and public opinion operate on legislative and executive branches of government. But only a small proportion of federal legislators and executives are "in the control of" an economic elite. At state and local levels, a larger proportion of legislators seek their positions to serve special economic interests, but even when they do, many of their votes are in accord with their ideological conception of what the public interest is.

There is a circularity in Mills's reasoning because of his beliefs that the top economic elite effects its control of American society secretly and that the political elite consists of lieutenants of the commanding economic elite. From these premises he deduces that the *actions* of the political elite are generally the only means by which the wishes and interests of the commanding economic elite can be ascertained by the outside observers, and that the words of the political elite are mere window dressing to mislead the masses into voting for them. There are several factual questions at issue here—the extent to which there is a discrepancy between the words and deeds of the political elite, and the extent to which the deeds of the political elite do not reflect the interests and wishes of the public. But aside from these factual questions, there is dubious logic in reasoning that the political elite constantly proves its subordination to the economic elite by its actions, where there is no independent way of ascertaining what the commanding economic elite really wants because of its secret modes of operating. The economic elite in fact does often expound its wishes—in the programs and campaigns of the National Association of Manufacturers, the United States Chamber of Commerce, and more specialized groups such as the American Medical Association. . . . [T]he President and the majority of the Congress more often go against these programs than support them, although the businessmen are more likely to get their way when they seek narrow economic advantages from the independent regulatory commissions and the military procurement agencies. Are the National Association of Manufacturers, the Chamber of Commerce, and the American Medical Association merely engaging in window dressing to fool the public as to their true wishes when they come out with a program or campaign?

Secrecy in politics has many functions other than the desire to hide the control that may be exercised by the economic elite on the politicians. The New York Reform Democratic party leader, Edward U. Costikyan,[3] says:

> The nature of politics and politicians is to reach decisions privately. This often leads the public to believe that secrecy is a screen to shield wrongdoing. It usually isn't. Generally it shields a desire for privacy, as well as some confusion, and some selfishness. . . .

Thus, the existence of secrecy in some political actions cannot by itself be taken as evidence that it hides business control of politics. Just how much secrecy there is in politics is an open question on which there is little evidence. Public ignorance of certain actions taken by politicians does not mean that there is secrecy; it often simply reflects the failure of the news media to report actions that were taken openly. Politicians interviewed by this author invariably stated, when asked about the frequency of the decisions they take in secret, that they occasionally found it expedient to act in secret, but that the secret usually "leaked out" in a matter of days or weeks. They all averred that the value of secrecy to them was temporary, and that they assumed, when they took secret actions, that the secret would likely ultimately become public. They also stated that many of the supposedly secret actions they took were not secret at all: newspaper and other mass media reporters were just not present, and when the news releases were finally issued, the reporters excused their own failure to be present by asserting that the decision-making had occurred secretly. . . .

2. Mills and his followers have been critical of those political scientists like Dahl who hold that political power is pluralistic in the United States. Our position is not simply that power is pluralistic in American society, but that the society itself is pluralistic. The different spheres of life do not interpenetrate each other in the way that in India, for example, religious values and institutions permeate the average man's political, economic, family, artistic,

educational, and other spheres of life. Or in the way that, in Hitler's Germany, or Stalin's Russia, political values similarly permeated all the other spheres of life. In the United States (and many other countries), practically every person has differentiated roles and values for the various spheres of life, and so power too usually does not significantly cross the boundaries of each sphere in which it is created. As Merton has put it: "Men with power to affect the economic life-chances of a large group many exert little interpersonal influence in other spheres; the power to withhold jobs from people may not result in directly influencing their political or associational or religious behavior."[4]

3. Since 1933, Democrats have won the great majority of the elections, naming all the presidents but one (Eisenhower),* dominating all the congresses but two (1946–48, 1952–54), and electing a considerable majority of the governors and state legislatures. Yet the majority of businessmen have strongly supported the Republican Party. Businessmen have not only not dominated the political scene, but have shown an increasing sense of frustration and bitterness at being "left out" in political decisions.

In 1960, the Committee on Economic Development conducted an attitude survey of bankers. One of the findings was that they felt that Congress ignored them and their interests. They pointed to the much lighter controls on their competitors, the savings and loan associations and the credit unions. In their belief this could be attributed to the "fact" that congressmen were more likely to place their savings in these latter associations than in banks, and that, because of the high rate of bank failures in the early 1930s, banks were still regarded with suspicion—in spite of the many reforms in procedure that banks had made since then.

The brief two years (1952–54) when the Republicans controlled both the presidency and the Congress must have seemed like a "Restoration" for the majority of businessmen, and it was during this atypical period that C. Wright Mills must have written the bulk of *The Power Elite*. But alienation from government increased during the late years of the Eisenhower presidency as the administration proved unable to achieve any of the major goals of the businessmen. They became even more antagonistic and truculent toward government when President Kennedy forced back the steel price rise ... and they went so far as to pull the Business Advisory Council out of its semiofficial relationship to the government. It was not until a politically extremist minority seized control of the majority of the Republican state organizations that a significant group of big businessmen exhibited a desire to take an accommodating position toward the Democrats. Big businessmen worked out a pragmatic relationship with President Lyndon Johnson[5] which

---

* Since this was written, there have been three other Republican presidents—Ford, Nixon and Reagan. In addition, Republicans took control of the U.S. Senate in 1980—*Editors.*

they had refused to do with Presidents Roosevelt, Truman, and Kennedy— but their subordinate role in the Johnson administration was shown by the fact that more welfare and "reform" legislation was passed by the 1964–65 Congress under Johnson's stimulation, than by any Congress since 1933.

4. Mills contends that the American top elite has a common provenance: he says that they are upper-class people, who attend the same preparatory schools and private colleges, associate with each other throughout their private lives, and pass on their power to their offspring. This picture is certainly not true for the top elected government officials. Very few sons of presidents, governors, and congressmen ever achieve top political positions. The men in these positions have the most diverse social origins. Of presidents in the twentieth century, only the two Roosevelts (sixth cousins to each other) were from the upper upper class, and only one came from a very wealthy family (Kennedy, whose family background is *nouveau riche*); Truman, Eisenhower, and Johnson could be said to have come from the lower middle class, and the others had somwhat higher middle-class family backgrounds. The Middle West provided as many presidents as did the East, and the small towns provided more than the opulent cities or suburbs. The majority did not attend the upper-class private schools or colleges. The great majority of the top elected officials of the United States have experienced a considerable amount of upward social mobility in comparison with their parents, not only in prestige and power, but also in education and wealth.

Studies by Newcomer, and by Warner and Abegglen, suggest that there is more social mobility in the economic elite than Mills claims.[6] In Newcomer's sample of big business executives in the eary 1950s, 7.5 percent were sons of workers, as compared to 4.2 percent for the executives of 1900; in Warner and Abegglen's study of 8,562 businessmen from 1900 to 1950 there was an increase of 8 percent in the proportion of executives whose fathers were laborers and a decrease of 10 percent in those whose fathers were owners of businesses. But Mills is almost completely wrong about the absence of social mobility among the political elite.

Dwight D. Eisenhower, General of the Armies and President of the United States, appointer of many top-level business executives to the leading decision-making posts in government, must have been considered by Mills as a leading member of the power elite. Yet he was one of the few in top decision-making posts who publicly warned against a "military-industrial complex" as a threat to the United States. On the significant occasion of his Farewell Address, this leader of the Establishment seemed to give support to one of C. Wright Mills's central theses:

> *In the councils of Government, we must guard against the acquisition of unwarranted influence, whether sought or unsought, by the military-industrial complex. The potential for the disastrous rise of misplaced power exists and will persist.*

We must never let the weight of this combination endanger our liberties or demo-cratic processes.

Many individuals not persuaded by the scholar Mills were persuaded by the President Eisenhower.[7] Yet a closer reading of Eisenhower's speech shows that he was on a different track than Mills. In the first place, Eisenhower placed the danger in the future; Mills had the economic-military power elite already in control of the nation. Second, Eisenhower was arguing for the autonomy of government; Mills identified the government as a tool of the elite. Third, Eisenhower—a leading figure in Mills's elite—was publicly denouncing the threat posed by that presumed elite, whereas Mills held that the members of the elite were like-minded and operated more or less in secret.

It is clear that Eisenhower was worried about the huge size of the armaments industry, and its consequent potential for using its great economic power to influence many areas of government, education, and science. . . . Eisenhower may also have worried about conflict of interest on the part of the nation's military leaders: as direct purchasers from the armaments industry, and as relatively low-paid government servants who could "retire" at an early age, were they not in danger of making decisions influenced by the fact that they could go into high-salaried jobs in one or another munitions firm after they retired? When Eisenhower made his statement, Congress was considering a bill to require retiring military procurement officers to wait two years before accepting a position in one of the supplying firms. But this may not be a long enough waiting period to prevent conflict of interest, and the law could not apply to civilians working for the Defense Department or to military officers not directly engaged in procurement. There were all sorts of ways of unduly influencing a military procurement officer: the military supply firms even set up a trade association, called the National Security Industrial Association, which has been in existence since World War II, to enhance their relationships with military leaders. Provision of information and gossip, wining and dining, and other standard techniques of lobbying were used on the military procurement officers. General Eisenhower was concerned about the conflict of interest on the part of his brother officers, and anxious to maintain the tradition of military independence and service.

Yet Eisenhower's conception of his role as President, as a mere enforcer of laws and mediator of the various conflicting forces in the executive branch, did much to enhance the very dangers he called attention to. It was his successors, Kennedy and Johnson, because they had a conception of the dominant and decisive role of the presidency, who set industry back several times when it sought an inflationary rise in prices, and whose appointed Secretary of Defense, Robert McNamara, maintained his dominance over the military in all matters. These presidents were political leaders, who saw a superordinate government as the check on any potential military-industrial complex. . . .

NOTES

1. The two political parties sometimes agree on almost identical specific pieces of legislation, but mainly in the areas of foreign policy and national defense, practically never in regard to their programs or actions with respect to an economic elite.
2. *New York Times*, April 5, 1966, p. 21.
3. *Behind Closed Doors: Politics in the Public Interest* (New York: Harcourt, Brace and World, 1966), Preface.
4. Robert K. Merton, "Patterns of Influence: A Study of Interpersonal Influence and of Communication Behavior in a Local Community," in Paul F. Lazarsfeld and Frank N. Stanton, eds. *Communication Research: 1948–1949* (New York: Harper, 1949), p. 217.
5. David T. Bazelton, "Big Business and the Democrats," *Commentary*, vol. 39 (May 1965), pp. 39–46.
6. Mabel Newcomer, *The Big Business Executive* (New York: Columbia University Press, 1955); W. Lloyd Warner and James C. Abegglen, *Big Business Leaders in America* (New York: Harper, 1955).
7. I do not know if Mills welcomed Eisenhower's statement. Among those who accepted it as verification of Mills's thesis were Fred J. Cook, *The Warfare State* (New York: Macmillan, 1962); and Marc Pilisuk and Thomas Hayden, "Is There a Military Industrial Complex Which Prevents Peace?", *Journal of Social Issues*, vol. 21 (July 1965), pp. 67–117. The latter mentions many others.